Human-Computer Interaction Series

T0143052

Human-Computer Interaction is a multidisciplinary field focused on human aspects of the development of computer technology. As computer-based technology becomes increasingly pervasive – not just in developed countries, but worldwide – the need to take a human-centered approach in the design and development of this technology becomes ever more important. For roughly 30 years now, researchers and practitioners in computational and behavioral sciences have worked to identify theory and practice that influences the direction of these technologies, and this diverse work makes up the field of human-computer interaction. Broadly speaking, it includes the study of what technology might be able to do for people and how people might interact with the technology.

In this series, we present work which advances the science and technology of developing systems which are both effective and satisfying for people in a wide variety of contexts. The human-computer interaction series will focus on theoretical perspectives (such as formal approaches drawn from a variety of behavioral sciences), practical approaches (such as the techniques for effectively integrating user needs in system development), and social issues (such as the determinants of utility, usability and acceptability).

For further volumes:
http//www.springer.com/series/6033

Desney S. Tan • Anton Nijholt

Editors

Brain-Computer Interfaces

Applying our Minds to Human-Computer Interaction

 Springer

Editors
Desney S. Tan
Microsoft Research
One Microsoft Way
Redmond
WA 98052
USA
desney@microsoft.com

Anton Nijholt
Fac. Electrical Engineering,
Mathematics & Computer Science
University of Twente
Enschede
The Netherlands
a.nijholt@ewi.utwente.nl

ISBN 978-1-4471-2571-6   ISBN 978-1-84996-272-8 (eBook)
DOI 10.1007/978-1-84996-272-8
Springer London Dordrecht Heidelberg New York

British Library Cataloguing in Publication Data
A catalogue record for this book is available from the British Library

Printed on acid-free paper

Springer is part of Springer Science+Business Media (www.springer.com)

Preface

Human-Computer Interaction (HCI) research used to be about the ergonomics of interfaces and, interfaces used to consist of a keyboard, a mouse and whatever could be displayed on the screen of a monitor, that is, the graphical user interface. Nowadays, when we talk about Human-Computer Interaction research, we are talking about multimodal interaction in environments where we research natural human behavior characteristics in general, rather than looking at keyboard and mouse interaction. The environments we live in support us in our activities. Sensor-equipped environments know about us, our activities, our preferences, and about our interactions in the past. This knowledge is obtained from our interaction behavior, behavior that can be observed and interpreted using knowledge that becomes available and that can be fused from cameras, microphones, and position sensors. This allows the environment to not only be reactive, but also proactive, anticipating the user's activities, needs and preferences.

Less traditional sensors are now being introduced in the Human-Computer Interaction field. The aim is to gather as much information as possible from the human interaction partner and the context, including the interaction history, that can be sensed, interpreted, and stored. This information makes it possible for the environment to improve its performance when supporting its users or inhabitants in their daily activities. These sensors detect our activities, whether we move and how we move and they can be embedded in our clothes and in devices we carry with us. In the past, physiological sensors have been used to evaluate user interfaces. How does the user experience a particular user interface? What can we learn from information about heart rate, blood pressure and skin conductivity about how a user experiences a particular interface? Such information can help in improving the design of an interface. At present we see the introduction of these physiological sensors in devices we carry with us or that are embedded in devices that allow explicit control of computer or computer controlled environments. Hence, this information can be used 'on-line', that is, to improve the real-time interaction, rather than 'off-line', that is, to improve the quality of the interface. This information gives insight in the user's affective and cognitive state and it helps us to understand the utterances and activities of the user. It can be used to provide appropriate feedback or to adapt the interface to the user.

Now we see the introduction of sensors that provide us with information that comes directly from the human brain. As in the case of the physiological sensors mentioned above, information from these neuro-physiological sensors can be used to provide more context that helps us to interpret a user's activities and desires. In addition, brain activity can be controlled by the user and it can be used to control an application. Hence, a user can decide to use his or her brain activity to issue commands. One example is motor imagery, where the user imagines a certain movement in order to, for example, navigate in a virtual or physical environment. On the other hand, an environment can attempt to issue signals from which it can become clear, by looking at the initiated brain activity, what the user is interested in or wants to achieve.

The advances in cognitive neuroscience and brain imaging technologies provide us with the increasing ability to interface directly with activity in the brain. Researchers have begun to use these technologies to build brain-computer interfaces. Originally, these interfaces were meant to allow patients with severe motor disabilities to communicate and to control devices by thought alone. Removing the need for motor movements in computer interfaces is challenging and rewarding, but there is also the potential of brain sensing technologies as input mechanisms that give access to extremely rich information about the state of the user. Having access to this information is valuable to Human-Computer Interaction researchers and opens up at least three distinct areas of research: controlling computers by using thought alone or as a complementary input modality, evaluating systems and interfaces, and building adaptive user interfaces.

Specifically, this book aims to identify and discuss

- Brain-computer interface applications for users with permanent and situational physical disabilities, as well as for able-bodied users; this includes application in domains such as traditional communication and productivity tasks, as well as in games and entertainment computing;
- Sensing technologies and data processing techniques that apply well to the suite of applications in which HCI researchers are interested;
- Techniques for integrating brain activity, whether induced by thought or by performing a task, in the palette of input modalities for (multimodal) Human-Computer Interaction

The Human-Computer Interaction field has matured much in the last several decades. It is now firmly rooted as a field that connects more traditional fields such as computer science, design, and psychology in such a way as to allow us to leverage and synthesize work in these spaces to build technologies that augment our lives in some way. The field has also built up well-defined methodologies for repeating this work across a series of disciplines. Simultaneously, neuroscience continues to advance sufficiently fast and brain-computer interfaces are starting to gain enough traction so that we believe it is a field ripe for collaboration with others such as HCI. In fact, we argue that the specific properties of the two fields make them extremely well suited to cross-fertilization, and that is the intent of this book. That said, we hope that the specific way we have crafted this book will also provide brain-computer interface researchers with the appropriate background to engage with HCI researchers in their work.

Acknowledgements   The editors are grateful to Hendri Hondorp for his help with editing this book.

Redmond/Enschede   *Desney Tan*
                                                                         Anton Nijholt

Contents

Contributors

Brendan Z. Allison Institute for Knowledge Discovery, Laboratory of Brain-Computer Interfaces, Graz University of Technology, Krenngasse 37/III, 8010 Graz, Austria, allison@tugraz.at

Nima Bigdely-Shamlo Swartz Center for Computational Neuroscience, Institute for Neural Computation, University of California San Diego, La Jolla, CA, USA

Benjamin Blankertz Berlin Institute of Technology, Franklinstr. 28/29, Berlin, Germany
Fraunhofer FIRST, Kekuléstr. 7, Berlin, Germany, blanker@cs.tu-berlin.de

Anne-Marie Brouwer TNO Human Factors, P.O. Box 23, 3769DE Soesterberg, The Netherlands, anne-marie.brouwer@tno.nl

Shih-Fu Chang Department of Electrical Engineering, Columbia University, New York, NY, USA, sfchang@ee.columbia.edu

Krysta Chauncey Computer Science Department, Tufts University, Medford, MA 02155, USA, krysta.chauncey@tufts.edu

Márton Danóczy Berlin Institute of Technology, Franklinstr. 28/29, Berlin, Germany, marton@cs.tu-berlin.de

Arnaud Delorme Swartz Center for Computational Neuroscience, Institute for Neural Computation, University of California San Diego, La Jolla, CA, USA
Université de Toulouse, UPS, Centre de Recherche Cerveau et Cognition, Toulouse, France
CNRS, CerCo, Toulouse, France, arno@ucsd.edu

J. Hunter Downs Archinoetics LLC, 700 Bishop St, Ste 2000, Honolulu, HI 96817, USA, hunter@archinoetics.com

Traci H. Downs Archinoetics LLC, 700 Bishop St, Ste 2000, Honolulu, HI 96817, USA, traci@archinoetics.com

Jan B.F. Erp   TNO Human Factors, P.O. Box 23, 3769DE Soesterberg, The
Netherlands, jan.vanerp@tno.nl

Sergio Fantini   Biomedical Engineering Department, Tufts University, Medford,
MA 02155, USA, sergio.fantini@tufts.edu

Siamac Fazli   Berlin Institute of Technology, Franklinstr. 28/29, Berlin, Germany,
fazli@cs.tu-berlin.de

Matti Gaertner   Team PhyPA, TU Berlin, Berlin, Germany
Department of Psychology and Ergonomics, Chair for Human-Machine Systems,
Berlin Institute of Technology, Berlin, Germany

Audrey Girouard   Computer Science Department, Tufts University, Medford,
MA 02155, USA, audrey.girouard@tufts.edu

Marc Grootjen   EagleScience, Lommerlustlaan 59, 2012BZ Haarlem, The
Netherlands, marc@eaglescience.nl

Hayrettin Gürkök   Human Media Interaction, University of Twente, Faculty of
EEMCS, P.O. Box 217, 7500 AE, Enschede, The Netherlands,
h.gurkok@ewi.utwente.nl

Barbara Hanna   Neuromatters, LLC, New York, NY, USA,
bhanna@neuromatters.com

Dirk Heylen   Human Media Interaction, University of Twente, Faculty of
EEMCS, P.O. Box 217, 7500 AE, Enschede, The Netherlands,
d.k.j.heylen@ewi.utwente.nl

Leanne M. Hirshfield   Computer Science Department, Tufts University,
Medford, MA 02155, USA, leanne.hirshfield@tufts.edu

Robert J.K. Jacob   Computer Science Department, Tufts University, Medford,
MA 02155, USA, robert.jacob@tufts.edu

Sabine Jatzev   Team PhyPA, TU Berlin, Berlin, Germany
Department of Psychology and Ergonomics, Chair for Human-Machine Systems,
Berlin Institute of Technology, Berlin, Germany

Christian Kothe   Team PhyPA, TU Berlin, Berlin, Germany
Department of Psychology and Ergonomics, Chair Human-Machine Systems,
Berlin Institute of Technology, Berlin, Germany, christiankothe@googlemail.com

Bram van de Laar   Human Media Interaction, University of Twente, Faculty of
EEMCS, P.O. Box 217, 7500 AE, Enschede, The Netherlands,
b.l.a.vandelaar@ewi.utwente.nl

Scott Makeig   Swartz Center for Computational Neuroscience, Institute for
Neural Computation, University of California San Diego, La Jolla, CA, USA,
smakeig@ucsd.edu

Rudolph Mappus BrainLab, School of Interactive Computing, Georgia Institute of Technology, Atlanta, USA, cmappus@gatech.edu

Yoky Matsuoka Department of Computer Science and Engineering, University of Washington, Washington, USA, yoky@u.washington.edu

Melody Moore Jackson BrainLab, School of Interactive Computing, Georgia Institute of Technology, Atlanta, USA, melody@cc.gatech.edu

Chet T. Moritz Department of Physiology and Biophysics and Washington National Primate Research Center, University of Washington, Washington, USA, ctmoritz@u.washington.edu

Christian Mühl Human Media Interaction, University of Twente, Faculty of EEMCS, P.O. Box 217, 7500 AE, Enschede, The Netherlands, c.muehl@ewi.utwente.nl

Klaus-Robert Müller Berlin Institute of Technology, Franklinstr. 28/29, Berlin, Germany, krm@cs.tu-berlin.de

Christa Neuper Institute for Knowledge Discovery, Laboratory of Brain-Computer Interfaces, Graz University of Technology, Krenngasse 37/III, 8010 Graz, Austria
Department of Psychology, University of Graz, Universitätsplatz 2/III, 8010 Graz, Austria, christa.neuper@uni-graz.at

Anton Nijholt Human Media Interaction, University of Twente, Faculty of EEMCS, P.O. Box 217, 7500 AE, Enschede, The Netherlands, a.nijholt@ewi.utwente.nl

Erin M. Nishimura Archinoetics LLC, 700 Bishop St, Ste 2000, Honolulu, HI 96817, USA, erin@archinoetics.com

Robert Oostenveld Donders Institute for Brain, Cognition and Behaviour, Radboud University Nijmegen, Nijmegen, The Netherlands, r.oostenveld@donders.ru.nl

Lucas C. Parra City College of New York, New York, NY, USA, parra@ccny.cuny.edu

Evan M. Peck Computer Science Department, Tufts University, Medford, MA 02155, USA, evan.peck@tufts.edu

Danny Plass-Oude Bos Human Media Interaction, University of Twente, Faculty of EEMCS, P.O. Box 217, 7500 AE, Enschede, The Netherlands, d.plass@ewi.utwente.nl

Mannes Poel Human Media Interaction, University of Twente, Faculty of EEMCS, P.O. Box 217, 7500 AE, Enschede, The Netherlands, m.poel@ewi.utwente.nl

Eric Pohlmeyer Department of Biomedical Engineering, Columbia University, New York, NY, USA, ep2473@columbia.edu

Florin Popescu Fraunhofer FIRST, Kekuléstr. 7, Berlin, Germany, florin.popescu@first.fraunhofer.de

Evan D. Rapoport Archinoetics LLC, 700 Bishop St, Ste 2000, Honolulu, HI 96817, USA, evan@archinoetics.com

Boris Reuderink Human Media Interaction, University of Twente, Faculty of EEMCS, P.O. Box 217, 7500 AE, Enschede, The Netherlands, b.reuderink@ewi.utwente.nl

Paul Sajda Department of Biomedical Engineering, Columbia University, New York, NY, USA, psajda@columbia.edu

Angelo Sassaroli Biomedical Engineering Department, Tufts University, Medford, MA 02155, USA, angelo.sassaroli@tufts.edu

Gerwin Schalk Wadsworth Center, New York State Dept. of Health, Albany, USA, schalk@wadsworth.org

Erin Treacy Solovey Computer Science Department, Tufts University, Medford, MA 02155, USA, erin.solovey@tufts.edu

Desney Tan Microsoft Research, One Microsoft Way, Redmond, WA 98052, USA, desney@microsoft.com

Marieke E. Thurlings TNO Human Factors, P.O. Box 23, 3769DE Soesterberg, The Netherlands
Utrecht University, Utrecht, The Netherlands, marieke.thurlings@tno.nl

Andrey Vankov Swartz Center for Computational Neuroscience, Institute for Neural Computation, University of California San Diego, La Jolla, CA, USA, avankow@ucsd.edu

Hans (J.A.) Veltman TNO Human Factors, P.O. Box 23, 3769DE Soesterberg, The Netherlands, hans.veltman@tno.nl

Jun Wang Department of Electrical Engineering, Columbia University, New York, NY, USA, jwang@ee.columbia.edu

Peter J. Werkhoven TNO Human Factors, P.O. Box 23, 3769DE Soesterberg, The Netherlands
Utrecht University, Utrecht, The Netherlands, peter.werkhoven@tno.nl

Alik S. Widge Department of Psychiatry, University of Washington, Washington, USA, alikw@u.washington.edu

Adam Wilson Department of Neurosurgery, University of Cincinnati, Cincinnati, USA, wilso3jn@uc.edu

Peter M. Wubbels   Archinoetics LLC, 700 Bishop St, Ste 2000, Honolulu, HI 96817, USA

Thorsten O. Zander   Team PhyPA, TU Berlin, Berlin, Germany
Department of Psychology and Ergonomics, Chair for Human-Machine Systems, Berlin Institute of Technology, Berlin, Germany,
thorsten.zander@mms.tu-berlin.de

Acronyms

AAT	Alpha Attenuation Test
ACT	Anatomically Correct Testbed
A-LOC	Almost Loss of Consciousness
ALS	Amyotrophic Lateral Sclerosis
AP	Average Precision
aPFC	Anterior PreFrontal Cortex
BCI	Brain-Computer Interaction
BIRT	Brain-Interface Run-Time
BMI	Brain-Machine Interaction
CAUS	Covert Aspects of User State
CBF	Cerebral Blood Flow
CI	Control Interface
CNV	Contingent Negative Variation
CSP	Common Spatial Patterns
DOF	Degrees of Freedom
ECG	ElectroCardioGram
ECoG	ElectroCorticoGraphic
EEG	ElectroEncephaloGraphy
EMG	ElectroMyoGram
EOG	ElectroOculoGram
ERD	Event Related Desynchronization
ERN	Error Related Negativity
ERP	Event Related Potentials
ERS	Event-Related Synchronization
FES	Functional Electrical Stimulation
FFT	Fast Fourier Transform
fMRI	functional Magnetic Resonance Imaging
FN	False Negative rate
fNIR	functional Near-InfraRed Sensing
fNIRS	functional Near-InfraRed Spectroscopy
FP	False Positive rate

GEQ	Game Experience Questionnaire
G-LOC	Gravity-induced Loss of Consciousness
GOMS	Goals, Operators, Methods and Selection rules
GUI	Graphical User Interface
HCI	Human-Computer Interaction
HSWM	High Spatial Working Memory
ICA	Independent Component Analysis
ITR	Information Transfer Rate
LDA	Linear Discriminant Analysis
LRP	Lateralized Readiness Potential
LSWM	Low Spatial Working Memory
MEG	MagnetoEncephaloGraphy
MMN	MisMatch Negativity
NIR	Near-InfraRed
NPC	Non-Player Character
OOI	Objects of Interest
PCT	Perceptual Control Theory
PET	Positron Emission Tomography
PFC	PreFrontal Cortex
PSoC	Programmable System-on-a-Chip
QDA	Quadratic Discriminant Analysis
RJB	Right Justified Box
RP	Readiness Potential
RSVP	Rapid Serial Visual Presentation
SCP	Slow Cortical Potential
SMR	SensoriMotor Rhythm
SPECT	Single Photon Emission Computed Tomography
SSEP	Somato Sensory Evoked Potential
SSVEP	Steady-State Visual Evoked Potentials
SWDA	Stepwise Discriminant Analysis
TLS	Total Locked-in Syndrome
TP	True Positive rate
TTD	Thought Translation Device
TTI	Target to Target Interval
UI	User Interface
VEP	Visually Evoked Potential
WM	Working Memory

Part I
Overview and Techniques

Chapter 1
Brain-Computer Interfaces
and Human-Computer Interaction

Desney Tan and Anton Nijholt

Abstract Advances in cognitive neuroscience and brain imaging technologies have started to provide us with the ability to interface directly with the human brain. This ability is made possible through the use of sensors that can monitor some of the physical processes that occur within the brain that correspond with certain forms of thought. Researchers have used these technologies to build brain-computer interfaces (BCIs), communication systems that do not depend on the brain's normal output pathways of peripheral nerves and muscles. In these systems, users explicitly manipulate their brain activity instead of using motor movements to produce signals that can be used to control computers or communication devices.

Human-Computer Interaction (HCI) researchers explore possibilities that allow computers to use as many sensory channels as possible. Additionally, researchers have started to consider implicit forms of input, that is, input that is not explicitly performed to direct a computer to do something. Researchers attempt to infer information about user state and intent by observing their physiology, behavior, or the environment in which they operate. Using this information, systems can dynamically adapt themselves in order to support the user in the task at hand.

BCIs are now mature enough that HCI researchers must add them to their tool belt when designing novel input techniques. In this introductory chapter to the book we present the novice reader with an overview of relevant aspects of BCI and HCI, so that hopefully they are inspired by the opportunities that remain.

D. Tan (✉)
Microsoft Research, One Microsoft Way, Redmond, WA 98052, USA
e-mail: desney@microsoft.com

A. Nijholt
University of Twente, PO Box 217, 7500 AE Enschede, The Netherlands
e-mail: anijholt@ewi.utwente.nl

D.S. Tan, A. Nijholt (eds.), *Brain-Computer Interfaces,*
Human-Computer Interaction Series,
DOI 10.1007/978-1-84996-272-8_1, © Springer-Verlag London Limited 2010

1.1 Introduction

For generations, humans have fantasized about the ability to communicate and interact with machines through thought alone or to create devices that can peer into person's mind and thoughts. These ideas have captured the imagination of humankind
in the form of ancient myths and modern science fiction stories. However, it is only
recently that advances in cognitive neuroscience and brain imaging technologies
have started to provide us with the ability to interface directly with the human brain.
This ability is made possible through the use of sensors that can monitor some of
the physical processes that occur within the brain that correspond with certain forms
of thought.

Primarily driven by growing societal recognition for the needs of people with
physical disabilities, researchers have used these technologies to build brain-
computer interfaces (BCIs), communication systems that do not depend on the
brain's normal output pathways of peripheral nerves and muscles. In these systems,
users explicitly manipulate their brain activity instead of using motor movements to
produce signals that can be used to control computers or communication devices.
The impact of this work is extremely high, especially to those who suffer from
devastating neuromuscular injuries and neurodegenerative diseases such as amyotrophic lateral sclerosis, which eventually strips individuals of voluntary muscular
activity while leaving cognitive function intact.

Meanwhile, and largely independent of these efforts, Human-Computer Interaction (HCI) researchers continually work to increase the communication bandwidth
and quality between humans and computers. They have explored visualizations and
multimodal presentations so that computers may use as many sensory channels as
possible to send information to a human. Similarly, they have devised hardware and
software innovations to increase the information a human can quickly input into
the computer. Since we have traditionally interacted with the external world only
through our physical bodies, these input mechanisms have mostly required performing some form of motor activity, be it moving a mouse, hitting buttons, using hand
gestures, or speaking.

Additionally, these researchers have started to consider implicit forms of input,
that is, input that is not explicitly performed to direct a computer to do something. In an area of exploration referred to by names such as perceptual computing or contextual computing, researchers attempt to infer information about
user state and intent by observing their physiology, behavior, or even the environment in which they operate. Using this information, systems can dynamically
adapt themselves in useful ways in order to better support the user in the task at
hand.

We believe that there exists a large opportunity to bridge the burgeoning research
in Brain-Computer Interfaces and Human Computer Interaction, and this book attempts to do just that. We believe that BCI researchers would benefit greatly from
the body of expertise built in the HCI field as they construct systems that rely solely
on interfacing with the brain as the control mechanism. Likewise, BCIs are now
mature enough that HCI researchers must add them to our tool belt when designing

novel input techniques (especially in environments with constraints on normal motor movement), when measuring traditionally elusive cognitive or emotional phenomena in evaluating our interfaces, or when trying to infer user state to build adaptive systems. Each chapter in this book was selected to present the novice reader with an overview of some aspect of BCI or HCI, and in many cases the union of the two, so that they not only get a flavor of work that currently exists, but are hopefully inspired by the opportunities that remain.

1.1.1 The Evolution of BCIs and the Bridge with Human Computer Interaction

The evolution of any technology can generally be broken into three phases. The initial phase, or proof-of-concept, demonstrates the basic functionality of a technology. In this phase, even trivially functional systems are impressive and stimulate imagination. They are also sometimes misunderstood and doubted. As an example, when moving pictures were first developed, people were amazed by simple footage shot with stationary cameras of flowers blowing in the wind or waves crashing on the beach. Similarly, when the computer mouse was first invented, people were intrigued by the ability to move a physical device small distances on a tabletop in order to control a pointer in two dimensions on a computer screen. In brain sensing work, this represents the ability to extract any bit of information directly from the brain without utilizing normal muscular channels.

In the second phase, or emulation, the technology is used to mimic existing technologies. The first movies were simply recorded stage plays, and computer mice were used to select from lists of items much as they would have been with the numeric pad on a keyboard. Similarly, early brain-computer interfaces have aimed to emulate functionality of mice and keyboards, with very few fundamental changes to the interfaces on which they operated. It is in this phase that the technology starts to be driven less by its novelty and starts to interest a wider audience interested by the science of understanding and developing it more deeply.

Finally, the technology hits the third phase, in which it attains maturity in its own right. In this phase, designers understand and exploit the intricacies of the new technology to build unique experiences that provide us with capabilities never before available. For example, the flashback and crosscut, as well as "bullet-time" introduced more recently by the movie the Matrix have become well-acknowledged idioms of the medium of film. Similarly, the mouse has become so well integrated into our notions of computing that it is extremely hard to imagine using current interfaces without such a device attached. It should be noted that in both these cases, more than forty years passed between the introduction of the technology and the widespread development and usage of these methods.

We believe that brain-computer interface work is just now coming out of its infancy, and that the opportunity exists to move it from the proof-of-concept and emulation stages into maturity. However, to do this, we will have not only have to continue the discovery and invention within the domain itself, but also start to build bridges and leverage researchers and work in other fields. Meanwhile, the human computer interaction field continues to work toward expanding the effective information bandwidth between human and machine, and more importantly to design technologies that integrate seamlessly into our everyday tasks. Specifically, we believe there are several opportunities, though we believe our views are necessarily constrained and hope that this book inspires further crossover and discussion. For example:

- While the BCI community has largely focused on the very difficult mechanics of acquiring data from the brain, HCI researchers could add experience designing interfaces that make the most out of the scanty bits of information they have about the user and their intent. They also bring in a slightly different viewpoint which may result in interesting innovation on the existing applications of interest. For example, while BCI researchers maintain admirable focus on providing patients who have lost muscular control an alternate input device, HCI researchers might complement the efforts by considering the entire locked-in experience, including such factors as preparation, communication, isolation, and awareness, etc.
- Beyond the traditional definition of Brain-Computer Interfaces, HCI researchers have already started to push the boundaries of what we can do if we can peer into the user's brain, if even ever so roughly. Considering how these devices apply to healthy users in addition to the physically disabled, and how adaptive system may take advantage of them could push analysis methods as well as application areas.
- The HCI community has also been particularly successful at systematically exploring and creating whole new application areas. In addition to thinking about using technology to fix existing pain points, or to alleviate difficult work, this community has sought scenarios in which technology can augment everyday human life in some way. We believe that we have only begun to scratch the surface of the set of applications that brain sensing technologies open, and hope that this book stimulates a much wider audience to being considering these scenarios.

The specific goals of this book are three-fold. First, we would like to provide background for researchers that have little (or no) expertise in neuroscience or brain sensing so that they gain appreciation for the domain, and are equipped not only to read and understand articles, but also ideally to engage in work. Second, we will present a broad survey of representative work within the domain, written by key researchers. Third, because the intersection of HCI/BCI is relatively new, we use the book to articulate some of the challenges and opportunities for using brain sensing in HCI work, as well as applying HCI solutions to brain sensing work. We provide a quick overview and outline in the remainder of this introductory chapter.

1.2 Brain Imaging Primer

1.2.1 Architecture of the Brain

Contrary to popular simplifications, the brain is not a general-purpose computer with a unified central processor. Rather, it is a complex assemblage of competing sub-systems, each highly specialized for particular tasks (Carey 2002). By studying the effects of brain injuries and, more recently, by using new brain imaging technologies, neuroscientists have built detailed topographical maps associating different parts of the physical brain with distinct cognitive functions.

The brain can be roughly divided into two main parts: the cerebral cortex and sub-cortical regions. Sub-cortical regions are phylogenetically older and include a areas associated with controlling basic functions including vital functions such as respiration, heart rate, and temperature regulation, basic emotional and instinctive responses such as fear and reward, reflexes, as well as learning and memory. The cerebral cortex is evolutionarily much newer. Since this is the largest and most complex part of the brain in the human, this is usually the part of the brain people notice in pictures. The cortex supports most sensory and motor processing as well as "higher" level functions including reasoning, planning, language processing, and pattern recognition. This is the region that current BCI work has largely focused on.

1.2.2 Geography of Thought

The cerebral cortex is split into two hemispheres that often have very different functions. For instance, most language functions lie primarily in the left hemisphere, while the right hemisphere controls many abstract and spatial reasoning skills. Also, most motor and sensory signals to and from the brain cross hemispheres, meaning that the right brain senses and controls the left side of the body and vice versa. The brain can be further divided into separate regions specialized for different functions. For example, occipital regions at the very back of the head are largely devoted to processing of visual information. Areas in the temporal regions, roughly along the sides and lower areas of the cortex, are involved in memory, pattern matching, language processing, and auditory processing. Still other areas of the cortex are devoted to diverse functions such as spatial representation and processing, attention orienting, arithmetic, voluntary muscle movement, planning, reasoning and even enigmatic aspects of human behavior such as moral sense and ambition.

We should emphasize that our understanding of brain structure and activity is still fairly shallow. These topographical maps are not definitive assignments of location to function. In fact, some areas process multiple functions, and many functions are processed in more than one area.

1.2.3 Measuring Thought with Brain Imaging

Regardless of function, each part of the brain is made up of nerve cells called neurons. As a whole, the brain is a dense network consisting of about 100 billion neurons. Each of these neurons communicates with thousands of others in order to regulate physical processes and to produce thought. Neurons communicate either by sending electrical signals to other neurons through physical connections or by exchanging chemicals called neurotransmitters. When they communicate, neurons need more oxygen and glucose to function and cause an increase in blood flow to active regions of the brain.

Advances in brain imaging technologies enable us to observe the electric, chemical, or blood flow changes as the brain processes information or responds to various stimuli. Using these techniques we can produce remarkable images of brain structure and activity. By inspecting these images, we can infer specific cognitive processes occurring in the brain at any given time.

Again, we should emphasize that with our current understanding, brain imaging allows us only to sense general cognitive processes and not the full semantics of our thoughts. Brain imaging is, in general, not mind reading. For example, although we can probably tell if a user is processing language, we cannot easily determine the semantics of the content. We hope that the resolution at which we are able to decipher thoughts grows as we increase our understanding of the human brain and abstract thought, but none of the work in this book is predicated on these improvements happening.

1.2.4 Brain Imaging Technologies

There are two general classes of brain imaging technologies: invasive technologies, in which sensors are implanted directly on or in the brain, and non-invasive technologies, which measure brain activity using external sensors. Although invasive technologies provide high temporal and spatial resolution, they usually cover only very small regions of the brain. Additionally, these techniques require surgical procedures that often lead to medical complications as the body adapts, or does not adapt, to the implants. Furthermore, once implanted, these technologies cannot be moved to measure different regions of the brain. While many researchers are experimenting with such implants (e.g. Lal et al. 2004), we will not review this research in detail as we believe these techniques are unsuitable for human-computer interaction work and general consumer use.

We summarize and compare the many non-invasive technologies that use only external sensors in Fig. 1.1 (see the Appendix of this Chapter). While the list may seem lengthy, only Electroencephalography (EEG) and Functional Near Infrared Spectroscopy (fNIRS) present the opportunity for inexpensive, portable, and safe devices, properties we believe are important for brain-computer interface applications in HCI work.

1.2.4.1   Electroencephalography (EEG)

EEG uses electrodes placed directly on the scalp to measure the weak (5–100 μV) electrical potentials generated by activity in the brain (for a detailed discussion of EEG, see Smith 2004). Because of the fluid, bone, and skin that separate the electrodes from the actual electrical activity, signals tend to be smoothed and rather noisy. Hence, while EEG measurements have good temporal resolution with delays in the tens of milliseconds, spatial resolution tends to be poor, ranging about 2–3 cm accuracy at best, but usually worse. Two centimeters on the cerebral cortex could be the difference between inferring that the user is listening to music when they are in fact moving their hands. We should note that this is the predominant technology in BCI work, as well as work described in this book.

1.2.4.2   Functional Near Infrared Spectroscopy (fNIRS)

fNIRS technology, on the other hand, works by projecting near infrared light into the brain from the surface of the scalp and measuring optical changes at various wavelengths as the light is reflected back out (for a detailed discussion of fNIRS, see Coyle et al. 2004). The NIR response of the brain measures cerebral hemodynamics and detects localized blood volume and oxygenation changes (Chance et al. 1998).

Since changes in tissue oxygenation associated with brain activity modulate the absorption and scattering of the near infrared light photons to varying amounts, fNIRS can be used to build functional maps of brain activity. This generates images similar to those produced by traditional Functional Magnetic Resonance Imaging (fMRI) measurement. Much like fMRI, images have relatively high spatial resolution (<1 cm) at the expense of lower temporal resolution (>2–5 seconds), limited by the time required for blood to flow into the region.

In brain-computer interface research aimed at directly controlling computers, temporal resolution is of utmost importance, since users have to adapt their brain activity based on immediate feedback provided by the system. For instance, it would be difficult to control a cursor without having interactive input rates. Hence, even though the low spatial resolution of these devices leads to low information transfer rate and poor localization of brain activity, most researchers currently adopt EEG because of the high temporal resolution it offers. However, in more recent attempts to use brain sensing technologies to passively measure user state, good functional localization is crucial for modeling the users' cognitive activities as accurately as possible. The two technologies are nicely complementary and researchers must carefully select the right tool for their particular work. We also believe that there are opportunities for combining various modalities, though this is currently underexplored.

1.3 Brain Imaging to Directly Control Devices

1.3.1 Bypassing Physical Movement to Specify Intent

Most current brain-computer interface work has grown out of the neuroscience and medical fields, and satisfying patient needs has been a prime motivating force. Much of this work aims to improve the lives of patients with severe neuromuscular disorders such as amyotrophic lateral sclerosis (ALS), also popularly known as Lou Gerig's disease, brainstem stroke, or spinal cord injury. In the latter stages of these disorders, many patients lose all control of their physical bodies, including simple functions such as eye-gaze. Some even need help with vital functions such as breathing. However, many of these patients retain full control of their higher level cognitive abilities.

While medical technologies that augment vital bodily functions have drastically extended the lifespan of these patients, these technologies do not alleviate the mental frustration or social isolation caused by having no way to communicate with the external world. Providing these patients with brain-computer interfaces that allow them to control computers directly with their brain signals could dramatically increase their quality of life. The complexity of this control ranges from simple binary decisions, to moving a cursor on the screen, to more ambitious control of mechanical prosthetic devices.

Most current brain-computer interface research has been a logical extension of assistive methods in which one input modality is substituted for another (for detailed reviews of this work, see Coyle et al. 2003; Vaughan 2003). When users lose the use of their arms, they typically move to eye or head tracking, or even speech, to control their computers. However, when they lose control of their physical movement, the physiological function they have the most and sometimes only control over is their brain activity.

1.3.2 Learning to Control Brain Signals

To successfully use current direct control brain-computer interfaces, users have to learn to intentionally manipulate their brain signals. To date, there have been two approaches for training users to control their brain signals (Curran and Stokes 2003). In the first, users are given specific cognitive tasks such as motor imagery to generate measurable brain activity. Using this technique the user can send a binary signal to the computer, for example, by imagining sequences of rest and physical activity such as moving their arms or doing high kicks. The second approach, called operant conditioning, provides users with continuous feedback as they try to control the interface. Users may think about anything (or nothing) so long as they achieve the desired outcome. Over many sessions, users acquire control of the interface without being consciously aware of how they are performing the task. Unfortunately, many users find this technique hard to master.

Other researchers have designed interfaces that exploit the specific affordances of brain control. One such interface presents a grid of keys, each representing a letter or command (Sutter 1992). Each row or column of the grid flashes in rapid succession, and the user is asked to count the number of flashes that occur over the desired key. The system determines the row and column of interest by detecting an event-related signal called the P300 response, which occurs in the parietal cortex about 300 milliseconds after the onset of a significant stimulus.

We believe that there remains much work to be done in designing interfaces that exploit our understanding of cognitive neuroscience and that provide the maximum amount of control using the lowest possible bit rate (for discussion of this and other research challenges in this area, see Wolpaw et al. 2002). We believe that expertise in human-computer interaction can be leveraged to design novel interfaces that may be generally applicable to brain-computer interfaces and low bit rate interactions.

1.3.3 Evaluation of Potential Impact

We are still at a very early stage in brain-computer interface research. Because current systems require so much cognitive effort and produce such small amounts of control information (the best systems now get 25 bits/minute), they remain useful mainly in carefully controlled scenarios and only to users who have no motor alternatives. Much work has to be done before we are able to successfully replace motor movement with brain signals, even in the simplest of scenarios.

While researchers believe that these interfaces will get good enough to vastly improve the lives of disabled users, not all are certain that brain-computer interfaces will eventually be good enough to completely replace motor movement even for able-bodied users. In fact, many researchers have mixed feelings on whether or not this is useful or advisable in many situations. However, we do foresee niche applications in which brain-computer interfaces might be useful for able-bodied people.

For example, since these interfaces could potentially bypass the lag in mentally generating and executing motor movements, they would work well in applications for which response times are crucial. Additionally, they could be useful in scenarios where it is physically difficult to move. Safety mechanisms on airplanes or spacecraft could benefit from such interfaces. In these scenarios, pilots experiencing large physical forces do not have much time to react to impending disasters, and even with limited bandwidth brain control could be valuable. Also, since brain control is intrinsically less observable than physical movement, brain-computer interfaces may be useful for covert operation, such as in command and control or surveillance applications for military personnel.

Brain-computer interfaces could also be successful in games and entertainment applications. In fact, researchers have already begun to explore this lucrative area to exploit the novelty of such an input device in this large and growing market. One interesting example of such a game is Brainball, developed at the Interactive Studio in Sweden (Hjelm and Browall 2000). In this game, two players equipped with EEG are seated on opposite sides of a table. Players score simply by moving a ball on the table into the opponent's goal. The unusual twist to this game is that users move the ball by relaxing. The more relaxed the EEG senses the user to be, the more the ball moves. Hence, rather than strategic thoughts and intense actions, the successful player must learn to achieve calmness and inactivity. At the time this book was written, various game companies (such as Mattel) have already released consumer devices (toys) that claim some form of EEG control, with multiple others pending release.

1.4 Brain Imaging as an Indirect Communication Channel

1.4.1 Exploring Brain Imaging for End-User Applications

As HCI researchers, we are in the unique position to think about the opportunities offered by widespread adoption of brain-computer interfaces. While it is a remarkable endeavor to use brain activity as a novel replacement for motor movement, we think that brain-computer interfaces used in this capacity will probably remain tethered to a fairly niche market. Hence, in this book, we look beyond current research approaches for the potential to make brain imaging useful to the general end-user population in a wide range of scenarios.

These considerations have led to very different approaches in using brain imaging and brain-computer interfaces. Rather than building systems in which users intentionally generate brain signals to directly control computers, researchers have also sought to passively sense and model some notion of the user's internal cognitive state as they perform useful tasks in the real world. This approach is similar to efforts aimed at measuring emotional state with physiological sensors (e.g. Picard and Klein 2002). Like emotional state, cognitive state is a signal that we would never want the user to intentionally control, either because it would distract them from performing their tasks or because they are not able to articulate the information.

People are notoriously good at modeling the approximate cognitive state of other people using only external cues. For example, most people have little trouble determining that someone is deep in thought simply by looking at them. This ability mediates our social interactions and communication, and is something that is notably lacking in our interactions with computers. While we have attempted to build computer systems that make similar inferences, current models and sensors are not sensitive enough to pick up on subtle external cues that represent internal cognitive state. With brain imaging, we can now directly measure what is going on in a user's brain, presumably making it easier for a computer to model this state.

Researchers have been using this information either as feedback to the user, as awareness information for other users, or as supplementary input to the computer so that it can mediate its interactions accordingly. In the following subsections, we describe threads that run through the various chapters, consisting of understanding human cognition in the real world, using cognitive state as an evaluation metric for interface design, as well as building interfaces that adapt based on cognitive state. We think that this exploration will allow brain imaging, even in its current state, to fundamentally change the richness of our interactions with computers. In fact, much like the mouse and keyboard were pivotal in the development of direct manipulation interfaces, brain imaging could revolutionize our next generation contextually aware computing interfaces.

1.4.2 Understanding Cognition in the Real World

Early neuroscience and cognitive psychology research was largely built upon case studies of neurological syndromes that damaged small parts of the brain. By studying the selective loss of cognitive functions caused by the damage, researchers were able to understand how specific parts of the brain mediated different functions. More recently, with improvements in brain imaging technologies, researchers have used controlled experiments to observe specific brain activations that happen as a result of particular cognitive activities. In both these approaches, the cognitive activities tested are carefully constructed and studied in an isolated manner.

While isolating cognitive activities has its merits, we believe that measuring brain activity as the user operates in the real world could lead to new insights. Researchers are already building wearable brain imaging systems that are suitable for use outside of the laboratory. These systems can be coupled with existing sensors that measure external context so that we can correlate brain activity with the tasks that elicit this activity. While the brain imaging device can be seen as a powerful sensor that informs existing context sensing systems, context sensing systems can also be viewed as an important augmentation to brain imaging devices.

Again, we believe that there are opportunities here that are currently underexplored. Using this approach, we are able not only to measure cognitive activity in more complex scenarios than we can construct in the laboratory, but also to study processes that take long periods of time. This is useful in tasks for which the brain adapts slowly or for tasks that cannot be performed on demand in sterile laboratory environments, such as idea generation or the storage of contextual memory cues as information is learned. Also, while neuroscience studies have focused on the dichotomy between neurologically disabled and normal patients, we now have the opportunity to study other individual differences, perhaps due to factors such as gender, expertise on a given task, or traditional assessment levels of cognitive ability. Finally, we believe that there exists the opportunity to study people as they interact with one another. This can be used to explore the neural basis of social dynamics, or to attempt to perform dynamic workload distribution between people collaborating on a project. Furthermore, having data from multiple people operating in the real world over long periods of time might allow us to find patterns and build robust cognitive models that bridge the gap between current cognitive science and neuroscience theory.

1.4.3 Cognitive State as an Evaluation Metric

In a more controlled and applied setting, the cognitive state derived from brain imaging could be used as an evaluation metric for either the user or for computer systems. Since we can measure the intensity of cognitive activity as a user performs certain tasks, we could potentially use brain imaging to assess cognitive aptitude based on how hard someone has to work on a particular set of tasks. With proper task and cognitive models, we might use these results to generalize performance predictions in a much broader range of scenarios.

For example, using current testing methods, a user who spends a huge amount of cognitive effort working on test problems may rate similarly to someone who spent half the test time daydreaming so long as they ended up with the same number of correct answers. However, it might be useful to know that the second user might perform better if the test got harder or if the testing scenario got more stressful. In entertainment scenarios such as games, it may be possible to quantify a user's immersion and attentional load. Some of the work in this book is aimed at validating brain imaging as a cognitive evaluation method and examine how it can be used to augment traditional methods.

Rather than evaluating the human, a large part of human-computer interaction research is centered on the ability to evaluate computer hardware or software interfaces. This allows us not only to measure the effectiveness of these interfaces, but more importantly to understand how users and computers interact so that we can improve our computing systems. Thus far, researchers have been only partially successful in learning from performance metrics such as task completion times and error rates. They have also used behavioral and physiological measures to infer cognitive processes, such as mouse movement and eye gaze as a measure of attention, or heart rate and galvanic skin response as measures of arousal and fatigue. However, there remain many cognitive processes that are hard to measure externally. For these, they typically resort to clever experimental design or subjective questionnaires which give them indirect metrics for specific cognitive phenomena. For example, it is still extremely difficult to accurately ascertain cognitive workloads or particular cognitive strategies used, such as verbal versus spatial memory encoding.

Brain sensing provides the promise of a measure that more directly quantifies the cognitive utility of our interfaces. This could potentially provide powerful measures that either corroborate external measures, or more interestingly, shed light on the interactions that we would have never derived from external measures alone. Various researchers are working to generalize these techniques and provide a suite of cognitive measures that brain imaging provides.

1.4.4 Adaptive Interfaces Based on Cognitive State

If we take this idea to the limit and tighten the iteration between measurement, evaluation, and redesign, we could design interfaces that automatically adapt depending on the cognitive state of the user. Interfaces that adapt themselves to available resources in order to provide pleasant and optimal user experiences are not a new concept. In fact, researchers have put quite a bit of thought into dynamically adapting interfaces to best utilize such things as display space, available input mechanisms, device processing capabilities, and even user task or context.

For example, web mechanisms such as hypertext markup language (HTML) and cascading style sheets (CSS) were implemented such that authors would specify content, but leave specific layout to the browsers. This allows the content to reflow and re-layout based on the affordances of the client application. As another example, researchers have built systems that model the user, their surroundings, and their tasks using machine learning techniques in order to determine how and when to best interrupt them with important notifications (Horvitz et al. 1998). In their work, they aim to exploit the computing environment in a manner that best supports user action.

Adapting to users' limited cognitive resources is at least as important as adapting to specific computing affordances. One simple way in which interfaces may adapt based on cognitive state is to adjust information flow. For example, verbal and spatial tasks are processed by different areas of the brain, and cognitive psychologists have shown that processing capabilities in each of these areas is largely independent (Baddeley 1986). Hence, even though a person may be verbally overloaded and not able to attend to any more verbal information, their spatial modules might be capable of processing more data. Sensory processes such as hearing and seeing, have similar loosely independent capabilities. Using brain imaging, the system knows approximately how the user's attentional and cognitive resources are allocated, and could tailor information presentation to attain the largest communication bandwidth possible. For example, if the user is verbally overloaded, additional information could be transformed and presented in a spatial modality, and vice versa. Alternatively, if the user is completely cognitively overloaded while they work on a task or tasks, the system could present less information until the user has free brain cycles to better deal with the details.

Another way interfaces might adapt is to manage interruptions based on the user's cognitive state. Researchers have shown that interruptions disrupt thought processes and can lead to frustration and significantly degraded task performance (Cutrell et al. 2001). For example, if a user is thinking really hard, the system could detect this and manage pending interruptions such as e-mail alerts and phone calls accordingly. This is true even if the user is staring blankly at the wall and there are no external cues that allow the system to easily differentiate between deep thought and no thought. The system could also act to minimize distractions, which include secondary tasks or background noise. For example, a system sensing a user getting verbally overloaded could attempt to turn down the music, since musical lyrics get subconsciously processed and consume valuable verbal resources. Or perhaps the cell phone could alert the remote speaker and pause the phone call if the driver has to suddenly focus on the road.

Finally, if we can sense higher level cognitive events like confusion and frustration or satisfaction and realization (the "aha" moment), we could tailor interfaces that provide feedback or guidance on task focus and strategy usage in training scenarios. This could lead to interfaces that drastically increase information understanding and retention.

1.5 The Rest of the Book

The chapters in this book are divided into four sections, which loosely parallel the goals of the book:

Part I, Overview and Techniques.

Chapter 2 (Neural Control Interfaces) opens the book by outlining some of the unique challenges and opportunities for designing BCI control interfaces. It presents a loose taxonomy of different factors that should be considered and provides a nice framework for pursuing work in this space. Chapter 3 (Could Anyone Use a BCI?) explores the phenomenon of "BCI illiteracy", the observation that most BCI systems do not typically work for all users. It uses this as grounding for discussion around standardized lingo and measurement metrics to facilitate discussions and comparisons across systems. Chapter 4 (Using Rest Class and Control Paradigms for Brain Computer Interfacing) addresses one specific technical challenge in BCI work, the Midas Touch problem. This is a classic HCI problem in which the control system must distinguish between intended commands and everyday actions, in this case thoughts. Chapter 5 (EEG-Based Navigation from a Human Factors Perspective) presents the analogy between designing BCIs and navigation devices, which include components of planning (cognition), steering (perception), and control (sensation). This provides an interesting way of considering the integration between human factors and BCI work.

Part II, Applications.

Chapter 6 (Applications for Brain-Computer Interfaces) presents a broad survey of applications for BCI systems and characterizes the range of possibilities for neural control. Among these are applications for assistive technologies, recreation, cognitive diagnostics and augmented cognition, as well as rehabilitation and prosthetics. Chapter 7 (Direct Neural Control of Anatomically Correct Robotic Hands) describes the potential to achieve dexterous control of prosthetic hands using BCIs. The chapter describes both the requirements for the BCI, as well as the match with a fully anthropomorphic robot hand that the authors have developed. Chapter 8 (Functional Near-Infrared Sensing and Environmental Control Applications) describes the relatively young fNIRS technology, as well as potential benefits in environmental-control BCIs. Chapter 9 (Cortically-Coupled Computer Vision) complements standard control work with a novel paradigm that extracts useful information processing using brain sensing technologies. Specifically, authors present visual search and im-age retrieval applications that use EEG to automatically decode whether an image is relevant or grabs a user's attention. Chapter 10 (Brain-Computer Interfaces and Games) surveys the state of the art of BCI in games and discusses factors such as learnability, memorability, efficiency, as well as user experience and satisfaction in this context.

Part III, Brain-Sensing in Adaptive User Interfaces.

Chapter 11 (Brain-based Indices for User System Symbiosis) introduces the concept of operator models and the usefulness of brain-based indices in creating computer systems that respond more symbiotically to human needs. Chapter 12 (Enhancing Human-Computer Interaction with Input from Active and Passive Brain-Computer Interfaces) describes the transition from direct control BCIs that provide explicit commands to passive BCIs that implicitly model user state as secondary input to adaptive systems. Chapter 13 (From Brain Signals to Adaptive Interfaces: Using fNIRS in HCI) ties several of the previous chapters together (e.g. Chapter 8 and 10) and describes details of fNIRS technology that are critical in considering the design of BCI-based adaptive systems.

Part IV, Tools.

Chapter 14 (Matlab-Based Tools for BCI Research) reviews freely available stan-dalone Matlab-based software, and drills into BCI-Lab as well as the Fieldtrip and Datasuite environments. Chapter 15 (Using BCI2000 for HCI-Centered BCI Re-search) rounds the book up with an overview of the BCI2000 system, a popular framework for implementing general-purpose BCIs and one that HCI researchers getting into the field could benefit from.

Appendix

Technique	Physical Property	Measurement Mechanism	Advantages	Disadvantages
Electro-encephelograph (EEG)	Electrical potential	Electrodes are placed carefully on the scalp in order to measure the weak (5-100 µV) electrical potentials generated by neural activity in the brain	• Portable, wearable • High temporal resolution (tens or hundreds of milliseconds)	• Low spatial resolution (at best 1-2 cm, usually more) due to noise added when signals move through fluid, bone, and skin. • Requires careful placement of electrodes directly on scalp
Magneto-encephelograph (MEG)	Magnetic potential	Measures magnetic fields generated by the electrical activity of the brain	• MEG enables much deeper imaging and is much more sensitive than EEG, since skull is almost completely transparent to magnetic waves	• Bulky and expensive equipment due to necessity for superconductivity
Positron Emission Tomography (PET)	Blood flow	Detects chemical activity of injected radioactive tracers by measuring gamma ray emissions		• Bulky and expensive equipment • Unsuitable for sustained use due to need to inject radioactive substances
Single Photon Emission Computed Tomography (SPECT)	Blood flow	Works like PET except that uses photomultiplier tubes to measure photons generated by gamma rays	• Slightly less expensive than PET	• Lower temporal and spatial resolution than PET • Bulky and expensive equipment • Unsuitable for sustained use due to need to inject radioactive substances
Functional Magnetic Resonance Imaging (fMRI)	Blood flow	Measures magnetic properties of blood to determine the decrease in deoxyhemoglobin to active brain regions (increased blood flow to these regions is not accompanied by proportional increase in oxygen consumption)	• High spatial resolution (~1mm-1cm)	• Low temporal resolution (5-8 seconds) because inflow of blood is not an immediate phenomenon • Bulky and expensive equipment due to need for superconducting magnets
Functional Near Infrared (fNIR)	Blood flow, Changes in cortical tissue	Measures the absorption and scattering of near infrared light directed into the brain to determine changes in tissue oxygenation (slow response) as well as changes in neuronal membranes during neuron firing (fast event related response)	• High spatial resolution (<1cm) • Similarity to fMRI allows transfer of knowledge • Inexpensive equipment • Portable, wearable • Does not require large amount of expertise to set up • Non-ionizing light safe for extended use	• Low temporal resolution (5-8 seconds) when using slow response measurements

Fig. 1.1 Overview of current functional brain imaging technologies

References

Baddeley AD (1986) Working Memory. Oxford University Press, New York

Carey J (ed) (2002) Brain Facts: A Primer on the Brain and Nervous System, 4th edn. Society for Neuroscience, Washington DC, USA

Chance B, Anday E, Nioka S, Zhou S, Hong L, Worden K, Li C, Murray T, Overtsky Y, Pidikiti D, Thomas R (1998) A novel method for fast imaging of brain function, non-invasively, with light. Opt Express 2(10):411–423

Coyle S, Ward T, Markham C (2003) Brain-computer interfaces: A review. Interdiscip Sci Rev 28(2):112–118

Coyle S, Ward T, Markham C, McDarby G (2004) On the suitability of near-infrared (NIR) systems for next-generation brain-computer interfaces. Physiol Meas 25:815–822

Curran E, Stokes MJ (2003) Learning to control brain activity: A review of the production and control of EEG components for driving brain-computer interface (BCI) systems. Brain Cogn 51:326–336

Cutrell E, Czerwinski M, Horvitz E (2001) Notification, disruption and memory: Effects of messaging interruptions on memory and performance. In: Hi-rose M (ed) Human-Computer Interaction–Interact '01. IOS Press, Amsterdam, pp 263–269

Hjelm SI, Browall C (2000) Brainball—Using brain activity for cool competition. In: Proceedings of NordiCHI 2000

Horvitz E, Breese J, Heckerman D, Hovel D, Rommelse K (1998) The Lumiere project: Bayesian user modeling for inferring the goals and needs of software users. In: Proceedings of the Fourteenth Conference on Uncertainty in Artificial Intelligence

Lal TN, Hinterberger T, Widman G, Schröder M, Hill NJ, Rosenstiel E, Elger CE, Schölkopf B, Birbaumer N (2004) Methods towards invasive human brain computer interfaces. In: Conference on Neural Information Processing Systems

Picard RW, Klein J (2002) Computers that recognize and respond to user emotion: Theoretical and practical implications. Interact Comput 14(2):141–169

Smith RC (2004) Electroencephalograph based brain computer interfaces. Thesis for Master of Engineering Science, University College Dublin

Sutter EE (1992) The brain response interface: Communication through visually induced electrical brain responses. J Microcomput Appl 15(1):31–45

Vaughan TM (2003) Guest editorial brain-computer interface technology: A review of the second inter-national meeting. IEEE Trans Neural Syst Rehabil Eng 11(2):94–109

Wolpaw JR, Birbaumer N, Mcfarland DJ, Pfurtscheller G, Vaughan TM (2002) Brain-computer interfaces for communication and control. Clin Neurophysiol 113:767–791

Chapter 2
Neural Control Interfaces

Melody Moore Jackson and Rudolph Mappus

Abstract The *control interface* is the primary component of a Brain-Computer Interface (BCI) system that provides user interaction. The control interface supplies cues for performing mental tasks, reports system status and task feedback, and often displays representations of the user's brain signals. Control interfaces play a significant role in determining the usability of a BCI, and some of the traditional human-computer interaction design methods apply. However, the very specialized input methods and display paradigms of a BCI require consideration to create optimal usability for a BCI system. This chapter outlines some of the issues and challenges that make designing control interfaces for BCIs unique.

2.1 Introduction

The *Control Interface* of a Brain-Computer Interface (BCI) system is described in (Mason and Birch 2003) as the component that translates the logical control signals produced by a neural signal classifier into semantic control signals to operate a device. Put more simply, the Control Interface (CI) is the component of the BCI system that the user observes during interaction to perform mental tasks and obtain performance feedback. Control Interfaces serve three main functions:

1. Making the state of the controlled device or application visible with a *Control Display*
2. Making the state of the user's neural signals visible via a *Neural Display*
3. Providing a representation of control tasks for the BCI

M. Moore Jackson (✉) · R. Mappus
BrainLab, School of Interactive Computing, Georgia Institute of Technology, Atlanta, USA
e-mail: melody@cc.gatech.edu

R. Mappus
e-mail: cmappus@gatech.edu

D.S. Tan, A. Nijholt (eds.), *Brain-Computer Interfaces,*
Human-Computer Interaction Series,
DOI 10.1007/978-1-84996-272-8_2, © Springer-Verlag London Limited 2010

Fig. 2.1 A binary speller
Control Display

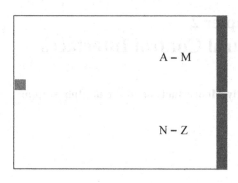

A control display provides visual and/or auditory cues for a control task as well as performance feedback for a BCI user. Control displays reflect the current state of the application or the device; for example, in a spelling program the control display contains the letters available for selection, and typically lists letters already selected. Figure 2.1 shows a binary speller such as described in Vaughan et al. (2001) and similar to Perelmouter and Birbaumer (2000). The two target alphabet ranges on the right side of the screen represent the control task (to select one of the ranges). The vertical position of the small square represents the normalized instantaneous amplitude of the targeted brain signal as the "cursor" moves horizontally across the screen at a constant rate. The selection occurs when the "cursor" reaches one of the targets, and the chosen target flashes to confirm. This simple control interface incorporates the control task, the state of the application, and a representation of neural activity for performance feedback.

This chapter provides an overview of control interface approaches, beginning with control tasks and their associated control and neural displays. We propose a classification of control interfaces and the types of information used to improve usability and performance in BCIs. We discuss traditional models of measuring usability of graphical interfaces and how they can apply in the context of BCI. The chapter concludes with the implications for designing control interfaces for general-use BCIs.

2.2 Background-Biofeedback

Control interface research began over a decade ago as biofeedback research; testing the hypothesis that operant conditioning of autonomic processes could be accomplished by providing physiological process information. The motivation for early biofeedback research was to explore whether displaying real-time physiological information such as blood pressure and heart rate would be sufficient to condition physiological processes. Controlling autonomic processes through conditioning suggested that behavioral therapies could be effective in treating chronic illnesses such as migraine headaches and hypertension.

While initial experiments showed great promise, validation studies were never successful, and biofeedback as the sole instrument for therapy was abandoned

(Roberts 1985). Today, BCIs routinely incorporate biofeedback in the form of neural signal representations. This neural biofeedback is essential for BCIs that require a user to learn to alter a particular brain signal (such as increasing the amplitude of motor cortical signals, Wolpaw et al. 2003) or to indicate the relative status of a brain signal (such as with functional Near Infrared based systems (Naito et al. 2007)).

Recent work has shown that biofeedback displays incorporated with BCIs show promise for new rehabilitation therapies. The barrier between autonomic and voluntary responses using respondent and operant conditioning is being challenged in areas like stroke rehabilitation and seizure management (Birbaumer 2006).

2.3 Control Tasks

A *control task* is a mental effort performed by a BCI user to voluntarily produce changes in brain signals. Control tasks take many forms, including imagined or physical movement, object visualization, focused attention, silent singing or counting, or calming thoughts. Control tasks can be divided into two main categories:

1. *Exogenous* (evoked) paradigms—the user focuses attention on a set of stimuli, which produce an autonomic response that can be detected by a BCI, and
2. *Endogenous* (self-generated) paradigms—the user performs a mental task, such as imagined movement or sub-vocal counting, to create changes in brain signals that can be detected by a BCI.

2.3.1 Exogenous Control Task Paradigms

In exogenous or evoked-response control, an external stimulus is required to cause brain signal changes. For example, the P300 response is activated in the parietal region of the brain 300 ms after the presentation of a visual or auditory stimulus (such as flashing the letters of the alphabet). The activation of the P300 response depends on attention, and a user indicates intent by attending to a particular stimulus (target letter) from a set of stimuli (the entire character set). The original interface paradigm for evoked responses that is still dominant in P300-based BCIs today is the Farwell and Donchin matrix for spelling (Farwell and Donchin 1988). The Farwell-Donchin BCI presents a user with an alphabet arranged in a square matrix. The system evokes a P300 response by randomly highlighting rows and columns of the matrix while measuring parietal responses. The user focuses attention on the desired letter, and each time the row or column containing that letter flashes, the P300 response occurs. At the end of a number of flashes, the intersection of the row and column in the matrix with the highest P300 response will indicate the desired target. P300-based BCI accuracies can reach 100% and many research groups have explored the nuances of optimally presenting stimuli (Allison and Pineda 2006;

Sellers and Donchin 2006). Current research in processing P300 aims to recognize single-trial P300 responses to decrease selection time (Salvaris and Sepulveda 2009; Solis-Escalante et al. 2006).

Another evoked-response approach for BCIs is Steady-state evoked potentials (SSVEPs). The SSVEP response is measured over visual cortex in response to steadily flashing stimuli. For example, an SSVEP control interface might consist of two checkerboxes displayed on a computer screen, one flashing at 10 Hz (representing the response "yes") and one flashing at 15 Hz (representing the response "no"). The user focuses attention on the checkerbox representing the desired response, and the corresponding oscillation can be detected in visual cortex. If the user attends to the 10 Hz checkerbox, after a number of samples the BCI will recognize the 10 Hz oscillations in visual cortex and choose the response "yes". Control interfaces using steady-state evoked potentials benefit from more differentiable states than the P300 response (Allison and Moore Jackson 2005; Bin et al. 2009) and have been applied to interfaces requiring multiple degrees of freedom such as gaming (Lalor et al. 2005; Moore Jackson et al. 2009).

Exogenous systems typically do not need to display any biofeedback; they typically only report task performance (i.e. the control outcome or selection itself). Sensory responses are autonomic, and therefore operant conditioning does not improve performance. Learned effects in exogenous control interfaces are usually a result of experience with the interface itself rather than a modulation of the observed response potentials.

2.3.2 Endogenous Control Task Paradigms

In an endogenous control interface, the user voluntarily performs a mental task that activates a particular part of the brain, such as silently singing or imagining hand movements. Endogenous responses do not require a stimulus, although prompts and cues may be used to improve response characteristics. Users can learn to improve brain signal responses; conditioning these voluntary responses is accomplished with biofeedback mechanisms.

Two of the first and most thoroughly studied endogenous control interface paradigms are Slow Cortical Potentials (SCPs) (Birbaumer 2006) and the mu-rhythm response (Wolpaw et al. 2003). These endogenous BCIs are based on voluntary, conditioned responses from users. SCP-based systems rely on operant conditioning to train users to shift the polarity (positive or negative) of their SCPs. Mu-based systems operate on actual or imagined movement reflected in the motor cortex; a mu-based BCI system measures the amplitude of the mu-band signal to effect control. Both SCP based and Mu-rhythm based BCIs have been demonstrated for cursor control and target selection (Birbaumer 2006; Schalk et al. 2008; Wolpaw et al. 2003). SCP and Mu-based BCIs are often used for target selection, such as spelling. In visual target acquisition tasks, the position of a pointer or cursor is manipulated using the endogenous input (such as a user imagining hand movement). The "right justified box" (RJB) task illustrated in Fig. 2.1 is a well-studied paradigm of target acquisition control used both for screening and testing (Schalk et al. 2004). In the one-dimensional case, the cursor moves across the screen at a constant rate of speed. Target areas are discretized regions of the right edge of the screen, each representing a selection alternative. The BCI user either performs or imagines movements such as finger tapping, which influences the y-position (height) of the cursor on the screen. The trial concludes when the cursor reaches the end of the screen, completing the selection based on the y-position of the cursor. Several manipulations of the task are regularly used in research. A similar paradigm allows selection in two and three dimensions, employing different imagined movement tasks. The size and number of targets can be manipulated as well. The effectiveness of the selection interface is also influenced by the relative sizes of the cursor and the targets, where Fitts's law appears to predict task performance (Felton et al. 2009). In the one-dimensional case, performance is affected by the rate of motion in the fixed x-direction as well as the target and cursor size. In the two-dimensional case, accuracy is determined by target and cursor size.

The mental task for indicating intent can also be varied. In a mu-rhythm motor imagery control setting, users may be instructed to imagine left hand movement to move the cursor left and right hand movement to move the cursor right. There are several aspects of an endogenous control interface that influence performance. Target regions may be placed in the middle of the screen, and the task is to maintain a cursor within a target for a predetermined time interval to indicate selection (a *dwell* task). The design of these interfaces has significant impact on performance (Felton et al. 2009). In the RJB task, the cursor moves across the screen; when the cursor reaches the end of the screen, the position of the cursor indicates the selection. The relative size of the destination regions affects the performance: smaller objective regions reduce overall performance but can provide higher confidence in ascertaining user intent.

Biofeedback plays a large role in shaping response performance in endogenous control interfaces. Operant conditioning of these responses determines performance accuracy for voluntary responses, and biofeedback positively affects training time. Feedback in these cases consists of performance information, task-related neural activity, and a reinforcement signal. Behavioral theory predicts the optimal schedule of reinforcement signals for training to improve task performance.

2.4 Cognitive Models of Interaction

How can we quantify the usability of a BCI? For graphical interfaces, cognitive models offer a means of assessing and predicting usability. Cognitive models predict the difficulty of interaction tasks by decomposing an interaction task into cognitive process components. For graphical interface interactions, component cognitive processes are measured in terms of response time. These components are well studied; their individual response times have relatively low between-subject variance, and therefore the sum of components represents total interaction response time and serves as a predictor for interaction difficulty where higher response time is positively correlated with task difficulty. Several task decomposition approaches exist today: the Human Information Processor (Card et al. 1986), activity theory (Nardi 1996), situated cognition (Clancey 1997), and goals, operators, methods, selection (GOMS) (John and Kieras 1996). While there is considerable empirical evidence for these approaches in traditional mouse-and-keyboard interaction assessment, there has been little validation of these methods in brain-computer interfaces. Perhaps the largest barrier to applying these methods to interface assessment is finding representations of component cognitive tasks in the sensing modality of the interface.

Consider the human information processor model of interaction, where the model of the brain is conceptually a collection of independent, task-specialized processors: cognitive, perceptual, and motor. These processors receive information from the visual image, working memory and long-term memory stores as they execute tasks. For example, the perceptual processor uses the visual image, which is information obtained from the visual sensory system. During task execution, processors access information from the information sources. Each processor has a cycle time and information stores each have a decay time. In the context of this model, BCIs directly measure these processors, so the task decomposition should provide predictions about the measurable differences in how these processors handle information. The problem with this model is that these processors are task-defined; a functional definition is required in terms of a BCI sensing modality. Anatomically, these processors represent integrations of disparate brain regions and therefore represent too coarse a model for BCI.

The GOMS model of interaction uses Goals, Operators, Methods and Selection to derive a response-time based representation of usability. In this method, the response times of tasks are gathered from population studies of activities. For instance, typing is a skill where the mean time to press a key depends on the relative skill level of the typist, and there is large variance between groups. "Typing" with a BCI may require a series of tasks, such as a binary selection, which could take up to five steps. The GOMS method represents too coarse of a level of model with respect to BCI, and therefore has little predictive power in the context of BCI usability.

2.5 Interaction Task Frameworks

A classic approach to classifying interaction tasks is rooted in differentiating the interaction tasks themselves. For graphical interfaces, Foley groups graphical interactions into basic interaction tasks and compound interaction tasks (Foley and Van Dam 1982). The basic interaction tasks are selection, text, quantify, and position. For graphical interfaces, these represent the set of possible actions a user can make with traditional input devices such as mice and keyboards.

2.5.1 Selection

Selection represents discrete choices from a set of possibilities. Typically, these possibilities are grouped and presented simultaneously, and the user interacts with the interface to select one of the finite set. In BCIs, selection is the most ubiquitous interaction task; selection is often employed to implement the other three interaction tasks. The most basic control tasks are the *binary selection*, which is a choice between one of two alternatives, and *n-ary selection*, a choice from several alternatives. In BCIs there are two common control tasks for binary selection. The first takes advantage of two spatially separate mental tasks causing differentiable activity in the brain. The second measures the activity level over one area of the brain, such as motor cortex, which can be increased and decreased with motor imagery. The second method can also be used for *n*-ary selection.

In the first approach, one of the mental tasks evokes brain activity in a target region of observation; the other task evokes activity in a spatially separate region, where the second task does not overlap activity with the first. A typical example of this design is language production versus mental rotation. Language production, while evoking activity in many cortical regions, is best measured over Broca's area (usually near the left temple). This activation pattern is contrasted with mental rotation, best measured over the parietal region on the top of the head. Users perform a sequence of these two tasks to indicate yes/no decisions. To indicate a positive response, the user performs a language production task such as sub-vocal counting or silently singing. To indicate a negative response, the user envisions a shape such as a Rubik's cube rotating in space. Each of these tasks is performed for a fixed time interval, sufficient to capture the activation patterns of the two tasks given the sensing modality. Typically, first order properties of the activation signals are used to determine which pattern is executed, and therefore which response the user makes.

There are several drawbacks to the binary selection method. First, the binary nature of the response sequence does not scale to more sophisticated communication. A user may indicate a number of symbols with these alternating sequences, but longer sequences are required to indicate intent. The symbol set must also have an ordering so that it can be predictably divided (a set of icons for, say, web browser controls would not work well in a binary selection interface). The fixed task time intervals themselves limit the speed with which a user may generate a symbol. These simple interfaces are often used with single channel sensor arrays.

N-ary selection can be implemented by measuring the amplitude of a signal (such as the mu signal generated by movement imagery), discretizing the signal with a number of progressive thresholds. This approach requires the user to be much more accurate with signal production, and relies heavily on biofeedback. However, the increased efficiency of selection makes this method more appealing than binary selection (Schalk et al. 2008).

Selections with evoked response BCIs such as P300 and SSVEP are similar to selections on a touch screen; by definition they require one selection step and therefore are more efficient than endogenous-response systems. Another advantage is that the entire selection space is displayed at once; no ordering is required as in binary selections.

2.5.2 Text and Quantify

Text and quantify in a BCI are both subsets of selection, where each alphanumeric character entered is a discrete choice of the character set represented on the input device. For graphical interfaces, typically the keyboard is the input device used to enter text or numeric values. Graphical controls for quantification are typically dials or sliders and often augmented with selection and text controls. Because there is no "typing" with a BCI, the methods for selection described above are employed to enter selections from an alphanumeric character set to implement text entry and quantify tasks.

2.5.3 Position

Position in a graphical interface means to move a cursor to a desired position. Position is used to implement drawing and other continuous (non-selection) tasks. In BCI systems, the position task could translate to more esoteric tasks, such as driving a wheelchair. The position interaction task for BCIs has not been fully explored. Although arguments can be made that evoked-response systems selection mechanism such as a Farwell-Donchin matrix indicates a position on a screen, the P300 paradigm cannot be used for drawing. The SSVEP response has been incorporated into a continuous-control BCI for a gaming environment (Moore Jackson et al. 2009) where the user positions an avatar by focusing attention on flashing stimuli in the desired direction of movement. A simple drawing system based on functional Near Infrared (fNIR) imaging provided positional control in a letter-drawing study (Mappus et al. 2009). More exploration of this control task for BCIs is needed to implement position requirements for creative expression and navigation.

2.6 Dialog Initiative

In user interface design, the *dialog initiative* determines whether the system initiates a control interaction, or the user does. Most command-line systems are system-initiated (the system prompts the user for a response); most graphical user interfaces are user-initiated (the user clicks on an icon to open an application). BCI systems have an additional issue: the brain generates signals constantly, such as the mu rhythm, and therefore a BCI system must know when the user intends to control the system. This issue is known as the "Midas touch problem"; as with King Midas, who turned everything to gold on his touch, BCIs interpret all brain signals in a specified domain as user intent. The ability to turn off neural input when the user does not wish to interact is a primary challenge in the field of BCI research.

In order to address this challenge, the BCI field makes a distinction between *synchronous* and *asynchronous* interaction. This differentiates systems that allow interaction in consistent, fixed time windows and those that are "interrupt driven" (initiated by the user). The distinction parallels the distinctions between exogenous and endogenous inputs.

2.6.1 Synchronous Interfaces

A *synchronous* interface allows interactions only in fixed time windows determined by the BCI system (system initiation). Exogenous control interfaces fit well in synchronous paradigms; evoking activity from a stimulus implies that the stimulus onset time is known and correlated with brain activity. Most BCI systems using evoked responses rely on this correlation, implementing synchronous paradigms where the stimulus onset times and display durations are fixed. This is not always the case for evoked responses, as animated stimuli can be displayed continuously and by attending to the animation the user evokes a response. Endogenous inputs may also be used in synchronous paradigms where precise event correlation is not needed. For example, the RJB paradigm requires the user to perform a mental task within a time window in order to make a selection, although the mu response is endogenous. Heuristically, synchronized interfaces are best suited for interactions involving selection; where a discrete choice from a set of possibilities is made within a time frame.

2.6.2 Asynchronous Interfaces

An *asynchronous* interface does not impose time windows for interaction; the user performs a mental task that initiates the interaction (user-initiation). Endogenous inputs fit well in asynchronous paradigms, where self-paced interaction is needed. In these cases, endogenous inputs with high recognition rates are critical. The mental task must be unique enough that it is unlikely to be detected by the BCI accidentally (such as imagining a rotating Rubik's cube). Mental tasks such as language production are poor for asynchronous control because of the likelihood of language processing evoked by the environment. Asynchronous paradigms are showing promise in general-purpose problems (Mason et al. 2006). Research focusing on BCI in the wild relies on asynchronous interaction; initiating and concluding interaction as well as eliminating "false positive" errors are essential for acceptable use.

2.6.3 User Autonomy

One barrier to adoption of BCI in general-use situations has to do with autonomy; for the user, this means when and at what rate to interact with the system.

In a setting where a sensor array is constantly sampling brain state and there is no fixed time course of interaction, the BCI must be able to differentiate intentful interaction from no interaction. Asynchronous interfaces address the problem of variable periods of inactivity during an interaction session (Borisoff et al. 2006; Scherer et al. 2008). Asynchronous interfaces improve BCI autonomy; as more sophisticated applications are adapted to BCI usage constraints and as BCI developers target more assistive technology settings, asynchronous interfacing becomes higher demand (Scherer et al. 2007).

Synchronous interfaces do not necessarily address the issue of indicating the beginning of interaction (i.e. turning on the system to begin with) or indicating the end of an interactive session. Two primary means of addressing this problem are using additional sensing channels and orthogonal mental tasks to recognize initiation and termination sequences of activity. Additional channels of interaction directly address asynchronous activity, but add complexity to the sensing system as well as cognitive load to the user. Work with asynchronous interfaces focuses on recognizing patterns of activity designated as initiation and termination sequences (Mason and Birch 2000).

Both cases improve autonomy; however, there is growing evidence from usability surveys and studies that these asynchronous switches must be accurate to be useful; users will not tolerate more than one false positive over several hours and will not use a system that makes it difficult to initiate interactions (high false negative rate) (Mason et al. 2006; Millán and Mouriño 2003; Scherer et al. 2007, 2008).

2.7 Improving BCI Control Interface Usability

Control interface design can be a critical factor in increasing the throughput of BCIs (Van Gerven et al. 2009). In a character selection task, character layout in conjunction with auto-completion and spell checking improves accuracy and lowers the key selection count for words (Felton et al. 2007). In target acquisition, relative area of cursor and target as well as rates of motion all affect task performance, particularly in dwell selection cases (McFarland et al. 2003).

McFarland and Wolpaw studied considerations between speed and accuracy tradeoffs in BCIs (McFarland and Wolpaw 2003). In this study, five participants manipulated a cursor in one- or two-dimensions. Target locations were one of four boxes arranged in a horizontal line. The task was to manipulate the cursor to the target box (bold outlined, while other boxes were light gray outlined) and dwell within the target for a fixed amount of time. The results of the study indicate performance in terms of achieving target locations is optimal when the distribution of target box selections is uniform.

Adaptive interfaces represent a novel approach to addressing BCI system throughput (Shenoy et al. 2006). By adaptively learning users' response characteristics, the BCI is able to better maintain a high level of performance accuracy. The drawback of adaptive systems is that they require repeated calibration sessions with a guided task, because in order to automatically "tune" the BCI system, perfect knowledge of the user's intent is required.

2.7.1 User Training

A subject-specific factor that affects user performance is the type and amount of training they receive (McFarland et al. 2005). The training process serves two purposes; first to make users aware of the interface dynamics and introduce them to the control paradigm, second to provide sufficient training data for a supervised learning method to classify input with sufficient accuracy to be a responsive interface for users. Conditioning in asynchronous, endogenous interfaces has a positive effect on enhancing generative responses. Finally, a converging set of evidence seems to indicate that directed conditioning affects synaptic plasticity in certain tasks and under certain neural conditions. The results of this work are challenging previous notions of the separation between operant and respondent conditioning. Achtman et al. presents usability results for Electrocorticographic (ECoG) data in an asynchronous task (Achtman et al. 2007). BCI applications in stroke rehabilitation show that BCI training produces lasting changes in neural responses where functionality is limited (Daly and Wolpaw 2008). In these cases the interface links brain activity with robotic control that serves as an assistive trainer for rehabilitation.

2.8 Conclusions

Control interfaces are a critical area of research in order for BCIs to be viable as general-purpose interaction methods. Studies have shown that the design and organization of a BCI control interface can significantly impact the usability of a BCI system. Many of the traditional design paradigms for interactive graphical systems have relevance to BCI control interfaces; however BCIs have additional unique challenges that make their control interfaces difficult to design. More studies are needed to solidify methods of user initiation for BCI interaction, and to solve the "Midas Touch" problem. More accurate classifiers are needed to improve selection accuracy. The area of continuous control needs much more work in order for BCIs to implement applications such as drawing or driving a vehicle. BCI control interfaces are even projected to impact rehabilitation by directing neural plasticity to "re-wire" the brain. BCIs have significantly improved the quality of life for people with severe physical disabilities by allowing them to communicate and control their environments. BCIs also have great potential as the ultimate hands-free control interface for mainstream applications. Although the BCI field has enjoyed dramatic progress in the last two decades, there is great promise and much work to be accomplished in the future as we strive to perfect our interaction methods through control interface research.

References

Achtman N, Afshar A, Santhanam G, Yu BM, Ryu SI, Shenoy KV (2007) Free-paced high-performance brain-computer interfaces. J Neural Eng 4(3):336–347

Allison B, Moore Jackson M (2005) Practical applications of brain computer interface systems using selective attention. Paper presented at the Human Computer Interaction International

Allison B, Pineda J (2006) Effects of SOA and flash pattern manipulations on ERPs, performance, and preference: Implications for a BCI system. Int J Psychophysiol 59:127–140

Bin GY, Gao XR, Yan Z, Hong B, Gao SK (2009) An online multi-channel SSVEP-based brain-computer interface using a canonical correlation analysis method. J Neural Eng 6:046002

Birbaumer N (2006) Breaking the silence: Brain-computer interfaces (BCI) for communication and motor control. Psychophysiology 43(6):517–532

Borisoff JF, Mason SG, Birch GE (2006) Brain interface research for asynchronous control applications. IEEE Trans Neural Syst Rehabil Eng 14(2):160–164

Card S, Moran T, Newell A (1986) The Model Human Processor: An Engineering Model of Human Performance. Xerox Palo Alto Research Center (PARC), Palo Alto, CA

Clancey W (1997) On Human Knowledge and Computer Representations. Press Syndicate of the University of Cambridge, Cambridge, UK

Daly JJ, Wolpaw JR (2008) Brain-computer interfaces in neurological rehabilitation. Lancet Neurol 7(11):1032–1043

Farwell LA, Donchin E (1988) Talking off the top of your head—toward a mental prosthesis utilizing event-related brain potentials. Electroencephalogr Clin Neurophysiol 70(6):510–523

Felton EA, Lewis NL, Wills SA, Radwin RG, Williams JC (2007) Neural signal based control of the dasher writing system. Paper presented at the Neural Engineering, 2007. CNE '07. 3rd International IEEE/EMBS Conference on

Felton EA, Radwin RG, Wilson JA, Williams JC (2009) Evaluation of a modified Fitts law brain-computer interface target acquisition task in able and motor disabled individuals. J Neural Eng 6(5):56002

Foley JD, Van Dam A (1982) Fundamentals of Interactive Computer Graphics. Addison-Wesley Pub. Co, Reading, Mass.

John B, Kieras D (1996) The GOMS family of user interface analysis techniques: Comparison and contrast. ACM Trans Comput Hum Interact 3(4):320–351

Lalor EC, Kelly SP, Finucane C, Burke R, Smith R, Reilly RB, et al (2005) Steady-state VEP-based brain-computer interface control in an immersive 3D gaming environment. Eurasip J Appl Signal Process 2005(19):3156–3164

Mappus R, Venkatesh G, Shastry C, Israeli A, Moore Jackson M (2009) An fNIR-based BMI for letter construction using continuous control. Paper presented at the Computer Human Interface (SIGCHI)

Mason SG, Birch GE (2003) A general framework for brain-computer interface design. IEEE Trans Neural Syst Rehabil Eng 11(1):70–85

Mason SG, Birch GE (2000) A brain-controlled switch for asynchronous control applications. IEEE Trans Biomed Eng 47(10):1297–1307

Mason SG, Kronegg J, Huggins J, Fatourechi M, Navarro K, Birch GE (2006) Evaluating the performance of self-paced brain computer interface technology

McFarland DJ, Wolpaw JR (2003) EEG-based communication and control: Speed-accuracy relationships. Appl Psychophysiol Biofeedback 28(3):217–231

McFarland DJ, Sarnacki WA, Wolpaw JR (2003) Brain-computer interface (BCI) operation: Optimizing information transfer rates. Biol Psychol 63(3):237–251

McFarland DJ, Sarnacki WA, Vaughan TM, Wolpaw JR (2005) Brain-computer interface (BCI) operation: Signal and noise during early training sessions. Clin Neurophysiol 116(1):56–62

Millán JR, Mouriño J (2003) Asynchronous BCI and local neural classifiers: An overview of the adaptive brain interface project. IEEE Trans Neural Syst Rehabil Eng 11(2):159–161

Moore Jackson M, Mappus R, Barba E, Hussein S, Venkatesh G, Shastry C, et al (2009) Continuous control paradigms for direct brain interfaces. Paper presented at the Human Computer Interaction International

Naito M, Michioka Y, Ozawa K, Ito Y, Kiguchi M, Kanazawa T (2007) A communication means for totally locked-in ALS patients based on changes in cerebral blood volume measured with near-infrared light. IEICE Trans Inf Syst E90-D7:1028–1036

Nardi B (1996) Context and Consciousness: Activity Theory and Human-Computer Interaction. MIT Press, Boston, MA

Perelmouter J, Birbaumer N (2000) A binary spelling interface with random errors. IEEE Trans Rehabil Eng 8(2):227–232

Roberts AH (1985) Biofeedback—research, training, and clinical roles. Am Psychol 40(8):938–941

Salvaris M, Sepulveda F (2009) Visual modifications on the P300 speller BCI paradigm. J Neural Eng 6(4)

Schalk G, McFarland DJ, Hinterberger T, Birbaumer N, Wolpaw JR (2004) BCI2000: A general-purpose, brain-computer interface (BCI) system. IEEE Trans Biomed Eng 51(6):1034–1043

Schalk G, Miller KJ, Anderson NR, Wilson JA, Smyth MD, Ojemann JG, et al (2008) Two-dimensional movement control using electrocorticographic signals in humans. J Neural Eng 5(1):75–84

Scherer R, Müller-Putz GR, Pfurtscheller G (2007) Self-initiation of EEG-based brain-computer communication using the heart rate response. J Neural Eng 4:L23–L29

Scherer R, Lee F, Schlögl A, Leeb R, Bischof H, Pfurtscheller G (2008) Toward self-paced brain-computer communication: Navigation through virtual worlds. IEEE Trans Biomed Eng 55(2):675–682

Sellers E, Donchin E (2006) A P300-based brain-computer interface: Initial tests by ALS patients. Clin Neurophysiol 117:538–548

Shenoy P, Krauledat M, Blankertz B, Rao RP, Müller KR (2006) Towards adaptive classification for BCI. J Neural Eng 3(1):R13–23

Solis-Escalante T, Gentiletti GG, Yanez-Suarez O (2006) Single trial P300 detection based on the empirical mode decomposition. Conf Proc IEEE Eng Med Biol Soc 1:1157–1160

Van Gerven M, Farquhar J, Schaefer R, Vlek R, Geuze J, Nijholt A, et al (2009) The brain-computer interface cycle. J Neural Eng 6(4):1–10

Vaughan TM, McFarland DJ, Schalk G, Sarnacki W, Robinson L, Wolpaw JR (2001) EEG-based brain-computer interface: Development of a speller. Paper presented at the Society for Neuroscience

Wolpaw JR, McFarland DJ, Vaughan TM, Schalk G (2003) The Wadsworth Center brain-computer interface (BCI) research and development program. IEEE Neural Syst Syst Rehabil Eng 11(2):203–207

Chapter 3
Could Anyone Use a BCI?

Brendan Z. Allison and Christa Neuper

Abstract Brain-computer interface (BCI) systems can provide communication and control for many users, but not all users. This problem exists across different BCI approaches; a "universal" BCI that works for everyone has never been developed. Instead, about 20% of subjects are not proficient with a typical BCI system. Some groups have called this phenomenon "BCI illiteracy". Some possible solutions have been explored, such as improved signal processing, training, and new tasks or instructions. These approaches have not resulted in a BCI that works for all users, probably because a small minority of users cannot produce detectable patterns of brain activity necessary to a particular BCI approach. We also discuss an underappreciated solution: switching to a different BCI approach. While the term "BCI illiteracy" elicits interesting comparisons between BCIs and natural languages, many issues are unclear. For example, comparisons across different studies have been problematic since different groups use different performance thresholds, and do not account for key factors such as the number of trials or size of the BCI's alphabet. We also discuss challenges inherent in establishing widely used terms, definitions, and measurement approaches to facilitate discussions and comparisons among different groups.

3.1 Why BCIs (Sometimes) Don't Work

Brain-computer interface (BCI) research has made great progress recently. Initial BCI research efforts focused primarily on validating proof of concept, usu-

B.Z. Allison (✉) · C. Neuper
Institute for Knowledge Discovery, Laboratory of Brain-Computer Interfaces, Graz University of
Technology, Krenngasse 37/III, 8010 Graz, Austria
e-mail: allison@tugraz.at

C. Neuper
Department of Psychology, University of Graz, Universitätsplatz 2/III, 8010 Graz, Austria
e-mail: christa.neuper@uni-graz.at

D.S. Tan, A. Nijholt (eds.), *Brain-Computer Interfaces,*
Human-Computer Interaction Series,
DOI 10.1007/978-1-84996-272-8_3, © Springer-Verlag London Limited 2010

ally by testing BCIs with healthy subjects in laboratories instead of target users in home or hospital settings (Pfurtscheller et al. 2000; Kübler et al. 2001; Wolpaw et al. 2002). BCIs have since provided practical communication for severely disabled users with no other way to communicate, and many new applications, signal processing approaches, and displays have been explored. Patients and healthy people have successfully used BCIs based on all three major noninvasive BCI approaches—P300 BCIs based on intermittent flashes, Steady State Visual Evoked Potential (SSVEP) BCIs based on oscillating lights, and Event Related Desynchronization (ERD) BCIs based on imagined movement. This progress and enthusiasm is reflected in the dramatic increase in peer reviewed publications, conference presentations and symposia, and media attention (Pfurtscheller et al. 2006, 2008; Allison et al. 2007; Nijholt et al. 2008). Amidst these positive developments, one major problem is becoming apparent: BCIs do not work for all users.

Ideally, any interface should work for any user. However, across the three major noninvasive BCI approaches, numerous labs report that very roughly 20% of subjects cannot attain control. This problem has been called "BCI illiteracy" e.g., Kübler and Müller (2007), Blankertz et al. (2008), Nijholt et al. (2008). Extensive efforts have been made to overcome this problem through various mechanisms, such as extensively training the subject and/or classifier, alternate displays or instructions, improved signal processing efforts, and error correction. They have only been partly successful. While these options can make BCIs work for some previously "illiterate" users, some people remain unable to use any particular BCI system (Allison et al. 2010b). There is no "universal BCI".

This problem may result from a possible reason why some users cannot generate the brain activity necessary to control a particular BCI. A small minority of subjects will probably never attain control with a given approach due to the structure of their brains. While all people's brains have the same cortical processing systems, in roughly the same locations, with similar functional subdivisions, there are individual variations in brain structure. In some users, neuronal systems needed for control might not produce electrical activity detectable on the scalp. This is not because of any problem with the user. The necessary neural populations are presumably healthy and active, but the activity they produce is not detectable to a particular neuroimaging methodology, such as EEG. The key neural populations may be located in a sulcus, or too deep for EEG electrodes, or too close to another, louder group of neurons. For example, about 10% of seemingly normal subjects do not produce a robust P300 (Polich 1986; Conroy and Polich 2007). These users would probably not benefit from training, alternate P300 tasks, or improved signal processing; their best hope is to switch to a BCI that relies on another signal, such as ERD or SSVEP.

There are other reasons why some users cannot use some BCIs. Some subjects produce excessive muscle artifact, or misunderstand or ignore the instructions on how to use a BCI. BCIs might fail because the people responsible for getting the BCI to work made mistakes resulting from inexperience, such as misusing the software or mounting the electrodes incorrectly. Some environments may produce excessive electrical noise that can impair signal quality.

These problems are generally surmountable, whereas individual variations in brain structure are quite difficult to change. This chapter does not address problems resulting from fundamental mistakes by subjects or BCI practitioners. That is, we assume subjects are following instructions, with properly prepared hardware and software, in a reasonable setting.

3.2 Illiteracy in Different BCI Approaches

What does it mean to say that some users "cannot use" some BCIs? As noted below, comparing illiteracy across different BCI articles is difficult because no standards exist, and various factors must be considered. Recent work that assessed the relationship between illiteracy and the severity of motor impairment used a threshold of 70% or other values (Kübler and Birbaumer 2008). This was an excellent article, and this threshold was adequate for establishing that the severity of impairment was not correlated with illiteracy, except in completely locked-in patients. However, a thorough and parametric assessment of illiteracy across the three major BCI approaches may be premature before some standards to assess illiteracy are developed.

BCI illiteracy is clearly not limited to any one research group or BCI approach. Anecdotal evidence suggests that ERD BCIs may entail greater illiteracy than BCIs based on evoked potentials (P300 and SSVEP). However, Kübler and Birbaumer (2008) (which did not assess SSVEP BCIs) did not find that ERD BCIs entailed higher illiteracy than P300 BCIs.

3.2.1 Illiteracy in ERD BCIs

ERD BCIs rely on EEG activity associated with different imagined movements. Some approaches rely on specific imagined movements, such as moving the left hand, right hand, or both feet (Pfurtscheller et al., 2006; Leeb et al., 2007; Blankertz et al., 2008; Scherer et al., 2004, 2008). Other approaches train users to explore different, often less specific, imagined movements until they find imagery that yields good results (Friedrich et al. 2009).

Hence, ERD BCIs can only function well if subjects can produce brain activity patterns that differ across different types of imagined movements. ERD BCIs rely on time frequency analysis; the raw EEG is transformed into an estimate of power at different frequencies by a mechanism such as a Fourier transform or autoregressive analysis. If the different movement classes (such as left hand vs. right hand) do not produce reliable and reasonably robust differences in power, at least at one or more frequencies and/or electrode sites, then effective communication will not be possible.

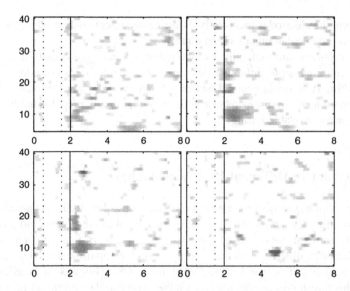

Fig. 3.1 These four panels present data from subject A, who attained very good control with an ERD BCI. In all panels, the *x*-axis represents the time from the beginning of the trial. A cue, which appeared 2 seconds after the beginning of the trial, instructed the subject to imagine either left or right hand movement. The *y*-axis shows the frequency. Blue reflects an increase in power, and red reflects a decrease in power, also called ERD. The *two left images* show activity over site C3, located over the left sensorimotor area, and the *two right images* show activity over site C4, located over the right sensorimotor area. The *top two images* reflect trials with imagined left hand movement, and the *bottom two images* present trials with imagined right hand movement. Images courtesy of Dr. Clemens Brunner

Figure 3.1 presents data from subject A, who could use an ERD BCI. The top two panels show activity over electrode sites C3 (top left panel) and C4 (top right panel) while the subject imagined left hand movement. In the top right panel, ERD is apparent at about 10 Hz, while there is no strong ERD in the top left panel. These top two panels show that left hand movement imagery reduced power at about 10 Hz over the right sensorimotor area, which occurs in most people (Pfurtscheller et al. 2006; Pfurtscheller and Neuper in press).

The bottom two panels of Fig. 3.1 show activity over sites C3 and C4 while the subject imagined right hand movement. These two panels instead show ERD over the left sensorimotor area. Therefore, an ERD BCI could determine whether the subject was imagining left or right hand movement by identifying characteristic activity in sites C3 and C4.

Figure 3.2 presents data from subject B, who could not use an ERD BCI. The top two panels do not differ very much from the bottom two panels. Hence, the classifier did not have any way to determine which hand the subject was thinking about moving.

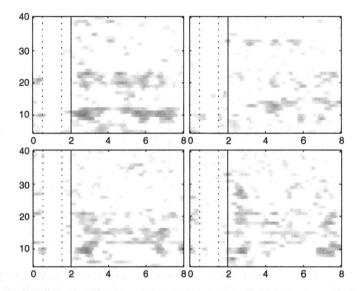

Fig. 3.2 These four panels present data from subject B, who was illiterate with an ERD BCI. The axes and shading are the as in Fig. 3.1. The *two left images* show activity over site C3, over the left sensorimotor area, and the *two right images* show over site C4, located over the right sensorimotor area. The *top two images* reflect trials with imagined left hand movement, and the *bottom two images* present trials with imagined right hand movement. Courtesy of Dr. Clemens Brunner

3.2.2 Illiteracy in SSVEP BCIs

SSVEP BCIs require subjects to focus their attention on one of (usually) two or more stimuli that each oscillate at different frequencies. This produces oscillations over visual areas at the same frequency as the oscillating stimulus, and often at one or more harmonics of that frequency as well (Pfurtscheller et al. 2006; Allison et al. 2008; Faller et al. 2010).

In an SSVEP BCI, the raw EEG is translated into an estimate of power at different frequencies, much like the procedure in an ERD BCI. The resulting spikes at specific frequencies can be used to determine which stimulus occupied the subject's attention. Therefore, SSVEP BCIs also depend on clear spikes in the power spectrum at specific frequencies. If these spikes are not apparent, or are too weak to distinguish from background noise, then the SSVEP BCI will not function accurately.

Figure 3.3 presents one literate subject (top 2 panels) and one illiterate subject (bottom two panels) who tried to use an SSVEP BCI. The left and right panels reflect the subject's desired to communicate left and right movement, respectively. There is a clear difference between the top two panels, and hence this subject attained almost perfect accuracy with an SSVEP BCI. However, there is no clear difference between the bottom two panels, and hence this subject could not attain performance above chance with this SSVEP BCI.

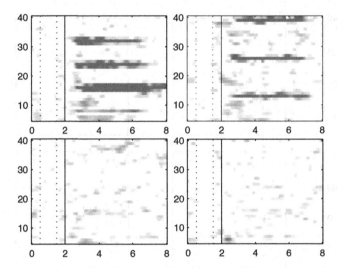

Fig. 3.3 These four panels present data from two subjects who tried to use an SSVEP BCI. All panels show data from electrode site O1, over the primary visual cortex. In all panels, the x-axis represents the time from the beginning of the trial. The cue that instructed the subject to focus on the 8 or 13 Hz LED appeared after 2 seconds. The y-axis shows the frequency. The *horizontal blue lines* reflect an increase in power. The *top two images* are from subject B, and the *bottom two images* are from subject A. The *two left images* were recorded when the subject focused on an 8 Hz LED (which could be used to move left), and the *two right images* were recorded when the subject focused on a 13 Hz LED (which could be used to move right). In the *top left panel*, there are clear power increases at 8 Hz and its harmonics of 16, 24, and 32 Hz. In the *top right panel*, there are clear power increases at 13 Hz and its harmonics of 26 and 39 Hz. Since there are very clear differences between the *top 2 panels*, subject B showed excellent control with this SSVEP BCI. However, neither of the *bottom two panels* shows these changes, and hence subject A was illiterate with this SSVEP BCI. Images courtesy of Dr. Clemens Brunner

Noteworthily, the two subjects shown in Fig. 3.3 are the same two subjects shown in Figs. 3.1 and 3.2. Subject A was literate with an ERD BCI, but illiterate with an SSVEP BCI. Subject B was literate with an SSVEP BCI, but illiterate with an ERD BCI.

3.2.3 Illiteracy in P300 BCIs

Like SSVEP BCIs, P300 BCIs rely on selective attention to visual stimuli (Allison and Pineda 2006; Sellers and Donchin 2006; Lenhardt et al. 2008; Kübler et al. 2009; Jing et al. 2010). However, in a P300 BCI, the stimuli flash instead of oscillate. Whenever a user focuses attention on a specific stimulus, a brainwave called the P300 may occur, whereas the P300 to ignored stimuli is much weaker.

P300 BCIs do not rely on time frequency analyses like ERD and SSVEP BCIs do. Instead, the raw EEG is time-locked to the onset of each flash, producing an event related potential or ERP. ERPs from several trials are usually averaged together to

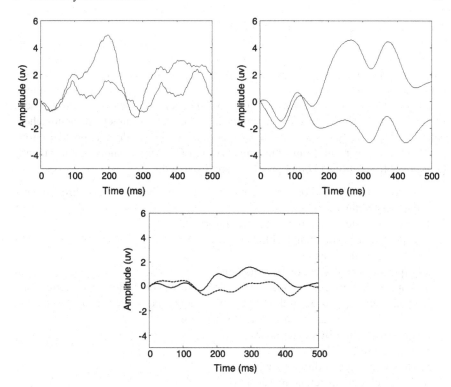

Fig. 3.4 ERP activity from three subjects who tried to use a P300 BCI. In all three panels, the
x-axis reflects the time after the flash began, and the y-axis reflects the amplitude of the ERP. Each
panel presents ERPs that were averaged over many trials; the solid and dashed lines are much
harder to distinguish on a single trial basis. The *top left panel* shows a subject who did not have a
strong P300. The solid and dashed lines look similar in the time window when the P300 is typically
prominent, which is about 300–500 ms after the flash. However, these two lines did differ during
an earlier time window. The *top right panel* shows a subject who did have a strong P300. The
bottom panel shows a subject whose ERPs look similar for target and nontarget flashes throughout
the time window. This subject was illiterate with a P300 BCI. Images courtesy of Dr. Jin Jing

improve accuracy. The classifier tries to identify which flash elicited a robust P300,
sometimes incorporating other ERPs as well. Ideally, only the target stimulus—
that is, the stimulus that the user is attending—elicits a robust P300. If none of
the flashes elicit an ERP that is reliably different from other ERPs, then effective
communication is not possible with that P300 BCI system.

Figure 3.4 contains ERPs for three subjects who tried to use a P300 BCI. In all
three panels, the solid line shows the ERP to a target flash, and the dashed line
shows the ERP to a nontarget flash. The top left panel shows a subject who had a
weak P300, although the target and nontarget flashes did vary earlier in the time
window. The right panel shows data from a literate subject. This subject's P300 is
clearly visible after only target flashes. The bottom panel shows an illiterate subject,
whose ERPs to target and nontarget flashes look similar.

3.3 Improving BCI Functionality

What can you do if someone cannot use a BCI? As noted, BCI illiteracy is essentially a problem of accuracy. The methods for improving accuracy presented here could make the difference between an ineffective system and a functional communication tool. Of course, improving accuracy could benefit literate users as well; since BCIs very rarely allow sustained communication at 100% accuracy, the approaches below could be useful to almost any BCI system. Again, we do not consider basic problems that may result from simple mistakes in BCI setup or a noisy environment. Four possible solutions to other problems are discussed:

1. Improve selection and/or classification of existing brain signals through improved algorithms
2. Use sensor systems that provide richer information
   a. Different neuroimaging technologies
   b. More or better sensors
3. Incorporate error correction or reduction
   a. Improved interfaces that make errors less likely and/or allow error correction
   b. Additional signals, from the EEG or elsewhere, that convey error
4. Generate brain signals that are easier to categorize
   a. Within existing BCI approaches
   b. Using novel BCI approaches
   c. By switching to a different approach
   d. By combining different approaches

3.3.1 Improve Selection and/or Classification Algorithms

Option 1 (improved algorithms) is by far the most heavily pursued. There have been four major data analysis competitions (e.g. Blankertz et al. 2004), but no competitions to (for example) produce the strongest ERD or develop the most discerning sensor system. Signal processing is the easiest component of a BCI to improve, since it requires no special equipment, data collection, device development, etc. Improved signal processing merits further study, and will probably continue to reduce but not eliminate "BCI illiteracy" (Blankertz et al. 2008; Brunner et al. 2010). Improved signal processing cannot help if the subject is not producing any detectable activity that could distinguish different mental states.

Since different people have different brain activity, customizing the classification algorithms for each user can dramatically improve accuracy with some subjects. This customization is now common; relatively few BCIs use the same parameters for all subjects. Hence, an emerging challenge is finding ways to automate this customization process, since a BCI could then customize itself without human intervention. As BCIs move outside the laboratory, and hence further away from experts who can customize BCIs for each user, software that can automatically configure classification algorithms and other parameters becomes increasingly important.

The top left panel of Fig. 3.3 presents a simple example of how a customized signal processing algorithm can improve performance, perhaps enough to make this subject literate. Some P300 BCIs use a linear classification technique that focuses on specific time periods after the flash, such as Stepwise Discriminant Analysis (SWDA). An SWDA classifier that used generic settings for all users would probably only evaluate time periods when the P300 is typically apparent, such as 300–500 ms after the flash. However, software might examine each subject's ERP, determine which time periods exhibit a strong difference between target and nontarget flashes, and adjust the classifier settings accordingly. In this example, the classifier could be automatically reprogrammed to focus more heavily on the time period about 200 ms after each flash.

The subject shown in the top left panel is not especially unusual. She shows a strong P200, which is a well-known ERP component that often precedes the P300 and can differ with selective attention (Allison and Pineda 2006). Indeed, the subject in the top right panel also has a strong P200, in addition to a strong P300. However, the subject in the bottom panel has a weak P200 and a weak P300. We could not identify any classifier settings that would make this subject proficient with a "P300" BCI.

3.3.2 Explore Different Neuroimaging Technologies

Option 2a (different neuroimaging technologies) needs more attention; no articles have thoroughly explored whether someone who cannot attain literacy with a BCI based on one neuroimaging approach might perform better with a different approach. This article focuses primarily on EEG-based BCIs, since over 80% of BCIs rely on the EEG (Mason et al. 2007). Other noninvasive methods might be effective when EEG based methods are not, but have other drawbacks such as cost or portability (Wolpaw et al. 2006; Allison et al. 2007).

Invasive BCIs can also be effective communication tools (Hochberg et al. 2006; Schalk et al. 2008; Blakely et al. 2009) and might also work when other methods do not. The brain's electrical activity is filtered, smeared, and diminished as it travels from the brain to the outer surface of the scalp. Signals recorded from sensors fixed on or in the brain might be easier to categorize, but entail neurosurgery, scarring, risk of infection, and ethical concerns that vary considerably across different users and their needs. Since some invasive BCIs may be able to detect activity from neurons within a sulcus, people who cannot use a noninvasive BCI because of their brain structure might attain better results with an invasive approach. This prospect merits further study, along with the possible benefits of combining noninvasive and invasive approaches (Wolpaw et al. 2002).

Option 2b (more or better sensors) has been heavily pursued, with little success. The conventional Ag/AgCl electrode, with electrode gel and skin abrasion, has not changed much in decades despite many efforts from academic and commercial groups. Dry electrodes might make caps more convenient (Popescu et al. 2007;

Sullivan et al. 2008), but even the most enthusiastic developers agree that the signals are at the very best comparable to gel based electrodes. The prospects of using additional electrodes and optimizing electrode locations are not new (Pfurtscheller et al., 1996, 2006). Furthermore, there are many drawbacks to adding more sensors, such as increased cost and preparation time.

3.3.3 Apply Error Correction or Reduction

Option 3 (error correction or reduction) could help improve BCIs in many ways. Since BCIs have generally failed to capitalize on fundamental principles from HCI research, there are many unexplored opportunities for improvement (Allison in press). However, like the two options already discussed, error reduction and correction cannot make all subjects proficient. Error related activity can be detected in the EEG, as well as other signals based on eye, heart, or other physiological signals (Schalk et al. 2000; Buttfield et al. 2006; Ferrez and Millán 2008). It can improve performance when a signal is poor but sometimes usable, but is useless if the subject cannot effect control at all. Similarly, software that prevents people from spelling impossible words or sending meaningless commands cannot help a subject who cannot convey anything in the first place (Allison in press).

3.3.4 Generate Brain Signals that are Easier to Categorize

Option 4a (clearer signals within a BCI approach) has been most heavily pursued within ERD BCIs, with considerable success. Many ERD BCI improvements from the Wolpaw lab stem from training subjects to produce more actionable information via ERD BCIs. Neuper et al. (2005) showed that instructing subjects to focus on first-person motor imagery (that is, imagining their own hand moving) could improve performance relative to third-person motor imagery (that is, imagining watching a hand move). Nikulin et al. (2008) claimed that a novel type of motor imagery based on "quasi-movements" could yield better performance than conventional ERD tasks.

Unlike ERD BCIs, there has been little success in generating clearer EEG signals with P300 or SSVEP BCIs. The original paradigm used in Farwell and Donchin (1988) already produced P300s that are about as big as some of the larger P300s in the literature. It is unlikely that a new paradigm to produce huge P3s will be developed, although novel displays, tasks, or other parameters might enhance other features such as the CNV (Farwell and Donchin 1988; Allison and Pineda 2006).

Paradoxically, some approaches to improve information transfer rate (ITR, also called bit rate or information throughput) in P300 BCIs might increase illiteracy. For example, changing the number or distribution of characters illuminated with each flash can improve P300 BCI ITR in some subjects—not by eliciting larger P300s, but by reducing the number of flashes required to identify each target character (Guger et al. 2009; Jing et al. 2010). However, methods that reduce the number of flashes also entail a shorter target to target interval (TTI), which can reduce P300 amplitude and potentially increase illiteracy (Gonsalvez and Polich 2002).

Conventional SSVEP BCIs already yield SSVEPs that differ considerably between target and nontarget events in most subjects. There seems to be no easy way to create SSVEP differences that are easier to recognize, though the number of events required to identify each target could be reduced. Other work showed that better displays or other parameters could create more recognizable SSVEPs and similar VEPs (Cheng et al. 2002; Wang et al. 2006; Allison et al. 2008; Bin et al. 2009).

Option 4a could also entail configuring a BCI to rely more heavily on the signals within a BCI approach that are easiest to categorize. This option has been explored with some BCIs that rely on imagination of different conventional mental tasks. For example, Millán and Mouriño (2003) first explored which of six mental tasks yielded the most discriminable EEG signals for each subject, and then configured a BCI system to control a robot using the three tasks that yielded the clearest signals.

A similar solution might work with ERD BCIs. Consider a BCI that detects foot imagery very poorly, but reliably detects hand imagery. This BCI might be only 10% accurate if the user usually tries to communicate via foot imagery, but 100% accurate if the user only uses hand imagery. Such a BCI should thus be configured to rely more heavily on hand imagery. This solution would reduce errors, but not eliminate them, unless the BCI is configured to operate without foot movement imagery, which limits its alphabet. There might be other reasons why the BCI was designed to include foot imagery. For example, foot movement might seem more natural if the goal is to walk forward (Leeb et al. 2007; Scherer et al. 2008) or control vertically scrolling letters (Scherer et al. 2004). On the other hand, keyboards are highly unnatural interfaces, since moving fingers across a keyboard has little intuitive connection to the message being sent, or indeed any natural activity. Further research should explore the importance of a congruent, literal mapping between mental task and desired outcome.

Improved feedback could make subjects more motivated and involved (Neuper and Pfurtscheller in press). Subjects might find immersive virtual feedback more absorbing than conventional feedback (Leeb et al. 2007; Scherer et al. 2008; Faller et al. 2010). Subjects who are more motivated or engaged could produce clearer brain signals (Nijboer et al. 2008; Nijboer and Broermann in press).

Presenting feedback through different modalities could also result in clearer brain signals. While most BCIs rely on visual stimuli, BCIs have also been developed based on auditory (Kübler et al. 2009) and tactile (Müller-Putz et al. 2006) stimuli. In healthy subjects, visual stimuli usually produce clearer brain signals. However, subjects who have trouble seeing might attain better results with a BCI based on auditory or tactile modalities. It may seem easy to determine whether a user can see, but this is not always true. Subjects who are locked in and cannot communicate have no way to report that they have trouble seeing the visual stimuli used in a BCI. Hence, if a subject who cannot communicate seems illiterate with a BCI based on visual stimuli, experimenters should consider an auditory or tactile BCI.

Option 4b (clearer signals with a novel BCI approach) is receiving more attention. Possibilities such as auditory streaming, imagined music, phoneme imagination, or conventional mental tasks like math or singing have not been tested across many subjects. A previously unknown or underappreciated task probably won't lead to a BCI that works for all users. Hence, all of the options presented so far should reduce but not eliminate illiteracy.

Option 4c is very rarely considered: give up on the current BCI approach and try another one. Many labs and researchers focus on only one approach, and thus lack both the tools and cognitive flexibility to explore other options. This option hinges on our belief that there will always be a small minority of users who can never use a specific approach, even after any or all of the above options have been implemented. This prospect was recently explored in the first controlled study devoted to comparing different BCI approaches within subjects. Our team at TU Graz recently compared data from offline simulations of SSVEP vs. ERD BCIs, which suggested that some subjects who could not effectively use an SSVEP BCI could use an ERD BCI, and vice versa (Allison et al. 2010b).

We have also confirmed this result with online BCIs. Figures 3.1–3.3 present clear examples of two subjects who were literate with only one of these two BCI approaches. Subject A was literate with an ERD BCI, but not an SSVEP BCI. Subject B was literate with an SSVEP BCI, but not an ERD BCI.

Allison et al. (2010b) also introduced a potential hybrid BCI that combines two BCI approaches (SSVEP and ERD), which addresses option 4d. A hybrid BCI would ideally have an adaptive classifier to learn how to appropriately weigh contributions from different signals. That is, with training, a hybrid BCI using signals X and Y would become the same as a BCI using signal X only if signal Y was uninformative. If subjects could use both signals, then X and Y could be combined to increase the dimensionality of control or improve the accuracy/speed tradeoff. Subjects A and B were both literate with our hybrid ERD/SSVEP BCI.

Options 4c and 4d, which both involve a different BCI approach, are underappreciated opportunities to provide communication for subjects who are not successful with the first approach they try. A new approach does not mean the subject cannot attain the same goals, such as spelling, moving a cursor, or controlling a robotic device. Major changes to display and feedback parameters may not be needed either. The subject must simply perform different mental tasks, such as paying attention to letters that flash instead of oscillate.

3.3.5 Predicting Illiteracy

There is currently no way to predict whether someone will be illiterate with a certain BCI approach. Illiteracy is only apparent after a subject tries to use a BCI. Researchers, carers, or others may also try to get the BCI working through some of the methods described above, and/or trial and error with additional BCI sessions. Therefore, considerable time and effort is necessary to diagnose illiteracy.

Additional research into BCI demographics might help identify factors that could predict whether someone will be proficient with a certain BCI approach, and could also help predict the best parameters for each user. Age, gender, personality traits, lifestyle and background, and other factors could help developers and other people find the best BCI for each user. People with a strong history of sports, dance, martial arts, or other movement oriented hobbies might perform better with BCIs based on imagined movement. People who play some types of computer games, or perform well on simple tests of visual attention, might perform better with BCIs that rely on visual attention.

Temporary factors like time of day, fatigue, or recent consumption of food, alcohol, caffeine, or drugs may be relevant. For example, Guger et al. (2009) found that people who reported less sleep the previous night performed better with P300 BCIs—a surprising finding that suggests a rather easy way to temporarily improve P300 BCI performance. Another study found that older subjects performed worse with SSVEP BCIs, but otherwise found no correlation between performance and many other factors (Allison et al. 2010a).

3.4 Towards Standardized Terms, Definitions, and Measurement Metrics

The term "BCI illiteracy" implies a connection between BCIs and language. BCI illiteracy is not limited to any alphabet of mental signals. That is, just as someone illiterate in German might be fluent in English, a person who cannot use an ERD BCI might communicate effectively through a SSVEP BCI. The graphemes or phonemes in written or spoken Japanese are incomprehensible to someone who only knows Arabic, and the mental tasks (also called "cognemes") in ERD BCIs are useless in SSVEP BCIs (Allison and Pineda 2006).

Like conventional illiteracy, BCI illiteracy is essentially a problem of accuracy. An illiterate reader or listener is someone who cannot interpret text or speech accurately. Also like conventional illiteracy, BCI illiteracy is a problem of scale that depends on the likelihood of correct communication by chance. A conventional illiterate is someone who can accurately communicate with about 0% accuracy, since the likelihood of correctly guessing the right word is very low because natural language vocabularies typically have tens of thousands of options. A person who can understand half the common words in a natural language might be considered reasonably competent. However, a BCI that correctly interprets the user's intended message only half the time is probably inadequate, since BCIs have smaller alphabets, perhaps as few as two elements.

This point underscores the first of many concerns with the term "BCI illiteracy": there is no accepted literacy threshold. That is, there are no guidelines that specify which accuracy threshold must be crossed before a subject is considered literate. For example, among BCIs that allow two choices, different articles use different thresholds (e.g. Perelmouter and Birbaumer 2000; Guger et al. 2003; Allison et al. 2008; Kübler and Birbaumer 2008). We used a threshold of 70% in two recent articles involving tasks that simulated a two choice BCI (Allison et al. 2010b; Brunner et al. 2010). Guger et al. (2003) was written before the term "BCI illiteracy" was coined, but refers to the 6.7% of subjects who attained less than 60% accuracy in a two-choice ERD task as "marginal." The article assumes that the 93.3% of subjects who attained better performance would be effectively literate. Had a threshold of 70% been used instead, the number of "marginal" (aka illiterate) subjects would have increased to 48.7%. Therefore, fairly small changes in the threshold can dramatically affect the percentage of subjects who are deemed literate.

This threshold depends on the number of choices in the BCI's alphabet, which is called N (Wolpaw et al. 2002). 65% accuracy is probably unacceptable in a BCI with two choices, but might be tolerable in a BCI with many more choices. However, regardless of N, there is no agreement on the best proficiency threshold. Sellers and Donchin (2006) criticized an earlier article for implying that a 36-choice BCI with almost 50% accuracy was a reasonable communication system. Only two of ten subjects in Friedrich et al. (2009) were considered illiterate by that paper's first author (Friedrich, personal communication, April 2009), although six subjects attained accuracy below 50% in a four-choice task.

Furthermore, the true "chance level" also depends on the length of the message or sequence of commands (Müller-Putz et al. 2008). While it may seem that chance performance with a two-choice BCI is 50%, this is effectively true only with infinity trials. The proficiency threshold should be higher if the user can only send one very short message.

Similarly, "BCI illiteracy" does not account for the possibility of improving accuracy by allowing more time for selections. In some cases, increasing the number of trials or the duration of each trial can improve accuracy, perhaps above the proficiency threshold. For example, P300 BCI articles often note that performance with single trials is typically below any reasonable proficiency threshold, but performance improves if data from many trials are averaged together (Farwell and Donchin 1988; Jing et al. 2010).

In summary, proficiency thresholds might not best be represented by a single number, but rather a formula that includes the number of choices, the number of trials, and the time allowed for each selection (Allison in press). Unfortunately, even after considering these factors, other challenges remain.

Some challenges with developing a standardized proficiency threshold are harder to address. A single formula cannot easily account for different types of errors, such as false positives or misses. Errors of omission or commission may be more or less confusing or frustrating for the user, designer, and/or listener. A proficiency threshold formula might be further complicated because some errors are more likely with certain signals, which was discussed in problem 4a above. Certain choices may be selected more often than others, which can complicate the standard formula for ITR (Wolpaw et al. 2002) and a standardized threshold approach.

A proficiency threshold is harder to determine with asynchronous BCI systems. In asynchronous BCI, the BCI system determines when messages or commands must be sent. This characteristic makes it relatively easy to determine whether a user correctly sent a message within the allotted time. However, in an asynchronous BCIs, users may communicate (or not) at their leisure (Millán and Mouriño 2003; Pfurtscheller et al. 2006). There might also be many different ways to accomplish a goal. For example, one user may navigate through a slalom course by turning after every step, while another might only turn once for each obstacle. Either solution would be correct. Any proficiency test for an asynchronous BCI should also ensure that a subject can avoid sending signals at certain times, which reflects effective communication of the "no control" state (Leeb et al. 2007; Scherer et al. 2008; Faller et al. 2010).

Further complicating the discussion, an "effective proficiency threshold" also depends on subjective factors. A subject who attains 69% accuracy with a two choice system might be classified as illiterate, but could still communicate if persistent and patient. A different subject might consider a two choice BCI useless if it does not provide at least 90% accuracy. That would be effectively illiterate, just like a decent French speaker who is so embarrassed by his accent, and/or by his periodic errors in French grammar, that he never speaks French. Other authors have noted that users may prefer a more accurate system over one that maximizes ITR (Kübler et al. 2001; Wolpaw et al. 2002; Allison et al. 2007).

Finally, illiteracy may vary within subjects with factors like time of day, mood, motivation, lighting, distraction, and testing environment. How should this be addressed? Can someone be literate in one setting, and illiterate in another?

3.4.1 The Relative Severity of Illiteracy

The discussion so far might suggest that "BCI illiteracy" is a fatal problem in BCI research. The severity of "BCI illiteracy" should also be considered in relation to other interfaces. Conventional interfaces are not universal either. Many millions of people cannot use keyboards, mice, cell phone keypads, and other conventional interfaces due to physical or other disability. This serious drawback has not prevented these interfaces from becoming mainstream communication tools. BCIs may also attain wider acceptance among disabled and healthy users even if they do not provide control for some people (Nijholt et al. 2008).

Similarly, ITR is a problematic way to compare BCIs, with many of the same problems as BCI illiteracy. For example, the formula for ITR does not account for types of errors, frequency of certain selections, subjective factors, preferences for higher accuracy over ITR, "extra time" such as the time between selections and breaks, and other issues. These concerns have been widely noted (e.g. Kübler et al., 2001; Wolpaw et al., 2002; Sellers and Donchin, 2006; Allison et al., 2007), yet ITR is still widely used in BCI articles.

3.4.2 (Re) Defining "BCI Illiteracy"

In addition to the problems with measuring illiteracy, there is no widespread agreement on the term itself. The term "BCI illiteracy" is still quite new. Its first publication outside of a conference presentation was in Kübler and Müller (2007). The Berlin group used the term "BCI aphasia" in prior conference presentations. Other terms that might be used include proficiency, reliability, or universality. Authors have described subjects' unacceptable performance as "bad" (Cheng et al. 2002), "marginal" (Guger et al. 2003), "low" (Allison et al. 2008) or "poor" (Leeb et al. 2007).

Extending the word "illiteracy" from natural languages to BCIs leads to intriguing comparisons, but can also be confusing. Since the word "illiteracy" refers to trouble reading or writing, it is unclear whether illiteracy results from the subject, classifier, or other factors. This distinction may be meaningful. As discussed above, different problems suggest different possible solutions.

"BCI illiteracy" implies that failure to use a BCI results from inadequate effort by the user, which is generally not true. Conventional illiteracy can typically be overcome by (for example) taking German classes. Hence, if someone cannot speak German, one might assume he is lazy, uninterested, or overly focused on other priorities (such as writing articles about BCIs). On the other hand, some subjects could never learn to use a particular BCI.

"Illiteracy" really reflects a problem connecting the different letters in an alphabet into meaningful communication. English, French, Spanish, Dutch, Flemish, Italian, and other languages have alphabets similar to the German alphabet, and native German speakers can recognize most letters in other Romance languages. Similarly, a native German speaker can produce the sounds used in most Romance languages. However, proficiency with the alphabet is only a precursor to literacy with a natural language. With BCIs, the real challenge is mastering the alphabet—the basic signals that convey information. Combining these signals into a vocabulary of messages or commands is then straightforward. There may be some cases when an individual signal can convey meaning (Allison et al. 2007), just as "I" or "a" are letters that are also English words, but such cases are rare.

3.5 Summary

The rapid increase in BCI research has exposed a problem that remains underappreciated: BCI illiteracy. This problem exists across the three prominent BCI approaches (P300, SSVEP, and ERD) and across different implementations of these approaches in different labs. Many options to reduce illiteracy have been explored. While these have been somewhat successful, some subjects will be unable to use a particular BCI approach, and these subjects might only attain proficiency by switching to another approach. Although we focused on EEG BCIs, BCI illiterates might benefit from switching to another imaging approach, and many of the problems, solutions, and terminological issues discussed here could be extended to non-EEG BCIs.

Hence, the answer to the question "Can anyone use a BCI?" depends on the interpretation of the question. For a specific BCI system, the answer is probably no. A "universal BCI" is unlikely in the near future; at least a minority of subjects will not be proficient any particular system. Fortunately, the answer becomes "probably" if the question is interpreted as: "Can anyone use at least one BCI?" It is unlikely that anyone would be unable to use all BCI approaches, so long as s/he is mentally capable of goal-directed action, receiving and understanding instructions and feedback, and forming messages or commands (Kübler and Birbaumer 2008). Therefore, while all the options presented above should be explored, more attention should be devoted to exploring different BCI approaches, especially hybrid BCIs, within subjects in real-world settings.

There are also many concerns with defining "BCI illiteracy". Some of these problems are unique to the term itself, while other problems create challenges in establishing any standards to assess this phenomenon. Ultimately, standards need to be established through discussion among established BCI research groups. Widely agreed terms, definitions, and measurement metrics will help future developers, authors, carers, users, and others unequivocally identify how to distinguish effective communication from illiteracy.

Acknowledgements   This work was supported in part by two grants: the Information and Communication Technologies Coordination and Support action "FutureBNCI", Project number ICT-2010-248320; and the Information and Communication Technologies Collaborative Project action "BrainAble", Project number ICT-2010-247447. We are grateful to Dr. Florin Popescu for suggesting the term "proficiency" as an alternative to "literacy", and to Prof. Dr. John Polich, Prof. Dr. Andrea Kübler, Dr. Femke Nijboer, and Dr. Günter Krausz for comments. We thank Dr. Clemens Brunner for help with Figs. 3.1–3.3, and Dr. Jin Jing for providing Fig. 3.4. We also thank Josef Faller for help with formatting, and we thank an anonymous reviewer for insightful comments.

References

Allison BZ (in press) Toward ubiquitous BCIs. In Graimann B, Allison BZ, Pfurtscheller G (eds) Brain-Computer Interfaces: Revolutionizing Human-Computer Interaction. Springer, Berlin

Allison BZ, Pineda JA (2006) Effects of SOA and flash pattern manipulations on ERPs, performance, and preference: Implications for a BCI system. Int J Psychophysiol 59:127–140

Allison BZ, Wolpaw EW, Wolpaw JR (2007) Brain computer interface systems: Progress and prospects. In: Poll E (ed) British Review of Medical Devices, Jul; 4(4):463–474

Allison BZ, McFarland DJ, Schalk G, Zheng SD, Moore Jackson M, Wolpaw JR (2008) Towards an independent SSVEP brain computer interface. Clin Neurophysiol 119(2):399–408

Allison BZ, Valbuena D, Lueth T, Teymourian A, Volosyak I, Gräser A (2010a) BCI demographics: How many (and what kinds of) people can use an SSVEP BCI? IEEE Trans Neural Syst Rehabil Eng. DOI 10.1109/TNSRE.2009.2039495

Allison BZ, Brunner C, Kaiser V, Müller-Putz G, Neuper C, Pfurtscheller G (2010b) A hybrid brain-computer interface based on imagined movement and visual attention. J Neural Eng 7(2):26007

Bin GY, Gao XR, Wang YJ, Hong B, Gao SK (2009) IEEE Comput Intell Mag 4(4):22 –26

Blakely T, Miller KJ, Zanos SP, Rao RP, Ojemann JG (2009) Robust long-term control of an electrocorticographic brain-computer interface with fixed parameters. Neurosurg Focus 27(1):E13

Blankertz B, Müller K-R, Curio G, Vaughan TM, Schalk G, Wolpaw JR, Schlögl A, Neuper C, Pfurtscheller G, Hinterberger T, Schröder M, Birbaumer N (2004) Progress and perspectives in detection and discrimination of EEG single trials. IEEE Trans Biomed Eng 51(6):1044–1051

Blankertz B, Losch Y, Krauledat M, Dornhege G, Curio G, Müller K-R (2008) The Berlin Brain-Computer Interface: Accurate performance from first-session in BCI-naive subjects. IEEE Trans Biomed Eng 55:2452–2462

Brunner C, Allison BZ, Krusienski DJ, Kaiser V, Müller-Putz GR, Neuper C, Pfurtscheller G (2010) Improved signal processing approaches for a hybrid brain-computer interface simulation. J Neurosci Methods 188(1):165–173

Buttfield A, Ferrez PW, Millán JR (2006) Towards a robust BCI: Error potentials and online learning. IEEE Trans Neural Syst Rehabil Eng 14(2):164–168

Cheng M, Gao XR, Gao SG, Xu DF (2002) Design and implementation of a brain-computer interface with high transfer rates. IEEE Trans Biomed Eng 49(10):1181–1186

Conroy MA, Polich J (2007) Normative variation of P3a and P3b from a large sample ($N = 120$): Gender, topography, and response time. J Psychophysiol 21:22–32

Faller J, Müller-Putz G, Schmalstieg D, Pfurtscheller G (2010) An application framework for controlling an avatar in a desktop based virtual environment via a software SSVEP brain-computer interface. Presence: Teleoperators and Virtual Environments 19(1):25–34

Farwell LA, Donchin E (1988) Talking off the top of your head: Toward a mental prosthesis utilizing event-related brain potentials. Electroencephalogr Clin Neurophysiol 70:510–523

Ferrez PW, Millán Jdel R (2008) Error-related EEG potentials generated during simulated brain-computer interaction. IEEE Trans Biomed Eng 55(3):923–929

Friedrich EVC, McFarland DJ, Neuper C, Vaughan TM, Brunner P, Wolpaw JR (2009) A scanning protocol for sensorimotor rhythm-based brain-computer interface. Biol Psychol 80:169–175

Gonsalvez CJ, Polich J (2002) P300 amplitude is determined by target-to-target interval. Psychophysiology 39(3):388–396

Guger C, Edlinger G, Harkam W, Niedermayer I, Pfurtscheller G (2003) How many people are able to operate an EEG-based brain-computer interface (BCI)? IEEE Trans Neural Syst Rehabil Eng 11:145–147

Guger C, Daban S, Sellers E, Holzner C, Krausz G, Carabalona R, Gramatica F, Edlinger G (2009) How many people are able to control a P300-based brain-computer interface (BCI)? Neurosci Lett 462(1):94–8

Hochberg LR, Serruya MD, Friehs GM, Mukand JA, Saleh M, Caplan AH, Branner A, Chen D, Penn RD, Donoghue JP (2006) Neuronal ensemble control of prosthetic devices by a human with tetraplegia. Nature 442(7099):164–171

Jing J, Allison BZ, Brunner C, Wang B, Wang X, Pfurtscheller G (2010) P300 Chinese input system based on PSO-LDA. Biomed Eng 55(1):5–18

Kübler A, Neumann N, Kaiser J, Kotchoubey B, Hinterberger T, Birbaumer N (2001) Brain computer communication: Self-regulation of slow cortical potentials for verbal communication. Arch Phys Med Rehabil 82:1533–1539

Kübler A, Müller K-R (2007) Toward brain-computer interfacing. In: An Introduction to Brain-Computer Interfacing. MIT Press, Boston, pp 1–25

Kübler A, Birbaumer N (2008) Brain-computer interfaces and communication in paralysis: Extinction of goal directed thinking in completely paralysed patients? Clin Neurophysiol 119(11):2658–2666

Kübler A, Furdea A, Halder S, Hammer EM, Nijboer F, Kotchoubey B (2009) A brain-computer interface controlled auditory event-related potential (P300) spelling system for locked-in patients. Ann NY Acad Sci 1157:90–100

Leeb R, Lee F, Keinrath C, Scherer R, Bischof H, Pfurtscheller G (2007) Brain-computer communication: Motivation, aim and impact of exploring a virtual apartment. IEEE Trans Neural Syst Rehabil Eng 15:473–482

Lenhardt A, Kaper M, Ritter HJ (2008) An adaptive P300-based online brain-computer interface. IEEE Trans Neural Syst Rehabil Eng 16(2):121–130

Mason SG, Bashashati A, Fatourechi M, Navarro KF, Birch GE (2007) A comprehensive survey of brain interface technology designs. Ann Biomed Eng 35:137–169

Millán Jdel R, Mouriño J (2003) Asynchronous BCI and local neural classifiers: An overview of the Adaptive Brain Interface project. IEEE Trans Neural Syst Rehabil Eng 11(2):159–161

Müller-Putz GR, Scherer R, Neuper C, Pfurtscheller G (2006) Steady-state somatosensory evoked potentials: Suitable brain signals for brain-computer interfaces? IEEE Trans Neural Syst Rehabil Eng 14(1):30 –37

Müller-Putz GR, Scherer R, Brunner C, Leeb R, Pfurtscheller G (2008) Better than random? A closer look on BCI results. Int J Bioelectromagn 10:52–55

Neuper C, Pfurtscheller G (in press) Neurofeedback training for BCI control. In: Brain-Computer Interfaces: Revolutionizing Human-Computer Interaction. Graimann B, Allison BZ, Pfurtscheller G (eds) Springer, Berlin

Neuper C, Scherer R, Reiner M, Pfurtscheller G (2005) Imagery of motor actions: Differential effects of kinesthetic and visual-motor mode of imagery in single-trial EEG. Brain Res Cogn Brain Res 25(3):668–677

Nijboer F, Broermann U (in press) Brain-computer interfaces for communication and control in locked-in patients. Toward ubiquitous BCIs. In: Graimann B, Allison BZ, Pfurtscheller G (eds) Brain-Computer Interfaces: Revolutionizing Human-Computer Interaction. Springer, Berlin

Nijboer F, Furdea A, Gunst I, Mellinger J, McFarland DJ, Birbaumer N, Kübler A (2008) An auditory brain-computer interface (BCI). J Neurosci Methods 167(1):43–50

Nijholt A, Tan D, Pfurtscheller G, Brunner C, Millán JR, Allison BZ, Graimann B, Popescu F, Blankertz B, Müller K-R (2008) Brain-computer interfacing for intelligent systems. IEEE Intell Syst 23:72–79

Nikulin VV, Hohlefeld FU, Jacobs AM, Curio G (2008) Quasi-movements: A novel motor-cognitive phenomenon. Neuropsychologia 46(2):727–742

Perelmouter J, Birbaumer N (2000) A binary spelling interface with random errors. IEEE Trans Rehabil Eng 8:227–232

Pfurtscheller G, Neuper C (in press) Dynamics of sensorimotor oscillations in a motor task. In: Graimann B, Allison BZ, Pfurtscheller G (eds) Brain-Computer Interfaces: Revolutionizing Human-Computer Interaction. Springer, Berlin

Pfurtscheller G, Flotzinger D, Pregenzer M, Wolpaw JR, McFarland D (1996) EEG-based brain computer interface (BCI). Search for optimal electrode positions and frequency components. Med Prog Technol 21(3):111–121

Pfurtscheller G, Neuper C, Guger C, Harkam W, Ramoser H, Schlögl A, Obermaier B, Pregenzer M (2000) Current trends in Graz Brain-Computer Interface (BCI) research. IEEE Trans Rehabil Eng 8(2):216–219

Pfurtscheller G, Müller-Putz GR, Schlögl A, Graimann B, Scherer R, Leeb R, Brunner C, Keinrath C, Lee F, Townsend G, Vidaurre C, Neuper C (2006) 15 years of BCI research at Graz University of Technology: Current projects. IEEE Trans Neural Syst Rehabil Eng 14:205–210

Pfurtscheller G, Müller-Putz GR, Scherer R, Neuper C (2008) Rehabilitation with brain-computer interface systems. IEEE Comput Mag 41:58–65

Polich J (1986) Normal variation of P300 from auditory stimuli. Electroencephalogr Clin Neurophysiol 65:236–240

Popescu F, Fazli S, Badower Y, Blankertz B, Müller K-R (2007) Single trial classification of motor imagination using 6 dry EEG electrodes. PLoS One 2(7):e637

Schalk G, Wolpaw JR, McFarland DJ, Pfurtscheller G (2000) EEG-based communication: Presence of an error potential. Clin Neurophysiol 111(12):2138–2144

Schalk G, Miller KJ, Anderson NR, Wilson JA, Smyth MD, Ojemann JG, Moran DW, Wolpaw JR, Leuthardt EC (2008) Two-dimensional movement control using electrocorticographic signals in humans. J Neural Eng 5(1):75–84

Scherer R, Müller GR, Neuper C, Graimann B, Pfurtscheller G (2004) An asynchronously controlled EEG-based virtual keyboard: Improvement of the spelling rate. IEEE Trans Neural Syst Rehabil Eng 51:979–984

Scherer R, Lee F, Schlögl A, Leeb R, Bischof H, Pfurtscheller G (2008) Toward self-paced brain-computer communication: Navigation through virtual worlds. IEEE Trans Biomed Eng 55(2):675–682

Sellers EW, Donchin E (2006) A P300-based brain-computer interface: Initial tests by ALS patients. Clin Neurophysiol 117(3):538–548

Sullivan TJ, Deiss SR, Jung T-P, Cauwenberghs G (2008) A brain-machine interface using dry-contact, low-noise EEG sensors. In: Proceedings of the IEEE International Symposium on Circuits and Systems (ISCAS'2008), Seattle, USA, pp 1986–1989

Wang Y, Wang R, Gao X, Hong B, Gao S (2006) A practical VEP-based brain-computer interface. IEEE Trans Neural Syst Rehabil Eng 14:234–240

Wolpaw JR, Birbaumer N, McFarland DJ, Pfurtscheller G, Vaughan TM (2002) Brain-computer interfaces for communication and control. Clin Neurophysiol 113:767–791

Wolpaw JR, Loeb GE, Allison BZ, Donchin E, do Nascimento OF, Heetderks WJ, Nijboer F, Shain WG, Turner JN (2006) BCI meeting 2005—Workshop on signals and recording methods. IEEE Trans Neural Syst Rehabil Eng 14:138–141

Chapter 4
Using Rest Class and Control Paradigms for Brain Computer Interfacing

Siamac Fazli, Márton Danóczy, Florin Popescu, Benjamin Blankertz, and Klaus-Robert Müller

Abstract The use of Electroencephalography (EEG) for Brain Computer Interface (BCI) provides a cost-efficient, safe, portable and easy to use BCI for both healthy users and the disabled. This chapter will first briefly review some of the current challenges in BCI research and then discuss two of them in more detail, namely modeling the "no command" (rest) state and the use of control paradigms in BCI. For effective prosthetic control of a BCI system or when employing BCI as an additional control-channel for gaming or other generic man machine interfacing, a user should not be required to be continuously in an active state, as is current practice. In our approach, the signals are first transduced by computing Gaussian probability distributions of signal features for each mental state, then a prior distribution of idle-state is inferred and subsequently adapted during use of the BCI. We furthermore investigate the effectiveness of introducing an intermediary state between state

This chapter is a slightly revised version of: S. Fazli, M. Danóczy, F. Popescu, B. Blankertz, K.-R. Müller: Using Rest Class and Control Paradigms for Brain Computer Interfacing. IWANN (1) 2009: 651–665.

S. Fazli (✉) · M. Danóczy · B. Blankertz · K.-R. Müller
Berlin Institute of Technology, Franklinstr. 28/29, Berlin, Germany
e-mail: fazli@cs.tu-berlin.de

M. Danóczy
e-mail: marton@cs.tu-berlin.de

B. Blankertz
e-mail: blanker@cs.tu-berlin.de

K.-R. Müller
e-mail: krm@cs.tu-berlin.de

F. Popescu · B. Blankertz
Fraunhofer FIRST, Kekuléstr. 7, Berlin, Germany

F. Popescu
e-mail: florin.popescu@first.fraunhofer.de

D.S. Tan, A. Nijholt (eds.), *Brain-Computer Interfaces,*
Human-Computer Interaction Series,
DOI 10.1007/978-1-84996-272-8_4, © Springer-Verlag London Limited 2010

probabilities and interface command, driven by a dynamic control law, and outline the strategies used by two subjects to achieve idle state BCI control.

4.1 Introduction

Non-invasive Brain Computer Interfacing (BCI) has recently become a hot topic with research activities outside its traditional fields medicine, psychology, neuroscience and rehabilitation engineering (Dornhege et al. 2007; Wolpaw et al. 2002; Kübler et al. 2001). As many novel applications beyond rehabilitation have emerged (Müller et al. 2008; Dornhege et al. 2007; Krepki et al. 2007) also other disciplines such as computer science have started to contribute with novel signal processing, machine learning, software and man machine interaction concepts (Blankertz et al. 2007b; Solovey et al. 2009). Furthermore novel sensors, amplifiers and open source software (Schalk et al. 2004; Sonnenburg et al. 2007) have increased the ease of handling BCIs and have therefore lowered the overall threshold for new groups to enter this highly interdisciplinary field of neuro-technology. In particular employing machine learning techniques allows a successful BCI communication for novices even from the first session (Tomioka and Müller, 2010; Blankertz et al., 2007a, 2008a): instead of several hundred hours of subject training now the machine learns to decode the brain states of BCI users individually (Blankertz et al., 2007a, 2008a; Dornhege et al., 2007). This concept of 'letting the machine learn' (instead of the subjects) was introduced by the Berlin Brain Computer Interface, adapting feature extraction and classification to data acquired in a so-called brief calibration phase (less than 5 minutes) where the subject is focussing to reproducibly generate certain brain states, e.g. imagery movements. The learning machine computes a statistical estimator from this calibration data which then allows to discriminate these learned brain states during the feedback part of the experiment where the subject can communicate with the machine by power of thought alone (see Blankertz et al. 2008a; Krauledat et al. 2006).

The practical versatility of BCI—this novel additional modality of interaction between man and machine—is yet far from explored (Dornhege et al. 2007; Müller et al. 2008; Blankertz et al. 2007b; Krepki et al. 2007). Note however that despite its bright future perspectives EEG based BCI faces a number of challenges that we would like to discuss following (Nijholt et al. 2008; Dornhege et al. 2007).

4.1.1 Challenges in BCI

First of all, the information transfer rate (ITR) achievable through EEG is approximately one order of magnitude lower than the one observed by invasive methods in monkey studies (Santhanam et al. 2006; Nicolelis 2001; Taylor et al. 2002). That said, the potential benefits of brain implant based BCI has so far not been demonstrated to be worth the associated cost and risk in the most disabled of patients, let alone in healthy users (Hochberg et al. 2006). EEG seems for now the only practical brain-machine interaction (BMI) choice (cost and ITR limitations hamper other non-invasive methods).

The most elementary of EEG-BCI challenges for healthy users is not—at first glance—a computational one. Standard EEG practice involves the tedious application of conductive gel on EEG electrodes in order to provide for accurate measurements of the micro-volt level scalp potentials that constitute EEG signals. Without "dry-cap" technology the proper set-up of BCI sessions in, say, a home environment, is too tedious, messy and therefore impractical. Marketing promises of impending "dry-cap" EEG have already made some media impact, while we have also presented "dry-cap" EEG-BCI design and performance in a controlled study (Popescu et al. 2007). All foreseeable systems, for reasons of ease-of-use and cost, use fewer electrodes than found on standard EEG caps. The computational challenges which we have addressed are (1) optimal placement of the reduced number of electrodes and (2) robustness of BCI algorithms to the smaller set of recording sites. With only 6 uni-polar electrodes we can achieve about 70% of full gel cap BCI performance at sites above the motor cortex, while being able to discount any potential influence of muscle and eye movement artifacts. Most other dry-cap challenges remaining are of an engineering design nature, excluding perhaps the computational reduction of artifacts produced not by unrelated electro-physiological activity but by measured low-frequency voltage variations caused by the physical movement of the head.

A long-standing problem of BCI designs which detect EEG patterns related to some voluntarily produced brain state is that such paradigms work with varying success among subjects/patients. We distinguish mental task based BCI such as "movement imagination" BCI from paradigms based on involuntary stimulus related potentials such as P300 which are limited to very specific applications such as typing for locked-in patients and require constant focus on stimuli extraneous to the task at hand. The peak performance to be achieved even after multiple sessions, varies greatly among subjects. Using a recent study (Blankertz et al. 2010) and other unreported data by many research groups, we estimate that about 20% of subjects do not show strong enough motor related mu-rhythm variations for effective asynchronous motor imagery BCI, that for another 30% performance is slow (<20 bits/min) and for up to 50% it is moderate to high (20–35 bits/min). It is still a matter of debate as to why BCI systems exhibit "illiteracy" in a significant minority of subjects and what in terms of signal processing and machine learning algorithms can be done about it. Our first steps using a fully adaptive approach for calibration seem promising.

So far most BCI systems are capable of performing asynchronously (self-paced), say, cursor control, however this can become tiring since the user is required to continuously imagine one of the two classes. Often the user does not intend to control anything but rather leave the BCI inactive, thus BCI usability would benefit from an "idle" or "rest" class where the cursor does not respond when no active class (from a set of two or more) is activated, on top the BCI being self-paced. The "idle" state may take one of two forms: a "relax" state where the subject stays still and tries to "think of nothing", or can do almost any other mental task than those which belong to the active classes, but the latter may not be intuitive. Remaining challenges are to find a classifier that can induce rest state without a "relax" cue and to optimize the relationship between classifier output and BCI command. Due to physiological variations in background EEG activity, where a main factor is fatigue, we believe that the introduction of a controller layer is necessary for maximal performance.

The remainder of the paper will discuss both rest class and control strategies in more detail. Note that we are well aware to only report first *conceptual* steps in this paper and empirical evidence drawn from two subjects only. Clearly, a broader exploration of this interesting direction will still have to come, along with larger subject studies.

4.1.2 Background on Rest Class and Controller Concepts

Relatively few results showing idle-state asynchronous BCI exist. Early neuro-feedback studies did feature an "idle" state, but required months of training on the part of subject to learn to modulate the slow cortical potentials required for classification and exhibited relatively low ITR (Birbaumer et al. 2003).

Among "rest-class" studies based on movement imagination, which offers intuitive control for gaming and prosthetics, the important measures of interface quality are the false positive (FP) rate, which is the probability of choosing an active class during "rest", the true positive rate (TP), meaning the probability of detecting the correct active class when movement imagination occurs or should occur. Other than accuracy measures, speed related measures of interest are the maximal time duration of correct idle state detection and the latency of correct responses to active states. Borisoff et al. (2004), Mason and Birch (2000) used a single active class vs. rest paradigm with FP rates of 3%, TP rates of 70%, and idle state lengths of 7 s in multiple normal subjects, and more limited success in spinal-cord injury patients, using nearest-neighbor classifiers on windowed band-power features. Also Millán and Mouriño (2003), Millán et al. (2006) have implemented a 2-active class rest-class interface based on Malahobnis distance classification of band-power features. After an earlier study in which rest-state was performed with eyes closed (doing so produces distinctive alpha wave EEG modulation), a follow-up study used "active relaxation" (Millán et al. 2006) and showed FP of 2%, TP of 70%, and 1.5 s of relax state. In the last specialized BCI data competition (Blankertz et al. 2006) a synchronous "relax"-vs.-active data set was addressed by the winning submission described in Wang et al. (2004).

The type of classifiers currently employed in BCI (linear discriminants (LDA) and combinations thereof, cf. Müller et al. (2001)) may partition the feature space in an overly simple manner, not allowing for "rest" class to be separated from active class regions with appropriate efficiency. To take a first step beyond linear methods we assigned continuous class membership probabilities, using compact principal component bandpower features instead of channel bandpower features as in Millán et al. (2006), and added an intermediate, continuously moving state which is driven by classifier output via a differential equation, which we call a "control law", such that when that intermediate state reaches a threshold, the output of the BCI interface changes. In the current approach, the classifier outputs a set of distances from each active class mean (or equivalently, a probability measure centered on the mean). We present feedback data using two active classes (left hand vs. right hand—or foot—movement imagination, "L" and "R") and an idle state. For the "active" classes the probabilities are of elliptical, Gaussian shapes. A given state (set of features) is either of higher probability (i.e. closer) to state L or R or far from both. Outside of both volumes is an outlier class, or the idle state. Stipulating that the idle state itself can be anywhere outside the "active" zones but also knowing where it lies preferentially, we place a "prior" on it as well—in between the active class zones, based on training data for "active" classes only. Training trials are recorded during cues to the subject to imagine "left" or "right" hand movements: no "idle" or "relax" trials are cued or recorded, and therefore the paradigm was not tuned to active relaxation. In subsequent feedback trials, i.e. actual asynchronous BCI control that is cued so that performance can be measured, all three probability distributions adapt and overlap, and the resulting posterior probabilities are fed into the "control law". Thus the subjects adapt their strategies based on feedback they receive while the classifier adapts also.

Post-hoc analysis was performed and is presented which outlines more efficient extraction of control signals could be achieved, for "rest" class inference as well as multi-class classification (i.e. for more than two mental tasks) by optimizing the control law on collected data. Also, we investigate the role of occipital alpha band power (a frequency range of 8–12 Hz around the cortical location related to visual processing) in the strategies used by two different subjects in achieving rest-class control. An increase in occipital alpha activity is traditionally associated with lack of attention to visual stimuli (Plotkin 1976), be it because of closing of the eyes while awake, in some phases of sleep, during a state of drowsiness, or during a general lack of focus on sensory stimuli, which occurs when subjects actively relax or do not perform any cognitive tasks (Plotkin 1976; Williamson et al. 1997). We used this phenomenon to help determine if the subjects "actively relaxed" or tried to modulate their active state EEG patterns more discernibly.

4.2 Methods

4.2.1 Experimental Paradigm

A 1D cursor control paradigm was reproduced in this study with two healthy volunteer subjects (both male). A standard DC amplifier set-up (BrainAmp128DC, Munich, Germany) was used (64 EEG channels, 4 bipolar EMG/EOG channels). In the first part of the experiment ("calibration session"), a sequence of 70 left/right cues was presented visually by means of a letter which appears in the middle of the computer screen. The subject was asked to imagine the cued class without moving either limbs or eyes. Apart from off-line checks, electromyograms and electro-oculograms were monitored.

In a second part of the experiment subjects were asked to move a cross displayed on the screen to a target represented by a bar on either the right or left side of the screen by imagining the corresponding class. The cross movement provided continuous performance feedback to the subjects. After training, 70 trials of normal, synchronous left/right target feedback trials were performed (no rest state, cursor moved as soon as the target was presented): this was done to ensure quality of common spatial patterns as well as to compare "usual" BCI performance to asynchronous performance. Cross-validation with LDA classifiers was used on the resulting Common Spatial Patterns (CSP) (Blankertz et al. 2008b; Lemm et al. 2005; Koles 1991) only on training trials.

The subject then performed 80 idle-to-active feedback trial attempts, in 4 blocks of 20 trials each. Each trial within the feedback phase consists of two separate parts. Within the first part no cue is presented to the subject for a period randomly varying (first subject: 8–12 sec, second subject: 10–20 sec), while the subject is instructed to relax. During this period the cursor is free to move, but not shown to the subject.

In general the cursor moves on a horizontal line, the center representing the relaxed state and respective edges active classes, e.g. left and right or left and foot. Not providing cursor feedback to the subject during this first part prevents the subject from steering the cursor stably into the middle by imagining movements. If during this "relax" period the subject reaches any target—without being aware of it—, an error is recorded and a new trial attempt begins. If neither of the two active classes are selected during the "relax" cue, the feedback progresses to the second part, where a visual cue (target on the left or right edge of the window) is presented, indicating the desired active class. In this second part the cursor is made visible to the subject. There is no time limit as to when a class has to be selected, but the subject is instructed to reach the cued target as fast as possible. After selection of any of the two active classes (the correct one or incorrect one) a new trial begins. The cursor does *not* represent an object whose position the subject is trying to control, it is merely a 1-D intermediate "state" which allows the subject to output a command when its position reaches the "left" or "right" boundaries.

4.2.2 Feature Extraction

A semi-automatic search for the time interval of the event-related desynchronization (ERDs) and frequency band whose power discriminates most between classes for each subjects generally selects the so-called mu- and beta-rhythms (10–25 Hz) in the motor cortex (Blankertz et al. 2007a; Pfurtscheller et al. 2006). Note that the lower part of this frequency range (the mu range) slightly overlaps the alpha range (8–12) Hz and that due to brain and scalp electrical conductivity EEG signals are known to be spatially "mixed", that is, a single source of electrical activity in the cortex can be recorded at multiple locations on the scalp, albeit with higher amplitudes at electrodes close to that cortical location. The discriminating frequency band search determined a band-pass filter which attenuated signal amplitude outside these bands thereby accomplishing a temporal "demixing". The resulting filtered multivariate signals, segmented in the ERDs time interval, are used to compute two covariance matrices Σ_1 and Σ_2 from the calibration data. The CSP algorithm (see e.g. Blankertz et al. 2007a; Lemm et al. 2005; Koles 1991) searches for a matrix W and a vector of n values $0 \leq d_i \leq 1$ which achieves:

$$W\Sigma_1 W^\top = D \quad \text{and} \quad W\Sigma_2 W^\top = I - D, \tag{4.1}$$

where n is the number of channels and D is a diagonal matrix with entries d_i. Using z-transform notation for digital signals, for any trial, the spatio-temporally de-mixed data is:

$$f(z) = WH(z)s(z). \tag{4.2}$$

Where x is the raw EEG signal and $H(z)$ is a diagonal matrix of identical band-pass filter transforms. The columns of the source to signal transform W^{-1} are called the Common Spatial Patterns (CSPs). The CSP decomposition can be thought of as a coupled decomposition of two matrices (for two classes) similar to a principal components analysis yielding eigenvectors and eigenvalues. As the eigenvalues d_i are equal to the power ratio of signals of class 1 by class 2 in the corresponding CSP filter (eigenvector in i-th column of matrix W), best discrimination is provided by filters with very high (i.e. near 1) or very low (i.e. near 0) eigenvalues. Accordingly CSP projections with the highest two and lowest two eigenvalues were chosen as features ($n = 4$).

4.2.3 Feature Processing

Let $x \in \mathbb{R}^n$ the input feature vector as determined by CSP ($n = 4$) and $y \in \{1, 0, -1\}$ be the class label. The prior distributions $p(x|y = i, \mu_i, \Sigma_i)$ for each class i are modelled as:

$$p(x|y = i, \mu_i, \Sigma_i) = \mathcal{N}(x|\mu_i, \Sigma_i) \quad \forall i, \tag{4.3}$$

where $\mathcal{N}(x|\mu, \Sigma)$ is the Gaussian density function with mean μ and variance Σ. We chose the distributions' parameters $\Theta = \{\mu_i, \Sigma_i\}$ by maximizing the logarithm of the data's joint likelihood:

$$\log \mathcal{L} = \sum_t \log P(y_t, x_t | \Theta) = \sum_t \log \frac{p(x_t | y_t, \Theta)P(y_t)}{p(x_t)}. \tag{4.4}$$

The maximum likelihood estimators for the parameters of a Gaussian probability density function are given by the empirical mean $\hat{\mu}$ and the empirical covariance

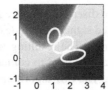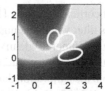

Fig. 4.1 Prior and posterior class membership probabilities during adaptation; after training, after 12, 24 and 36 trials, from left to right. In each panel, the *top white ellipse* is left class, the *middle ellipse* is rest class and the *bottom ellipse* is right class 68% confidence region. The classifier output $[1 - P(y = 0|\boldsymbol{x})][P(y = +1|\boldsymbol{x}) - P(y = -1|\boldsymbol{x})]$, see (4.11), is encoded as gray-scale, with the light area having a high probability for "rest" and dark (top and right) areas having high probabilities for "left" or "right". Only the largest and smallest CSP projections (the x and y axes of the plots above) are shown for visualization purposes, as they are the two most relevant of the four features. The two right-angled lines on the leftmost panel indicate the method of selecting the rest class prior mean: the minimum of movement class means in each CSP projection, corresponding to minimal bandpower difference

matrix $\hat{\Sigma}$:

$$\hat{\boldsymbol{\mu}} = \frac{1}{n} \sum_{t=1}^{n} \boldsymbol{x}_t \quad \text{and} \quad \hat{\Sigma} = \frac{1}{n} \sum_{t=1}^{n} (\boldsymbol{x}_t - \hat{\boldsymbol{\mu}})(\boldsymbol{x}_t - \hat{\boldsymbol{\mu}})^\top. \tag{4.5}$$

Training data give us the CSPs which decompose each training trial, yielding a population of 4-dimensional vectors $\boldsymbol{x}$ for each of the two movement (i.e. active) classes, by taking the logarithm of the variance of each of the 4 chosen CSP projections over a (moving) time window of 800 ms.

As we have chosen not to collect training data for the rest class, we must instead initialize the parameters of its probability distribution heuristically. If in rest state, we expect both hemispheres to generate roughly the same power in the alpha and beta band. We therefore initialize each component of the rest state's mean at the minimum of the respective means of the two active classes for each CSP component (see Fig. 4.1, leftmost panel). The rest state's initial covariance matrix is set to the average of the covariance matrix of the two active classes.

4.2.4 Adaptation

In order to track non-stationarities in feedback BCI performance, we adapt by iteratively adding each new data point to the empirical means and covariance matrices. We make use of the sequential formulas for updating means:

$$\mu_{n+1} = \frac{1}{n+1} \sum_{t=1}^{n} \boldsymbol{x}_t + \frac{1}{n+1} \boldsymbol{x}_{n+1} = \frac{n}{n+1} \mu_n + \frac{1}{n+1} \boldsymbol{x}_{n+1} \tag{4.6}$$

Substituting the fraction $1/(n+1)$ by the constant α we introduce a forgetting factor (i.e. we compute leaky average):

$$\mu_{n+1} = (1-\alpha)\mu_n + \alpha x_{n+1}. \tag{4.7}$$

For the covariance matrix Σ, we implement a similar procedure (covariance estimation with forgetting factor). In the following, the notation $x^{2\top} = x\,x^\top$ signifies a vector's outer product with itself.

$$\Sigma_{n+1} = \frac{1}{n+1}\sum_{t=1}^{n}(x_t - \mu_{n+1})^{2\top} + \frac{1}{n+1}(x_{n+1} - \mu_{n+1})^{2\top}. \tag{4.8}$$

Substituting the leaky mean estimate for μ_{n+1} from (4.7) yields:

$$\Sigma_{n+1} = \frac{n}{n+1}\Sigma_n + (x_{n+1} - \mu_n)^{2\top} \times \left[\alpha^2\frac{n}{n+1} + (1-\alpha)^2\frac{1}{n+1}\right]. \tag{4.9}$$

For the sequential estimation of Σ, too, we introduce a constant β for $1/(n+1)$, thereby weighting data points with a possibly different forgetting factor as above:

$$\Sigma_{n+1} = (1-\beta)\Sigma_n + (x_{n+1} - \mu_n)^{2\top} \times [\alpha^2(1-\beta) + (1-\alpha)^2\beta]. \tag{4.10}$$

Thus the probability density functions of the active classes adapt to feedback trials in a straightforward fashion. The prior for the rest class (i.e the outlier class) is formed by choosing the mean as a combination of the active class means (see Fig. 4.1) while the covariance is the mean of the two active class covariances. The adaptation proceeds similarly as for the active classes, described above.

4.2.5 Determination of Cursor Speed

The (left/right) cursor position c, which is also the "cross" sometimes presented to the subject and is the "intermediate state" given by the control law, is calculated by numerically integrating its time derivative, the cursor speed $\dot{c}$. The cursor speed depends directly on the current class membership probabilities:

$$\dot{c} = (1-p_0)s(p_{+1} - p_{-1}) - p_0\frac{c}{\tau}, \tag{4.11}$$

where $p_i = P(y = i|x)$.

This reduces to the simple rate control law $\dot{c} = s(p_{+1} - p_{-1})$ with the speed constant s if the probability of the rest state is zero. However, if the rest-state probability is non-zero, the exponential decay term $-p_0 1/\tau\, c$ pulls back the cursor to its middle position $c = 0$ with the time constant τ, thereby effectively avoiding the accumulation of small movements to either side.

Table 4.1 Main classification results for 1D feedback. Band stands for the frequency band, selected by a heuristic. xval stands for cross-validation error of training trials and TP is the accuracy of the two active classes

Subject	A	B
classes	left-right	left-foot
band [Hz]	[9 22.5]	[11 13]
xval [%]	1.5 ± 4.2	6.4 ± 5.6
time/trial [s]	2.23	2.98
TP [%]	94.3	88.9
ITR [bit/min]	11.7	7.04

Table 4.2 Idle state feedback results. Idle state timeout stands for the time the subject was required to stay in the idle state without activating any classes, FP stands for the percentage of trials, where an active class was selected during the required idle-state period. To illustrate effectiveness of adaptivity in our classifier, in FP* the first 5 trials were disregarded, showing higher performance after most of the adaptation occurred

Subject	A	B
Idle state timeout [s]	10 ± 2	15 ± 5
FP [%]	11.2	18.7
FP* [%]	7.8	13.7
TP [%]	100	96.9
Activation time [s]	6.00	17.24
Under 10 sec [%]	91.3	55.3

4.3 Results

The accuracy of classification for synchronous feedback is given in Table 4.1. ITRs of 11.7 and 7 bits/min were achieved by the two subjects. Table 4.2 summarizes the average results of the 4 individual asynchronous feedback sessions. Note that most asynchronous trials reach target under 5 s for Subject A. The shape and adaptive response of the classifier are shown in Fig. 4.1.

4.3.1 Alpha Power

Alpha power was calculated from raw EEG data sampled at 100 Hz from the six occipital electrodes PO3, POz, PO4, O1, Oz, O2. After applying a band-pass butterworth filter in the alpha band ranging between 8–12 Hz, the log variance of the resulting signal was calculated and averaged over channels over shifting causal time windows of 800 ms (same windowing as in CSP calculation fed into the classifier). Then, mean and standard deviation of the average alpha power per trial was evaluated for each class (Table 4.3). The p-values shown for the t-test of the mean difference show no statistical difference between either active class and the rest class.

Table 4.3 Per-class alpha power for both subjects. The column pVal shows the p-Value for the hypothesis that the alpha powers of each active class and the rest class are distributed with the same mean. The hypothesis can not be rejected at the 5% level for any of the classes and subjects

Subject A					Subject B				
class	N_{trials}	mean	stdev	pVal	class	N_{trials}	mean	stdev	pVal
left	34	4.63	0.69	0.36	left	32	1.70	0.89	0.64
right	37	4.59	0.68	0.23	right	33	2.00	1.31	0.03
rest	80	4.74	0.59	–	rest	80	1.63	0.52	–

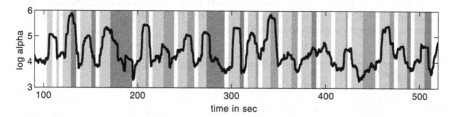

Fig. 4.2 Trace of occipital alpha for a sample experimental session. *Vertical bars* are cued rest (*light grey*) left (*dark grey*) and right (*medium grey*) states

Figure 4.2 shows actual traces of alpha power along with labeled bars indicating detected states for a typical session. The spaces between bars correspond to time between cued trials. Although alpha power is being modulated it is not significantly higher in the rest state than active states.

4.3.2 Post-hoc Optimization of Meta-Parameters

We investigate whether we could have attained higher performance if we had chosen other meta-parameters, these being the decay time constant τ, the moving window size w and cursor speed constant s. For this the EEG recordings, transduced into CSP component traces, were fed off-line into a simulated controller and adaptive classifier having different meta-parameter values. Through a combination of brute-force parameter search followed by downhill-simplex minimization, the following two performance cost functions were evaluated:

$$\text{cost} \sim \sum_i \begin{cases} v|c|^{e_X} & \text{if } y_i = 0 \text{ (i.e. state 'X'),} \\ \Theta(\theta + c)(\theta + c)^{e_{LR}} & \text{if } y_i = -1 \text{ (i.e. state 'L'),} \\ \Theta(\theta - c)(\theta - c)^{e_{LR}} & \text{if } y_i = +1 \text{ (i.e. state 'R').} \end{cases} \quad (4.12)$$

Optimization variables v, e_X and e_{LR} control the trade-off between accuracy and speed, Θ is the Heaviside step function (see Fig. 4.3)

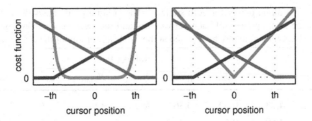

Fig. 4.3 The two cost functions used for optimization. A weighted integral of trajectory over time is computed with weights as functions of cursor state as shown for each class. The sum over all trials is minimized. *Left* "slow but accurate" cost function ($e_X = 10$, $e_{LR} = 1$), *right panel* "fast but less accurate" ($e_X = 1$, $e_{LR} = 1$) cost function for each of the three classes (left: dark grey, right: medium grey, rest: light grey). Vertical scaling is arbitrary. The variable v (see (4.12)) is selected to scale the function at the threshold to equal values

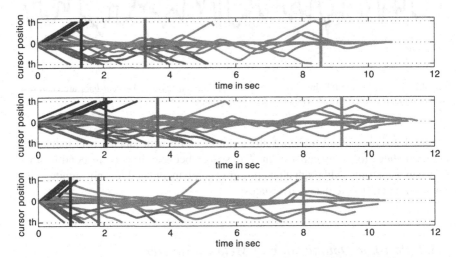

Fig. 4.4 (Data in Table 4.4) *Top*: original trajectories for one subject. *Middle*: "slow but accurate" optimized trajectories. *Bottom*: "fast but less accurate" optimized trajectories. The *vertical bars* indicate average time to hit in each class. *Light grey*: rest, *medium grey*: right, *dark grey*: left. Note that in the middle panel there are no false positives, the rest trajectory which seems to hit threshold is in fact slightly below it

The resulting traces, before and after optimization, for Subject A are shown in Fig. 4.4. The traces shown correspond to the intermediate state (the cursor). Intersection of threshold (θ) means that a L or R command is given. First note that one of the active states is detected much faster than the other, within 2 s. This is consistent with both subjects reporting that they had less difficulty moving the cursor in one direction than another. The hypothetical trajectories that "would have been" from parameters optimized by the different cost functions differ. In one case (the first cost function) the rest state is more robust (i.e. the cursor trajectories are further from the threshold and the FP rate is lower) and using the second cost function the active classes would have responded faster, but with a rest class that is less robust.

Table 4.4 (Data for Fig. 4.4) Control law parameters and results for original experiment (orig) and after the two optimizations, for accuracy (slow) and for speed (fast). The control law parameters are: Window size w [msec], speed constant (s), decay rate ($1/\tau$), TP rate, FP rate, activation time tAct [sec] and rest state duration tRst [sec]

	Subject A						
	w	s	$1/\tau$	TP	FP	tAct	tRst
orig	1000	0.70	0.20	100%	10%	2.30	8.56
slow	546	0.31	0.14	100%	0%	2.81	9.19
fast	1547	1.14	0.50	100%	20%	1.45	8.02

4.4 Conclusion and Outlook

The study reported success in an asynchronous feedback BCI paradigm using minimal subject training involving a "rest" class. It incorporated several features postulated to be important in "switch" type classification. One was the classifier type: adaptive as to account for rest state non-stationarities (see also von Bünau et al. 2009; Shenoy et al. 2006; Sugiyama et al. 2007), and distance-based rather than linear-partition based such that it could classify "rest" state as outlier (distant) from either active state. Although the adaptation scheme used involves merely a leaky average of covariance and mean of class-conditional probability densities, our results show that performance increases quickly with practice. The free design parameters of this transduction algorithm are the coefficients of the implemented control law and the learning rates of the leaky running average.

Fortunately, the current heuristic search for the initial adaptability meta-parameters was rather quick: an adaptive system needs to be neither excessively adaptive or inert with respect to the process it needs to track (in this case, the behavior of the subject), and for the control law, the cursor needed to be responsive but not so fast as to reach thresholds in less than 2–3 sec: data from prior experiments was used to choose these. Post-hoc analysis revealed that optimizing control law parameters for each subject could be useful, however there is a fundamental trade-off that is due to the integrative nature of the control law: one can make the interface more responsive but at a higher risk of sending inadvertent commands. Furthermore, the off-line analysis must be interpreted with caution: as users are active learners their behavior would adapt if the meta-parameters changed. Thus in future studies we aim to make this optimization run on-line, adaptively, such that the interface changes behavior gradually, allowing stable convergence of combined user and interface performance. Long term adaptation, over many sessions and many days, is also a future direction of research. An anecdotal note: the classifier was robust to the subject sometimes moving, or talking during the "rest" state, which suggests that this is in part an "idle" state.

The classification scheme we have employed makes "anything other than active state" detection possible, as it is based on "distance" from a particular mental state and an "outlier" cutoff or competition between distances. Future studies will therefore consider also non-parametric outlier models (e.g. Müller et al. 2001).

The benefit of adaptation and lack of explicit rest class training is the following: instead of collecting training data by instructing the subject to relax, or recording the other mental tasks which do not correspond to commands but which the subject may otherwise perform during BCI use, we only train the active classes, and through cued performance which provides feedback or performance, we allow the subject to find the approach that works best for him/her. The classifier then adapts to the strategy chosen or changes therein. Although they could have chosen to "think of nothing", and one of the subjects reported that he sometimes attempted to do so, this was not evidenced by the available physiological measure of active relaxation, namely occipital alpha-band EEG activity. This could be seen as further evidence that the rest state detected was an idle state and not a relaxation state—without objective measures, no matter what the subjects report it is difficult to tell between the two. It remains to be seen whether the optimized control law, then placed in an un-cued "real-world" BCI use environment translates to effective rest-state BCI control which allows the subject to attend to other tasks than BCI commands. As such, new paradigms must be designed in which the BCI performance is quantified against various levels of background cognitive workload.

Concluding, we envisage an EEG BCI scenario in which users purchase an affordable computer peripheral which is simply placed on the head and requires no gel. Novel users undergo a one-time calibration procedure which takes maximally 5 minutes, ideally even less (Krauledat et al. 2008; Fazli et al. 2009). They then proceed to use the BCI system in a game environment, to control a robot or wheelchair, and the performance of the system slowly adapts to the users' brain patterns, reacting only when they intend to control it. At each repeated use, parameters from previous sessions are recalled and re-calibration is rarely, if ever, necessary. We strongly believe such a system, capable of an average performance of about >20 bits/min, is achievable within the next few years. Clearly, challenges as the ones discussed above need to be met, in order to bring EEG BCI technology closer to becoming a commonplace computer peripheral.

Acknowledgements The studies were partly supported by BFNT, BMBF FKZ 01IBE01A/B, by DFG MU 987/3-1 and by the EU under PASCAL2. This publication only reflects the authors' views.

References

Birbaumer N, Hinterberger T, Kübler A, Neumann N (2003) The thought-translation device (TTD): Neurobehavioral mechanisms and clinical outcome. IEEE Trans Neural Syst Rehabil Eng 11(2):120–123

Blankertz B, Müller KR, Krusienski DJ, Schalk G, Wolpaw JR, Schlögl A, Pfurtscheller G, Millán JdR, Schröder M, Birbaumer N (2006) The BCI competition III: Validating alternative approaches to actual BCI problems. IEEE Trans Neural Syst Rehabil Eng 14(2):153–159

Blankertz B, Dornhege G, Krauledat M, Müller KR, Curio G (2007a) The non-invasive Berlin Brain-Computer Interface: Fast acquisition of effective performance in untrained subjects. Neuroimage 37(2):539–550

Blankertz B, Krauledat M, Dornhege G, Williamson J, Murray-Smith R, Müller KR (2007b) A note on brain actuated spelling with the Berlin Brain-Computer Interface. In: Stephanidis C (ed) Universal Access in HCI, Part II, HCII 2007. LNCS, vol 4555. Springer, Berlin, pp 759–768

Blankertz B, Losch F, Krauledat M, Dornhege G, Curio G, Müller KR (2008a) The Berlin brain-computer interface: Accurate performance from first-session in BCI-naive subjects. IEEE Trans Biomed Eng 55(10):2452–2462

Blankertz B, Tomioka R, Lemm S, Kawanabe M, Müller KR (2008b) Optimizing spatial filters for robust EEG single-trial analysis. IEEE Signal Process Mag 25(1):41–56. DOI 10.1109/MSP.2008.4408441

Blankertz B, Sannelli C, Halder S, Hammer EM, Kübler A, Müller K-R, Curio G, Dickhaus T (2010) Neurophysiological predictor of SMR-based BCI performance. NeuroImage 51(4):1303–1309. DOI 10.1016/j.neuroimage.2010.03.22

Borisoff JF, Mason SG, Bashashati A, Birch GE (2004) Brain-computer interface design for asynchronous control applications: Improvements to the LF-ASD asynchronous brain switch. IEEE Trans Biomed Eng 51(6):985–992

Dornhege G, Millán JdR, Hinterberger T, McFarland D, Müller KR (eds) (2007) Towards Brain-Computer Interfacing. MIT Press, Cambridge

Fazli S, Popescu F, Danóczy M, Blankertz B, Müller KR, Grozea C (2009) Subject independent mental state classification in single trials. Neural Netw 22(9):1305–1312

Hochberg LR, Serruya MD, Friehs GM, Mukand JA, Saleh M, Caplan AH, Branner A, Chen D, Penn RD, Donoghue JP (2006) Neuronal ensemble control of prosthetic devices by a human with tetraplegia. Nature 442:164–171

Koles ZJ (1991) The quantitative extraction and topographic mapping of the abnormal components in the clinical EEG. Electroencephalogr Clin Neurophysiol 79:440–447

Krauledat M, Losch F, Curio G (2006) Brain state differences between calibration and application session influence BCI classification accuracy. In: Proceedings of the 3rd International Brain-Computer Interface Workshop and Training Course 2006. Verlag der Technischen Universität Graz, Graz, pp 60–61

Krauledat M, Tangermann M, Blankertz B, Müller KR (2008) Towards zero training for brain-computer interfacing. PLoS ONE 3:e2967

Krepki R, Blankertz B, Curio G, Müller KR (2007) The Berlin brain-computer interface (BBCI)—towards a new communication channel for online control in gaming applications. Multimedia Tools Appl 33(1):73–90. DOI 10.1007/s11042-006-0094-3

Kübler A, Kotchoubey B, Kaiser J, Wolpaw JR, Birbaumer N (2001) Brain-computer communication: Unlocking the locked in. Psychol Bull 127:358–375

Lemm S, Blankertz B, Curio G, Müller KR (2005) Spatio-spectral filters for improving the classification of single trial EEG. IEEE Trans Biomed Eng 52:1541–1548

Mason SG, Birch GE (2000) A brain-controlled switch for asynchronous control applications. IEEE Trans Biomed Eng 47(10):1297–1307

Millán JdR, Mouriño J (2003) Asynchronous BCI and local neural classifiers: An overview of the Adaptive Brain Interface project. IEEE Trans Neural Syst Rehabil Eng 11(2):159–161

Millán JdR, Renkens F, Mouriño J, Gerstner W (2006) Non-invasive brain-actuated control of a mobile robot by human EEG. In: 2006 IMIA Yearbook of Medical Informatics. Schattauer Verlag, Stuttgart

Müller KR, Mika S, Ratsch G, Tsuda K, Schölkopf B (2001) An introduction to kernel-based learning algorithms. IEEE Trans Neural Netw 12(2):181–201. DOI 10.1109/72.914517

Müller KR, Tangermann M, Dornhege G, Krauledat M, Curio G, Blankertz B (2008) Machine learning for real-time single-trial EEG-analysis: From brain-computer interfacing to mental state monitoring. J Neurosci Methods 167:82–90

Nicolelis MA (2001) Actions from thoughts. Nature 409:403–407

Nijholt A, Tan D, Pfurtscheller G, Brunner C, Millán JdR, Allison B, Graimann B, Popescu F, Blankertz B, Müller KR (2008) Brain-computer interfacing for intelligent systems. IEEE Intell Syst 23(3):72–79. DOI 10.1109/MIS.2008.41

Pfurtscheller G, Brunner C, Schlögl A, Lopes da Silva FH (2006) Mu rhythm (de)synchronization and EEG single-trial classification of different motor imagery tasks. Neuroimage 31(1):153–159

Plotkin WB (1976) On the self-regulation of the occipital alpha rhythm: control strategies, states of consciousness, and the role of physiological feedback. J Exp Psychol Gen 105(1):66–99

Popescu F, Fazli S, Badower Y, Blankertz B, Müller KR (2007) Single trial classification of motor imagination using 6 dry EEG electrodes. PLoS ONE 2(7):e637

Santhanam G, Ryu SI, Yu BM, Afshar A, Shenoy KV (2006) A high-performance brain-computer interface. Nature 442:195–198

Schalk G, McFarland DJ, Hinterberger T, Birbaumer N, Wolpaw JR (2004) BCI2000: A general-purpose brain-computer interface (BCI) system. IEEE Trans Biomed Eng 51(6):1034–1043. DOI 10.1109/TBME.2004.827072

Shenoy P, Krauledat M, Blankertz B, Rao RP, Müller KR (2006) Towards adaptive classification for BCI. J Neural Eng 3:13–23

Solovey ET, Girouard A, Chauncey K, Hirshfield LM, Sassaroli A, Zheng F, Fantini S, Jacob RJ (2009) Using fnirs brain sensing in realistic HCI settings: Experiments and guidelines. In: UIST '09: Proceedings of the 22nd Annual ACM Symposium on User Interface Software and Technology. ACM, New York, NY, USA, pp 157–166. DOI 10.1145/1622176.1622207

Sonnenburg S, Braun ML, Ong CS, Bengio S, Bottou L, Holmes G, LeCun Y, Müller KR, Pereira F, Rasmussen CE, Rätsch G, Schölkopf B, Smola A, Vincent P, Weston J, Williamson R (2007) The need for open source software in machine learning. J Mach Learn Res 8:2443–2466

Sugiyama M, Krauledat M, Müller KR (2007) Covariate shift adaption by importance weighted cross validation. J Mach Learn Res 8:985–1005

Taylor DM, Tillery SI, Schwartz AB (2002) Direct cortical control of 3D neuroprosthetic devices. Science 296:1829–1832

Tomioka R, Müller KR (2010) A regularized discriminative framework for EEG analysis with application to brain-computer interface. NeuroImage 49(1):415–432

von Bünau P, Meinecke F, Kiraly F, Müller KR (2009) Estimating the stationary subspace from superimposed signals. Phys Rev Lett 103:214101

Wang Y, Zhang Z, Li Y, Gao X, Gao S, Yang F (2004) BCI competition 2003—data set IV: An algorithm based on CSSD and FDA for classifying single-trial EEG. IEEE Trans Biomed Eng 51(6):1081–1086

Williamson SJ, Kaufman L, Lu ZL, Wang JZ, Karron D (1997) Study of human occipital alpha rhythm: The alphon hypothesis and alpha suppression. Int J Psychophysiol 26(1–3):63–76

Wolpaw JR, Birbaumer N, McFarland DJ, Pfurtscheller G, Vaughan TM (2002) Brain-computer interfaces for communication and control. Clin Neurophysiol 113:767–791

Chapter 5
EEG-Based Navigation from a Human Factors Perspective

Marieke E. Thurlings, Jan B.F. van Erp,
Anne-Marie Brouwer, and Peter J. Werkhoven

Abstract In this chapter we discuss Brain-Computer Interfaces (BCIs) as navigation devices from a Human Factors point of view. We argue that navigation is more
than only steering a car or a wheelchair. It involves three levels: planning, steering
and control, linked to cognition, perception and sensation, respectively. We structure the existing BCIs along those three levels. Most existing BCIs focus on the
steering level of navigation. This is a remarkable observation from a Human Factors perspective because steering requires a very specific subclass of control devices
that have a high bandwidth and a very low latency like joysticks or steering wheels;
requirements that can not be met with current BCIs. We recommend exploring the
potential of BCIs for the planning level, e.g. to select a route, and for the control
level, e.g. based on possible collision-related potentials.

5.1 Introduction

The field of Brain-Computer Interfacing (BCI) has its origin in the medical domain
and is a relatively young research area. However, over the last few years, some remarkable achievements have been obtained. For instance, a study from the University of Pittsburg shows that monkeys can get cortical control over a prosthetic arm

M.E. Thurlings (✉) · J.B.F. van Erp · A.-M. Brouwer · P.J. Werkhoven
TNO Human Factors, P.O. Box 23, 3769DE Soesterberg, The Netherlands
e-mail: marieke.thurlings@tno.nl

J.B.F. van Erp
e-mail: jan.vanerp@tno.nl

A.-M. Brouwer
e-mail: anne-marie.brouwer@tno.nl

P.J. Werkhoven
e-mail: peter.werkhoven@tno.nl

M.E. Thurlings · P.J. Werkhoven
Utrecht University, Utrecht, The Netherlands

D.S. Tan, A. Nijholt (eds.), *Brain-Computer Interfaces,*
Human-Computer Interaction Series,
DOI 10.1007/978-1-84996-272-8_5, © Springer-Verlag London Limited 2010

Fig. 5.1 The picture shows a typical situation when we are coming hands short and our eyes and ears are over-occupied

for self-feeding (Velliste et al. 2008). The corresponding video of one of the monkeys feeding itself via this invasive BCI (electrodes are implanted into the brain) has impressed many.

In recent years, the developed knowledge and techniques in the original BCI field has resulted in spin-offs outside medical applications. For instance, research has started for applications in space shuttles (Trejo et al. 2006), for the air force (Middendorf et al. 2000) and in gaming (see Chapter 10 of this Volume). BCI research is pre-eminently a multidisciplinary field: Neuro-science, medical disciplines, computer science, signal processing, machine-learning, engineering and psychology are all involved. Slightly neglected is the field of Human Factors, even though its expertise on how to facilitate the interaction between humans and machines could potentially be of great benefit to the development of BCIs (Van Erp and Werkhoven 2006). In this chapter we take a Human Factors perspective on human navigation processes and discuss how BCIs are, and can be used as alternative input devices. Navigation in the real or in the virtual world is an example of an interaction that is often complex. Especially when our eyes and ears are over-occupied or when both our hands are involved in other tasks (e.g. when driving through an unknown town while answering a telephone call) navigation can be a challenging feat (see Fig. 5.1).

5.1.1 Human Navigation Models

Navigation is more than steering a car or a wheelchair. This is illustrated by several navigation models and theories. One of them is Prenav (Van Erp et al. 2006) which aims to describe human behaviour in navigation and control (see Fig. 5.2 for a simplified version). This model focuses on the classic information-processing loop from sensation to perception to decision and finally to action; with a feedback loop to sensation via the environment. Sensation is the low-level processing of input via the senses, the stage before our brain interprets the input and attributes meaning to it, which is called perception.

According to Prenav, two shortcuts can break the serial order of these steps. The first is the sensation-action shortcut. This shortcut concerns reflexive action and

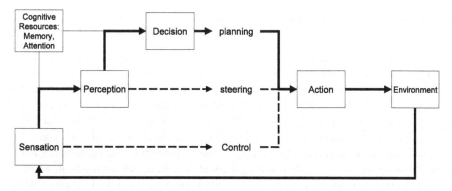

Fig. 5.2 A simplified version of the model Prenav. This model explains human behaviour in navigation and control. The *dashed lines* reflect the possible shortcuts as described in the text

completely sidesteps the need for cognitive resources (e.g. we immediately dive away if someone throws a rock at us). The second shortcut goes from perception directly to action, therewith bypassing the decision process. Behaviour on that level is also stimulus driven but not reflexive as described above. This shortcut links to trained behaviour that occurs without our full attention, for example shifting gears, stopping for a traffic light. The loop and its shortcuts are related to three levels of navigation that we call planning, steering and control:

- *Planning* corresponds to knowledge-based behaviour (Rasmussen 1983), leading to the choice of a goal and planning a route. It requires conscious analytic decisions, information on the environment, landmarks, etc. Operating GPS-based navigation devices is an example of the planning level.
- *Steering* is linked to pursuit tracking and rule-based behaviour, for example setting a specific course, speed or lead distance, stopping for a red traffic light or changing lanes on the highway. It is conscious behaviour requiring cognitive processing but without the results having to be stored in memory.
- *Control* refers to compensatory tracking and skill-based behaviour, for example maintaining a chosen course, speed or lead distance. It represents sensory motor performance and is linked to reflexive behaviour and (highly trained) skills. It for example enables one to ride a bike in the presence of sudden wind blows, to drive between road markings sheer effortless and to break hard for crossing children.

The Prenav model helps to assess the intuitiveness of a navigation device or display. According to Prenav intuitive refers to minimal use of cognitive resources, i.e. in navigation a device or display that automatically triggers the required reaction and uses the sensation-action or perception-action shortcut. As will become clear in the next sections, many BCI applications in navigation are not based on an intuitive mapping between for instance required navigation input and mental task.

5.1.2 BCI as a Navigation Device

For patients who lack control over their limbs, the usefulness of a navigation BCI is evident (Birbaumer and Cohen 2007). However, also for healthy users an alternative or additional navigation device may be of interest. Most of the time we interact with systems using our hands, but in certain situations it may be convenient to have an additional control channel as illustrated by the development of eye movement and voice based control devices (see also Fig. 5.1). Situations where an extra control channel may be convenient include flying a plane, where pilots need their hands not only for navigating but also for assessing flight information, and driving a car, where we need our hands to steer, shift gears, control the navigation device, adjust the car radio and answer the phone. Preferably, an alternative input device is intuitive, thereby alleviating the demand for cognitive resources. The Nintendo *Wii*® is a good example of this. With respect to our discussion of navigation levels in the previous section, note that the requirements of a navigation device depend on the level of navigation that it is used for.

In this chapter we will make an inventory of existing EEG-based BCIs according to the navigation level they apply to. To further structure this endeavour, we make use of the three categories of BCIs as defined by Zander (Zander et al. 2008, see also Chapter 11 of this Volume): active, reactive and passive.

These categories are based on the user's effort and task to control the BCI. In active BCIs users actively manipulate their brain signals in order to control the BCI. In the reactive type, users can give a command by modulating attention to external stimuli, so-called probe stimuli. A passive BCI analyses brain signals without the user needing to perform specific mental tasks. Table 5.1 outlines the structure of our inventory, providing examples of BCIs that would fit in the different cells. Our overview aims to give an insight into the current focus and white spots in BCI research and to outline directions for future research to broaden the applications. First, we will start by devoting a few more words to the different categories of BCIs.

5.1.3 A Short Overview of the Different Types of BCIs

5.1.3.1 Active BCIs

Active BCIs are based on users actively performing cognitive tasks, such as motor imagery (e.g. imagined movement of the left hand or the right foot), imagined word association and mental calculation. Usually participants have to train to be able to perform the mental tasks in such a way that the system can correctly classify them. To achieve optimal performance, this training period may take months. After the brain signals have been classified, they are translated into a system command, such as turn left or right, stop or continue. The match between mental task and resulting navigation action is often arbitrary, violating the aim for intuitive navigation controls.

Table 5.1 Nine navigation BCIs based on matching BCI type with navigation level including a conceivable example

	Planning level	Steering level	Control level
	Active planning BCIs	*Active Steering BCIs*	*Active control BCIs*
Active BCIs	Motor imagery to select a destination from a list	Mental calculations for leftright decisions at junction	Motor imagery to correct for course deviations or collision threats
	Reactive planning BCIs	*Reactive steering BCIs*	*Reactive control BCIs*
Reactive BCIs	A P300 speller to enter a destination in a navigation system	A SS(V)EP[a]-BCI with four flickering checker-boards around an avatar to stear it left, right, back and straight ahead in a virtual environment	A BCI that corrects for deviations in a path by utilizing P300s, evoked by attention modulation to P300-stimuli
	Passive planning BCIs	*Passive steering BCIs*	*Passive control BCIs*
Passive BCIs	Distilling and using the neural correlates of the brain's goal selection and route planning processes[b]	Distilling and using left versus right decisions from the brain	Utilizing possible ERPs[c] evoked by relevant events such as impeding collisions and line crossings

[a]Steady State (Visual) Evoked Potential

[b]See Section 5.1.4.1 for discussion on this type of BCI

[c]Event Related Potential

5.1.4 Reactive BCIs

Reactive BCIs in general are event driven and measure brain responses to visual, tactile or auditory (probe) stimuli. These responses can be modulated by the user through focussing attention to the stimulus of interest. In contrast to active BCIs, the advantage of reactive BCIs is that they do not require user training. The disadvantage is that the user depends on external cues to give a command. The P300 and SSEP are both features that can be elicited in the EEG by focusing attention to a specific stimulus.

The P300, also referred to as the P3, is the third positive peak in the EEG that occurs approximately 300 ms after the onset of a stimulus that stands out from other stimuli. The stimulus can stand out because it is physically different from other stimuli (stimulus driven, as in an oddball-paradigm), or because the observer attends to that particular stimulus (task driven). The ERP that is elicited in the first paradigm is also referred to as the P3a, while the one elicited by the second type of paradigm is referred to as the P3b (Polich 2007). In general P3s are measured most clearly at Fz, Cz and Pz as defined by the 10-20 system.

With the P300-matrix speller, (Farwell and Donchin 1988) exploited the P300 for the first time in a BCI. In this P300-matrix speller, letters and numbers are placed in a 6×6 matrix. Rows and columns flash after each other in random order. Every time a row or column flashes that contains the symbol the user is focusing on, a P300 is (potentially) elicited. In this way, users can spell words and communicate with their environment.

The SSEP is a feature in the EEG that can be elicited by focusing on a stimulus that is presented with a certain constant flicker frequency. The fundamental frequency of the initiating source can be found in the EEG (Regan 1989) as well as its harmonics (Müller-Putz et al. 2005). If multiple stimuli are provided simultaneously with different frequencies, the attended frequency will dominate the unattended frequency in the observer's EEG. This is of particular interest for BCI applications. A commonly used method to detect a SSEP response is to apply a Fast Fourier Transformation on the EEG signal and search for high amplitudes in the frequency bins corresponding to the frequencies of the stimuli provided. If a SSEP is detected, a command signal can be issued.

In principle, the SSEP can be elicited by stimuli in the visual, tactile and auditory modality. SSVEPs are recorded over the visual cortex. In the visual domain, frequencies between 5–20 Hz elicit the highest SSVEPs (Herrmann 2001). SSVEPs have been used in several BCI studies, the main reasons being that the signal is robust and that no training is required. Drawbacks mentioned are that SSVEPs depend on gaze, which means that users should be able to move their eyes or heads to control a SSVEP-BCI, and that the task environment should allow to do so. Some studies have shown that adjusting gaze is not required, because SSVEPs are (also) spatial attention modulated (Morgan et al. 1996; Müller et al. 1998; Kelly et al. 2005; Allison et al. 2008). However, recent data from our own lab (Thurlings et al. 2009) suggest that covert attention to visual stimuli presented at an angle larger than three degrees does not elicit robust SSVEPs. This leaves a SSVEP-BCI application with covert attention rather unlikely. Because most BCI research aims to improve the quality of life of patients, of whom many cannot control their muscles, this can be a problem.

5.1.4.1 Passive BCIs

Traditionally, passive BCIs are aimed at detecting changes in a cognitive state or an (affective) user state that spontaneously occurs during task execution (see Chapter 12 of this Volume). This type of BCI is mainly applied to enhance or facilitate other tasks or interactions and not so much for voluntary control. However, these latter applications are under development, for instance game control based on alpha activity in neuro-feedback therapies.

In navigation, this type of BCI might use the (spontaneous) brain signals that occur when the user decides on the preferred route to take (planning level) or whether to turn left or right at a junction (steering level). One other kind of passive signal that can be useful in navigation is the error potential. It occurs whenever a non-intended outcome is detected as a result of a self-generated or machine-generated error. Note that according to Zander, even though this signal needs an external stimulus (i.e., 'an error'), it is passive rather than reactive because this signal is generated without effort (Zander et al. 2008), see Chapter 11 of this Volume. One can speculate about the existence of ERPs similar to the error potential that are linked to (the control level of) navigation events such as line crossings or impeding collisions.

5.2 BCIs Operating on a Planning Level of Navigation

5.2.1 Active Planning BCIs

No studies were found that investigate the use of active BCIs for planning tasks. An example of such a BCI is a system that allows one to select the kitchen as a goal by imagining tongue movement, the study room by performing a mental calculation task and the living room by performing mental word association.

5.2.2 Reactive Planning BCIs

A few reactive BCI navigation applications operate on a planning level. We distinguish P300-based and SSEP-based applications. A reactive BCI for planning is the P300-BCI for control in a virtual apartment by Bayliss (2003). Five semitransparent spheres superimposed five controllable objects, such as a lamp and a television. These spheres flashed sequentially while observers focussed their attention on the sphere associated with the to-be-manipulated object. In addition to the basic concept, it was investigated whether there is an effect of viewing the environment on a computer monitor or in a virtual environment. No effect on the P300 was found, although the subjective experiences did differ in the two different settings.

Bell et al. (2008) described an interesting system that allows a person to give a goal-oriented command, such as 'pour a drink'. This was accomplished through a humanoid robot that took pictures of possible 'goals' in the environment. The pictures were presented on a screen, and the borders flashed up sequentially, eliciting P300s when the focused option was flashed. After the selection, the robot could hypothetically carry out the command. The system enabled the user to select a command from four options in 5 sec with 95% accuracy and it achieved a bit rate of 24 bits/min. An additional finding was that the system's performance was the same for four or six pictures presented on the screen.

Valbuena et al. (2007) studied a SSVEP-BCI that operates on a planning level, with seven possible choices. With this application, navigation in a menu system containing certain goal-oriented tasks, such as 'pour a drink', was explored. To this end, four flickering stimuli were used, which were linked to navigation commands through the folders in a window like the arrow keys on a keyboard. By navigating through the folders, in total seven goals could be selected. Average classification accuracy was 96% and it took 2.38 sec per command.

5.2.3 Passive Planning BCIs

Future passive planning BCIs might be able to distil the neural correlates of the brain's goal selection and route planning processes. Please note that of the going definitions of BCI categories, such a BCI could be classified both as active and as passive. We consider passive the most appropriate categorization since there is no arbitrarily chosen mental task involved as a means to communicate planning, instead the BCI is tapping into the naturally occurring brain signals during planning and decision making. We are not aware of any group currently pursuing such a BCI.

5.3 BCIs Operating on a Steering Level of Navigation

5.3.1 Active Steering BCIs

Imagining motor movement is a mental task that has been intensively studied in the context of BCI. Both the Wadsworth BCI (Wolpaw et al. 2003) and the Graz BCI (Pfurtscheller et al. 2003) make use of mu and beta rhythms in the EEG. The maximum amplitude of these rhythms can be modified when well-trained participants are actively imagining motor movement. Imagined right and left limb movements can be distinguished, as can imagined foot and hand movements. The motor imagery principle has been used to drive a cursor on a screen (usually 1D, but 2D is also possible) or a neuro-prosthetic device. Well-trained participants can obtain information transfer rates of about 20–25 bits/minute. The examples mentioned so far link one type of imagined movement to one direction of motion while another type of imagined movement results in another direction of motion. However, 1D movement in a virtual environment is also possible by using one type of motor imagery for moving and another type for stopping (Leeb et al. 2006; Pfurtscheller et al. 2006). In these studies, foot movement imagery resulted in moving forward with constant speed in a projected virtual street. The motion was stopped when participants imagined moving their hands. The participants had at least four months experience in using the Graz BCI preceding the experiment. Each of them went through a number of training sessions with the goal to set up a personal classifier able to discriminate online and in real-time between two mental states. Training required focussing attention to the task-relevant parts of the body and away from task-irrelevant parts of the body.

Besides moving one's own body within a real or virtual environment, moving a cursor is a widely investigated task within active navigation BCIs. An appealing example is Brain Pong, where each user moves his or her own cursor 'bat' up and down using motor imagery in order to block an approaching ball (Müller and Blankertz 2006). It has even been shown that all functions of a mouse can be replicated by an active BCI, using three sets of sensorimotor rhythm features (McFarland et al. 2008).

In most active BCI studies, participants are cued when to perform certain tasks. These BCIs are called synchronous. Asynchronous BCIs do not require allotted time intervals for performing mental tasks. Millán and colleagues have done many studies on asynchronous brain-controlled robots based on mental tasks. In one study they enabled a robot to execute six possible navigation tasks, taking three mental states supplemented with four perceptual states of the environment as determined by the robots sensory reading (Millán et al. 2004). In another study, they built an asynchronous active BCI to control a wheelchair. Participants were asked to drive a simulated wheelchair from a starting point to a goal following a pre-specified path. They imagined left hand movement to turn left, they relaxed to go forward and performed a word association task to turn right (Galán et al. 2008).

One final example, though originally designed for communication rather than navigation, is the Hex-o-Spell by the Berlin BCI group (Blankertz et al. 2007). In the Hex-o-Spell application, users select letters by means of motor imagery. Interesting and relevant for navigation, is the fact that the Hex-o-Spell paradigm is not based on Cartesian coordinates but on polar coordinates. This setup allows the selection of options in fewer steps: Six hexagons containing five letters (or symbols) are each positioned around a circle that contains an arrow. Two motor imagery states as classified by the system control the rotation and the length of the arrow. A hexagon is selected when an arrow of sufficient length points towards it. After the selection of a hexagon, the letters that it contains move individually to the different hexagons. They take the place of the groups of letters and offer a new choice to the user. A similar principle was applied to a navigation task in a virtual environment (Ron-Angevin et al. 2009). At each junction in a virtual labyrinth a circle was presented with a rotating bar in the middle. Instead of a hexagon with letters, directions were selected.

5.3.2 Reactive Steering BCIs

Besides using P300s for communication, several groups work on applications to control cursor movement with a P300-BCI. Ma et al. (2007) investigated the feasibility of a BCI that uses four sequentially flashing probe stimuli around a cursor. Participants had to focus on the stimulus that corresponded with the desired direction of motion of the cursor. Offline analyses resulted in an information transfer rate of 5.4 bit/min for high intensity stimuli and 4.6 bit/min for low intensity stimuli. The difference in information transfer between high and low intensity stimuli corresponded to a high, respectively low P300 amplitude (Ma et al. 2007).

Another navigation application of a P300-BCI, is the wheelchair reported by Pires et al. (2008). For this application, a screen is fixed on a wheelchair, showing eight arrows that present the possible directions the user can choose. A ninth cue in the middle of the arrows, corresponded with 'no movement'. Pires and colleagues mention the importance of evaluating such a BCI not just by error rate, but also by the amount of false positives and false negatives. A false positive would cause the wheelchair to move into the wrong direction, while a false negative only slows down the system. Obviously the first has much more impact and should be avoided. Performance was seven commands/min, although it was only tested with two persons.

For reactive BCIs, tactile probe stimuli can be an interesting alternative to visual and auditory ones. The auditory and visual channels are often already in use for other purposes. With tactile stimuli, control of gaze is not required and tactile stimuli can be delivered by a device that is invisible and inaudible to others. For navigation, tactile stimuli have the advantage that they correspond naturally with spatial information, e.g. with movement directions when applied around the waist (Van Erp 2005). Users can focus their attention on the tactile stimulus that corresponds to the direction in which they want to move, possibly eliciting a useful P300 signal. This idea was tested in the TNO tactile P300 BCI (Brouwer and Van Erp 2008). An online classification algorithm was able to classify the attended location reliably, irrespective of the number of tactile devices worn around the waist (2, 4 or 6).

Trejo et al. (2006) demonstrate with the 'Think Pointer BCI System' the possibility of 2D cursor control, allowing navigation over a moving map. Participants selected a desired movement direction by focusing on one of four flickering checkerboards that corresponded with the commands up, down, left and right. Obtained accuracies were between 80 and 100%.

Martinez et al. (2007) also show the feasibility of an online SSVEP navigation BCI. In a game, four flickering checkerboards were located at each side of a car and moved along with it. The car was on a fixed path. A direction command could be given by focussing on one of the stimuli (left, right, up and down). An average of 96.5% success rate with a bit rate of 30 bits/min was achieved.

5.3.3 Passive Steering BCIs

As with passive planning BCIs, we are not aware of work on passive steering BCIs. An example of employing a passive BCI for subtasks of the planning level would be a BCI that utilizes error potentials for correcting wrong selections. The work by Schalk et al. (2000) is a step towards such a BCI. They explored a BCI using motor imagery to move a cursor to a word (in this case, 'YES' or 'NO', but LEFT and RIGHT would be similar). This part of the BCI is active. As BCIs typically cannot obtain 100% classification accuracy, participants using this system did not always select the target they intended. Results showed that such a mistake was followed by an error potential. It was suggested that these error potentials could be used to improve the accuracy and communication speed of the system. Zander and colleagues used error potentials to enhance performance in a game where players had to rotate a letter presented on a monitor into a desired orientation using buttons on a keyboard (i.e. this part is not a BCI). In some cases, the button command was followed by an incorrect response of the computer, eliciting an error potential. When the error potential was used to correct the movement of the letter (even though the classifier detecting errors did not work 100% correct) total performance was better than when players had to correct for the errors manually (Zander et al. 2008) It was demonstrated in a similar task where participants had to steer a tactile cursor to a tactile target that tactile error potentials show up in the EEG as well, both for self-generated and computer-generated errors (Lehne et al. 2009).

5.4 BCIs Operating on a Control Level of Navigation

No papers were found that describe a system that works on a control level of navigation (e.g. keeping a chosen course or speed). For this level we have searched for BCI studies that investigate the use of low level compensatory tracking behaviour, or reflexive behaviour caused by for instance impeding collisions.

5.5 Discussion

In the introduction we explained the three levels involved in the process of navigation: planning, steering and control. We also described three types of BCIs: active, reactive and passive. In the previous sections, we gave an overview of navigation BCIs ordered along navigation level and BCI type. Table 5.2 summarises the results. This table reflects the existing concentration of BCIs on the steering level of navigation. Striking is the lack of navigation BCIs on the control level, therefore we will start the discussion with that level.

For this categorization we focussed on BCI applications developed for navigation. In principle BCI applications can be used also for other purposes than the reason they were created. As we mentioned, a communication BCI can also be used as a navigation BCI.

5.5.1 Control Level

As Table 5.2 illustrates, no work has been done yet on the control level of navigation (i.e. the level where perception and cognition are not involved). The automated corrections at this level are an important part of the navigation process and ensure that we hit the brakes in a split second and that we can keep our car neatly on course while thinking about something completely different. One could argue that a BCI that can tap into this automatic sensation-action loop could be of large value to user groups that require an alternative control device and can benefit from these automated or reflexive corrections. If these corrections can not take place at the level of the sensation-action loop, disturbances will increase until they are large enough to be corrected at the steering level. However, this level includes a cognitive component and the latency will be larger.

Table 5.2 Overview of the current navigation BCIs categorised into the nine types described in Table 5.1

	Planning level	Steering level	Control level
	Active planning BCIs	*Active steering BCIs*	*Active control BCIs*
Active BCIs	None	Leeb et al. (2006); Pfurtscheller et al. (2006); Millán et al. (2004); Galán et al. (2008); McFarland et al. (2008); Ron-Angevin et al. (2009)	None
	Reactive planning BCIs	*Reactive steering BCIs*	*Reactive control BCIs*
Reactive BCIs	P3: Bell et al. (2008) SSVEP: Valbuena et al. (2007)	Visual P3: Ma et al. (2007); Pires et al. (2008); SSVEP: Trejo et al. (2006); Martinez et al. (2007) TactileP3: Brouwer and Van Erp (2008)	None
	Passive planning BCIs	*Passive steering BCIs*	*Passive control BCIs*
Passive BCIs	None	None[a]	None

[a]With the exception of using ERN signals to correct wrongly interpreted steering inputs

An interesting research question is whether brain responses to for instance near collisions or other events related to the control level of navigation can be detected and interpreted by a BCI. These BCIs will be of the passive kind since they use brain signals that are automatically generated and in normal circumstances used to execute corrective actions.

5.5.2 Steering Level

Most navigation BCIs operate on a steering level of navigation. This is a remarkable observation from a Human Factors perspective because this level of navigation requires a very specific subclass of control devices that have a high bandwidth and a very low latency like joysticks or steering wheels. Designing alternative input devices for this level is challenging and many devices including for instance BCIs, keyboards and voice operated devices seem not very well suited for the job. When these devices are used at the steering level, the lack of bandwidth and/or the large delays result(s) in a stepwise steering pattern also known as bang-bang control, i.e., moving a cursor step by step to reach an end goal. This makes the process slow and complex, requiring the user to think about each step and unnecessarily using cognitive resources.

If we take a closer look at the steering level, we see that decisions are mainly event driven (e.g., turn right at a specific landmark, cross the street at the traffic light, change lanes when you are close to the car in front of you, etc.), or in terms of BCIs: reactive. It would be an interesting endeavour to look for the event driven neural correlates in the brain that actually control our steering behaviour to see if these can be used in a reactive BCI.

5.5.3 Planning Level

On the planning level of navigation, we actively think and make a decision to set a goal and choose a route. If we could communicate this goal and decisions directly with a BCI this would lead to more intuitive interaction. It is not immediately clear whether such a BCI should be called active or passive. Because it would not require specific mental activity in order to generate the proper brain signals, we prefer to call such a BCI passive.

Although distilling the navigation goal without additional user effort from the brain will probably not happen in the next decades, some studies started the exploration of reactive goal-oriented navigation interfaces in contrast to the steering interfaces. Actually, all existing BCIs used at a planning level are reactive BCIs: With an additional task (focussing on an external stimulus) one can select the navigation goal. Current technology would also be suited to implement an active planning BCI, for instance one in which motor imagery is used for goal selection: Imagine tongue movement to go to the kitchen.

5.5.4 Sensory Modalities

Reactive BCIs rely on probe stimuli, usually presented visually and sometimes auditory. However the risk of sensory overload is eminent for the visual and auditory channel, especially when navigation is part of a multi-task environment (Van Erp and Padmos 2003, see also Fig. 5.1). As mentioned earlier, an interesting alternative is to use the tactile channel. This is barely explored yet, although it is an appealing option for both healthy users and patients since it does not require control of eye movements. Interesting in the context of navigation is that tactile displays have widely proven their usefulness, predominantly because information coded by location on the body translates itself easily into spatial information (Van Erp 2005; Van Erp and Van Veen 2004; Van Erp et al. 2007).

5.6 Conclusion and Recommendations

As we argued in this chapter, navigation from a Human Factors perspective is more than steering a car or a wheelchair. Navigation comprises three levels, planning, steering and control involving respectively cognition, perception and sensation. This is reflected by the different control devices, ranging from a steering wheel and joystick at the control level to a keyboard or touch screen to program a navigation system at the planning level. A BCI-based navigation device could also be implemented at these levels. Interestingly enough, the vast majority of the navigation BCIs replaces traditional control devices at the steering level of navigation, a level that puts high demands on the bandwidth and latency of the control device. We recommend aiming for automating tasks at the steering level and exploring BCIs for the planning level and for the control level. This would result in a navigation BCI in which the user enters the destination and only corrects anomalies (i.e. course deviations) or emergency situations (impeding collisions) but leaves the steering level (turn at junctions) to the automat. The usefulness of the first part (a goal-oriented approach) is also being recognised by researchers focussing on patient applications (Wolpaw 2007). The second part requires a whole new approach and must be aimed at identifying brain signals that are based on: ERPs related to course deviations or collisions etc, or any other pattern related to the control level of navigation.

If navigation BCIs are used as additional input devices, another issue that should be resolved is the relation between cognitive effort and type of BCI (especially active versus reactive). It is hypothesised that reactive BCIs use less cognitive resources than active BCIs but future studies should compare these two types in combination with performing other tasks.

We believe that expanding BCI based navigation beyond the steering level will be of benefit to both patients and healthy user groups.

Acknowledgements   The authors gratefully acknowledge the support of the BrainGain Smart Mix Programme of the Netherlands Ministry of Economic Affairs and the Netherlands Ministry of Education, Culture and Science. This research has been supported by the GATE project, funded by the Netherlands Organization for Scientific Research (NWO) and the Netherlands ICT Research and Innovation Authority (ICT Regie).

References

Allison BZ, McFarland DJ, Schalk G, Zheng SD, Jackson MM, Wolpaw JR (2008) Towards an independent brain-computer interface using steady state visual evoked potentials. Clin Neurophysiol 119(2):399–408

Bayliss JD (2003) Use of the evoked potential P3 component for control in a virtual apartment. IEEE Trans Neural Syst Rehabil Eng 11(2):113–116

Bell CJ, Shenoy P, Chalodhorn R, Rao RPN (2008) Control of a humanoid robot by a noninvasive brain-computer interface in humans. J Neural Eng 5(2):214–220

Birbaumer N, Cohen LG (2007) Brain-computer interfaces: Communication and restoration of movement in paralysis. J Physiol 579(3):621–636

Blankertz B, Krauledat M, Dornhege G, Williamson J, Murray-Smith R, Müller K-R (2007) A note on brain actuated spelling with the Berlin brain-computer interface. In: Lecture Notes in Computer Science (including subseries Lecture Notes in Artificial Intelligence and Lecture Notes in Bioinformatics). LNCS, vol 4555. Springer, Berlin, pp 59–768. (Part 2)

Brouwer A-M, Van Erp JBF (2008) A tactile P300 BCI and the optimal number of tactors: Effects of target probability and discriminability. In: Proceedings of the 4th International Brain-Computer Interface Workshop and Training Course 2008. Verlag der Technischen Universität Graz, Graz, pp 280–285

Farwell LA, Donchin E (1988) Talking off the top of your head: Toward a mental prosthesis utilizing event-related brain potentials. Electroencephalogr Clin Neurophysiol 70(6):510–523

Galán F, Nuttin M, Lew E, Ferrez PW, Vanacker G, Philips J, Millán JdR (2008) A brain-actuated wheelchair: Asynchronous and non-invasive brain-computer interfaces for continuous control of robots. Clin Neurophysiol 119(9):2159–2169

Herrmann CS (2001) Human EEG responses to 1–100 Hz flicker: Resonance phenomena in visual cortex and their potential correlation to cognitive phenomena. Exp Brain Res 137(3–4):346–353

Kelly SP, Lalor EC, Finucane C, McDarby G, Reilly RB (2005) Visual spatial attention control in an independent brain-computer interface. IEEE Trans Biomed Eng 52(9):1588–1596

Leeb R, Keinrath C, Friedman D, Guger C, Scherer R, Neuper C, Garau M, Antley A, Steed A, Slater M, Pfurtscheller G (2006) Walking by thinking: The brainwaves are crucial, not the muscles! Presence: Teleop Virtual Environ 15(5):500–514

Lehne M, Ihme K, Brouwer A-M, van Erp JBF, Zander TO (2009) Error-related EEG patterns during tactile human-machine interaction. In: Proceedings of ACII-ABCI 2009

Ma Z, Gao X, Gao S (2007) Enhanced P300-based cursor movement control. In: Lecture Notes in Computer Science (including subseries Lecture Notes in Artificial Intelligence and Lecture Notes in Bioinformatics). LNAI, vol 4565. Springer, Berlin, pp 120–126

Martinez P, Bakardjian H, Cichocki A (2007) Fully online multicommand brain-computer interface with visual neurofeedback using SSVEP paradigm. Comput Intell Neurosci 2007:94561

McFarland DJ, Krusienski DJ, Sarnacki WA, Wolpaw JR (2008) Emulation of computer mouse control with a noninvasive brain-computer interface. J Neural Eng 5(2):101–110

Middendorf M, McMillan G, Calhoun G, Jones KS (2000) Brain-computer interfaces based on the steady-state visual-evoked response. IEEE Trans Rehabil Eng 8(2):211–214

Millán JDR, Renkens F, Mouriño J, Gerstner W (2004) Noninvasive brain-actuated control of a mobile robot by human EEG. IEEE Trans Biomed Eng 51(6):1026–1033

Morgan ST, Hansen JC, Hillyard SA (1996) Selective attention to stimulus location modulates the steady-state visual evoked potential. Proc Nat Acad Sci USA 93(10):4770–4774

Müller KR, Blankertz B (2006) Towards noninvasive brain-computer interfaces. IEEE Signal Process Mag 23(5):126–128

Müller MM, Picton TW, Valdes-Sosa P, Riera J, Teder-Sälejärvi WA, Hillyard SA (1998) Effects of spatial selective attention on the steady-state visual evoked potential in the 20–28 Hz range. Cogn Brain Res 6(4):249–261

Müller-Putz GR, Scherer R, Brauneis C, Pfurtscheller G (2005) Steady-state visual evoked potential (SSVEP)-based communication: Impact of harmonic frequency components. J Neural Eng 2(4):123–130

Pfurtscheller G, Neuper C, Müller GR, Obermaier B, Krausz G, Schlögl A, Scherer R, Graimann B, Keinrath C, Skliris D, Wörtz M, Supp G, Schrank C (2003) Graz-BCI: State of the art and clinical applications. IEEE Trans Neural Syst Rehabil Eng 11(2):177–180

Pfurtscheller G, Leeb R, Keinrath C, Friedman D, Neuper C, Guger C, Slater M (2006) Walking from thought. Brain Res 1071(1):145–152

Pires G, Castelo-Branco M, Nunes U (2008) Visual P300-based BCI to steer a wheelchair: A Bayesian approach. In: Proceedings of the 30th Annual International Conference of the IEEE Engineering in Medicine and Biology Society, EMBS'08—'Personalized Healthcare through Technology', art no 4649238, pp 658–661

Polich J (2007) Updating P300: An integrative theory of P3a and P3b. Clin Neurophysiol 118(10):2128–2148

Rasmussen J (1983) Skills, rules, and knowledge; signals, signs, and symbols, and other distinctions in human performance models. IEEE Trans Syst Man Cybern SMC-13(3):257–266

Regan D (1989) Human Brain Electrophysiology: Evoked Potentials and Evoked Magnetic Fields in Science and Medicine

Ron-Angevin R, Díaz-Estrella A, Velasco-Álvarez F (2009) A two-class brain computer interface to freely navigate through virtual worlds (Ein Zwei-Klassen-Brain-Computer-Interface zur freien Navigation durch virtuelle Welten). Biomed Tech 54(3):126–133

Schalk G, Wolpaw JR, McFarland DJ, Pfurtscheller G (2000) EEG-based communication: Presence of an error potential. Clin Neurophysiol 111(12):2138–2144

Thurlings ME, Brouwer A-M, Van Erp JBF, Werkhoven P (2009) SSVEPs for BCI? The effect of stimulus eccentricity on SSVEPs. Annual Meeting Society for Neuroscience

Trejo LJ, Rosipal R, Matthews B (2006) Brain-computer interfaces for 1-D and 2-D cursor control: Designs using volitional control of the EEG spectrum or steady-state visual evoked potentials. IEEE Trans Neural Syst Rehabil Eng 14(2):225–229, art no 1642775

Valbuena D, Cyriacks M, Friman O, Volosyak I, Gräser A (2007) Brain-computer interface for high-level control of rehabilitation robotic systems. In: 2007 IEEE 10th International Conference on Rehabilitation Robotics, ICORR '07, art no 4428489, pp 619–625

Van Erp JBF (2005) Presenting directions with a vibrotactile torso display. Ergonomics 48(3):302–313

Van Erp JBF, Padmos P (2003) Image parameters for driving with indirect viewing systems. Ergonomics 46(15):1471–1499

Van Erp JBF, Van Veen HAHC (2004) Vibrotactile in-vehicle navigation system. Transp Res Part F: Traffic Psychol Behav 7(4–5):247–256

Van Erp JBF, Werkhoven P (2006) Validation of principles for tactile navigation displays. In: Proceedings of the Human Factors and Ergonomics Society, pp 1687–1691

Van Erp JBF, Duistermaat M, Philippens IHCHM, Van Veen HAHC, Werkhoven PJ (2006) Brain machine interfaces: Technology status, applications and the way to the future. In: Proceedings of the Human Factors and Ergonomics Society, pp 752–756

Van Erp JBF, Eriksson L, Levin B, Carlander O, Veltman JA, Vos WK (2007) Tactile cueing effects on performance in simulated aerial combat with high acceleration. Aviat Space Environ Med 78(12):1128–1134

Velliste M, Perel S, Spalding MC, Whitford AS, Schwartz AB (2008) Cortical control of a prosthetic arm for self-feeding. Nature 453(7198):1098–1101

Wolpaw JR (2007) Brain-computer interfaces as new brain output pathways. J Physiol 579(3):613–619

Wolpaw JR, McFarland DJ, Vaughan TM, Schalk G (2003) The Wadsworth Center brain-computer interface (BCI) research and development program. IEEE Trans Neural Syst Rehabil Eng 11(2):204–207

Zander TO, Kothe C, Welke S, Rötting M (2008) Enhancing human-machine systems with secondary input from passive brain-computer interfaces. In: Proc of the 4th Int BCI Workshop & Training Course. Graz University of Technology Publishing House, Graz, Austria

Part II
Applications

Chapter 6
Applications for Brain-Computer Interfaces

Melody Moore Jackson and Rudolph Mappus

Abstract Brain-computer Interfaces (BCIs) have been studied for nearly thirty years, with the primary motivation of providing assistive technologies for people with very severe motor disabilities. The slow speeds, high error rate, susceptibility to artifact, and complexity of BCI systems have been challenges for implementing workable real-world systems. However, recent advances in computing and biosensing technologies have improved the outlook for BCI applications, making them promising not only as assistive technologies but also for mainstream applications. This chapter presents a survey of applications for BCI systems, both historical and recent, in order to characterize the broad range of possibilities for neural control.

6.1 Introduction

The original and still prevalent motivation for Brain-computer Interface (BCI) research has been to provide assistive technology for people with severe physical disabilities, particularly locked-in syndrome (complete paralysis and inability to speak) caused by strokes or chronic diseases such as Amyotrophic Lateral Sclerosis (ALS). The explosion of computing power in recent years and the evolution of technologies providing better classification and more effective interactions has led to greatly expanded possibilities for neural control. While not comprehensive because of space constraints, this chapter provides an overview and examples of applications that have been developed and studied for brain-computer interface control, categorizing them into four main areas. We begin with an overview of BCI applications in assistive technology, including communication, environmental control, mobility (including robotics). We then cover BCIs for recreation, including gaming, virtual reality,

M. Moore Jackson (✉) · R. Mappus
BrainLab, School of Interactive Computing, Georgia Institute of Technology, Atlanta, USA
e-mail: melody@cc.gatech.edu

R. Mappus
e-mail: cmappus@gatech.edu

D.S. Tan, A. Nijholt (eds.), *Brain-Computer Interfaces,*
Human-Computer Interaction Series,
DOI 10.1007/978-1-84996-272-8_6, © Springer-Verlag London Limited 2010

and creative expression. The next category revolves around cognitive diagnostics and augmentation, including computational user experience and attention monitoring, among others. The last category surveys the exciting possibilities for BCI in rehabilitation and prosthetic control.

6.2 BCIs for Assistive Technology

Restoring the ability to communicate, controlling the environment, and providing mobility are critical concerns for people with severe physical disabilities. These three areas have been the focus of the majority of BCI research.

6.2.1 Communication

One of the most critical needs for people with severe physical disabilities is restoring the ability to communicate. Perelmouter and Birbaumer (2000) showed that even people with total locked-in syndrome (TLS) report having a good quality of life if they can communicate with family, friends, and caregivers.

6.2.1.1 Yes/No Communication

The most rudimentary communication is the ability to reliably say "yes" or "no". Many early BCI communication systems were based on users learning to regulate aspects of brain rhythms with mental tasks. One of the earliest BCIs for communication was the Wadsworth Center's "Right Justified Box" paradigm in which users learned to modulate their mu rhythm using motor imagery to select one of two targets (Vaughan et al. 2001). The EEG-based Thought Translation Device (Kubler et al. 2001) was based on regulating Slow Cortical Potentials to move a cursor up or down, which could be interpreted as "yes" or "no". More recently, Naito et al. (2007) describes a study in which more than 40 locked-in ALS patients tested a brain-computer interface based on functional near infra-red imaging (fNIR) in order to communicate. Their "Kokoro Gatari" ("teller of hearts" in Japanese, see Fig. 6.1) system measures changes in blood oxygenation over Broca's area, the language center of the brain, in response to language imagery such as sub-vocal counting.

6.2.1.2 Spellers

Spelling is an essential part of communicating, and there have been a myriad of speller implementations with brain-computer interfaces. A simple strategy is to implement a binary speller with the yes/no systems described above, dividing the alphabet selection space in half progressively until the desired letter is attained, resulting in an average speed of one character every two minutes (Perelmouter and Birbaumer 2000), see Fig. 6.2.

Fig. 6.1 The Kokoro Gatari fNIR-based BCI display (Naito et al. 2007) showing biofeedback of the hemodyamic response to mental tasks, resulting in a "yes"

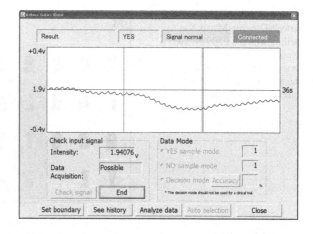

Fig. 6.2 A binary speller using the "Right Justified Box" paradigm as described in Vaughan et al. (2001). The cursor on the left travels at a constant rate across the screen; the user modulates mu rhythm with motor imagery to move the cursor up or down to select letters or letter ranges

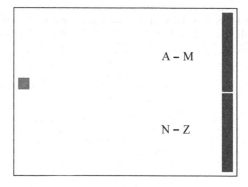

The Hex-o-Spell application (Blankertz et al. 2006) employs a dial to select one of six target letters, attaining typing speeds of more than seven characters per minute. Another early approach that has now been studied extensively is the "Farwell-Donchin Matrix" (Farwell and Donchin 1988), which measures the P300 evoked response when letters of the alphabet arranged in a matrix are flashed in random order, originally achieving 2.3 characters per minute with up to 95% accuracy (Fig. 6.3). Current research in this area is exploring methods to reduce the number of flashes needed to make a selection, with the goal of achieving single-stimulus (one flash) selection (Li et al. 2009). Integrating predictive spellers such as Dasher with BCIs (Blankertz et al. 2007) has been proposed to significantly improve spelling speed.

6.2.1.3 Web Browsers

Access to the Internet could be life-changing for people with severe physical disabilities. The web provides capabilities for education, financial management, communication, and even employment. Several research groups have explored BCI-controlled web browsers. The *BrainBrowser* (Fig. 6.4) described in Moore et al.

Fig. 6.3 An example of a
Farwell-Donchin Matrix for
spelling with the P300 evoked
response as described in
Farwell and Donchin (1988).
The highlighted column is
currently being flashed

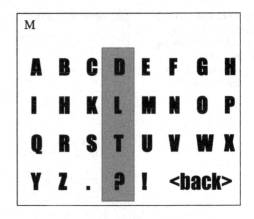

Fig. 6.4 The BrainBrowser
neurally controlled web
browser

(2004) was based on modulating mu rhythms over motor cortex to select browsing commands such as "next" and "previous". Users selected links by increasing their mu amplitude with motor imagery to move to the next link, and using a dwell select (pause for a dwell interval of two seconds) to traverse the link. A more recent version of the BrainBrowser currently in experiments utilizes P300-based BCIs, flashing the controls and links in random order for direct selection. Karim et al. (2006) detail a study with the *Descartes* web browser, first developed in 1999, which is based on users regulating Slow Cortical Potentials (SCPs). The browser incorporated biofeedback of a yellow ball that moved to indicate the level of SCP amplitude. Browser control was implemented as a binary decision tree with choices between commands such as writing an email or surfing the net. Links were selected in a similar manner, arranging them in a list that could be traversed with SCP modulation.

6.2.2 Environmental Control

Another important challenge for people with severe physical disabilities is controlling devices in the environment, for example, a television, a thermostat, or video
recorder. Cheng et al. (2002) describes an SSVEP-based BCI that allows users to
employ the discrete selection capabilities of an SSVEP control interface to dial numbers to place a phone call. Adams et al. (2003) describes the Aware 'Chair project,
which focused on integrating environmental control such as radio, lights, and television into a communication device mounted on a wheelchair.

6.2.3 Mobility

Naturally, one of the most profound assistive technologies BCI systems could provide to people with severe motor disability is restoring movement. The BCI research
community has devoted significant effort to developing methods for controlling mobility applications, such as driving wheel-chairs and manipulating remote robots.

6.2.3.1 Wheelchair Control

Early work in mobility employed small mobile robots to simulate wheelchair navigation tasks. Millán et al. (2004) describe a mental-task based BCI that operated
a mobile robot to navigate in a home environment. Blatt et al. (2008) details the
LURCH project, studying a "smart wheelchair" with gross-grain neural navigation
capabilities (selecting "go to the kitchen" rather than specifying individual turns or
movements).

The ongoing Aware 'Chair project (see Fig. 6.5, described in Adams et al. 2003)
incorporates similar gross-grain navigational capabilities plus temporal and spatial
contextual prediction based on user habits and preferences. For example, the Aware
'Chair can present the user with an option to navigate to the living room just before
the time of the user's favorite television show.

More recently, Toyota Central R&D labs has created a neurally-controlled
wheelchair that operates in near real-time to process discrete navigation commands,
with accuracy up to 95% (Toyota 2009). Iturrate et al. (2009) describe a P300-based
BCI that sends discrete movement commands to a wheelchair that has autonomous
navigation and obstacle avoidance systems.

6.2.3.2 Robotics

Controlling robots with thought has long been a popular science fiction concept.
Recent work with BCIs, however, has shown that robotic control is indeed possible
with brain signals. Applications for neurally-controlled robots currently center on

Fig. 6.5 The Aware 'Chair as described in Adams et al. (2003), integrating communication, navigation, and environmental control. Photo credit: Stanley Leary

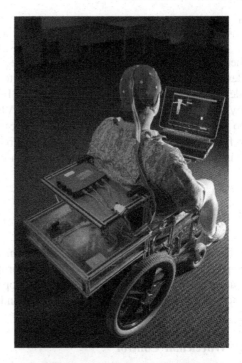

Fig. 6.6 A coffee-making robot controlled by P300 signals, described in Vora et al. (2005). Photo: Stanley Leary

assistive technologies—"helper" robots—but BCI control has been proposed for military and industrial applications as well. One of the earliest BCI-controlled robots is described in Vora et al. (2005). The experiment explored the effects of real-world feedback (the movement of the robot) in conjunction with a P300-based BCI, which depends on user attention. The robot was configured to perform the steps to make coffee, such as getting powdered coffee, sugar, and cream, and stirring the mixture with a spoon, see Fig. 6.6. The results showed that users can effectively attend to real-world feedback while operating an attention-based BCI.

Bell et al. (2008) describe a humanoid robot controlled by a similar P300-based BCI. Users select discrete commands via the BCI to cause the robot to perform simple tasks, such as picking up an object and moving it to another location. Selection accuracy for a user-specific classifier was reported to be 95%.

6.3 BCIs for Recreation

As BCIs became more effective and new systems provided higher bandwidth, BCI control for mainstream applications such as games, virtual reality, and creative expression became possible. Originally recreational applications for BCIs were targeted at people with motor disabilities, and there is still considerable interest in this area in the BCI community. However, recently a number of simple mainstream game controllers primarily based on BCIs have become available on the market. While it is generally accepted that BCIs in their current state cannot replace traditional controllers such as joysticks or control buttons, BCIs have been incorporated into games as auxiliary hands-free control channels as well.

6.3.1 Games

A recent comprehensive survey of the capabilities and challenges of BCIs for game control may be found in Nijholt et al. (2009). As stated in the survey, early BCI-controlled games focused on diagnostic brain signal detection, such as measuring a user's attention or relaxation to affect game components. More recently, games employing BCI in a more active control modality have gained popularity. One of the early systems to implement brain signal control for gaming was the Berlin BCI (Krepki et al. 2003) which later included a simple "Brain Pong" game and a "Pacman"-style game, controlled by modulating Slow Cortical Potentials (Krepki et al. 2007). Lalor et al. (2005) describe the 3D immersive game "Mindbalance", a simulation of a character walking a tightrope, controlled by SSVEP with flashing checkerboard stimuli. Mason et al. (2004) incorporate the LF/ASD asynchronous switch BCI into a maze-following game in which the player activates the BCI at decision points in the game to determine the navigation path.

The "BrainBasher" game (Oude Bos and Reuderink 2008), also described in Section 10.4.1 in this Volume, compared the motor-imagery BCI control with a physical keyboard version of the game, employing a user-satisfaction survey to discover that users found the BCI-based game to be more engaging and interesting than the traditional-input version. Another motor-imagery game, called "RLR" (Zander et al. 2008) requires the user to rotate a shape until it matches a template.

BCIs that detect attention and relaxation (typically alpha rhythms over frontal cortex) are popular for game control. The "LazyBrains" game (Bohenick and Borden 2008) combines a simple BCI with a game engine to allow users to navigate a virtual world. "BrainBall" (Moberg Research 2009) uses a similar paradigm in a competitive scenario where multiple players attempt to raise their alpha rhythm amplitude by relaxing.

Often games are incorporated into BCI systems as training programs. The "Dolphin Trainer" from Archinoetics, Inc. (Rapoport et al. 2008) teaches users to modulate their hemodynamic response to raise or lower a dolphin avatar controlled by an fNIR-based BCI. The dolphin targets goldfish, which are introduced at varying

Fig. 6.7 The "Epoc" headset from Emotiv Inc. (2009) implementing "virtual telekenesis"

Fig. 6.8 The ReaCTor Cave virtual environment (Pfurtscheller et al. 2006)

height levels. The user moves the vertical position of the dolphin to the height of the next target goldfish swimming across the screen, with the objective of steering the dolphin to intersect the path of the oncoming goldfish.

Commercial organizations such as NeuroSky (NeuroSky Inc. 2009) offer products such as the "Mindset", a simple EEG-based BCI device. The Mindset controls a variety of applications, including a brainwave visualizer and a game called "NeuroBoy", a virtual world in which the player can focus or relax to achieve goals in the game. Emotiv (Emotiv Inc. 2009) is another commercial company that markets a simple device, the "Epoc", based on EEG, EOG, and facial EMG to control applications (see Fig. 6.7). Their "Stonehenge" game challenges users to reassemble fallen pieces of Stonehenge using motor movements.

6.3.2 Virtual Reality

Virtual Environments are often placed in the category of games; however there are several in the BCI research world that have more practical purposes. The early work in virtual environments is described in Bayliss and Ballard (2000), which details a study of a P300 BCI controlling a virtual apartment and a virtual driving simulator.

Subsequent work as detailed in Pfurtscheller et al. (2006) incorporates the ReaCTor "cave" environment, an immersive virtual world which the user navigates using a BCI (see Fig. 6.8). The subject can "walk" through the virtual world by imagining foot movement, and can "touch" things in the virtual world by imagining reaching and hand movement.

6.3.3 Creative Expression

Another goal in assistive technology beyond restoring basic communication and environmental control capabilities is to improve quality of life by providing outlets for creative expression. BCIs have been studied in the contexts of both music and visual art.

6.3.3.1 Music

The Plymouth Brain-Computer Music Interface (BCMI) project (Miranda et al. 2005) provides a control interface to generate music from EEG signals. The BCMI piano study incorporates a BCI with a music engine, which is influenced by the output of a classifier that identifies the most prominent frequency in the brain signal. Different dominant frequencies control the musical output in different ways. The study reports efforts towards training users to produce specific EEG patterns to further control music production.

6.3.3.2 Visual Art

Rapoport et al. (2008) describes an fNIR-based BCI with training program that assists users in learning how to control their hemodynamic response for creative expression. The BrainPainting application (Archinoetics 2009) was originally developed for an artist who was locked in as a result of ALS. She was able to create visual art by imagining language tasks (silently singing to increase the response, or reciting nonsense syllables to decrease response) to influence the colors and shading of abstract art with a painting program. (See the BrainPainting "Navajo Nightfall", by Peggy Chun (Archinoetics 2009) in Chapter 8, Fig. 8.7 of this Volume).

6.4 BCIs for Cognitive Diagnostics and Augmented Cognition

In addition to assistive technology and rehabilitation therapies, BCIs have been developed to aid in diagnosing, influencing, and augmenting cognitive function. Often *neurofeedback*, representations of a user's brain signals or brain state, have been incorporated into applications to give insight into cognitive processes. From detecting comas to monitoring attention for safety-critical tasks, diagnostic BCIs have played a role in recent research.

Mainstream applications for BCIs have led to new frontiers in the fields of augmented cognition (AugCog) and the subfield of computational user experience. AugCog research studies real-time assessment of a user's cognitive state and workload in order to adjust work tasks to accommodate the user's mental capacity (Schmorrow et al. 2009). AugCog also includes "intelligence amplification", providing information to augment human reasoning or problem solving abilities.

6.4.1 Coma Detection

The Thought Translation Device (Birbaumer et al. 2003) described above has also been proposed as a diagnostic tool for people who appear to be in a vegetative state or coma. The TTD can assess cognitive function by measuring the event related brain potentials (ERPs) of various stimuli. Cognitive function is present if there is a response to the ERP stimuli (ERP differentiation can be achieved). The chances of regaining consciousness and recovering from a coma may be assessed by a patient's ERP response which could provide critical information to families and caregivers of people in a locked-in state.

6.4.2 Meditation Training

Eskandari and Erfanian (2008) describes a BCI that teaches users to control changes in their EEG rhythms by meditating during mental task exercises. Analyzing the EEG time-frequency signals for subjects in the meditation group showed an event-related desynchronization (ERD) of beta rhythm during the resting state. The control group did not display this ERD. Learning to meditate improved BCI classification accuracy from 70% in the control group to accuracies as high as 98% in the meditation group.

6.4.3 Computational User Experience

Computational user experience involves classifying mental workload as a usability testing method for human-computer interaction designs. Studies have shown that mental workload during HCI usability tests can be classified with a BCI resulting in up to 99% accuracy (Grimes et al. 2007). Cutrell and Tan (2008) describes a system for assessing "passive input", collecting and classifying the cognitive state of the user. This cognitive state can provide a wealth of information about the user, from mental workload to interest in a task or even emotional state (such as frustration or satisfaction). Cutrell and Tan propose that this cognitive state information could be used to perform automated adaptation of system interfaces to accommodate the

Fig. 6.9 The MEG-based
BCI described in Birbaumer
and Cohen (2007) controlling
a hand prosthetic

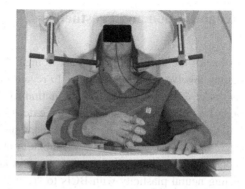

user's current mental abilities. Tan (2006) describes work with a simple EEG-based BCI that classifies mental tasks, including differentiating components of playing the video game Halo (rest, navigation, and engaging another player). The results of this work are intended to advance the state of the art in usability testing for human computer interaction.

6.4.4 Visual Image Classification

Another diagnostic BCI application developed in recent years is employing EEG-based BCIs for automatically classifying visual images by measuring human brain signal responses to visual stimuli. Rather than asking subjects to explicitly sort through images to locate a specific target image, a BCI measures brain response while subjects passively view images. Studies have shown that target images can be identified with BCIs with greater than 90% accuracy (Gerson et al. 2006; Nijholt et al. 2008). Another study described in Kapoor et al. (2008) showed that images of objects in specific categories—animals, faces, or inanimate objects—can be automatically categorized by an EEG-based BCI as a human subject passively views the visual stimuli. This system achieved classification accuracy of over 90%.

6.4.5 Attention Monitoring

Measuring alertness in safety-critical jobs requiring intense, prolonged concentration such as air traffic control and long-haul truck driving can prevent accidents and save lives. Nijholt et al. (2008) report that BCI monitoring of alpha rhythms are more effective as a measure of alertness than behavioral measures, and proposes BCI monitoring to assess drowsiness. Systems that detect user drowsiness could automatically revise workload or inform the user that he or she should rest.

6.5 Rehabilitation and Prosthetics

Perhaps one of the most significant and promising applications for BCIs currently under study involves creating therapies to regain motor control lost from diseases such as stroke. Neural control of rehabilitation robots, for example, could provide treatments for people whose paralysis is too extensive for traditional therapies. Clanton et al. (2005) describe efforts to model hand and arm movement in preparation for integrating with neural control. Matsuoka et al. (2006) details the design of a brain-controlled robotic hand. Several research groups are exploring the possibility of directing neural plasticity with BCIs to "re-wire" the brain. Daly and Wolpaw (2008) describes two strategies for restoring movement in paralyzed patients with BCIs: to train the patient to produce more "normal" motor brain signals, and to train the patient to control a device that implements movement. The earliest work in the latter area is described in Pfurtscheller et al. (2005). A subject paralyzed from spinal cord injury learned to regulate sensorimotor rhythms to control functional electrical stimulation (FES) of arm and hand muscles to perform simple tasks such as grasping a glass. Birbaumer and Cohen (2007) describes a system based on magnetoencephalography (MEG) that allows a user to imagine movement of a hand, increasing or decreasing sensorimotor rhythm amplitudes (Fig. 6.9). The BCI responds by opening or closing the user's hand, which is resting in a simple prosthetic. Four of five paralyzed stroke patients were able to open and close their hand voluntarily with the MEG BCI.

Preliminary work in progress described in Moore Jackson (2008) centers on a BCI interface to a rehabilitation robot, the KINARM (BKIN Technologies). Able-bodied subjects wearing an EEG-based BCI train a classifier to recognize arm-reaching tasks with a variety of targets in a 2-dimensional plane (Fig. 6.10). When the classifier is trained, users move the robot (and consequently, the user's arm) by imagining reaching for targets; the BCI adapts to the subjects' brain signals to implement the movement of the robot.

Research in the area of BCI and rehabilitation is promising both for neural prosthetics, and for understanding neuro-plastic effects of BCIs.

Fig. 6.10 The KINARM™ robot for upper limb movement controlled by a BCI as described in Moore Jackson (2008)

6.6 Conclusions

Research and development in Brain Computer Interfaces has exploded in the last ten years, both in the technologies available and the number of organizations involved in the field. BCIs have now evolved beyond laboratory experimental systems and some are now offered as commercial products. No longer the realm of science fiction, BCIs are becoming a viable and effective alternative for assistive technology and a plethora of mainstream applications. New paradigms of interaction open even more possibilities for BCI and create new fields of study, such as neural imaging for computational user experience.

However, many obstacles remain for BCI researchers. BCIs are still notoriously slow and error-prone compared to traditional input technologies. More research is essential in order to develop techniques to reduce both neural and environmental artifacts, to reduce error rates, and to increase accuracy. For BCI systems to be feasible for mainstream real-world use in the home and office, they must be simple, small, wearable, and unobtrusive. New sensor technologies such as dry EEG electrodes and fNIR emitter/detectors must be perfected. Adaptive systems must be sufficient to automatically calibrate and "tune" BCIs to an individual's brain signal patterns without expert assistance. These are daunting challenges, but as the BCI field matures, effectiveness and accuracy are increasing. The BCI field is rapidly approaching critical mass to develop the human-computer interaction methods of the future.

References

Adams L, Hunt L, Moore M (2003) The aware system: Prototyping an augmentative communication interface. Paper presented at the Proceedings of the Rehabilitation Engineering Society of North America (RESNA)

Archinoetics Inc (2009) BrainPainting, from http://www.archinoetics.com/

Bayliss J, Ballard D (2000) A virtual reality testbed for brain-computer interface research. IEEE Trans Rehabil Eng 8(2):188–190

Bell C, Shenoy P, Chalodhorn R, Rao R (2008) Control of a humanoid robot by a noninvasive brain-computer interface in humans. J Neural Eng 5:214–220

Birbaumer N, Cohen L (2007) Brain-computer interfaces: Communication and restoration of movement in paralysis. J Physiol 579:621–636

Birbaumer N, Hinterberger T, Kubler A, Neumann N (2003) The thought-translation device (TTD): Neurobehavioral mechanisms and clinical outcome. IEEE Trans Neural Syst Rehabil Eng 11(2):120–123

Blankertz B, Dornhege G, Krauledat M, Müller KR, Kunzmann V, Losch F et al (2006) The Berlin brain-computer interface: EEG-based communication without subject training. IEEE Trans Neural Syst Rehabil Eng 14(2):147–152

Blankertz B, Krauledat M, Dornhege G, Williamson J, Murray-Smith R, Müller KR (2007) A note on brain actuated spelling with the Berlin brain-computer interface. Universal Access in HCI, Part II, 4555:759–768

Blatt R, Ceriani S, Dal Seno B, Fontana G, Matteucci M, Milgliore D (2008) Brain control of a smart wheelchair. Paper presented at the 10th International Conference on Intelligent Autonomous Systems

Bohenick A, Borden J (2008) LazyBrains, 2008, from http://www.voxel6.com/

Cheng M, Gao X, Gao S, Xu D (2002) Design and implementation of a brain-computer interface with high transfer rates. IEEE Trans Biomed Eng 49(10):1181–1186

Clanton S, Laws J, Matsuoka Y (2005) Determination of the arm orientation for brain-machine interface prosthetic. In: Proceedings of the 14th IEEE Intl Workshop on Robot and Human Interactive Communication, pp 422–426

Cutrell E, Tan D (2008) BCI for passive input in HCI. Paper presented at the Computer Human Interaction—ACM SIGCHI 2008

Daly J, Wolpaw J (2008) Brain-computer interfaces in neurological rehabilitation. Lancet Neurol 7:1032–1043

Emotiv Inc (2009) Emotiv Epoc, from http://www.emotiv.com/

Eskandari P, Erfanian A (2008) Improving the performance of brain-computer interfaces through meditation practicing. Paper presented at the Engineering in Medicine and Biology Society

Farwell LA, Donchin E (1988) Talking off the top of your head: Toward a mental prosthesis utilizing event-related potentials. Electroencephalogr Clin Neurophysiol 70:510–523

Gerson AD, Parra LC, Sajda P (2006) Cortically-coupled computer vision for rapid image search. IEEE Trans Neural Syst Rehabil Eng 14(2):174–179

Grimes D, Tan D, Hudson S, Shenoy P, Rao R (2007) Feasibility and pragmatics of classifying working memory load with an electroencephalograph. CHI 2008:835–844

Iturrate I, Antelis J, Kubler A, Minguez J (2009) Non-invasive brain-actuated wheelchair based on a P300 neurophysiological protocol and automated navigation. IEEE Trans Robot 25(2):367–381

Kapoor A, Shenoy P, Tan D (2008) Combining brain computer interfaces with vision for object categorization. In: CVPR08, pp 1–8

Karim A, Hinterberger T, Richter J, Mellinger J, Neumann N, Flor H, et al (2006) Neural Internet: Web surfing with brain potentials for the completely paralyzed. Neurorehabil Neural Repair 20(4):508–515

Krepki R, Blankertz B, Curio G, Müller K-R (2003) The Berlin brain-computer interface. Paper presented at the 9th International Conference on Distributed Multimedia Systems (DMS 03)

Krepki R, Blankertz B, Müller K-R, Curio G (2007) The Berlin brain-computer interface (BBCI)—towards a new communication channel for online control in gaming applications. Multimed Tools Appl 33(1):73–90

Kubler A, Kotchoubey B, Kaiser J, Wolpaw J, Birbaumer N (2001) Brain-computer communication: Unlocking the locked-in. Psychol Bull 127(3):358–375

Lalor EC, Kelly SP, Finucane C, Burke R, Smith R, Reilly R, et al (2005) Steady state VEP-based brain-computer interface control in an immersive 3D gaming enivonment. EURASIP J Appl Signal Process 19:3156–3164

Li K, Sankar R, Arbel Y, Donchin E (2009) P300 single trial independent component analysis on EEG signal. In: Foundations of Augmented Cognition: Neuroergonomics and Operational Neuroscience. Lecture Notes in Computer Science, vol 5638. Springer, Berlin, pp 404–410

Mason SG, Bohringer R, Borisoff JF, Birch GE (2004) Real-time control of a video game with a direct brain-computer interface. J Clin Neurophysiol 21(6):404–408

Matsuoka Y, Afshar P, Oh M (2006) On the design of robotic hands for brain-machine interface. Neurosurg Focus 20(5:E3):1–9

Millán JdR, Renkens F, Mouriño J, Gerstner W (2004) Noninvasive brain-actuated control of a mobile robot by human EEG. IEEE Trans Biomed Eng 51(6):1026–1033

Miranda E, Brouse A, Boskamp B, Mullaney H (2005) Plymouth brain-computer music interface project: Intelligent assistive technology for music-making. Paper presented at the International Computer Music Conference

Moberg Research (2009) BrainBall, from http://www.mobergresearch.com/brainball.html

Moore Jackson M (2008) Direct brain interfaces for healing games. Paper presented at the SIGCHI 2008 Brain-Computer Interface Workshop

Moore MT, Ope, Yadav, Yadav, Amit (2004) The BrainBrowser, a brain-computer interface for internet navigation. Paper presented at the Society for Neuroscience, San Diego, CA

Naito M, Michioka Y, Ozawa K, Ito Y, Kiguchi M, Kanazawa T (2007) A communication means for totally locked-in ALS patients based on changes in cerebral blood volume measured with near-infrared light. IEICE Trans Inf Syst E90-D(7):1028–1036

NeuroSky Inc. (2009). MindSet, from http://www.neurosky.com/

Nijholt A, Tan D, Pfurtscheller G, Brunner C, Millán JdR, Allison B, et al (2008) Brain-computer interfacing for intelligent systems. IEEE Intell Syst 23(3):72–79

Nijholt A, Oude Bos D, Reuderink B (2009) Turning shortcomings into challenges: Brain-computer interfaces for games. Entertain Comput 1(2):85–94

Oude Bos D, Reuderink B (2008) Brainbasher: A BCI game. In: Markopoulos P, Hoonhout J, Soute I, Read J (eds) Extended Abstracts of the International Conference on Fun and Games 2008, Eindhoven, Netherlands, October 2008. Eindhoven University of Technology, Eindhoven, pp 36–39

Perelmouter J, Birbaumer N (2000) A binary spelling interface with random errors. IEEE Trans Rehabil Eng 8(2):227–232

Pfurtscheller G, Leeb R, Keinrath C, Friedman D, Neuper C, Guger C, et al (2006) Walking from thought. Brain Res 1071:145–152

Pfurtscheller J, Rupp R, Müller G, Fabsits E, Korisek GHG, et al (2005) Functional electrical stimulation instead of surgery? Improvement of grasping function with FES in a patient with C5 tetraplegia. Unfallchirurg 108(7):587–590 (German)

Rapoport E, Nishimura E, Zadra J, Wubbels P, Proffitt D, Downs T, et al (2008) Engaging, non-invasive brain-computer interfaces (BCIs) for improving training effectiveness and enabling creative expression. Hum Factors Ergon Soc Annu Meet Proc 52(7):591–594

Schmorrow D, Estabrooke I, Grootjen M (eds) (2009) Foundations of augmented cognition: Neuroergonomics and operational neuroscience. In: 5th International Conference, FAC 2009 Held as Part of HCI International 2009, San Diego, CA, USA, July 19–24, 2009. Lecture Notes in Computer Science, vol 5638. Springer, Berlin, p 850. ISBN 978-3-642-02811-3

Tan D (2006) Brain-computer interfaces: Applying our minds to human-computer interaction. Paper presented at the ACM SIGCHI—Workshop

Toyota (2009). Real-time control of wheelchairs with brain waves—a new signal processing technology for brain machine interface (BMI) application. Press Release from Toyota Central R&D Labs

Vaughan TM, McFarland DJ, Schalk G, Sarnacki WA, Robinson L, Wolpaw JR (2001) EEG-based brain-computer interface: development of a speller application. Society for Neuroscience Abstracts, vol 26

Vora J, Allison B, Moore M (2005) Discrete control of a robotic arm with a P300-based brain-computer interface. Paper presented at the Third International Brain-Computer Interface Meeting

Zander TO, Kothe C, Jatzev S, Dashuber R, Welke S, de Fillippis M, et al (2008) Team PhyPA: Developing applications for brain-computer interaction. Paper presented at the Computer Human Interaction (SIGCHI), Florence, Italy

Chapter 7
Direct Neural Control of Anatomically Correct Robotic Hands

Alik S. Widge, Chet T. Moritz,
and Yoky Matsuoka

Abstract This chapter presents a potential method of achieving dexterous control of a prosthetic hand using a brain-computer interface (BCI). Major control successes with invasive BCIs have been achieved by recording the activity of small populations of neurons in motor areas of the cortex. Even the activity of single neurons can be used to directly control computer cursors or muscle stimulators. The combination of this direct neural control with anthropomorphic hand prostheses has great promise for the restoration of dexterity. Based on users' requirements for a functional hand prosthesis, a fully anthropomorphic robot hand is required. Recent work in our laboratories has developed two new technologies, the Neurochip and the Anatomically Correct Testbed (ACT) Hand. These technologies are described and some examples of their performance are given. We conclude by describing the advantages of merging these approaches, with the goal of achieving dexterous control of a prosthetic hand.

7.1 Introduction

As described elsewhere in this book, brain-computer interfaces (BCIs) have a wide range of future possibilities for improving quality of life after nervous system insults. Perhaps the earliest example of invasive BCIs occurred over 40 years ago,

A.S. Widge (✉)
Department of Psychiatry, University of Washington, Washington, USA
e-mail: alikw@u.washington.edu

C.T. Moritz
Department of Physiology and Biophysics and Washington National Primate Research Center,
University of Washington, Washington, USA
e-mail: ctmoritz@u.washington.edu

Y. Matsuoka
Department of Computer Science and Engineering, University of Washington, Washington, USA
e-mail: yoky@u.washington.edu

D.S. Tan, A. Nijholt (eds.), *Brain-Computer Interfaces,*
Human-Computer Interaction Series,
DOI 10.1007/978-1-84996-272-8_7, © Springer-Verlag London Limited 2010

when monkeys were trained to drive an electrical meter with the activity of single neurons recorded from motor cortex (Fetz 1969). With the invention of desktop computers and improved electrode technology, the field re-emerged in its present form. Impressive demonstrations of rodents and primates using neural activity to control external devices rapidly followed (Chapin et al. 1999; Serruya et al. 2002; Taylor et al. 2002). Monkeys could be trained to control the movement of a cursor on a computer screen using the activity of groups of single neurons (Santhanam et al. 2006; Serruya et al. 2002; Taylor et al. 2002). This rapidly progressed to demonstrations of reaching and grasping movements of neurally-controlled robot arms (Carmena et al. 2003; Velliste et al. 2008) and of primates controlling muscular functional electrical stimulation (FES) using cortical signals (Moritz et al. 2008; Pohlmeyer et al. 2009).

Neural control of computer cursors and interfaces has now advanced into human clinical trials (Hochberg et al. 2006). There remain significant challenges, however, in creating a clinically useful invasive BCI. Based on animal experiments, we can reasonably expect a subject to smoothly control a cursor or position a robotic manipulator in 3D space and achieve basic grasp (Velliste et al. 2008). While this demonstrates control of three to four degrees of freedom (DOFs), achieving dexterous, 22-DOF hand movement may be a challenge. If we hope to reach full human-level dexterity with BCI, developing actuators that can explore this full control space, as well as BCI controllers that can drive those actuators, remains a valuable endeavor.

In this chapter we suggest a direct neural control strategy for a biologically-inspired robotic manipulator that may achieve human-level dexterity. Our thesis is that there are advantages to simultaneously leveraging the learning capacity of the brain and the mechanical properties of anthropomorphic actuators (human-like artificial hands). By designing a maximally anthropomorphic system, we believe that more effective BCIs can be realized, bringing greater clinical benefit to patients with nervous/musculoskeletal injuries. Here we summarize key aspects of the field and argue in favor of our proposed BCI/prosthesis platform, providing specific examples of technologies from our laboratories that can serve as a testbed for this hypothesis.

7.2 Cortical Interface Technology and Control Strategies

To control any prosthetic with BCI, neural signals must reliably be extracted from the cortex and converted into control signals for the actuator. As the number of usable signals is limited, a high-DOF BCI must make efficient use of available data. Two main strategies exist for BCI control of motor prostheses: *population decoding* (extracting each controlled variable from the activity of the entire neural population) and *direct control* (mapping each recorded neuron directly to one controlled variable). In this section, we present the advantages and limitations of each strategy, concluding with an argument that direct control may be preferable when controlling high-DOF actuators such as hands.

7.2.1 Interface Technologies

We concern ourselves here with BCI techniques involving invasive recording of individual neurons (*single units*). There are many BCI designs (see previous Chapters of this Volume) that utilize either the electroencephalogram (EEG) or electrocorticogram (ECoG), particularly for cursor control. While these less invasive technologies show good results, to date single unit recording provides a greater number of independent control signals. Invasive BCIs are thus the most relevant technology to discuss when considering control of high-DOF actuators.

Stable, long-term recording of single neuron activity has become easier with the advent of high-density (up to 100 recording sites) microelectrode arrays created with silicon microfabrication technology (Maynard et al. 1997; Vetter et al. 2004). However, the number of electrodes recording stable neural signals can vary greatly, anywhere from about 10 to over 100 (Ganguly and Carmena 2009; Truccolo et al. 2008), and usually decreases over time (Kim et al. 2008). The underlying mechanism remains under investigation (Biran et al. 2005; McConnell et al. 2009), and there are many efforts underway to mitigate this effect. Particularly promising strategies include drug-releasing electrodes (Papageorgiou et al. 2006), biomolecular coatings that "fool" the host rejection/foreign-body response (Azemi et al. 2008), and conductive polymer electrodes that modulate the local immune response while also providing improved electrical properties (Cui and Zhou, 2007; Widge et al., 2007a, 2007b).

7.2.2 Control Strategies: Population Decoding

In multiple areas of the cortex, subpopulations of cells are preferentially active when movements are made in a particular ("preferred") direction. This was originally described by Georgopoulos and colleagues, who further found that recording of multiple cells with varying preferred directions could then be used to construct a "population vector" reflecting a monkey's arm movement (Georgopoulos et al. 1986). Population decoding BCIs extend this concept to predict a subject's movement intention from populations of neural activity. Typically the decoder is "trained" or calibrated during actual or imagined movements before BCI control by monitoring neural activity during pre-specified movements and deducing appropriate weights. Some decoders are subsequently updated on-line during BCI control to compensate for changes in neural activity as the brain learns the task (Carmena et al. 2003; Serruya et al. 2002).

Population decoding provides an "instant" and effective method of converting stochastic neural activity into useful BCI control. The activity and direction tuning of any individual neuron can be quite noisy, and thus a combination of many cells is used to "average out" the noise (Nicolelis and Lebedev 2009). Present decoders can predict motor intention with an accuracy of about 60–86% (as shown in Fig. 7.1) (Carmena et al. 2003; Kim et al. 2008). Such decoders

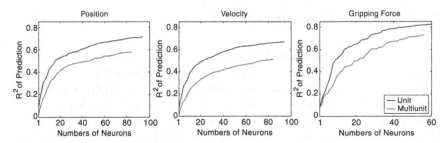

Fig. 7.1 Contributions of greater numbers of isolated neurons (units) or multi-unit neural activity to predictions of hand position, velocity, and gripping force. Random neuron dropping curves represent the average prediction accuracy (R^2 a function of number of neurons used for decoding. Typically, performance does not improve nearly as fast once at least 20 neurons are in the population. Well-isolated single-units predict movement parameters approximately 20% better than multi-unit admixtures. Figure modified and reproduced with permission of author and under Creative Commons attribution license from Carmena et al. (2003)

underlie many recent achievements in invasive BCIs, including primates making skilled reaches/grasps with neurally-controlled robot arms (Kim et al. 2006; Velliste et al. 2008) and tetraplegic human patients successfully controlling cursors and assistive devices (Hochberg et al. 2006; Truccolo et al. 2008).

Despite these impressive examples, population decoding may have limitations when scaling to higher dimensions (cf. Fetz 2007). First, even large populations of neurons do not perfectly predict movement intentions. Prediction accuracy seems to asymptote around 60–80%, suggesting that adding additional neurons will not improve control (Fig. 7.1, adapted from Carmena et al. 2003). Second, large populations of neurons likely contribute redundant information to the decoder. The neuron dropping curves of Fig. 7.1 also illustrate that performance does not begin to decline steeply until only 10–20 randomly selected neurons remain. Third, information may be lost when averaging together large numbers of neurons to drive a small number of variables. Finally, population decoders use only neurons that exhibit directional tuning, which represents only a subset of the population. Data from un-tuned neurons is effectively discarded. Thus, population decoding may not make the most efficient use of available data, which could pose a challenge when greater numbers of control channels are needed to drive complex actuators. While multiple parameters (e.g., endpoint position, velocity and grasp aperture) can be simultaneously decoded from the same population of neurons, significant interference will likely occur when controlling the many degrees of freedom required for a hand prosthesis.

7.2.3 Control Strategies: Direct Control

An alternative to population decoding is direct control, a strategy that may leverage the substantial learning capacity of the brain for control of high-DOF BCIs. In a direct control system, activity from a single neuron or small group of neurons is directly linked to the control of a single degree of freedom, such as a muscle group or joint of a robotic actuator. Renewed interest in direct control has recently arisen, as studies of population decoding demonstrated the role of brain remapping/learning in the successful operation of such prostheses. As performance improved in monkeys performing a BCI cursor control task, cortical neurons were found to alter their directional tuning to better fit the fixed decoder (Taylor et al. 2002). Furthermore, when a similar decoder's parameters were randomly perturbed, cells within the population could be observed altering their tuning direction and degree of tuning to restore good performance (Jarosiewicz et al. 2008).

Thus, direct control may offer a solution to the redundancy challenges described above for population decoding, opening the way for control of more degrees of freedom. The fundamental advantage is that while population decoding depends on the use of directionally tuned neurons, direct control BCIs can begin with any active neuron and train that cell to the task at hand. We have recently demonstrated this paradigm using a cortically-controlled muscle stimulation task (Fig. 7.2(A)). Macaques were first trained to control a cursor on a computer screen using activity from cells recorded from motor cortex, but whose activity was not necessarily correlated with limb movements. Motor and sensory signals between the subjects' arms and the brain were then blocked by infusion of local anesthetic through a perineural catheter. With the arm effectively paralyzed, activity from the previously-trained cortical cells was used to drive functional electrical stimulation (FES) delivered to the wrist muscles. Despite no prior correlation between many of these cells and the desired wrist movements, the monkeys were able to modulate cell activity to control FES and produce the necessary wrist torques to match targets presented on a screen (Moritz et al. 2008). Monkeys could also simultaneously control multiple cells con-

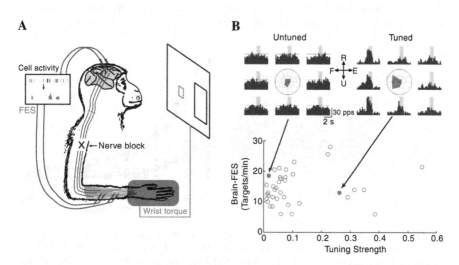

Fig. 7.2 Direct control of paralyzed muscles by cortical neurons. (**A**) Schematic of experiment where monkeys learned to volitionally modulate arbitrary neurons in motor cortex to control stimulation delivered to paralyzed wrist muscles after nerve block. (**B**) Monkeys learned to control both directionally tuned and un-tuned neurons equally well to restore functional torques to a paralyzed wrist. Adapted from Moritz et al. (2008) with permission of Nature Publishing Group

nected to antagonist muscles about the wrist. Importantly, nearly all neurons tested could be trained to control FES equally well regardless of their original association to movement (Fig. 7.2(B)).

Based on this finding, we believe that direct control strategies may be able to maximize information recorded from neurons available on chronic arrays. Only about one-third of primary motor cortex neurons show strong direction tuning (Evarts 1968), and thus a population decoder may effectively discard up to two-thirds of its recordable cells. Direct control is able to use nearly all recorded neurons, even those that exhibit no directional tuning.

A key feature of direct control is improving performance through the use of feedback. Monkeys viewing the activity of single neurons readily learn to differentially modulate their activity (Fetz and Baker 1973). Similarly, a tetraplegic human can control the activity of a single neuron when provided with visual feedback (Hochberg et al. 2006). Further, when human subjects were asked to control an on-screen cursor using forearm EMG activity, they rapidly achieved accurate performance regardless of whether the linkage between specific muscles and cursor directions was intuitive or perversely non-intuitive (Radhakrishnan et al. 2008). Figure 7.3 shows the fairly smooth trajectories reached with this non-intuitive mapping after only an hour of practice.

The nature of neural feedback under direct control may also make training easier for a BCI user. During population decoding, it may be difficult for individual neurons to reshape their activity based on task performance, because each cell's contribution to the movement is masked and diffused through the decoder's averaging (Fetz 2007). Furthermore, because advanced decoders update their weightings often, the brain is not able to discover a consistent mapping between neuronal firing and actuator behavior. Conversely, in a direct control strategy, individual neurons

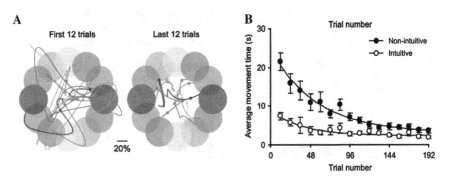

Fig. 7.3 Control of a computer cursor using myoelectric (EMG) signals under direct control with a non-intuitive mapping. (**A**), trajectories from first 12 and last 12 trials from a block of 192 trials with a non-natural mapping between arm surface EMGs and cursor direction. Note the substantial improvement in shape of trajectories (and thus time to target) in a short time even in this difficult task. (**B**), comparison of performance in intuitive and non-intuitive mappings. Although performance was initially much worse using non-intuitive control, subjects rapidly learned the novel transform to achieve similar control within a single session. Figures reprinted with permission from Radhakrishnan et al. (2008)

are directly linked to specific actuators or DOFs, which may allow the brain to engage in very naturalistic feedback learning. Since the mapping is fixed, cells are also free to maximize their modulation without having to compensate for changes in the decoder. This stable substrate should not be undervalued—a recent study demonstrated that when a population decoder's parameters were held constant and linked only to a set of stably recordable neurons across several days, performance on a cursor-control task reached nearly 100% (Ganguly and Carmena 2009). Most notably, the same level of performance was achieved even when the decoder weights were randomized, demonstrating that a consistent transform is far more important than the neuron's original direction or depth of tuning.

Despite these advantages, direct control also has several limitations. Perhaps the most notable is a high vulnerability to instability in individual neuron recordings, since each control variable is linked to one or a small group of neurons. Recent advances in electrode technology permit the same neurons to be recorded for several weeks (Jackson et al. 2007), but unstable recordings remain a challenge for all invasive BCI. We propose to buffer against the loss of any single neuron by taking advantage of the redundancy of the neuromuscular system. For example, if four single neurons each directly control one of four synergist flexors (in either a biological or robotic hand), loss of one or two neurons would be tolerable. The remaining neurons could compensate while new cells were isolated and trained. Monkeys and humans can learn to volitionally control isolated neurons within several minutes (Hochberg et al. 2006; Moritz et al. 2008), suggesting that new neurons could be easily added to replace those lost due to recording instability.

Another criticism of the direct control approach is the stochastic variability of single neuron action potentials, or neural noise. Single neurons' activity may require some filtering or averaging across time to reduce this variability. The mechanical properties of the output actuator (e.g., stimulated muscles or robotic motors) may act as a filter to reduce neural noise. For example, the slow time-constants of muscle effectively smooth the resulting force when single neurons are used to control stimulation (Moritz et al. 2008). The mechanical properties of biologically inspired robots may similarly filter stochastic neural activity to achieve smooth movements.

While population decoding controlling a simple prosthetic gripper will likely be the first BCI-based prosthetic hand, we believe that direct control may provide more robust BCI control of high-DOF prostheses. We suggest that the best solution involves direct control of an actuator that mimics the mechanical properties of human anatomy. Such an anatomically accurate prosthesis is ideal for direct control, as neurons can be used to directly control the many (and partially redundant) "muscle motors", and the mechanics of the hand will in turn act to filter this potentially noisy control signal. Our labs have developed two key technologies, the Neurochip and the Anatomically Correct Testbed (ACT) hand, that we are in the process of combining to demonstrate this approach.

7.3 Neurochip: A Flexible Platform for Direct Control

Exploration of direct control as a BCI strategy has been limited by suboptimal hardware. The basic need is for a "neural router" that acquires signals from cortical neurons and routes them to arbitrary effectors (motors, stimulators, etc.). Rack-mounted hardware does the job, but tethers the subject to the experimental rig. To implement direct control for free-roaming subjects, a fully integrated and wireless system is required. We have developed a miniaturized, battery-powered, autonomous system, the "Neurochip", partly as a platform for direct control BCI experimentation.

The original Neurochip is described in Mavoori et al. (2005), while the next-generation version is presented in Zanos et al. (2009) and shown in Fig. 7.4. Briefly, input from implanted electrodes (microwires, silicon arrays, ECoG or EMG) is bandpass filtered, preamplified, and passed to a Programmable System-on-a-Chip (PSoC) for digitization and processing. The PSoC includes a dual time-amplitude window spike discriminator to detect consistent spike waveforms. The Neurochip can be programmed with stimulation contingencies such that a detected event (action potential or other activity) triggers real-time stimulation delivered to another site, or a signal delivered to an external device. Onboard memory stores both raw neural signals and average activity, recording more than 24 hours of data at moderate sampling rates or when utilizing the real-time discriminator to compress neural data to spike times and waveforms.

An infra-red interface permits two-way communication and configuration. By using a "smart" microprocessor that can automatically adjust clock speed and turn modules off when not needed, the Neurochip is able to maximize battery life. Autonomous stimulation experiments, with the neuro-stimulator continuously available, may be run for over 24 hours; extension of the run requires only a quick battery change. When only recording is required, we have achieved 60 hours of un-tethered operation in freely-behaving primates. Each device is primarily constructed from off-the-shelf components, lowering both development time and unit cost. Although the current version is limited to three parallel channels, it could relatively simply be scaled up as needed for direct control of a high-DOF robot limb.

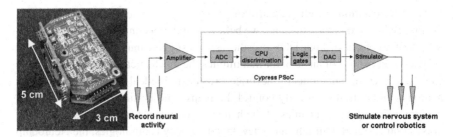

Fig. 7.4 The Neurochip 2, able to autonomously and simultaneously process three input channels and drive three stimulation channels for 24 hours using only on-board power (battery not shown)

7.4 Anatomical Prosthetic Design

During the past century, artificial limbs have advanced in both appearance and functionality. However, artificial upper extremities still do not meet patients' needs. Commercial myoelectrically-controlled prosthetic arms, effectively the "state of the art", are basically unused by 50% of their owners (Silcox et al. 1993). Furthermore, they do not offer nearly the same breadth of control space as a human hand/arm. To achieve widespread acceptability, a prosthetic must succeed in three domains: cosmesis, comfort, and control.

Cosmesis refers to the overall appearance of a prosthetic device. There is strong societal pressure to be "normal", a large part of which is looking "normal". Unless an upper limb prosthesis is extremely close to the original anatomy, it cannot be hidden with sleeves or gloves. Thus, patients often eschew unappealing hook or claw prostheses in favor of pleasing but immobile silicone hands. Current prostheses also move in an "unnatural" fashion, which many observers find uncanny and disconcerting. The ideal upper extremity prosthesis thus should look, feel, and move as much as possible like an actual human hand.

Comfort refers to the burden of use. While problems can arise in donning and doffing the prosthesis, ease of connection to the control interface, protection against dirt and environmental hazards, and heat/noise from mechanical components, the greatest difficulty is usually with weight. A standard robot hand/arm design might put motors directly at the actuated joints. While simple in terms of power train, such a design places much of the weight at the end of a lever arm, thus increasing the subjective burden and the user's fatigue. A better design would attempt to mimic human anatomy, in which force-generating components (i.e., muscles) are kept closer to the torso, and distal actuators (i.e., fingers) are driven through a system of tendons.

Most important is *controllability*, the ability to perform daily tasks. Existing prostheses often use non-paralyzed muscles/joints to generate control signals (Kilgore et al. 2008; Kuiken et al. 2007). As this only affords a few control signals, prostheses generally compensate by permitting the user to select from a few "primitive" hand postures, rather than attempting to reach the entirety of hand configuration space. Such a strategy leaves the user unable to truly control how he/she interacts with objects. Furthermore, if the prosthesis takes a form different from the human hand, a patient must re-learn strategies for grasping and manipulating. While some motivated and resourceful users can be quite functional, others find themselves unable to adapt, and ultimately give up on their prosthesis.

We therefore propose that an ideal upper extremity motor prosthesis will be anthropomorphic, i.e. contain salient features of the human anatomy that produce the appearance, movements, and function of a human hand. This naturally leads to improved cosmesis, since a human-like hand will move in more human-like ways. If the prosthesis follows human anatomy, motors will be located more proximally, leading to greater comfort. Finally, although an anthropomorphic hand has many more DOFs to master, it may ultimately improve controllability.

Several hands have been designed to attempt this goal. The Robonaut (Bluethmann et al. 2003), Cog (Matsuoka 1997), JPL/Stanford (Salisbury and Craig 1982), and Utah/MIT (Jacobsen et al. 1986) hands all offer some anthropomorphic qualities. While these hands are anthropomorphic in many ways, there is no natural mapping from the muscles. Furthermore, they have the correct number of joints and fingers, but it is not clear if those are the salient features of human hands which enable dexterous behavior. Further development was needed to create a device that is truly able to replicate the critical properties of a human hand.

Another advantage of anthropomorphic design is that biological limbs include substantial non-linearities arising from the mechanical properties of muscle and tendon, as well as from transforms applied to neural signals as they pass from brain to muscle. Motor control signals from the brain are optimized for the filtering and amplifying properties of the complete musculoskeletal system. When designing a BCI prosthetic arm/hand, one must create software that accounts for these expectations and effectively decodes the brain's intent. If the actuator instead reproduces the mechanical properties of human tissue, it may be better suited to the control signals being generated in motor cortex, and the decoding algorithm can be simpler.

7.5 The Anatomically Correct Testbed (ACT) Hand

7.5.1 General Overview

We have worked to develop a new anthropomorphic robotic hand as a platform for both prostheses and studies of manipulation. While not all anatomical details may be necessary for prosthetic applications, we are learning many salient features that should be useful to achieve natural cortical control of a high-DOF hand. The current version of the ACT Hand is shown in Fig. 7.5, demonstrating both its humanoid appearance and ability to grasp a wide variety of objects. The ACT Hand is the only artificial hand to date that mimics, accurately and in detail, the anatomy of a human hand.

The mechanics of the ACT Hand are described in detail in Matsuoka et al. (2006), whereas control, kinematics, and sensing systems are elsewhere (Deshpande et al. 2009; Koterba and Matsuoka 2006). To construct the initial prototype and mimic anatomy faithfully, a cadaver hand was studied and each bone reconstructed using computer-aided design. Subtle bumps and asymmetry on the bone surface have been shown to matter for efficient control (Deshpande et al. 2008). Joints between the artificial bones have also been matched in size to the original joint spaces, range of motion, and placement and number of kinematic axes (Vande Weghe et al. 2004). Similarly, extensive studies were undertaken of the precise anatomy and spring properties of the human tendon web, with careful choice of materials to match these properties (Wilkinson et al. 2003). In system identification experiments and computational simulations of the actuated mechanism, the ACT Hand data remained within one standard deviation of (and often almost identical to) measurements from a cadaver hand (Deshpande et al. 2008).

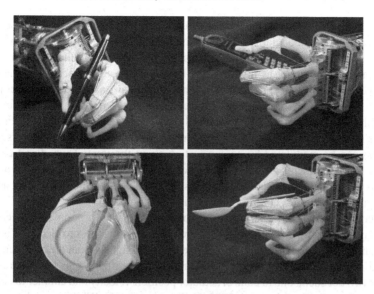

Fig. 7.5 Example postures illustrating the ACT Hand grasping several household objects. Particular attention was paid to the replication of human bone structure, including the weight of each finger element, and to the anatomy of the flexor/extensor tendon web. Note the natural appearance of each grasp posture, a consequence of faithfully modeling actual hand kinematics

Human motor control exploits the passive dynamics of the actuator to achieve more dexterous movements, and involves strategies (such as co-contraction of antagonist muscles to increase joint stiffness) that require a specific motor architecture. By replicating some of those features, we believe that prosthesis control will be simplified and will feel more natural to the user, because cortical neural signals are optimized to drive the human hand structure. Some evidence for this hypothesis has already emerged from simulations. When increasingly more complicated aspects of the low-level muscular system were taken into account, a simulated limb was able to maintain more stability in the face of perturbations (Loeb et al. 1999). Our own experiments found similar results when we attempted to predict human index finger joint angle. Predictors using raw EMG activity (as a proxy for neural activity) were inferior to those that first estimated joint torques by filtering EMG activity with a model of musculoskeletal mechanics (Afshar and Matsuoka 2004). The ACT Hand implements those same filters implicitly in its structure and mechanics, and thus should offer more stability and functionality than existing prostheses.

7.5.2 Anatomically Correct Hands Under Direct Neural Control

It is relatively easy to imagine connecting a fully anthropomorphic hand to a direct control BCI. Assuming that one has a set of cortical electrodes capable of recording at least 22 single neurons, the output of each can be connected to an arbitrarily-chosen muscle motor actuating one hand/finger DOF. If the damping and non-linear force generation properties of human muscles are faithfully replicated in the artificial hand, they will act as inbuilt filters to reduce the effects of noise/variability in the neural activity. Redundancy between motors in an anatomically correct prosthetic would allow the user to continue being functional in daily activities even if one of the controlling neurons is temporarily lost due to electrode instability. Finally, if pairs of single neurons are directly connected to antagonist muscle motors, joint stiffness can be modulated by co-contraction about the joint. Thus, direct control of muscle-like elements provides precise force and position control, but also allows the user to change joint impedance to resist external perturbations (a critical aspect of normal human motor control in uncertain situations).

In contrast, controlling an anthropomorphic hand with a population decoding BCI may prove quite difficult. Although there will be robustness to electrode issues, the challenge is generating many independent control signals from the recorded population. To date, strategies for controlling reach-and-grasp systems involve training at least two decoders, one to control actuator position/velocity and another to control gripper actuation (Carmena et al. 2003; Velliste et al. 2008). While a population may be able to drive two decoders simultaneously, it is unclear whether this would scale to 20 or more, particularly when some of those decoders would be controlling functionally antagonistic actuators. An additional group of decoders would be needed to control joint stiffness. One might expect that each decoder would be driven primarily by a small subpopulation that happens to correlate highly with that decoder's DOF. Such decoders may work fairly well, but are effectively a direct control strategy in disguise.

7.6 Synthesis: Visions for BCI-Based Prosthetics

We have described recent progress in the development of single unit-based BCI systems and anthropomorphic hand prostheses. Each of these technologies independently represents a major step forward. Both population decoding and direct control BCIs have achieved significant results in the laboratory, and population decoding has reached human users. We hypothesize that direct control may eventually offer full human-level dexterity, because it can make more efficient use of neural data and may scale better for high-DOF actuators. By leveraging the brain's tremendous capacity for learning, direct control designs may allow more rapid development and deployment of novel BCIs. Anthropomorphic prostheses, particularly in the upper limb/hand domain, offer improved cosmetic appearance and greater user comfort. By incorporating the passive mechanical properties and mimicking the salient kinematic features of the human hand, they are expected to be easier to control.

The true value of these two lines of research becomes more apparent when they are linked together such that cortical signals are used to directly control the motors of an anatomically correct hand. Under direct control, the user's brain can learning optimal mappings between each hand muscle-motor and the activity of each controlling neuron. This can be done implicitly, without the need to carefully design a decoder. Based on existing data, it seems feasible that subjects can rapidly learn to modulate individual cells to control individual motors, even though the cells being employed need not have a prior relation to hand control. At the same time, the passive behavior of the actuator will enhance stability and filter out some of the noise inherent to direct control signals, producing more natural movements. Thus, the combination of a direct control with the ACT Hand has the potential to restore full dexterous capability to a BCI prosthesis user.

Even as we move towards high-functionality, high-DOF prostheses, the solutions to today's problems also create new research challenges. There remains a question of how to further design interfaces to be more "natural" for the user. The ACT Hand represents one example of how, by optimizing the design of the actuator, a prosthesis can be made easier for the subject to use. "Unnatural" mappings can be learned for simple 2D cursor-control tasks (Radhakrishnan et al. 2008), but the same data (seen in Fig. 7.3) suggest that logical neuron-actuator mapping may help learning speed. This, in turn, has implications for scaling BCIs to higher-DOF actuators. Thus, the human-computer interaction community may be able to suggest further strategies to make prosthetic use as naturalistic and intuitive as possible. We are hopeful that the use of these intuitive and direct control signals to drive biomimetic prostheses will restore dexterous movements to individuals following limb-loss or nervous system injury.

References

Afshar P, Matsuoka Y (2004) Neural-based control of a robotic hand: Evidence for distinct muscle strategies. IEEE Int Conf Robot Autom 2:4633–4638

Azemi E, Stauffer WR, Gostock MS, et al (2008) Surface immobilization of neural adhesion molecule L1 for improving the biocompatibility of chronic neural probes: In vitro characterization. Acta Biomater 4:1208–1217

Biran R, Martin DC, Tresco PA (2005) Neuronal cell loss accompanies the brain tissue response to chronically implanted silicon microelectrode arrays. Exp Neurol 195:115–126

Bluethmann W, Ambrose R, Diftler M, et al (2003) Robonaut: A robot designed to work with humans in space. Auton Robot 14:179–197

Carmena JM, Lebedev MA, Crist RE, et al (2003) Learning to control a brain-machine interface for reaching and grasping by primates. PLoS Biol 1:193–208

Chapin JK, Moxon KA, Markowitz RS, et al (1999) Real-time control of a robot arm using simultaneously recorded neurons in the motor cortex. Nat Neurosci 2:664–670

Cui XT, Zhou DD (2007) Poly(3) (4-ethylenedioxythiophene) for chronic neural stimulation. IEEE Trans Neural Syst Rehabil Eng 15:502–508

Deshpande A, Balasubramanian R, Lin R, et al (2008) Understanding variable moment arms for the index finger MCP joints through the ACT hand. IEEE Int Conf Robot Autom 776–782

Deshpande A, Ko J, Matsuoka Y (2009) Anatomically correct testbed hand control: Muscle and joint control strategies. IEEE Int Conf Robot Autom 2287–2293

Evarts EV (1968) Relation of pyramidal tract activity to force exerted during voluntary movement. J Neurophysiol 31:14–27

Fetz EE (1969) Operant conditioning of cortical unit activity. Science 163:955–958

Fetz EE (2007) Volitional control of neural activity: Implications for brain-computer interfaces. J Physiol 579:571–579

Fetz EE, Baker MA (1973) Operantly conditioned patterns on precentral unit activity and correlated responses in adjacent cells and contralateral muscles. J Neurophysiol 36:179–204

Ganguly K, Carmena JM (2009) Emergence of a stable cortical map for neuroprosthetic control. PLoS Biol 7:e1000153

Georgopoulos AP, Schwartz AB, Kettner RE (1986) Neuronal population coding of movement direction. Science 233:1416–1419

Hochberg LR, Serruya MD, Friehs GM, et al (2006) Neuronal ensemble control of prosthetic devices by a human with tetraplegia. Nature 442:164–170

Jackson A, Mavoori J, Fetz EE (2007) Correlations between the same motor cortex cells and arm muscles during a trained task, free behavior, and natural sleep in the macaque monkey. J Neurophysiol 97:360–374

Jacobsen S, Iversen E, Knutti D, et al (1986) Design of the Utah/MIT dextrous hand. IEEE Int Conf Robot Autom 3:96–102

Jarosiewicz B, Chase SM, Fraser GW, et al (2008) Functional network reorganization during learning in a brain-computer interface paradigm. Proc Natl Acad Sci USA 105:19486–19491

Kilgore KL, Hoyen HA, Bryden AM, et al (2008) An implanted upper-extremity neuroprosthesis using myoelectric control. J Hand Surg Am 33:539–550

Kim HK, Biggs SJ, Schloerb DW, et al (2006) Continuous shared control for stabilizing reaching and grasping with brain-machine interfaces. IEEE Trans Biomed Eng 53:1164–1173

Kim S, Simeral J, Hochberg L, et al (2008) Neural control of computer cursor velocity by decoding motor cortical spiking activity in humans with tetraplegia. J Neural Eng 5:455–476

Koterba S, Matsuoka Y (2006) Flexible, high density, artificial skin with triaxial force discernment. IEEE Int Conf Robot Autom

Kuiken TA, Miller LA, Lipschutz RD, et al (2007) Targeted reinnervation for enhanced prosthetic arm function in a woman with a proximal amputation: A case study. Lancet 369:371–380

Loeb GE, Brown IE, Cheng EJ (1999) A hierarchical foundation for models of sensorimotor control. Exp Brain Res 126:1–18

Matsuoka Y (1997) The mechanisms in a humanoid robot hand. Auton Robot 4:199–209

Matsuoka Y, Afshar P, Oh M (2006) On the design of robotic hands for brain-machine interface. Neurosurg Focus 20:1–9

Mavoori J, Jackson A, Diorio C, et al (2005) An autonomous implantable computer for neural recording and stimulation in unrestrained primates. J Neurosci Methods 148:71–77

Maynard EM, Nordhausen CT, Normann RA (1997) The Utah Intracortical Electrode Array: A recording structure for potential brain-computer interfaces. Electroencephalogr Clin Neurophysiol 102:228–239

McConnell GC, Rees HD, Levey AI, et al (2009) Implanted neural electrodes cause chronic, local inflammation that is correlated with local neurodegeneration. J Neural Eng 6:056003

Moritz CT, Perlmutter SI, Fetz EE (2008) Direct control of paralysed muscles by cortical neurons. Nature 456:639–643

Nicolelis MAL, Lebedev MA (2009) Principles of neural ensemble physiology underlying the operation of brain-machine interfaces. Nat Rev Neurosci 10:530–540

Papageorgiou DP, Shore SE, Sanford C, Bledsoe J, et al (2006) A shuttered neural probe with on-chip flowmeters for chronic in vivo drug delivery. J Microelectromech Syst 15:1025–1033

Pohlmeyer EA, Oby ER, Perreault EJ, et al (2009) Toward the restoration of hand use to a paralyzed monkey: Brain-controlled functional electrical stimulation of forearm muscles. PLoS One 4:e5924

Radhakrishnan SM, Baker SN, Jackson A (2008) Learning a novel myoelectric-controlled interface task. J Neurophysiol 100:2397–2408

Salisbury J, Craig J (1982) Articulated hands: Force control and kinematic issues. Int J Robot Res 1:4

Santhanam G, Ryu SI, Yu BM, et al (2006) A high-performance brain-computer interface. Nature 442:195–198

Serruya MD, Hatsopoulos NG, Paninski L, et al (2002) Brain-machine interface: Instant neural control of a movement signal. Nature 416:141–142

Silcox D, Rooks M, Vogel R, et al (1993) Myoelectric prostheses. A long-term follow-up and a study of the use of alternate prostheses. J Bone Joint Surg Am 75:1781–1789

Taylor DM, Helms Tillery SI, Schwartz AB (2002) Direct cortical control of 3D neuroprosthetic devices. Science 296:1829–1832

Truccolo W, Friehs GM, Donoghue JP, et al (2008) Primary motor cortex tuning to intended movement kinematics in humans with tetraplegia. J Neurosci 28:1163–1178

Vande Weghe M, Rogers M, Weissert M, et al (2004) The ACT hand: Design of the skeletal structure. IEEE Int Conf Robot Autom

Velliste M, Perel S, Spalding MC, et al (2008) Cortical control of a prosthetic arm for self-feeding. Nature 453:1098–1101

Vetter RJ, Williams JC, Hetke JF, et al (2004) Chronic neural recording using silicon-substrate microelectrode arrays implanted in cerebral cortex. IEEE Trans Biomed Eng 51:896–904

Widge AS, Matsuoka Y, Kurnikova M (2007a) In silico insertion of poly(alkylthiophene) conductive polymers into phospholipid bilayers. Langmuir 23:10672–10681

Widge AS, Jeffries-El M, Cui X, et al (2007b) Self-assembled monolayers of polythiophene conductive polymers improve biocompatibility and electrical impedance of neural electrodes. Biosens Bioelectron 22:1723–1732

Wilkinson D, Weghe M, Matsuoka Y (2003) An extensor mechanism for an anatomical robotic hand. IEEE Int Conf Robot Autom

Zanos S, Richardson AG, Shupe L, et al (2009) The Neurochip-2: A programmable, implantable system for recording neural signals and delivering contingent electrical stimuli in freely behaving monkeys. 2009 Neuroscience Meeting Planner, Program No 664.615

Chapter 8
Functional Near-Infrared Sensing (fNIR) and Environmental Control Applications

**Erin M. Nishimura, Evan D. Rapoport,
Peter M. Wubbels, Traci H. Downs,
and J. Hunter Downs III**

Abstract Functional near-infrared (fNIR) sensing is a relatively young brain imaging technique, yet one that holds great promise for brain-computer interfaces. Measuring essentially the same signals as functional magnetic resonance imaging (fMRI), fNIR acts as a single-point monitor of oxy- and deoxy-hemoglobin concentrations for localized sensing with greatly lowered costs and hardware requirements. As an optical sensing technique, fNIR is more robust to ambient electrical noise that affects the electroencephalogram (EEG) signal. The reduced hardware requirements and robustness in noisy environments make fNIR well-suited for brain-computer interface systems as it poses few physical restrictions on the operator and can be implemented in a wide range of applications and scenarios.

8.1 Near Infrared Sensing Technology

Relying on the known optical properties of the interaction between near-infrared (NIR) light and oxy- and deoxy-hemoglobin, near-infrared sensing is a non-invasive technology that monitors even minute fluctuations in tissue oxygenation (Cope 1991). In between visible and infrared light, NIR light (750 nm–2500 nm) is relatively weakly absorbed and scattered (Schmidt 1999). Oxy- and deoxy-hemoglobin, present in all living human tissue, have distinct absorption spectra of near-infrared light. It is these distinct properties that are used to calculate the concentrations of

E.M. Nishimura (✉) · E.D. Rapoport · P.M. Wubbels · T.H. Downs · J.H. Downs III
Archinoetics LLC, 700 Bishop St, Ste 2000, Honolulu, HI 96817, USA
e-mail: erin@archinoetics.com

E.D. Rapoport
e-mail: evan@archinoetics.com

T.H. Downs
e-mail: traci@archinoetics.com

J.H. Downs III
e-mail: hunter@archinoetics.com

D.S. Tan, A. Nijholt (eds.), *Brain-Computer Interfaces,*
Human-Computer Interaction Series,
DOI 10.1007/978-1-84996-272-8_8, © Springer-Verlag London Limited 2010

oxy- and deoxy-hemoglobin in tissue based on the differential changes in received NIR light passed through this tissue.

For continuous wave or continuous intensity NIR sensing, multiple wavelengths of NIR light are time-modulated and emitted at a constant output intensity. The intensity of the received light after passing through tissue is a measure of the attenuation changes caused by the tissue for each wavelength. These received intensities are converted to oxy- and deoxy-hemoglobin concentrations using a modified Beer-Lambert equation (Franceschini et al. 2002).

Near-infrared sensing, while promising as a non-invasive and relatively inexpensive monitor of oxy- and deoxy-hemoglobin, is a relatively young technology. There exist known problems when fielded that have yet to be adequately addressed, namely motion artifacts that distort the optical signal. However, as a relatively young technology, the possibilities for near-infrared sensing and potential applications, as well as its shortcomings, have not yet been fully explored.

Outputting relative regional oxy- and deoxy-hemoglobin, near-infrared sensing can provide a means for continuous physiological monitoring or can be applied to the cortical surface for relatively inexpensive, portable functional brain imaging.

8.1.1 Physiological Monitoring

As a monitor of tissue oxy- and deoxy-hemoglobin fluctuations, near-infrared sensing can be used as a physiologic sensor in applications that must monitor oxygenation as a correlate to an event or extreme environments. A direct application is early G-LOC (gravity-induced loss of consciousness) detection in high-speed flight. G-LOC is believed to be caused by the reduced cerebral blood flow that results from exposure to high G forces. This decrease in blood flow to the brain lowers the oxygenation level in brain tissues, contributing to the onset of G-LOC and A-LOC (almost loss of consciousness) (Kobayashi 2002). Brain cells function on a high utilization rate of oxygen; a decreased oxygenated blood supply to the brain due to gravitational forces leads to G-LOC within a few seconds (Glaister 1988). Monitoring decreases in oxy-hemoglobin concentrations in the brain that precede the onset of G-LOC can lead to early detection and potential prevention of this condition.

In addition to providing access to gross oxy- and deoxy-hemoglobin changes, NIR sensing can also detect passive vital signals. These vital signs unavoidably affect oxy- and deoxy-hemoglobin levels, with the dominant signals consisting of oscillations from the heartbeat and respiration. The heartbeat propagates changes in oxy- and deoxy-hemoglobin concentrations throughout the body tissue, resulting in changes in tissue transparency for NIR wavelengths outside of the isobestic point. Thus, the heartbeat signal is present in fNIR imaging as a pulse waveform, with the inflection points determined by the systolic pressure wave (Gratton and Corballis 1995). The use of the NIR signal for heartbeats would enable measurement from a single-site sensor, rather than multiple sensor sites as required by electrocardiogram (ECG)-based measures.

8.1.2 Functional Brain Imaging

Applied to the scalp, NIR sensing detects regional oxy-hemoglobin changes on the cortical surface. Lagging several seconds after the onset of neuronal activity, a hemodynamic and metabolic response leads to increases in blood flow and an increase in the concentration of oxy- relative to deoxy-hemoglobin in the area of the brain being used by that activity (Chance et al. 1998). These oxygenation changes in the area of the brain being used by this neuronal activity can be monitored and detected through the NIR oxy- and deoxy-hemoglobin signals. Therefore, functional near-infrared sensing can sense cognitive activity based on rises in oxy-hemoglobin concentrations in the area of the brain being used by that activity.

While NIR sensing measures physiologic signals that are similar to those measured by fMRI, the hardware required for near-infrared sensing can be much more compact and less costly. Although NIR sensing does not offer the same spatial resolution as fMRI, the potentially portable nature of the technology lends itself to mobile and more real-world applications in natural environments.

8.2 The OTIS System

The OTIS system is a continuous-wave near-infrared sensing system developed by Archinoetics that monitors relative oxy- and deoxy-hemoglobin concentrations for both physiologic and functional brain imaging applications (Nishimura et al. 2007). Several iterations of the system have been created, with the latest system shown below in Fig. 8.1.

This system is wireless, battery-powered, and wearable, with a focus on comfort for long-term wear while allowing for adjustability of the optics for optimal NIR signals. All of the optics, communications, and embedded processing are contained within the sensor enclosure shown. Because of the small size and wireless feature of the system, this device is suitable for flight applications, allowing for helmet

Fig. 8.1 The latest OTIS system that is wearable, wireless, battery powered, and includes 3-axis accelerometry in addition to near-infrared sensing

(a)   (b)   (c)

Fig. 8.2 Several generations of the OTIS system

Fig. 8.3 Custom NIR sensor for verbal cognitive activity detection and analysis (front view on left, showing the slip for a strap, and back view on right, showing the optics that must be placed against the skin)

integration without compromising any safety features of the helmet. The system also meets the safety features required for integration into a flight platform, including the elimination of any tethering to the cockpit for communications or power (Nishimura et al. 2009).

This most recent system iteration has evolved from past device generations, shown in Fig. 8.2. Figure 8.2a is a two-channel system per sensor, with the processing enclosure supporting up to two sensors. Figure 8.2b is an eight-channel system. Figure 8.2c shows an early system design that utilized fiber optics with an electronics enclosure.

Power minimization allows for the current system to be powered through a rechargeable battery, eliminating the need for a connection to an external power source. Miniaturization of the electronics led to a smaller overall profile. While smaller in size, this latest device iteration also provides 3-axis accelerometry data for analysis of sensor motion for motion artifact detection and/or removal and larger scale acceleration that may be reflective of extreme environments.

An alternative form factor has been designed for making contact with the head without a helmet. Figure 8.3 shows a design for a functional brain imaging application, specifically for analysis of Broca's area where hair penetration for skin coupling is not required due to the location of that region. The enclosure holds a strap in place to aid in the coupling the sensor to the head without a helmet.

8.3 Basic BCI Applications

The key to applying the functional brain imaging capabilities of near-infrared sensing to human-computer interfaces is the accurate detection of regional changes in oxy-hemoglobin concentrations caused by cognitive activity controlled by the operator. Detection of these controlled cognitive activities can provide a means of non-physical and non-vocal control.

Basic human-computer interaction through functional near-infrared sensing (fNIR) was done through simple interfaces with cognitive activity detection algorithms. While fundamental in nature, these interfaces provide binary switches that can lead to more complex controls.

8.3.1 Hemodynamic Response Detection

The most direct approach to using the fNIR system for cognitive control is through detection of the hemodynamic response that is the physiologic change in response to cognitive activity. Detecting a hemodynamic response in near-real-time requires either detection of the signal change or statistical comparison to the expected time course of the oxy-hemoglobin concentration response to tasks that are associated with the region of the brain being monitored (active tasks) and to tasks that are not associated with this region (inactive tasks). An estimate of the expected time course can be created by applying hemodynamic response modeling techniques used in fMRI, given the timing of the active and inactive tasks used (Rajapakse et al. 1998). However, differences in responses between individuals and even between trials within the same individual affect the robustness of these detection techniques in practice.

8.3.2 Yes/No Response

A more robust technique for accurately interpreting operator intent is a comparison between two task periods, one in which the operator is performing an "active" task, and one in which the operator is performing an "inactive" task. By comparing these two periods to determine which is the "active" task period, a more accurate determination of user intent can be made, rather than change detection in a relative signal that is required for direct hemodynamic response detection.

A confidence score, between 0 and 1, is calculated based on the comparison between the fNIR signal for the two periods. If the two periods are too similar for a determination, the confidence score is near 0.5 and an "unsure" output is displayed.

Applying this approach to BCI's, the result is a reliable on/off switch for translation into cognitively-controlled communication or environmental manipulation. Figure 8.4 illustrates an "active" task period followed by an "inactive" task period (a) and an "inactive" task period followed by an "active" task period (b) with high confidence.

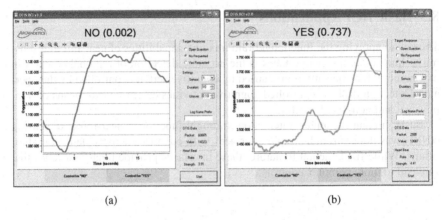

(a)   (b)

Fig. 8.4 The OTIS BCI application graphs oxygenation data in real-time and then provides the state determination at the end of the trial. The "NO" screenshot on the left shows the hemodynamic response while the subject performs the active task followed by the inactive task (the order is reversed in the "YES" screenshot on the right). The scores at the top reflect the confidence in the yes/no determination, where 0 is a strong "NO", 1 is a strong "YES", and 0.5 is inconclusive

8.4 Environmental Control with fNIR

Basic fNIR applications can be extended for more complex environmental control and communications using a non-vocal and non-physical means of control, namely control through modulated cognitive tasks. This is ideal for individuals with locked-in syndrome. Chronic locked-in syndrome is a severe neurological condition that results in varying degrees of paralysis, yet often there may be little or no effect on cognitive function. There are several known causes of locked-in syndrome, including brainstem injury, stroke, or ALS (amyotrophic lateral sclerosis), commonly known as Lou Gehrig's Disease. Individuals afflicted with locked-in syndrome vary in their range of motor functions, from voluntary eye movements to involuntary movements to complete paralysis (Leon-Carrion et al. 2002; Feldman 1971).

Interfaces that rely on fNIR as the means for control can be used by locked-in individuals for applications ranging from basic control of electronics to creative expression. Several are described in the sections to follow, in addition to the software that enables such applications. Many of these applications are based on the real-time cognitive activation level detected by the fNIR signal that is controllable by the cognitive activity of the operator.

8.4.1 Software Framework for Control Applications

These more advanced brain-computer interfaces that rely on the fNIR signal are enabled by a custom, modular software application (BIRT) that offers an interface to the Archinoetics' OTIS system and XML-based pipeline configuration. Several environmental control applications have been created as BIRT modules for use with fNIR through an add-on platform for integration of 3rd-party applications.

8.4.1.1 BIRT

The primary software for acquiring and utilizing data from the fNIR system is the Windows-based Brain-Interface Runtime (BIRT) application. BIRT is a highly configurable tool that loads XML-based pipeline files that dynamically (at run-time) load modules, filters, or user interfaces for handling data that is received from the fNIR system. This modular architecture facilitates both in-house and third-party development because the different components can be developed in isolation and then incorporated with only a minimal amount of additional code (required for the module to acquire and distribute data).

The pipelines that BIRT loads can be easily created through a graphical user interface by non-technical personnel who wish to modify how the data will be processed or utilized. This feature enables experimental psychologists on the different teams to make changes to the BIRT process chain without requiring software modifications or assistance from a software engineer. Similar applications can be developed for use with other fNIR systems by modifying the data acquisition modules based on the raw data output format of the system to be used.

8.4.1.2 Platform for 3rd Party Interfacing

With the goal of facilitating collaborative software development, BIRT also includes functionality that allows developers to program in languages other than those in the .NET framework. Through making a socket connection to the BIRT, any application on any operating system can easily consume fNIR data in real-time.

In order to facilitate community development of rich, animated brain-computer interfaces, BIRT also provides the ability for people to create applications in Adobe Flash. By loading a Flash template that already contains all the necessary ActionScript to connect to BIRT, animators and other non-programmers can easily create BCI games and rich media in the most ubiquitous platform for this type of media. Since BIRT integrates with Flash, people with artistic and design talents, who might not otherwise be able to develop BCIs, are able to contribute to the software development process.

An additional benefit of providing Flash integration is that, teamed with basic knowledge of ActionScript, it is a good platform for rapid prototyping, particularly for user interfaces requiring animation. Full-scale applications can be built without extensive time commitment and by people with relatively little programming experience. This allows undergraduate students in computer science classes or other novice programmers to build BCIs while providing them an understanding of the challenges and opportunities in building assistive technologies for disabled individuals.

For Flash interfaces to work as BCIs, processed fNIR data is sent from the BIRT processing chain into Flash. A BIRT module, included with the application, allows pipeline creators to load any Flash application to consume the data. A working Flash application template with full source code is also included to show Flash developers how to use the fNIR signal to control visual objects and numeric variables within Flash. For example, the relative strength of cognitive activity determines the depth of a swimming dolphin (please see the "Dolphin Trainer" section for a screenshot and more in-depth description).

A custom algorithm is used to convert the relative oxy-hemoglobin concentration from the fNIR system to a measure of cognitive activation, normalized to a value between zero and one (with higher numbers reflecting higher levels of cognitive activity in the cortical region of interest). This normalized output from the fNIR signal provides a consistent input for the Flash programmer and eliminates any requirements for any advanced understanding of the fNIR technology. All this serves to simplify the development process for the Flash developer, enabling development by a wider range of programmers and designers.

8.4.2 Electronics/Appliance Control

An interface that links the fNIR system output to its surroundings for environmental interaction can offer paralyzed and disabled operators more control over their lives, and also enrich the way able-bodied users manipulate their world. This was developed using home automation transmitters and receivers that allow control over nearly any electronic device. A module was created that translates an fNIR-based switch, based on the yes/no responses described previously, into controls for the electronics, such as turning on a lamp.

Interfacing with more complex home automation transmitters and receivers, operators are able to activate saved sequences of commands through the fNIR interface, such as dimming the ambient lights, turning on their TV, turning up the volume, then switching to their favorite channel. By combining multiple transmitters and receivers, the system provides the flexibility to control an unlimited number of IR devices with everything from simple on/off commands, to more complicated sequences.

8.4.3 Dolphin Trainer

An application called the "Dolphin Trainer" was developed to demonstrate integration with Flash and the potential for engaging users with rich, animated BCIs (Fig. 8.5). Any cognitive task can be used to control the dolphin, as long as the placement of the sensor corresponds to the cortical area that is activated by that task. Dolphin Trainer provides a video game-like experience in which the user raises and

Fig. 8.5 The Dolphin Trainer application, demonstrating a more enjoyable, goal-oriented, video game application that enables flexible scripting to train and evaluate subjects' abilities to control BCIs

lowers the dolphin to eat the fish as they move from right-to-left across the screen. The fish may be added randomly, manually, or via scripting. The overall score is displayed and the difficulty can be adjusted. In the scripting method, patterns of fish can be created to train or test the subject's ability to control the BCI. For example, by placing repeating sets of three fish (displayed in a vertical column) and instructing the user to always select the green fish, an experimenter could assess how well the subject could manipulate the BCI's signal to reach each of the three corresponding levels.

8.4.4 Dolphin Interface for Communication/Control

Taking the Dolphin Trainer one step further, the selection of a fish can also launch a developer-specified action. At the basic level, some fish have words trailing behind them, enabling a subject to answer a multiple choice question or spell out a sentence. Additionally, fish can be associated with commands that are sent to other software applications or to objects in the real-world environment (see Fig. 8.6). For example, in one instantiation, the selection of a colored fish triggers a robotic arm to pick up a board game piece of the corresponding color. This could be expanded to allow a BCI user to play checkers with a friend on an actual game board, use a set of paint-brushes, or manipulate other objects typically requiring hands.

8.4.5 Brain Painting for Creative Expression

Another example of an engaging BCI is a painting program, which also simultaneously trained people on the skills required to use a BCI for communication and environmental control. The program allows a user to create complex color gradients that were directly mapped to the relative level of activity in the brain area of

Fig. 8.6 The Dolphin Trainer application being used in conjunction with a robot that can manipulate pieces on a board game. The user raises and lowers the dolphin to eat a fish causing the robot moves the game piece of that color

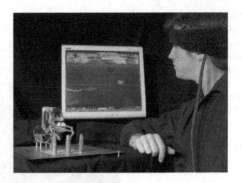

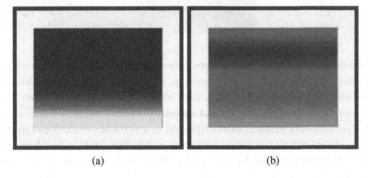

(a)   (b)

Fig. 8.7 Some of the first brain painting by world famous watercolor artist Peggy Chun (who has ALS and is fully paralyzed except for her eyes)

interest. A high level of activity is mapped to one color and a low level to another (colors are chosen by the user prior to data collection). The canvas is filled line by line, from top to bottom. The speed and sensitivity of the program can by varied to achieve different effects, with a single painting taking from ten seconds through several minutes (or even hours).

The first regular user of Brain Painting was the late watercolor painter, Peggy Chun, who was a world famous artist who had ALS and yet continued to paint even after she became paralyzed. The software was refined and enhanced through consultations with Mrs. Chun, who assisted in developing strategies for maximizing the artistic appeal of the resulting works. She also painted the first set of brain paintings (Fig. 8.7).

To create these paintings, Mrs. Chun first selected two colors, then designated one color as the "active" color that is displayed when she performs the cognitive task that activates the fNIR signal. In this case, the sensor was placed over Broca's Area, so her active task was subvocal singing. The other color was designated as the "inactive" color for display when performing a task that doesn't activate Broca's Area (cloud visualization). Mrs. Chun then controlled the color gradient, from the top of the digital canvas to the bottom, through modulating between the active and inactive tasks.

As Brain Painting users practice they often become better able to control the BCI and have a greater ability to produce the painting they intend. Mrs. Chun's talents as a watercolor artist certainly helped her envision an attractive composition, but she would not have been able to achieve her vision without practice using the BCI. Considering the target population for BCIs are often locked-in and severely disabled people who would otherwise not have any ability to express themselves creatively or do anything actively enjoyable, there is tremendous inherent value in providing these sorts of applications.

8.5 Conclusion

Near-infrared sensing, monitoring oxy- and deoxy-hemoglobin concentrations, can provide an effective means for control in a brain-computer interface without requiring any physical or vocal action. The gradient cognitive activation levels it can provide allows for higher resolution control interfaces. Because it is both non-invasive and portable, the Archinoetics' OTIS fNIR sensing system is ideal for BCI applications ranging from in-flight use to creating brain-controlled digital painting. Such a variety of applications benefit the warfighter as well as the locked-in operator.

As a relatively immature and emerging technology, there is considerable research that must still be done in the areas of artifact removal and reliable cognitive activity detection for robust use in real-world environments. However, the newness of the technology also leaves opportunity for innovative exploration. There is much room for refinement and discovery with fNIR technology and applications, especially as a means for non-vocal and non-physical human-computer interaction.

References

Chance B, Anday E, Nioka S, Zhou S, Hong L, Worden K, Li C, Murray T, Ovetsky Y, Pidikiti D, Rhomas R (1998) A novel method of fast imaging of brain function, non-invasively, with light. Opt Express 2(10)

Cope M (1991) The development of a near-infrared spectroscopy system and its application for non-invasive monitoring of cerebral blood and tissue oxygenation in the newborn infant. PhD Thesis, Dept of Medical Physics and Bioengineering, University College London

Feldman MH (1971) Physiological observations in a chronic case of "locked-in" syndrome. Neurology 21(5):459–478

Franceschini MA, Boas DA, Zourabian A, Diamond SG, Nadgir S, Lin DW, Moore JB, Fantini S (2002) Near-infrared spiroximetry: Noninvasive measurements of venous saturation in piglets and human subjects. J Appl Physiol 92:372–384

Glaister MB (1988) Current and emerging technology in G-LOC detection: Noninvasive monitoring of cerebral microcirculation using near infrared. Aviat Space Environ Med 59:23–28

Gratton G, Corballis PM (1995) Removing the heart from the brain: Compensation for the pulse artifact in the photon migration signal. Psychophysiology 32:292–299

Kobayashi A (2002) Pilot cerebral oxygen status during air-to-air combat maneuvering. Aviat Space Environ Med 73(9):919–924

Leon-Carrion J, Van Eeckhout P, Dominguez-Morales Mdel R, Perez-Santamaria FJ (2002) The locked-in syndrome: A syndrome looking for therapy. Brain Inj 16(7):571–582

Nishimura EM, Stautzenberger JP, Robinson W, Downs TH, Downs JH III (2007) A new approach to functional near-infrared technology. IEEE Eng Med Biol Mag 26:25–29

Nishimura EM, Russell CA, Stautzenberger JP, Ku H, Downs JH III (2009) In-helmet oxy-hemoglobin change detection using near-infrared sensing. Hum Comput Interact 4:514–513

Rajapakse JC, Kruggel F, Maisog JM, von Cramon DY (1998) Modeling hemodynamic response for analysis of functional MRI time-series. Hum Brain Mapp 6:283–300

Schmidt FEW (1999) Development of a time-resolved optical tomography system for neonatal brain imaging. PhD Thesis, Dept of Medical Physics and Bioengineering, University College London

Chapter 9
Cortically-Coupled Computer Vision

Paul Sajda, Eric Pohlmeyer, Jun Wang,
Barbara Hanna, Lucas C. Parra,
and Shih-Fu Chang

Abstract We have developed EEG-based BCI systems which couple human vision and computer vision for speeding the search of large images and image/video databases. We term these types of BCI systems "cortically-coupled computer vision" (C3Vision). C3Vision exploits (1) the ability of the human visual system to get the "gist" of a scene with brief (10's–100's of ms) and rapid serial (10 Hz) image presentations and (2) our ability to decode from the EEG whether, based on the gist, the scene is relevant, informative and/or grabs the user's attention. In this chapter we describe two system architectures for C3Vision that we have developed. The systems are designed to leverage the relative advantages, in both speed and recognition capabilities, of human and computer, with brain signals serving as the medium of communication of the user's intentions and cognitive state.

P. Sajda (✉) · E. Pohlmeyer
Department of Biomedical Engineering, Columbia University, New York, NY, USA
e-mail: psajda@columbia.edu

E. Pohlmeyer
e-mail: ep2473@columbia.edu

J. Wang · S.-F. Chang
Department of Electrical Engineering, Columbia University, New York, NY, USA

J. Wang
e-mail: jwang@ee.columbia.edu

S.-F. Chang
e-mail: sfchang@ee.columbia.edu

B. Hanna
Neuromatters, LLC, New York, NY, USA
e-mail: bhanna@neuromatters.com

L.C. Parra
City College of New York, New York, NY, USA
e-mail: parra@ccny.cuny.edu

D.S. Tan, A. Nijholt (eds.), *Brain-Computer Interfaces,*
Human-Computer Interaction Series,
DOI 10.1007/978-1-84996-272-8_9, © Springer-Verlag London Limited 2010

9.1 Introduction

Today we are faced with more information on a daily basis than ever before. Constantly evolving digital recording devices that can capture large amounts of spatial and/or temporal data, ever increasing digital storage capacities and multitudes of multimedia applications are just a few factors that create this "information tsunami". Searching for something of interest, making rapid decisions and being attentive to relevant information are becoming increasingly complex tasks.

Various technologies, driven by diverse fields of research, have been developed to assist us in consuming information. Yet the fact is that the human capacity to analyze information and make inferences about our surrounding environment remains unsurpassed. For example, our ability to recognize objects is extraordinarily robust, and with trillions of neuronal connections, our brain can react extremely fast to an external stimulus: we respond to the information we receive in the "blink of an eye" (Gladwell 2005), before we are even aware of it.

Recently we, as well as others, have been investigating the application of brain computer interfaces (BCI) for dealing with issues in image search, retrieval and triage (Gerson et al. 2006; Parra et al. 2008; Kapoor et al. 2008; Bigdely-Shamlo et al. 2008). Our group has developed an approach which we term *cortically coupled computer vision* (C3Vision) where the goal is to synergistically couple computer vision with human vision, via on-line real-time decoding of EEG while users' view images as a rapid serial visual presentation (RSVP) (Gerson et al. 2006). As well as being a method for maximizing throughput, the use of RSVP is motivated by our ability to make very rapid and accurate decisions. The ability of the human visual system to do this has sometimes been characterized as getting the "gist" of a scene (Oliva 2005) in a few hundred milliseconds. The C3Vision approach exploits our ability to decode EEG signals that are related to detection and recognition in rapidly shown images (Thorpe et al. 1996; Keysers et al. 2001; Gerson et al. 2006). One of the key signals we exploit in our system is the P300. The P300 is an evoked response in the EEG which reflects perceptual "orienting" or shift of attention which can be driven by the content of the sensory input stream (Linden 2005).

In this chapter we review our work in C3Vision, focusing on two architectures we have developed. The first architecture is tailored to a visual search problem, where a user must find targets in an extremely large image (on the order of 30 K × 30 K pixels). For this case computer vision serves as a pre-processor to select potential areas of interest, creating chips (or regions of interest—ROIs) of these areas which are subsequently presented to the user via RSVP while the user's EEG is decoded to generate an "interest score" used to rank or prioritize the ROIs (see Fig. 9.1A). Given this first step "triage", the user can proceed to search the large image with the added capability of jumping to locations in the scene which grabbed his/her's attention during the RSVP EEG decoding phase. In Section 9.3 we describe this system and demonstrate results for remote sensing.

The second architecture, presented in Section 9.4, addresses an image retrieval application, using EEG decoded during RSVP presentation to generate an interest

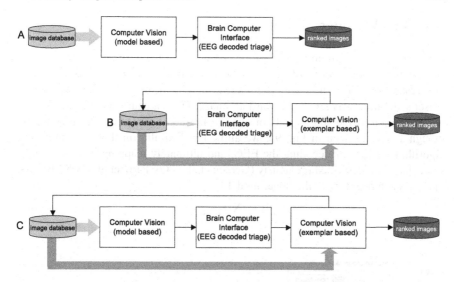

Fig. 9.1 Strategies for integrating computer vision with EEG-based image triage. The goal is to re-rank images in a database so that the result is a dense ranking, with images of interest at the front of the database, given an initial ranking that is sparse. In system A a very large database is processed by model based computer vision to generate a candidate set of images that might be of interest to the user. The computer vision model is tuned to have a high sensitivity at the cost of specificity. The user is presented with rapid sequences of images labeled as potentially interesting by computer vision while high-spatial density EEG ($\approx$64 channels) is recorded. An EEG decoder is trained on data collected from subjects while they look at imagery from an unrelated database and pay attention for target specific or "interesting" imagery in the rapid sequences. The trained EEG decoder is used to process EEG signals while the user observes the barrage of images in the sequence, with the result being an interest score used to re-rank the database. This leads to a dense ranking of the database (note dark gray vs light gray, indicating the database has become more dense in term of the "concentration" of interesting images). System B starts by randomly sampling the database and passing on the samples as rapid sequences to a human user. Note that in this case, the volume of imagery assessed by the human is small, compared with the computer vision in System A, due to speed and fatigue limitations. However an advantage of System B is that the human is able to look for images which are specifically of interest to him/her and which might be difficult to define in terms of a prior model for computer vision. The EEG interest score is used to re-rank images and pass labels to an exemplar based computer vision system which then propagates predicted labels into the database and returns a re-ranking based on the propagated labels. System C combines systems A and B so that computer vision operates both at the front end and back end of the system

score usable for training a feature based computer vision system (see Fig. 9.1B). The computer vision system derives training labels from the EEG interest score and propagates them to re-rank the image database and retrieve for the user those images which match what grabbed his/her attention. Below we begin by describing how we decode the EEG and map it to an "interest score". For additional technical details readers are referred to Gerson et al. (2006), Parra et al. (2008), Wang et al. (2009b), Sajda et al. (2010).

9.2 The EEG Interest Score

Given an RSVP paradigm for presenting a rapid sequence of images to the subject, we simultaneously record EEG, using 64 scalp electrodes, and map the activity to an "interest score" for each image. The interest score is meant to reflect how much of a user's attention was directed toward an image. From a neuro-science perspective it can be seen as the single-trial correlate of the P300-related orienting response, though as can be seen in Fig. 9.2 we allow for flexibility in this definition. The algorithm we use for decoding the EEG, and ultimately mapping it to an interest score, has been described previously (Gerson et al. 2006; Parra et al. 2008). Briefly, our approach begins with the linear model,

$$y_t = \sum_i w_i x_{it} \tag{9.1}$$

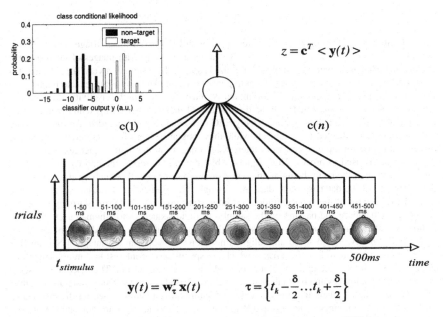

Fig. 9.2 Using hierarchical discriminant component analysis to construct EEG interest scores. Shown is the forward model for the discriminating component at each time window, which can also be seen as the normalized correlation between the component activity in that window and the data (Parra et al. 2005). The series of 10 spatial maps thus shows that the spatial distribution of the forward model of the discriminant activity changes across time. Activity at 300–400 ms has a spatial distribution which is characteristic of a P3f, which has been previously identified by our group and others (Gerson et al. 2005; Makeig et al. 1999) during visual oddball and RSVP paradigms. In addition, the parietal activity from 500–700 ms is consistent with the P3b (or P300) indicative of attentional orienting. Other significant discriminant signals can be found at earlier and later time and often vary from subject to subject and the specifics of the experimental paradigm, e.g. presentation speed. The 10 components characterized by the scalp maps are linearly integrated to form a single classification score, which can be represented via the class-conditional histograms. This classification score is used as the "interest score" in our C3Vision systems

where x_{it} represents the electrical potential measured at time t for electrode i on the scalp surface, while w_i represents the spatial weights which will be learned based on a set of training data. The goal is to combine voltages in the electrodes linearly such that the sum y is maximally different between two conditions—e.g. "target of interest" vs "distractor". We also assume that this maximally discriminant activity is not constant but changes its spatial distribution within the second that follows the presentation of an image—i.e. we assume a stationarity time T of approximately 100 ms. Thus we find distinct optimal weight vectors, w_{ki} for each 100 ms window following the presentation of the image (index k labels the time window):

$$y_{kt} = \sum_i w_{ki} x_{it}, \quad t = T, 2T, \ldots, (k-1)T, kT. \tag{9.2}$$

These different y_{kt} are then combined in an average over time to provide the optimal discriminant activity over the entire second of data, with the result being our "interest score", y_{IS} for the image

$$y_{IS} = \sum_t \sum_k v_k y_{tk}. \tag{9.3}$$

For on-line implementation purposes we use the method of Fisher Linear Discriminants to train coefficients w_{ik} within each time window of time. The coefficients v_k are learned using penalized logistic regression after all exemplars have been observed. Because of the two step process of first combining activity in space, and then again in time, we have termed this algorithm "Hierarchical Discriminant Component Analysis". Figure 9.2 plots the spatial filters that are learned for each time window and shows the subsequent hierarchical integration which enables us to construct interest scores, based on the classifier output. Note in the figure that the scores distribute as a function of whether the image was a target of interest or not.

9.3 C3Vision for Remote Sensing

We first consider architecture A in Fig. 9.1 with computer vision followed by RSVP and EEG decoding. The application we will consider is for remote sensing. In remote sensing, analysts must search images that are several hundreds of giga-pixels in size. In particular, intelligence analysts routinely search very large satellite images in order to find and monitor objects and regions of interest (Fig. 9.3A). As part of their work-flow, analysts use specialized software (e.g. Remoteview, by Overwatch Systems) that lets them rapidly load, display and zoom/pan such images. They conduct their searches using various strategies depending on their level of experience and expertise. Figure 9.3B shows for example the raster scanning search pattern followed by an image analyst during a test. Given the size of the images, this typical search process can be lengthy and inefficient. For example a trained analyst may need 60 minutes to complete the review of a 30 K × 30 K image, and may only identify the targets of interest in the last few minutes of the review. However, searches

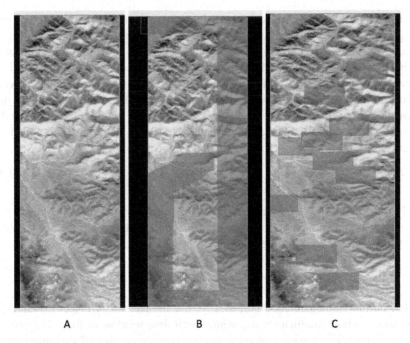

A   B   C

Fig. 9.3 **A**. Satellite image to be searched. **B**. Traditional search approach shows a smooth and continuous path. **C**. Search in which areas are prioritized by EEG triage. *Shaded areas* in **B** & **C** represent regions analyzed by the analyst

could be significantly enhanced and accelerated with means to prioritize the search, and help analysts focus their attention on regions with high target probability.

Leveraging the high sensitivity of computer vision with the high specificity of human visual recognition, we have developed a C3Vision Remote Sensing System, based on the architecture of Fig. 9.1A. In this system potential target regions are automatically identified by computer vision and image chips centered on potential targets are generated and then presented as RSVP to the user. Centering the image chips on potential targets improves the detection performance during the triage, as targets are better foveated when presented to the analysts at a rapid pace. The EEG scores computed during the RSVP are used to prioritize which regions of the image should be searched first, leading to search patterns like those shown in Fig. 9.3C.

Using C3Vision in this way improves on the analysts' typical work-flow by offering a first pass in which they can very rapidly review thousands of image chips extracted from the large satellite image and identify those that will be of most interest to them, as shown in Fig. 9.4. They can then move to a more in-depth second pass during which they can review high priority areas first, thus accelerating and managing their search more efficiently.

This architecture combines three major components: 1. computer vision based automated region selection and target detection; 2. real-time recording and decoding of EEG signals and 3. the interface used to exploit the prioritized image analysts.

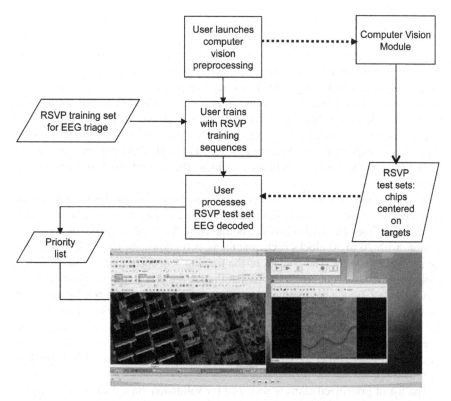

Fig. 9.4 Analyst work-flow with the C3Vision architecture. Potential target regions are automatically identified, and image chips constructed with potential targets centered on those regions. Image chips are triaged using rapid image presentation and classification of neural activity. The results are then reviewed by order of priority in existing specialized software with the help of a dedicated visualization interface

While there is a vast body of computer vision research on object/region detection, the C3Vision architecture itself is agnostic to the choice of a particular method. Such a choice is best guided by the task for which the system is used. The scenario presented here involves targets classes that are known a priori, enabling the use of a model based approach. In particular, we have implemented and tested a framework that extracts low-level features specific to aerial object classes. The framework then infers object classes with a grammar-based reasoning engine that uses domain knowledge and the relationship between object features (see Sajda et al. 2010 for more details). As the image size is typically large and the target detection needs only to be within a few pixels, target detection is only performed on a subsample of image pixels, for example a uniform grid with user specified density. The detection framework associates a confidence score with each pixel in the subsample. Image chips are generated based on those detections with a score exceeding a predefined, task-based threshold.

The image chips are then presented to the analyst as RSVP, using a pace of 5 to 10 Hz (i.e. 200–100 ms per image). While they are presented, EEG signals are recorded using a 64 electrode EEG recording system (ActiveTwo, Biosemi, Germany) in a standard 10–20 montage and at a 2048 Hz sampling rate. Image chips are presented in blocks, typically 100 image chips long. Since detection performance can degrade when target occurrences are too seldom or too frequent, each block is constructed to satisfy a certain target prevalence. In particular, for each block, a number of image chips are randomly drawn from the computer vision list, based on expected true and false positive rates, and additional chips are drawn from a pool of "distractors" in order to achieve the desired block size and prevalence.

As the EEG stream is acquired, a classifier based on the hierarchical discriminant component analysis, described above, assigns an EEG interest score to each image chip in real time. The EEG classifier is trained at the beginning of a presentation session, with 20 to 30 blocks each containing two known but randomly placed (in the sequence) targets. The content of the training sequences can be related to the content of the test sequences to better familiarize the user to the paradigm and targets. However, from a neuro-physiological perspective, training is not dependent on the choice of imagery, since the classifier is in fact tuned to P300 events. To further help users modulate their responses and obtain better training, feedback can be given at the end of each block, for example by providing a visual indication of how the classifier can re-order the target images within a block based on the EEG interest scores.

The list of prioritized chips is reviewed for validation via a dedicated visualization interface that interacts directly with the analysts' dedicated software. Analysts validate target locations by clicking on corresponding x, y coordinates, which can then be saved in analyst specific products such as shape files. The visualization interface controls the software's viewport, forcing it to show areas centered on the x, y coordinates of the original large image corresponding to the centers of the chips by descending order of EEG interest. Those "jumps" can be triggered by user inputs (e.g. pressing a next button) or be automatically paced. Analysts experimenting with the system have provided positive feedback on both approaches, reporting that the latter helps them rapidly focus their decisions, while the former gives them greater control over the review process.

The architecture has been tested in the course of four semi-operational tests, involving a minimum of 4 image analysts each and imagery from a variety of sensors: EO-gray-scale cameras, EO-color cameras and SAR. Here we show the results of tests where each analyst had to perform three search tasks: 1. look for POLs (Petroleum Oil Lubricant storage); 2. look for airfields in a SAR image; 3. look for buildings in a large EO gray-scale image. For each search task, the times at which image analysts had clicked on a target pixel location was recorded for both baseline and image assisted searches. As a result, several metrics were computed to compare baseline and assisted searches: area throughput at matched sensitivity, i.e. the number of pixels searched per unit time while keeping the baseline and assisted number of targets found the same, detection rate, i.e. the number of targets found over time,

Table 9.1 Throughput comparison between baseline search and C3Vision for the remote sensing application

	Task 1 (POLs—MSI)	Task 2 (Airfields—SAR)	Task 3 (Buildings—EO)
Avg throughput improvement	3.21	11.01	3.16
Standard deviation	0.42	3.48	0.52

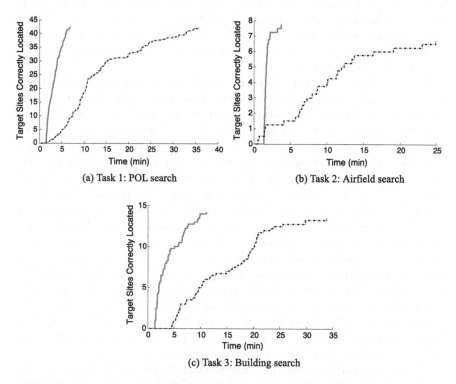

(a) Task 1: POL search

(b) Task 2: Airfield search

(c) Task 3: Building search

Fig. 9.5 Average number of target detections as a function of time across subjects and for each task. *Dashed lines* are for baseline and *solid lines* are using C3Vision

and sensitivity. For each task, the system was shown to improve on the baseline area throughput by at least 300% on average (see Table 9.1), as well as on the baseline detection rates (see Fig. 9.5). At the same time, the overall sensitivity and number of false positives were kept the same or moderately improved upon, highlighting the capacity of the system to drastically accelerate search without degrading detection performance.

9.4 C3Vision for Image Retrieval

Due to explosive growth of visual content on the Web, such as personal photographs and video, there is an emerging need for efficient and accurate systems to rapidly analyze visual information. One of the ultimate goals for automated computer vision or media content analysis is to detect and recognize objects, scenes, people, and events in images or videos. A common framework used in such efforts is to learn object models from a pool of training data, which may have been wholly or partly annotated over pre-defined object classes. Such a learning framework has been shown to be powerful. However, it is limited in its scalability to large-scale applications. One of the main barriers is the dependence on the manual annotation process, which is laborious and time consuming. To overcome this, efforts have been reported using interactive annotation with relevance feedback and active learning in order to reduce the required manual input.

We consider a C3Vision system for image retrieval using the architecture shown in Fig. 9.1B (and more specifically in Fig. 9.6A). In this architecture, neural signals measured via EEG are used to detect generic objects of interest (OOI) presented in a series of images, while computer vision exploits the EEG labels within the context of a graph-based visual pattern mining algorithm. For the EEG-based OOI detection, only a relatively small subset of images (on the order of few hundred) is first randomly sampled from a larger image database and presented as visual stimuli to the subject. From this window into the larger image collection, the EEG interest detector can identify a small set of highly ranked images to be used as a group of 'pseudo positive' labels for the pattern discovery module. This module then refines and propagates the labels throughout the entire database of images, returning a larger set of images related to those to which the subject showed the greatest interest. In this way, subject participation is minimized, yielding just sufficient information for the neural state decoder and the pattern mining module to effectively infer objects that have attracted a users attention and generate labels for all the images in the collection. Thus, while subjects are only required to review a small subset of the database (avoiding long EEG recording sessions and fatigue), they can still obtain access to a large number of images that interest them.

The imagery used to test the image retrieval architecture was taken from the Caltech 101 database. This database is a well known set of images that are commonly used to evaluate object detection and recognition algorithms (Fei-Fei et al. 2004). It is composed of 101 different image categories, with all the images having been taken from the web. As the categories have large intra class variation and represent a diverse set of image types, while still only consisting of images that have been well-defined, it provides a good testbed for the image retrieval architecture. The Caltech images do vary considerably in both resolution in scale, however. To control for any such fluctuations in image size impacting the subjects' visual responses and fixation capabilities during the RSVP, we selected a subset of categories from the Caltech 101 database to serve as the experimental database. These categories all contained images of similar scale and resolutions, and the images could easily be re-scaled to a consistent size (with negligible distortion) to provide the desired uniformity in the

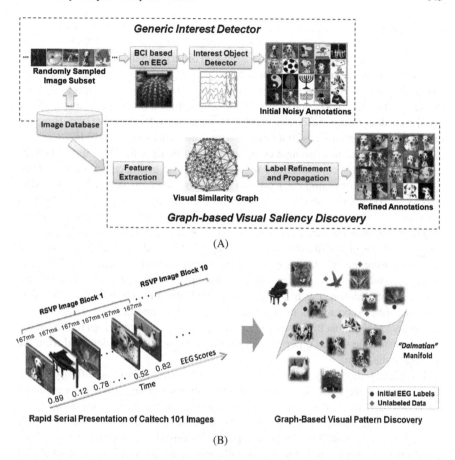

(A)

(B)

Fig. 9.6 System design for image retrieval. (**A**) Images are sampled from the image database and presented as RSVP to the user while EEG is simultaneously recorded. EEG interest scores are calculated and used to rank the samples based on their score. Concurrently, the entire image database is mapped to a graph structure based on image-based feature similarity. The graph structure is than provided labels derived from the EEG interest scores and these labels are propagated in the graph to re-rank the entire image database. Since the labels derived from EEG interest scores are considered noisy, there is a label refinement/sensitivity analysis step which is used to maximize the value of the labels. (**B**) From the perspective of the graph based model, the interest scores derived from EEG during the RSVP presentation of images can be seen as improving the discovery of manifolds in the feature space of the images. These manifolds represent object categories which are of interest to the user and which are similar in terms of the feature space in which they reside

visual input during the RSVP. The experimental database thus consisted of 62 of the Caltech 101 database categories for a total of 3798 images (42% of the total Caltech 101 images).

Each test sequence involved the users being presented with 1000 images randomly selected from the 62 categories. The images were shown in 10 blocks of 100 images each, with the images within each block being shown at 6 Hz for the RSVP.

During each test sequence, the users were instructed to look for images from one of three target categories: Starfish, Chandeliers, and Dalmatians. The RSVP sequence of 1000 images were then repeated (in a random order) with the participant being instructed to attend to images from the next target category. The ordering of the target categories was varied between subjects. All EEG data from four subjects (who were familiar with EEG work, but who had not been exposed to this experiment), were again recorded during these tests using a 64 channel system (ActiveTwo, Biosemi, Germany) in a standard 10–20 montage, with a sampling rate of 2048 Hz.

The hierarchical discriminate component analysis algorithm was used to create the interest detector component of the image retrieval architecture, see Fig. 9.6A. The format of the training data used to create the detector matched the test data (blocks of 100 images, shown at 6 Hz), with the training images being taken from the Caltech 256 database to differentiate the training and testing data. Similarly to the testing data though, only a subset of relatively similarly sized Caltech 256 images were used for the training database, with several 101 categories that are typically part of the 256 database also having been removed. Typically 25–30 blocks of images (with exactly 2 target images randomly positioned within each block) were presented during the training session, with the subjects being instructed to attend to either soccer balls or baseball gloves as the training target category. The 20 images ranked most highly by the interest detector were then given to the pattern discovery module so that other images similar to those could be identified from the full image database.

The pattern discovery subsystem starts with construction of an affinity graph, which captures the pairwise visual content similarity among nodes (corresponding to images) and the underlying subspace structures in the high dimensional space (as shown in the right part of Fig. 9.6B). Such a construction process is done offline before user interaction. The small set of pseudo positive labels generated by the EEG based interest detector is fed to the initially unlabeled graph as assigned labels for a small number of nodes, which are used to drive the subsequent processes of label identification, refinement, and propagation. Graph based semi-supervised learning techniques (Wang et al. 2008) play a critical role here since we will rely on both the initial labels and the large pool of unlabeled data points throughout the diffusion process.

Assume that the generic interest detector outputs the EEG score $\mathbf{e} = \{e_1, e_2, \ldots, e_n\}$ from a RSVP sequence $\mathcal{X} = \{\mathbf{x}_1, \mathbf{x}_2, \ldots, \mathbf{x}_n\}$ shown to the subject.[1] Previous work has shown that the existing semi-supervised methods cannot handle cases with extremely noisy labels (Wang et al. 2009a). In order to refine the noisy EEG scores, our method first extracts the salient image pattern and recovers the visual consistency among the top ranked images. In other words, an improved interest measurement $\mathbf{f}$ is estimated using an image based representation and initial EEG scores as $\{\mathcal{X}, \mathbf{e}\} \rightarrow \mathbf{f}$. We formulate the following process of EEG label refinement and visual pattern mining.

---

[1]For an RSVP image sequence, the decoded EEG score vector $\mathbf{e} = \{e_1, e_2, \ldots, e_n\}$ is usually normalized as $e_i \in [0, 1], i = 1, \ldots, n$.

1. Convert the image representation to a visual similarity graph $\mathcal{X} \rightarrow \mathcal{G} = \{V, E, W\}$, where vertices V are the image samples $\mathcal{X}$ and the edges E with weights W measure the pairwise similarity of images.

2. Transfer the interest scores to pseudo EEG labels $\mathbf{e} = \{e_1, e_2, \ldots, e_n\} \rightarrow \mathbf{y} = \{y_1, y_2, \ldots, y_n\}$. In other words, a binarization function $g(\cdot)$ is applied to convert EEG scores to EEG labels as $\mathbf{y} = g(\mathbf{e})$, where $y_i \in \{1, 0\}$ and $y_i = 1$ for $e_i > \epsilon$, otherwise $y_i = 0$. The value ϵ is called interest level for discretizing the EEG scores.[2]

3. Apply the bivariate regularization framework to define the following risk function

$$E_\gamma(\mathbf{f}, \mathbf{y}) = \mathcal{Q}(\mathbf{f}, \mathbf{y}) + \gamma \mathcal{V}_\mathcal{G}(\mathbf{f}) \tag{9.4}$$

which imposes the tradeoff between the smoothness measurement $\mathcal{V}_\mathcal{G}(\mathbf{f})$ of function $\mathbf{f}$ and empirical error $\mathcal{Q}(\mathbf{f}, \mathbf{y})$. Specifically, the function smoothness is evaluated over the undirected graph $\mathcal{G}$.

4. Alternatively minimize the above risk function with respect to $\mathbf{f}$ and $\mathbf{y}$ to finally achieve the optimal $\mathbf{f}^*$

$$\mathbf{f}^* = \arg\min_{\mathbf{f}, \mathbf{y}} E_\gamma(\mathbf{f}, \mathbf{y}). \tag{9.5}$$

Finally, the propagated label predictions over the entire graph can be used to generate annotations for every single image in the collection, or to re-rank the images based on the detection scores. The top ranked results, as shown in Fig. 9.7B, are expected to be more accurate (in terms of both precision and recall) than the baseline of using EEG based detection alone.

The Caltech 101 image search experiments clearly demonstrated how the C3Vision architecture was able to improve on image identification over chance or even just using EEG detection alone (Wang et al. 2009b). The results were quantified in terms of their average precision (AP), a metric commonly used in information retrieval, and which approximates the area under the precision recall curve (Wang et al. 2009b). For example, the full system achieved 69.1% AP for one subject searching for Dalmatians, as compared to 33.73% when using EEG interest detection alone, and 1.76% for chance. The precision recall curves for this particular case are shown in Fig. 9.7A, with Fig. 9.7B illustrating how the density of target images was increased using the full architecture (bottom panel) versus simply using the EEG scoring (top panel). Overall, the combined EEG-pattern discovery module showed significant improvement in eight of the twelve trials (4 subjects searching for 3 target categories), with AP's in those cases ranging between 25–69% (mean: 42.5%). By comparison, chance levels were 1.76% (Dalmatian), 2.26% (Starfish), 5.11% (Chandelier/Menorah), and the average APs for the EEG detection alone was 15.7%. Furthermore, even in cases where the EEG detection was below 10% AP, the label refinement process was still able to significantly improve the image annotation accuracy.

---

[2]In practice, the value of ϵ is set dynamically to achieve a fixed-number l of EEG positive labels, i.e. $\sum_i y_i = l$.

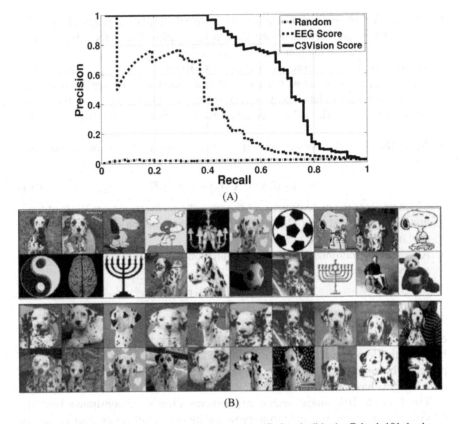

Fig. 9.7 Results for image retrieval for the object class "Dalmatian" in the Caltech 101 database. (**A**) Precision-recall curves for random sampling, retrieval using the EEG interest score alone and the results using EEG + the computer vision based transductive graph (i.e. C3Vision). Note that the C3Vision case results in a >5× increase in recall while maintaining a 100% precision, over the EEG score ranking alone. (**B**) Top 20 images for one subject, showing (a) ranking by interest scores from EEG detector; (b) ranking by scores after label refinement in transductive graph. Adapted from Wang et al. (2009b)

9.5 Conclusions

The C3Vision framework we describe has potentially many applications in multimedia search and image retrieval. However there are several technical challenges that remain. The results we have described have investigated essentially feedforward one-pass processing, namely there is no feedback between the computer vision system and human (or vice versa). However more recent work by our group has shown that feedback can be used to improve the precision of retrieval, though this comes at the cost of also changing the prevalence of objects of interest in the sample and thus the potential magnitude of the neural target related signal (e.g. P300). More generally, the issue of feedback brings up the interesting problem of co-learning. The human subject, the computer vision system and the EEG decoder can all potentially adapt in a feedback loop and we are currently investigating co-learning strategies which will improve convergence to high precision recall.

Our approach in developing C3Vision has been to leverage the complementary strengths of rapid, general-purpose scene analysis by humans and the ability of computers to process vast amounts of information. Unique to our approach is that we create an interface between the two vision systems via real-time EEG-based communication channel. A current challenge in BCI system design is that state-of-the-art decoding enables relatively low bit rates—40–60 bits per minute—far below what other communication mediums might offer. For BCI's which focus on assisting those with neurological disease and disability, particularly those that look to assist people that are "locked-in", such a low bandwidth channel is better than no channel at all and thus can substantially improve quality of life. However if BCI systems are going to make an impact in applications in which users are essentially neurologically healthy individuals, then the low bit rate channel of EEG must be exploited with some ingenuity. For example, in our BCI applications, we are looking at ways in which the bits that we can obtain via the EEG channel are very difficult to measure from other channels, for example by monitoring behavior via eye-tracking and/or button/keyboard responses. Future work will continue to investigate approaches that exploit this low bandwidth channel in ways that give us access to information about otherwise latent cognitive states of the user.

Acknowledgements This research was funded by DARPA (contract NBCHC080029). The views, opinions, and/or findings contained in this document are those of the authors and should not be interpreted as representing the official views or policies, either expressed or implied, of the Defense Advanced Research Projects Agency or the Department of Defense. Aerial images are provided by DigiGlobe.

References

Bigdely-Shamlo N, Vankov A, Ramirez RR, Makeig S (2008) Brain activity-based image classification from rapid serial visual presentation. IEEE Trans Neural Syst Rehabil Eng 16(5):432–441. DOI 10.1109/TNSRE.2008.2003381

Fei-Fei L, Fergus R, Perona R (2004) Learning generative visual models from few training examples: An incremental Bayesian approach tested on 101 object categories. In: IEEE CVPR 2004, Workshop on Generative-Model Based Vision

Gerson A, Parra L, Sajda P (2005) Cortical origins of response time variability during rapid discrimination of visual objects. Neuroimage 28(2):342–353

Gerson AD, Parra LC, Sajda P (2006) Cortically-coupled computer vision for rapid image search. IEEE Trans Neural Syst Rehabil Eng 14:174–179

Gladwell M (2005) Blink: The Power of Thinking Without Thinking. Little, Brown and Company: Time Warner Book Group, New York

Kapoor A, Shenoy P, Tan D (2008) Combining brain computer interfaces with vision for object categorization. In: Proc IEEE Conference on Computer Vision and Pattern Recognition CVPR 2008, pp 1–8. DOI 10.1109/CVPR.2008.4587618

Keysers C, Xiao DK, Foldiak P, Perrett D (2001) The speed of sight. J Cogn Neurosci 13(1):90–101

Linden D (2005) The P300: Where in the brain is it produced and what does it tell us? Neuroscientist 11(6):563–576

Makeig S, Westerfield M, Jung TP, Covington J, Townsend J, Sejnowski T, Courchesne E (1999) Independent components of the late positive response complex in a visual spatial attention task. J Neurosci 19:2665–2680

Oliva A (2005) Gist of the scene. In: Encyclopedia of Neurobiology of Attention. Elsevier, San Diego, CA, pp 251–256

Parra L, Christoforou C, Gerson A, Dyrholm M, Luo A, Wagner M, Philiastides M, Sajda P (2008) Spatiotemporal linear decoding of brain state: Application to performance augmentation in high-throughput tasks. IEEE Signal Process Mag 25(1):95–115

Parra LC, Spence CD, Gerson AD, Sajda P (2005) Recipes for the linear analysis of EEG. Neuroimage 28(2):326–341

Sajda P, Parra L, Christoforou C, Hanna B, Bahlmann C, Wang J, Pohlmeyer E, Dmochowski J, Chang SF (2010) In a blink of an eye and a switch of a transistor: Cortically-coupled computer vision. Proceedings of the IEEE 98(3):462–478

Thorpe S, Fize D, Marlot C (1996) Speed of processing in the human visual system. Nature 381:520–522

Wang J, Jebara T, Chang SF (2008) Graph transduction via alternating minimization. In: International Conference on Machine Learning (ICML)

Wang J, Jaing YG, Chang SF (2009a) Label diagnosis through self tuning for web image search. In: IEEE Computer Society Conference on Computer Vision and Pattern Recognition (CVPR), Miami Beach, Florida, USA

Wang J, Pohlmeyer E, Hanna B, Jiang YG, Sajda P, Chang SF (2009b) Brain state decoding for rapid image retrieval. In: ACM MultiMedia, Beijing, China, pp 945–954

Chapter 10
Brain-Computer Interfacing and Games

**Danny Plass-Oude Bos, Boris Reuderink, Bram van de Laar,
Hayrettin Gürkök, Christian Mühl, Mannes Poel, Anton Nijholt,
and Dirk Heylen**

Abstract Recently research into Brain-Computer Interfacing (BCI) applications for healthy users, such as games, has been initiated. But why would a healthy person use a still-unproven technology such as BCI for game interaction? BCI provides a combination of information and features that no other input modality can offer. But for general acceptance of this technology, usability and user experience will need to be taken into account when designing such systems. Therefore, this chapter gives an overview of the state of the art of BCI in games and discusses the consequences of applying knowledge from Human-Computer Interaction (HCI) to the design of BCI for games. The integration of HCI with BCI is illustrated by research examples and showcases, intended to take this promising technology out of the lab. Future

D. Plass-Oude Bos (✉) · B. Reuderink · B. van de Laar · H. Gürkök · C. Mühl · M. Poel · A. Nijholt · D. Heylen
Human Media Interaction, University of Twente, Faculty of EEMCS, P.O. Box 217, 7500 AE, Enschede, The Netherlands
e-mail: d.plass@ewi.utwente.nl

B. Reuderink
e-mail: b.reuderink@ewi.utwente.nl

B. van de Laar
e-mail: b.l.a.vandelaar@ewi.utwente.nl

H. Gürkök
e-mail: h.gurkok@ewi.utwente.nl

C. Mühl
e-mail: c.muehl@ewi.utwente.nl

M. Poel
e-mail: m.poel@ewi.utwente.nl

A. Nijholt
e-mail: a.nijholt@ewi.utwente.nl

D. Heylen
e-mail: d.k.j.heylen@ewi.utwente.nl

D.S. Tan, A. Nijholt (eds.), *Brain-Computer Interfaces,*
Human-Computer Interaction Series,
DOI 10.1007/978-1-84996-272-8_10, © Springer-Verlag London Limited 2010

research needs to move beyond feasibility tests, to prove that BCI is also applicable in realistic, real-world settings.

10.1 Introduction

Brain-computer interfacing (BCI) research has been motivated for years by the wish to provide paralyzed people with new communication and motor abilities, so that they can once again interact with the outside world. During the last couple of years, BCI research has been moving into applications for healthy people. Reasons for this range from providing applications to increase quality of life to the commercial benefits of such a large target group (Nijholt et al. 2008a). The area of games, especially, receives a lot of interest, as gamers are often among the first to adopt any new technology (Nijholt and Tan 2007). They are willing to put the effort into learning to work with it, if it may eventually provide some advantage. Besides, a large part of the general population plays games, little though it may be. As these abled users have many other interaction modalities at their command, they have a lot more requirements for such an interface than the people for which this is the only option to interact with the external world. Brain-computer interaction is slower and less accurate than most modalities that are currently available. Furthermore, BCIs often require a lot of training. Why would a healthy person want to use BCI in games?

Current BCI games are often just proofs of concept, where a single BCI paradigm is the only possible means of control, such as moving a paddle in the game Pong to the left or right with imaginary movement of the hands (Krepki et al. 2007). These BCIs are weak replacements for traditional input devices such as the mouse and keyboard: they cannot achieve the same speed and precision. The information transfer rate (ITR) of BCIs is still around up to 25 bits per minute (Wolpaw et al. 2002), which is incomparable with keyboard speeds of over 300 characters per minute.[1] Due to these limitations, there is still a big gap between these research games and games developed by the games industry at this time.

Current (commercial) games provide a wide range of interactions: with your avatar in the virtual world, with other gamers and non-player characters, as well as with objects in the game environment. This is also reflected in the game controllers for popular consoles. For example, the PlayStation® DualShock™ 3 controller has fourteen buttons, two analog thumb-controlled mini-joysticks plus motion-sensing functionality. The Nintendo® Wiimote™ has ten buttons, can sense acceleration along three axes and contains an optical sensor for pointing. Apparently this still provides too few interaction possibilities, as this controller is often combined with a nunchuck, which has an analog stick, two additional buttons, and another accelerometer.

---

[1]Due to different ITR measures used in BCI, a comparison between keyboard and BCI is hard to make. The entropy of written English text is estimated to be as low as 1.3 bit per symbol (Cover and Thomas, 2006, page 174). A rate of 300 characters per minute would therefore correspond to roughly 400 bits per minute.

Although a large number of inputs is needed for interaction with games nowadays, this also poses a problem. The more input options you have, the more of an effort it is to learn and remember what each input is for. Even the options that are currently provided may not be sufficient for what developers envision for rich interaction in future games. To make it easier for the gamer, companies and research groups are very interested in more natural methods of interaction. If the gamer can interact with the game world in a way similar to the real world, then learnability and memorability may no longer be an issue. The popularity of motion sensors in current game controllers reflects this, as they enable gamers to make gestures that should come naturally with whatever it is that they would like to do in the game. Microsoft®'s Project Natal is a prime example of this movement towards natural interaction, using gestures, speech, and even real-world objects (Microsoft® 2009).

We can take this trend towards natural interaction one step further. Like our thoughts, computer games do not take place in the real world, and are not constrained to what is physically possible. Therefore, it would make sense to express ourselves directly in the game world, without mediation of physically limited bodily actions. The BCI can bypass this bodily mediation—a fact well appreciated by those Amyotrophic Lateral Sclerosis (ALS) patients who now have the ability to communicate with others and their environment despite their full paralysis—enabling the gamers to express themselves more directly, and more naturally given a game context.

As an example, consider the following. Even though we know there is no such thing as magic, in a game world we have no problem with the idea and possibility of casting spells. Although our minds readily accept these new abilities because we are confined to interacting via the real world, we have to press buttons to make things happen in the super-realistic world of the game. If, however, the game were to have access to our brain activity, then perhaps it would be possible to interact with the game world in ways that would be realistic considering the rules of that particular environment. Being able to merge in such a way with the super-realism of the game world should increase presence (Witmer and Singer 1998), but also memorability as the relations between user action and in-game action become more direct. However, using a BCI to bypass physical interaction may seem unnatural, as we are used to converting our thoughts into bodily actions. The implication is that when using brain activity directly, one needs to be more aware of this activity and to develop new levels of control.

Developing control over brain signals is as necessary when signals are used passively to enhance the game experience, for example, by guiding the player towards a state of flow (Csikszentmihalyi 1990). From brain activity the user's mental state can be derived, which makes it possible for applications to respond to this state. When the mental state is known, it can be manipulated via the game to keep the user in equilibrium, where skill and challenge are well matched (see Fig. 10.1). Alternatively, the game could incorporate the user's mood into the story, for example by the appropriate adaptation of interactions with non-player characters (NPCs).

Summarized, to make BCI an acceptable interaction modality for healthy users, it should enhance the user experience by offering something that current interaction modalities do not. Brain activity can provide information that no other input

Fig. 10.1 Flow diagram,
based on Csikszentmihalyi
(1990)

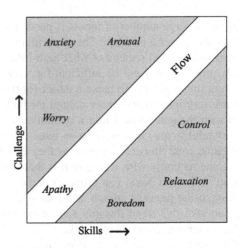

modality can, in a way that comes with its own unique features. Like speech it is hands-free, but as no external expression is required, the interaction is private. And similar to the way in which exertion interfaces that require physical effort will make you more fit, the use of specific BCI paradigms could make you more relaxed and focused. This, in turn, could result in higher intelligence, and better coping with stress (Doppelmayr et al. 2002; Tyson 1987). The following sections will discuss what can be learned from current BCI research prototypes and commercial applications and how BCI can be applied in such a way that it does not violate the usability of the system but actually improves the interaction. Cases and ideas from our own research at the Human Media Interaction (HMI) group at the University of Twente will be provided as concrete examples.

10.2 The State of the Art

The first BCI game was created by Vidal (1977). In this game, the user can move in four directions in a maze, by fixating on one of four fixation points displayed off-screen. A diamond-shaped checkerboard is periodically flashed between the four points, resulting in neural activity on different sites of the primary visual cortex. Using an online classification method, this visually evoked potential (VEP) is recognized, and used to move in the maze. Despite being the first game, its performance is remarkable with an information transfer rate (ITR) of above 170 bits/min on average. Using online artifact rejection and adaptive classification, the approach used by Vidal was far ahead of its time. Much lower ITRs of 10–25 bits per minute are often reported as the state of the art in reviews (Wolpaw et al. 2002). One reason to not include Vidal in these overviews could be that the operation of this BCI depends the ability to make eye movements.

A much simpler approach to integrate brain signals in games is based on the interpretation of broadband frequency power of the brain, such as the alpha, beta, gamma and mu-rhythm. A classic example is Brainball (Hjelm et al. 2000; Hjelm 2003), a game that can be best described as an anti-game. Using a headband, the EEGs of the two players is measured and a relaxation score is derived from the ratio between the alpha and beta activity in the EEG signal. The relaxation score is used to move a steel ball across the table away from the most relaxed player; when the ball is almost at the opponent's side, and players realize they are winning, then get excited and lose. Another example we would like to mention is the experiment of Pope and Palsson (2001), in which children with attention deficit hyperactive disorder (ADHD) were treated using neurofeedback. One group used standard neurofeedback, another group played Sony Playstation™ video games where the controller input was modulated by a neurofeedback system developed by NASA; correct brain-wave patterns were rewarded with a more responsive controller. Other neurofeedback games are listed in the overview in Table 10.1. Characteristic of these neurofeedback games is that the player has to discover how to control aspects of brain activity to play the game. Mastering control over brain signals is often the goal of the game, as opposed to using a BCI as an input device similar to a gamepad or a joystick. While conceptually simple, neurofeedback games do aim at providing a user experience that cannot be provided using other modalities.

In contrast to neurofeedback games, motor-control based BCIs are often used as (traditional) input devices. For example, Pineda et al. (2003) used the mu-rhythm power on the motor cortices to steer a first person shooter game, while forward/backward movement was controlled using physical buttons. No machine learning was involved; the four subjects were trained for 10 hours over the course of five weeks, and learned to control their mu-power. Another movement controlled BCI game is the Pacman game by Krepki et al. (2007). The detection of movement is based on the lateralized readiness potential (LRP), a slow negative shift in the electroencephalogram (EEG) that develops over the activated motor cortex starting some time before the actual movement onset. In this game, Pacman makes one step each 1.5–2 seconds, and moves straight until it reaches a wall or receives a turn command. Users report they sometimes had the feeling that Pacman moves in the correct direction before the user was consciously aware of this decision. This indicates a new level of interaction that can be enabled only by a BCI.

Both the neurofeedback and the motor controlled games use BCIs based on induced activations, meaning that the user can initiate actions without depending on stimuli from the game. Evoked responses, on the other hand, where the application measures the response to a stimulus, require a tight coupling between the game that presents the stimuli and the BCI.

An example of a evoked response is the P300, an event related potential (ERP) that occurs after a rare, task-relevant stimulus is presented. Bayliss used a P300 BCI in both a virtual driving task and a virtual apartment (Bayliss 2003; Bayliss et al. 2004). In the virtual apartment, objects were highlighted using a red translucent sphere, evoking a P300 when the object the user wanted to select was highlighted. A more low-level evoked paradigm is based on steady-state visually evoked potentials (SSVEPs), where attention to a visual stimulus with a certain frequency is measured as a modulation of the same frequency in the visual cortex. In

Table 10.1 Overview of BCI games. Work is sorted by paradigm: F represents feedback games, in which the user has to adapt the power of the different rhythms of his brain, M stands for recognition of motor tasks, including motor planning, imaginary and real movement, P300 is the P300 response to task relevant stimuli and VEPs are visually evoked potentials. In the sensors column, E indicates EEG sensors, O indicates the use of EOG measurements, and M indicates EMG measurements. The number of (EEG) sensors is indicated in column NS, the number of classes for control is listed in the NC column. The last column contains the accuracy of recognition. Due to differences in the number of classes and trial lengths, these accuracies cannot be used to compare individual studies

Work	Type	Paradigm	Sensors	NS	NC	A
Lee et al. (2006)	Game	?	invasive			
Wang et al. (2007)	Game	?	E			
Sobell and Trivich (1989)	Visualization	F	E			
Nelson et al. (1997)	Game	F	E, M			
Allanson and Mariani (1999)	Game	F	E			
Cho et al. (2002)	Virtual reality	F	E	3	2	
Tschuor (2002)	Visualization	F	E	32	2	85%
Hjelm (2003), Hjelm et al. (2000)	Game	F	E			
Palke (2004)	Game	F	E	1		
Mingyu et al. (2005)	Game	F	E	3	1D	
Kaul (2006)	Visualization	F	E, M, O	3		
Lin and John (2006)	Game	F	E	1		
Shim et al. (2007)	Game	F	E	4	2	
Lotte et al. (2008)	Game	F/M	E	1	2	
Vidal (1977)	Game	VEP	E	5	5	80%
Middendorf et al. (2000)	Game	VEP	E	2	3	88%
Bayliss and Ballard (2000)	Virtual reality	P300	E		2	85%
Bayliss (2003)	Virtual reality	P300	E	5	2	
Bayliss et al. (2004)	Virtual reality	P300	E	7	2	85%
Lalor et al. (2004, 2005)	Game	VEP	E	2	2	80%
Martinez et al. (2007)	Game	VEP	E	6	5	96%
Finke et al. (2009)	Game	P300	E	10	2	66%
Jackson et al. (2009)	Game	VEP	E	2	4	50%
Pineda et al. (2003)	Game	M	E	3	1D	
Leeb et al. (2004)	Virtual reality	M	E	4	2	98%
Leeb and Pfurtscheller (2004)	Virtual reality	M	E		2	
Mason et al. (2004)	Game	M	E	12	2	97%
Leeb et al. (2005)	Virtual reality	M	E	6	2	92%
Kayagil et al. (2007)	Game	M	E	1	4	77%
Krepki et al. (2007)	Game	M	E	128	2	100%
Scherer et al. (2007)	Game	M	E, M, O	3	2 + 2	
Bussink (2008)	Game	M	E	32	4	45%
Lehtonen et al. (2008)	Game	M	E	6	2	74%
Oude Bos and Reuderink (2008)	Game	M	E	32	3	
Zhao et al. (2009)	Game	M	E	5	4	75%
Tangermann et al. (2009)	Game	M	E	64	2	

the MindBalance game by Lalor et al. (2004, 2005), a SSVEP is evoked by two different checkerboards, inverting at 17 Hz and 20 Hz. The attention focused on one of the checkerboards is used to balance an avatar on a cord in a complex 3D environment. One advantage of the evoked responses over induced BCI paradigms is that it allows easy selection of one out of multiple options by focussing attention on a stimulus. For example, a 2D racing game with four different directional controls using SSVEP was created by Martinez et al. (2007), and in a similar fashion a shooter was controlled in Jackson et al. (2009).

We have seen a series of games based on neurofeedback, games based on the imagination of movement, and games based on evoked potentials. Of these BCI paradigms, the neurofeedback games exploit the unique information a BCI can provide best. For example, Brainball uses relaxation both as game goal, and as means of interaction. Using traditional input modalities this game simply could not exist. In contrast, BCI games that are based on evoked potentials replace physical buttons with virtual, attention activated triggers which do not change the game mechanics significantly. These games could be improved by using evoked potentials to measure the state of the user, and use the state as new information source as opposed to as a button. By assigning a meaning to the mental action of concentrating on a game element, for example devouring a bacteria in Bacteria Hunt (Mühl et al. 2010), the user state itself becomes part of the game mechanics. The same holds for games using imagined movement. These games replace movement to interact with buttons with (slow) imagined movement, without adding much other than novelty.

While interesting, most of the BCI games are proofs of concept. The speed of these games is often decreased to allow for BCI control, reducing fast-paced games into turn-based games. In recent publications we see a trend towards more fine-grained control in games using BCI interfaces, Zhao et al. (2009) and Jackson et al. (2009) focus on smooth, application specific interpretation of BCI control signals. The role of precise timing is also gaining attention, as shown in a pinball experiment of Tangermann et al. (2009). We now need to continue this trend to move beyond feasibility tests, and focus on the role that BCI can play in improving the gaming experience.

10.3 Human-Computer Interaction for BCI

While BCI has until recently been an exploratory field of research, it might be profitable to take some insights from Human Computer Interaction (HCI) into account. Of course, fundamental research on hardware, signal processing, machine learning and neurophysiology are a prerequisite for a BCI. However, advances in the usability area are a direction of research that might be just as important for the acceptance and widespread usage of BCIs. In this section we will look at learnability, memorability, efficiency and effectiveness, error handling, and satisfaction, which are the main concepts of usability according to Nielsen (1993). We will look at the most relevant guidelines in these concepts and elaborate on them in the context of BCI games.

10.3.1 Learnability and Memorability

In HCI, one of the most important aspects of a software program or interface is how intuitive it is in its usage. Learnability is defined by ISO 9126 as the effort that is required to learn the application (International Organization for Standardization 1991). Is a user able to use it straight out of the box, or is training needed to use the interface? Memorability is closely related to learnability and deals with remembering an interface (Nielsen 1996). Obviously, when an interface is intuitive and easier to learn, the user will also remember the interface better.

Concerning BCIs, one needs to separate different forms of training that are often needed for use of the BCI, namely training the user to use the right mental task to control the game (interface training), training the user to reliably perform the mental tasks (user training), and training a BCI system to recognize user specific brain signals (system training).

User training is an important factor for getting users to start working with a BCI. As performing a mental task to communicate with a computer is new for most people and as the mental tasks are also new for everybody, it has to be made clear to the users what is expected of them if they want to use a BCI. One illustrative example of this is when using a Motor-Imagery-based BCI. A user is told to imagine movements of his hands for example. But to a lot of naive users it is unclear what is actually meant by imagining. Should they visualize the movement? Should they feel their hand moving? Or should they see someone else's hand moving? Most of the time the sensation of moving ones hand is preferred, as this elicits the event-related desynchronization (ERD) often used as a feature for detecting this mental task (McFarland et al. 2000).

It is certain that for research and comparison of BCIs, all users need to perform the mental task in the same way, id est, they need to be thoroughly and consistently instructed. For more practical applications, this may as well be important. Users might not overcome the first step of performing the mental task in the right way and lose motivation because the BCI is not working properly. It is known from literature that some users are unable to use certain paradigms—this is called BCI illiteracy (Guger et al. 2003), see also Chapter 3 of this Volume. One reason for this problem might be the way in which the relevant part of the cortex is folded in relation to the scalp (Nijholt et al. 2008b). However, user training can be used to overcome some types of BCI illiteracy, namely, those related to incorrect execution of the task by the user. Training to perform the wanted brain activity consistently, for example using feedback, can help to improve performance (Hwang et al. 2009). Of course user training can be a tedious process, especially because performance can sometimes decrease instead of increase (Galán et al. 2007). Moreover, it is important to keep the user motivated through the process. To keep the user motivation high and the task clear, an intuitive mapping from mental task to in-game action is vital. One example of such an intuitive mapping is explained on page 168. The intuitive mapping of the state of relaxation to the shape of the player's avatar is helping the users use this modality to their advantage. This type of BCI is of a more passive one. Very little or no training at all is needed to use the system. This is often the case with passive BCI's as opposed to active BCI's (see also Chapter 11 of this Volume).

One promising way to combine different techniques is the so-called online "on-the-job" training (Vidaurre et al. 2006). Users get clear instructions how to perform a certain task while at the same time the BCI system gathers data to train its classifier. For games, this online training might consist of some tutorial in which the game itself is explained, or in which the users play some kind of minigame.

10.3.2 Efficiency and Effectiveness

As seen in Sections 10.1 and 10.2, the speed and accuracy of active BCIs (the user intentionally makes an action) does not yet even approach that of traditional game controllers. The advantage of using a BCI for direct control should then be in something other than efficiency (doing things with the least amount of effort). In this case the BCI should not be a replacement for using the keyboard and/or mouse. So if the efficiency cannot be high enough because of technical limitations, the effectiveness (doing the right things) could be higher. In other words: a BCI application should give the user the feeling that the BCI has an added value. In the design of a game, one could think of certain bonuses when using a BCI, or relieving the user of some extra buttons to push by performing this task through the BCI.

However, the low transfer and high error rates are not so much a problem for passive BCIs that try to estimate the user state (Zander et al. 2009). This information is acquired without the active participation of the user and can be used to derive meta-information about the context in which the HCI takes place. Applications can adapt the way they present information or react to user input depending on the users' psychological state in terms of attention, workload, or emotion. A specific example of such a user state sensed by passive BCIs is reaction on machine or user errors, as we will see in the next section.

10.3.3 Error Handling

As with the majority of modalities in HCI that try to extract information from the human body, BCI is one of the modalities that has a fairly high level of error rates. As can be seen in Section 10.2, error rates are typically around 25% and more. When we also consider users that can make errors, error handling becomes an important factor in designing games which use BCI.

Error handling consists of two parts: error prevention and error correction. Error prevention consists of taking measures to prevent an error of ever happening. Within the context of BCI this can be done by applying better classification algorithms, smoothing, hysteresis and artifact filtering (see page 169).

For this section error, correction is of particular interest. With the use of error related negativity (ERN) it is possible to detect that a user is conscious of his error and undo the previous movement (Ferrez and Millán 2008). One way to implement this in the design of a game is to use it as a "rewind" function which breaks the strict timeline often incorporated into games. This calls for creative game design but can also lead to more immersive games. The user can interact with the game in a completely different way. This kind of interaction might even be applied without the user being aware of it: at some point the user will be conscious of his fault and the BCI will have recognized it already. In other applications it can be used as a more classical method of error correction and/or improve the system's perceived accuracy.

10.3.4 Satisfaction

Satisfaction is often said to be heavily influenced by acceptance and success of the system (Rushinek and Rushinek 1986; Goodwin 1987) which can be attributed to the system's effectiveness and efficiency. Of course, there are also social aspects and the personal preferences of the user involved (Lucas 1975; Ives et al. 1983; Hiltz and Johnson 1990).

In the context of BCI games we can consider satisfaction to be the end result of all of the design choices that were made, the functionality of the game, the ease with which the user could learn and memorize the control of the BCI and with what accuracy they could control the game. In other words, satisfaction can be seen as everything the user experienced during the game.

The user satisfaction after playing a game can be measured, for example, by using a post-game questionnaire (IJsselsteijn et al. 2008) for quantitative, or by interviewing the user for a more qualitative, analysis. Both can lead to interesting findings on the BCI game. For an example of a quantitative analysis, in van de Laar et al. (2009) it was found that users liked the challenge of imagining movements, but were also quickly mentally tired by performing this task.

Besides using the quite reliable method of administering questionnaires to measure the user experience, an interesting possibility to measure certain parts of the user experience is to let the BCI itself measure whether the user is satisfied or not. In Garcia Molina et al. (2009) it is shown that certain moods can be recognized. Especially if the system then adapts itself, depending on what the user feels, such a kind of feedback loops can be helpful in creating a satisfying user experience. This system might be able to make certain choices in HCI design or in the machine learning and classifying techniques it uses, specific for every user. This might open up completely new ways of playing and interacting with games. In turn, this would lead to user-specific games with fine-tuned parameters for different aspects of the game. With such a great feature implemented, BCI games will have an advantage over traditional games which will boost acceptance and popularity.

10.4 BCI for Controlling and Adapting Games

So far in this chapter we have discussed BCI games generally in the context of HCI research. In this section we would like to narrow the focus down to the research conducted and applications developed within our research team at the Human Media Interaction research group of the University of Twente. We will touch on the critical issues of user experience, affective BCI games, BCI for controlling games, intuitiveness and multi-modality in BCI games.

10.4.1 User Experience

Today, BCI research is still investigating the extent of the performance this technique can achieve. A lot of research effort is spent on improving speed and accuracy, but in spite of the many BCI applications created for healthy people, the HCI aspect of them is still often overlooked. As already stated in the previous section, how the user feels about using a particular BCI paradigm, and about using it for a particular task, can have a great influence on the acceptance of this new technology.

BCIs for healthy users have to deal with a different environment, and therefore different challenges, different from BCIs for patients. Differences in the environment can be split into the effect the environment has on external user behaviour during gameplay (moving, shouting, sweating), and more internal effects (changes in the user state due to the game, such as, frustration, boredom or anger).

In our research group, a simple platform has been developed to test and demonstrate BCI in a game environment. BrainBasher, as this setup is called, was initially used to compare the user experience for keyboard interaction with imaginary-movement control (Oude Bos and Reuderink 2008). More recently, it was used to compare imaginary and actual movement as paradigms to control the game (van de Laar et al. 2009). See the case description below:

10.4.1.1 Application: BrainBasher

In 2008, we conducted research to find out what the differences were in user experience and in performance, between real and imagined movement in a BCI game. This was one of the first BCI studies in which not only the speed and accuracy of the paradigms used was considered, but also the user's affect through the use of a post-game questionnaire. The BCI game used for this research was BrainBasher (Oude Bos and Reuderink 2008). The goal of this game is to perform specific brain actions as quickly as possible. For each correct and detected action you score a point.

The goal is to score as many points as possible within the limited amount of time. For the actual-movement task users must lay both hands on the desk in front of them. When the appropriate stimulus appears they have to perform a simple tapping movement with their whole hand. When performing the imagined movement task, users are instructed to imagine (feeling) the same movement, without actually using any of their muscles.

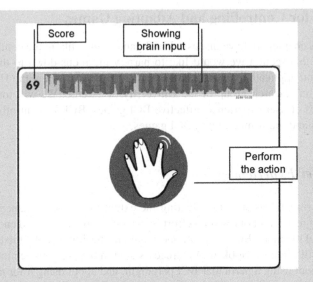

A screen capture of a BrainBasher game session, showing the score, the current target task, and feedback on previous and current brain activity.

Twenty healthy persons participated as test subjects in this study. The average age across the group was 26.8 years, 50% was male and 50% was female.

Our experiment consisted of two conditions: actual movement and imagined movement. The order of performing actual and imagined movement was randomly assigned for each subject respecting equal groups for each order. Each part consisted of one training session, in order to create a user-specific classifier, followed by one game session, after which the subject filled in a user experience questionnaire. This questionnaire was designed based on the Game Experience Questionnaire (GEQ) developed at the Game Experience Lab in Eindhoven (IJsselsteijn et al. 2008).

Results show that differences in user experience and in performance between actual and imagined movement in BCI gaming do exist. Actual movement produces a more reliable signal while the user stays more alert. On the other hand, imagined movement is more challenging.

10.4.2 Passive BCI and Affect-Based Game Adaptation

Despite the increasing numbers of controller buttons and various ways to provide input to the computer, HCI in its common form is a highly asymmetrical exchange of information between user and machine (Hettinger et al. 2003). While the computer is able to convey a multitude of information, users are rather limited in their possibilities to provide input. Specifically, the flexible incorporation of information on contextual factors, such as the users' affective or cognitive states, into the interaction remains difficult. Such flexibility might be seen as one of the hallmarks of a natural interaction between humans, and would add great value when available in HCI, in particular to improve the user experience. For example, when humans are playing together, one can realize that the other is bored or frustrated and subsequently adapt their behaviour accordingly to motivate the other player again.

There are multiple ways to optimize user experience in games. Saari et al. (2009) introduce the term "psychological customization" and suggest the manipulation of the story line or the presentation of games to realize a user-specific affective adaptation. Knowledge about the user profile, task and context can be used to regulate the flow of emotions as narrative experiences, to avoid or limit negative emotions harmful to user experience (or health), to respond to observed emotional states (e.g., to maintain challenge), or to deliberately create new combinations of emotional, psychological states and behaviour. For the online adaptation to the user during the game, however, a reliable and robust estimation of the affective user state is imperative. Unfortunately, despite their increasing computational capacities and sensory equipment (camera and microphone), modern computers are limited in their capability to identify and to respond appropriately to the user state.

Some applications try to take user states into account using indirect measures, mostly behavioural indicators of efficiency. Examples are speed boosts for players that are fallen behind in racing games ("rubber banding"), to keep them engaged, or the adaptation of number and strength of opponents in first person shooter games according to the performance of the player. These techniques make assumptions about the relation between in-game performance and user states. And while these assumptions might hold most of the time and for most of the users, they are only rough estimations and can lead to misinterpretations of user states. Such behavioural estimates could be complemented by more direct methods of user state estimation.

10.4.2.1 User State Estimation

The automatic recognition of affective user states is one of the main goals of the field of affective computing (Picard 1997), and great efforts have led to promising results for user state estimation via behavioural and physiological signals. The principal possibility of deriving information about affective user states was shown for visible and audible behaviour (Zeng et al. 2007). Alternatively, and especially in the absence of overt behaviour, one can observe physiological responses of the user, for example heart rate, respiration, or perspiration to derive the user's affective state (Picard et al. 2001; Benovoy et al. 2008; Kim and André 2008). Interestingly, it was shown that game-related user states, such as boredom, flow, and frustration, can be differentiated via physiological sensors (van Reekum et al. 2004; Mandryk et al. 2006; Chanel et al. 2008; Nacke and Lindley 2008; Tijs et al. 2009). However, all of those measurements are indirect and thus potentially modulated by a number of factors. Behaviour, for example, can be scarce in HCI or biased due to the (social) context. Physiological signals are influenced by exercise, caffeine and other factors. Neuro-physiological sensor modalities on the other hand, while not being free of those influences, enable a more direct recording of affective experience.

Affective neuro-science has shown the capability of EEG to discriminate between affective states (Davidson 1992; Müller et al. 1999; Keil et al. 2001; Marosi et al. 2002; Aftanas et al. 2004). These neural correlates of affective processes are explained and predicted by cognitive appraisal theories (e.g. Sander et al. 2005). These associations between EEG and affective processes suggest the viability of neurophysiology-based affect classification. Accordingly, several studies showed that such a classification is in principle possible (Chanel et al. 2006, 2009; Lin et al. 2009). Chanel et al. (2006) even showed that EEG contributes additional information about the affective state to physiological sensor modalities, and that a fusion of both sensor modalities delivers the best classification performance.

It has to be noted that many of those (neuro-)physiological studies are still done in a very simple and controlled context. This has implications for the applicability of the techniques in a real-life context. As in other BCI fields, affective BCI also has to deal with artifacts and other noise sources in order to deliver robust and reliable measurements. Additionally, the complexity of affective and cognitive processes requires special care in design and analysis of such experiments inducing specific user states to ensure the validity of the induced states (van den Broek et al. 2009; Fairclough 2009). So, if measurements are to be collected in more realistic scenarios, the risk of possible confounds increases and endangers the reliability of the psychophysiological inferences intended.

Two fundamental issues associated with the reliability of affect classification are those of specificity and generality. That is, it is important to identify physiological markers or patterns that are specific to the target emotions (e.g., independent of the method of elicitation), but that general over different contexts (e.g., laboratory versus real world). Especially for neuro-physiological measures, the independence of measurements from a specific elicitation or the tasks participants are performing cannot be assumed. To test it, experiments could use carefully constructed multimodal stimuli (Mühl and Heylen 2009) to manipulate affective states via different stimulus modalities. On the other hand, a measurement of physiological correlates in the context of different tasks and environments might provide evidence for their context-independence. In this respect, computer games offer an interesting research tool to induce affective states, as they have the potential to immerse players into their world, leading to affective reactions.

10.4.2.2 Application: AlphaWoW

In Alpha-World of Warcraft (alphaWoW) affective signals couple the mood of the player to her avatar in an immersive game environment. Alpha activity recorded over the parietal lobe is used to control one aspect of the game character, while conventional controls are still used for the rest.

World of Warcraft® is a very popular massively-multiplayer online roleplaying game (Blizzard Entertainment®, Inc 2008). For our application, the user plays a druid who can shape-shift into animal forms. In bear form, with its thick skin, the druid is better protected from physical attacks, and is also quite the fighter with sharp claws and teeth.

In her normal elf form, she is much more fragile, but can cast effective spells for damage to knock out enemies from a distance as well as to heal herself. In alphaWoW, the shifting between these shapes is controlled by the user's alpha activity.

A user playing World of Warcraft using both conventional controls and brain activity to control her character in the game.

How changes in alpha activity are experienced by the user, depends on the location where the activity is measured. According to Cantero et al. (1999), high alpha activity measured over the parietal lobe is related to a relaxed alertness. This seems a beneficial state of mind for gaming, especially compared to drowsiness, which is said to be measured frontally. The premises for mapping alpha to shape-shifting in the game was that the opposite of this relaxed state would be some kind of sense of stress or agitation. Agitation would have a natural relation to the bear form, as the bear is eager to fight, whereas the relaxed alertness would be a good match for the mentally-adept night elf.

An example of a game that is used to induce mental states is the Affective Pacman game (Reuderink et al. 2009). This games induces frustration in users by manipulating the keyboard input and the visual output. During the experiment, users regularly rate their emotions on the valence, arousal and dominance dimensions (Morris 1995). In addition to these ratings, important events in the game—such as dying, scoring points and advancing a level—are all stored, and can be analyzed for correlations with the EEG and physiological sensors.

10.4.2.3 The Application of User State Estimates

Once the measurability and classifiability of specific psychological concepts, for example boredom, engagement and frustration, are shown in a context related to a specific application, the recognition technique can be integrated in a cybernetic control loop. The determination of the reaction of the application now allows the incorporation of the current user state. With models guiding the dynamic behaviour of the application according to the effect aimed for (potentially a specific user state or positive experiences in general), affective-BCI-enriched interaction could be a more natural, efficient, and enjoyable activity.

Combining behaviour dependent and independent indicators of user state might lead to more robust and more reliable state recognition and thus to more effective game adaptations. Affective BCI could qualify for such a system as a fast and sensitive method to directly measure affective states. Evidence for the value of the adaptation of game difficulty based on physiologically determined anxiety level was found by Liu et al. (2009) in the form of a reduced anxiety level, higher user satisfaction, increased feeling of challenge, and higher performance. A similar result was found in a study monitoring facial expressions to discriminate between positive and negative affective states (Obaid et al. 2008).

The neuro-physiological inference of the user's affective and cognitive state might also help to increase safety and efficiency in work environments. This particular perspective will be discussed in Chapter 12 of this Volume.

10.4.3 BCI as Game Controller

While using a BCI to measure mental state is the most valuable way to integrate BCIs in games—a new information source is tapped—a BCI can be useful as a traditional game controller. To act as a game controller, the predictions of the BCI need to be translated into meaningful commands in a way that enables fluent game play. This implies that commands have to operate at the correct time scale, are issued with minimal delays, and are invariant to changes in user state. We will now explore these implications in more detail.

10.4.3.1 The Time Scale of a BCI

The time scale on which commands are issued needs to be congruent with the game. For example, in slow-paced games, fewer commands are issued during a unit of time, and the BCI output can be interpreted in a similar slow fashion by filtering out the fast changes in the BCI output. A faster-paced game might require quick responses, and hence short spikes in output are required for control. The slow changes in the output would work counter-productively, as they would make the game biased to a specific action. Some BCI paradigms are inherently more suitable for slow games (sensorimotor-cortex rhythms), others are more suitable for fast-paced action (the lateralized readiness potential, LRP). See Table 10.2.

An example of a game that requires operation on a small timescale is Affective Pacman (see Application: Affective Pacman). Control in our Affective Pacman game is analyzed using the lateralized readiness potential (LRP). For this game, multiple commands are usually issued within one second. This requires a BCI that can respond quickly but is insensitive to changes that take place on the minute scale.

Table 10.2 Overview of BCI paradigms information transfer rates (ITR), and the timescale they operate on, sorted on latency. This table is based on the median values for the ITR and the latency from Tonet et al. (2008, Table 2). As LRP was not presented in the overview of Tonet et al., we used numbers from Krepki et al. (2007) to illustrate negative latencies. EMG was added as reference modality

Paradigm	ITR (bits/min)	Latency (sec)
LRP	20.	−0.120
P300	28.2	1.58
ERD/ERS	28.8	1.5
SSVEP	26.4	2.10
Sensorimotor cortex rhythms	16.8	2.20
SCP	3.6	65.75
(EMG)	(99.6)	(0.96)

Alternatively, AlphaWoW (see Application: AlphaWoW) is an example of a game that operates on a large time scale. Alpha power requires at least a few seconds to be measured accurately. Therefore the game is most sensitive to changes in this time range; faster and slower changes are attenuated. Due to its time scale, alpha activity is less fit for fast-paced commands.

In order to adapt the system to changes in brain activity that occur over a longer period of use, and also to individual differences in brain activity, z-score normalization is applied to the measured alpha band power values. As a result, even if a user has a tendency for, for example, high alpha values, they will still be able to change into a bear. This is because the system looks at changes relative to the observed situation. The game is sensitive to medium-term changes, and adjusts itself for long-term changes and differences between subjects.

In addition, short term changes—due to noise and artifacts—could result in frequent, involuntary shape shifting. In alphaWoW, three methods are applied to deal with this issue and make the interaction more deliberate: smoothing, hysteresis, and dwelling. With smoothing, the current value of alpha power is not only dependant on the latest measurement, but also on the two previous ones. However, the most recent band power value is still the most influential. This attenuates peaks caused by outliers. Hysteresis is applied to the mapping from alpha value to changing into elf or bear form. Alpha below a certain threshold results in a change to bear, and alpha above a certain level transforms the user into elf form. In between these levels no change occurs, giving the user some leeway, and only letting the more extreme values have an effect. Finally, the user also has to stay in the range of effect for a little while for the shape-shift to occur. This dwelling also reduces the effect of unintentional peaks in the values. Dwelling has not been applied to BCI before, but is not an unknown method for other interaction modalities, such as for pointing in gesture recognition (Müller-Tomfelde 2007). The combination of these measures make alphaWoW sensitive to intended changes, and robust against unintended short-term changes in the BCI output.

With alphaWoW, we have seen a few ways to adapt the time scale of the BCI to a game. Due to the nature of shape-shifting, small delays are not much of a problem in alphaWoW. But for other games, the latency will have a huge impact on gameplay. Some latency is inherent in BCI control, as the brain signals need to be observed over a period before they can be analyzed. But in some paradigms, such as the LRP for actual movement, preparation can be observed before the actual action takes place. These characteristics could be exploited for fluent gameplay, resulting in potentially *negative latencies* (Krepki et al. 2007). For slower paradigms, the only solution may be to backfit the command in the game history, resulting in only a visual delay, and not a semantic one. The translation of a working BCI to meaningful game commands will be the most challenging, and most import, aspect of building BCIs for games.

10.4.3.2 Influence of Mental State on BCI

A more complex challenge for BCI control is posed by the influence the content of the game can have on the mind of the player. It is very likely that the mental state of the player changes, as players often play games to relax, or are frustrated when they cannot win. This variability in user state cannot be eliminated, as it is the core of experiencing video games. The influence of mental state on BCIs is well known in the BCI community; changes in the ongoing EEG signal are often attributed to boredom (Blankertz et al. 2007). Boredom during training can be eliminated to a degree by making training part of the game environment. Frustration is another mental state that will occur frequently during game-play, for example, caused by a challenge that is too difficult, or due to a BCI controller that malfunctions. This makes the influence frustration has on the EEG signal a very relevant and interesting topic. It has also been proposed to use the influence emotions might have on measured brain activity to enhance BCI operation, for example, by using emotion-eliciting pictures as SSVEP stimuli (Garcia Molina et al. 2009).

10.4.3.3 Application: Affective Pacman

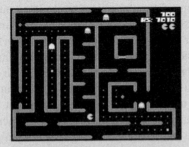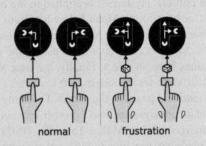

normal   frustration

Affective Pacman is a Pacman clone, controlled using only two buttons; one to turn clockwise, and one to turn counter clockwise. For short periods, the buttons act unreliable to induce frustration.

In our Affective Pacman game (Reuderink et al. 2009), we induced frustration in a Pacman game to measure the potential influence of frustration on BCI performance. Frustration was induced by simulating a malfunctioning keyboard for a few minutes, interspersed with periods of normal game control. Self assessments indicate more negative mental states during the frustration condition.

Results indicate increased BCI accuracy during the frustration condition for ERD/ERS based classification.[2] For the (better performing) LRP classification, no influence of frustration was found. User frustration does not seem to pose a problem for BCI operation, but more research is needed to investigate if this generalizes to other context and other BCI paradigms.

To counter the effect of boredom on the (necessary) training of BCI systems, the training can be made part of the game (Nijholt et al. 2009). During the start-up phase of the game, players can start playing using more traditional modalities such as keyboard and mouse. During this phase, the BCI collects training data, with ground-truth based on events in the game. A simple approach would be to use the key presses as ground truth for an actual-movement paradigm. The computer collects training data until a BCI can be trained with sufficient performance. BCI control is then enabled, while still allowing the user to continue playing with the keyboard. Slowly the influence of the keyboard can be decreased, until the player is playing using only the BCI. This approach keeps the online situation very similar to the training period, reducing the surface for generalization errors. More interesting game events can be used as well, for example, when the user casts spells by imagining (an EEG recognizable) spell, and subsequently presses the relevant button. This creates training data in a similar fashion, with EEG examples tied to ground truth (the button). When the BCI recognizes the spell successfully, the spell is cast before the button is pressed, again allowing a gentle transition from training to online performance.

10.4.4 Intuitive BCI

There are many BCI prototype examples where the mapping between mental task and the in-game action are not intuitive. Lotte et al. (2008) map the task of imaginary foot movement to floating an object in the air. The Berlin BCI selects the best pair of mental tasks to map to two controls in the applications—without any respect to what actions it might actually get mapped to (Blankertz et al. 2008). This lack of logic in the mapping may reduce the measured performance, as the subjects will have to mentally translate what they want to do into the mental action they have to perform. The less natural this translation, the more time and effort it will take to actually perform the task. It does not help with the memorability of the mapping either.

---

[2]To be published.

The BCI paradigms that are currently most common have only a limited applicability when one is trying to find intuitive mappings between the task and the in-game action. P300 and SSVEP are intuitive for visual, auditory, or haptic selection. Imaginary movement of the left hand is easily mapped onto moving your avatar to the left, and movement of the right hand to the right. But at the moment, there are not many alternatives. This means that it is important to keep our eyes open to possible new paradigms that might match all kinds of game interactions.

Beyond waiting for neuro-scientists to come up with the next best thing based on knowledge from cognition and neurophysiology, another option is to look at it from the user point of view. What would the user like to map to certain in-game actions, and is that perhaps something that can be recognized from EEG measurements? As users will not have knowledge about the neurophysiology that would help in choosing mental tasks that might be detectable, many of the ideas that they come up with may not work. On the other hand, when something does work, it will probably be more natural to use, considering the source.

Although people do take suitability of the task for the in-game action into account, the effort it takes to perform the task adds more weight to their preference. When the participant is given feedback as to how well the system can detect the mental task, that information outweighs all other considerations. One can imagine however that there is a break-even point from where the task takes more effort than users are willing to spend, even if the detection was certain to be correct. And even though the detection is this important to the user, one has to realize that although the detection can be improved with better hardware and better software, the mental task will remain the same.

10.4.4.1 Application: IntuiWoW

Based on some informal, open discussions we have had with a small selection of World of Warcraft® players, we decided to try the following three paradigms, to be applied to the same shape-shifting action as used in alphaWoW:

1. Inner speech: the user casts a spell in their mind, e.g. "I call upon the great bear spirit" to change into bear form, and "Let the balance be restored" to change back into the basic elf form.
2. Association: to change into a bear, the user tries to feel like a bear. To change into an elf, the user tries to feel like an elf.
3. Mental state: the user goes into bear form, they stress themselves out, and to return to elf form they relax. This task is similar to the tasks used in AlphaWoW, but this time it is not explicitly related to alpha power.

A series of experiments with these three paradigms was run for five weeks, with fourteen participants returning each week. The first week all participants were asked to just perform the tasks, without getting any feedback as to how well the system was recognizing any of it. In the last week everybody was given feedback, and in between half the group was given feedback and half was not.

Results indicate interesting differences between the feedback and non-feedback groups. The mental state paradigm was well-liked by the feedback group, because of the accurate recognition by the system, but disliked by the non-feedback group because of the effort it took to perform this task. Also, people did not like to put themselves into a stressed state voluntarily. On the other hand, inner speech was liked by the non-feedback group as it was most like a magic spell, and took very little effort and concentration to do. Participants also considered this task to be the most easy to interpret. However, the feedback group quickly discovered that the current system was not well-equipped to detect this task, quickly moving this paradigm to the bottom of their list of preference. The association task set seemed generally well-liked, as people felt it fitted well with the game. It encourages the player to become one with the character they are playing, and to immerse in the game world.

10.4.5 Multimodal Signals, or Artifacts?

In order to measure clean brain signals, BCI experiments are usually conducted in isolated rooms, where the subjects are shielded from electrical noise and distractions. Healthy subjects are instructed to behave like ALS patients; they are not allowed to talk, to move or blink their eyes, as these activities would interfere with the brain signals and the cognitive processes being studied. But such laboratory-based controlled setups are far from a natural environment for gamers (Nijholt et al. 2009). To realize the ultimate automatic intuitive "think & play" game console (Lécuyer et al. 2008), experiments should be conducted in a realistic HCI setting, which implies first a natural game environment, such as a private home or even outdoor public place, and second natural behaviour of the user.

In an ordinary computer game, the players would be situated in a home environment and express themselves—willingly or not—through mimics, gestures, speech and in other ways. The increase in body movement imposed or allowed by the game results in an increase in the player's engagement level (Bianchi-Berthouze et al. 2007), so the reactions and movements would become more intense as the game gets immersive. Players would regularly receive auditory or visual feedback from the game. Additionally, in multi-player games, players interact with each other by means of talking, listening, and the like.

10.4.5.1 Application: Bacteria Hunt

During the eNTERFACE'09 Summer Workshop on Multimodal Interfaces, we started a project to build a multi-modal, multi-paradigm, multi-player BCI game. The project resulted in the Bacteria Hunt game in which the aim is to control an amoeba using arrow keys and to eat as many bacteria as possible. Three versions of the game were implemented. In the basic non-BCI version, eating is accomplished by moving the amoeba on a bacterium and pressing the space key. In the second version, the relative alpha power of the player is also used. The high alpha measured at the parietal lobe is related to a relaxed alertness (Cantero et al. 1999). In the game, the more relaxed the player is, the easier it is to control the amoeba. The third version adds a second BCI paradigm into the game: SSVEP. Eating is now performed by concentrating on a flickering circle that appears when the amoeba is on a bacterium.

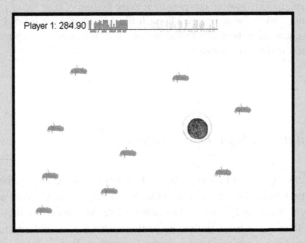

A screen shot of the Bacteria Hunt game

The non-BCI version of the game allows the comparison of BCI and other modalities with respect to features such as enjoyment, ease, and exertion. The second version enables exploration of how well BCI can be used together with another modality—keyboard in this case—and what implications this might have on concentration and performance matters. And by the third version of the game the critical issues that may arise due to using different BCI paradigms together—namely, the alpha power and the SSVEP—such as overlapping measurement sites and frequencies, ability to extract and decode information produced by complex brain activity can be investigated.

The feasibility of using BCI technology has already been proven with many applications (Section 10.2). The time has come to explore how BCIs can function in combination with other modalities, and whether it is realizable to use BCIs in real HCI environments. Recently, there was a study defining a set of guidelines to employ fNIRS in realistic HCI settings (Solovey et al. 2009). Another attempt was Bacteria Hunt, a multi-modal, multi-paradigm BCI game utilizing EEG, built and demonstrated during the eNTERFACE'09 workshop (Mühl et al. 2010). We argue that this kind of research needs to be extended to cover multiple users, different modalities, different contexts, and different BCI paradigms and signal types.

Using EEG-based BCIs in combination with other modalities poses a few extra challenges due to the nature of EEG. One of these problems is that EEG sensors tend to pick up other electrical signals as well, such as electrical activity caused by eye movements (electrooculogram, EOG), and electrical activity from muscle contraction (electromyogram, EMG). Especially BCI based on potentials, as opposed to BCIs based on band power (such as ERD/ERS based BCIs) can suffer from the big amplitude change caused by eye movements and eye blinks. As we cannot ask that a player stops eye movement and blinking altogether, the negative impact of eye movements has to be removed from the signals. In contrast to medical BCIs, we do not have to remove all eye movement in our recordings, decreasing the negative influence should be enough.

There are two main approaches when dealing with occular artifacts. The first is to simply remove EEG episodes contaminated with eye movements. For some games, where the BCI is applied to detect long-term changes, such as mental state, this method can be applied. As a result, the game then needs to be able to deal with missing episodes. The other approach, filtering, is applicable to a wider range of applications. Removing the EOG signal has an additional benefit; consciously blinking, or even suppressing movement is known to cause a Readiness Potential (RP).[3] Allowing the user to move their eyes freely could potentially reduce the number of non-task related RPs, making the EOG movements simpler to interpret and remove. One huge drawback associated with filtering the EOG artifacts is the need for additional sensors to record the activity of the eyes. EEG headsets designed for gamers often do not contain sensors specifically placed at traditional EOG locations. This poses the technical challenge of removing EOG influence without the use of these sensors.

Another challenge that BCIs will face when applied to games is the influence of speech, facial expressions and movement. The EMG signal, characterized by a high-power signal in a broad frequency range, has a profound impact on the EEG recordings. While speech and facial expressions are easier to suppress during game play than eye movements, a BCI that can work robustly while the player laughs and talks is preferable.

So far we have approached the EOG and EMG signals as noise, that has to be removed from the EEG signal. But if we can identify the influence of EOG and EMG signals, as is required to perform filtering, these signals can be isolated, and used as a separate eye gaze or muscle modality. In this context, the artifact becomes another signal, and can be used as an additional source of information.

In IntuiWoW, one of the reasons mental state is so easy to recognize, is because many users tense up facial and neck muscles to enter a more stressed state, and relax these for the relaxed state. The EEG system is sensitive to this muscle activity, and as a result the BCI pipeline can easily classify these clear muscle tensions into the two states. For these users, the actual brain activity related to these states will mostly be ignored. In medical BCI, often aimed at paralyzed people, a system that uses muscle activity in order to distinguish different user states is considered useless. The patients who might end up using the system will not be able to produce

---

[3]Whether automatic eye movements and blinks also display a RP remains to be seen (Shibasaki and Hallett 2006).

this muscle activity, so the system will not work for them. The healthy subjects in our experiment did not experience this as a problem, however. The system recognized their mental state, even though it may have been an external expression of it. They were just amazed that they could control their avatar by changing their mental state, and did not care about whether it was a "pure BCI" or not. We propose that the usability and user experience are more important when looking at the general population as a user group, than the consideration of only using brain activity for the interaction.

10.5 Conclusions

Applications for healthy people are becoming more and more important in BCI research. Gamers are a large potential target group, but why would a healthy person want to use BCI when it has still so many issues (delays, bad recognition, long training time, cumbersome hardware)? BCI needs to prove it can be used in distinctive new ways that will make it a valuable addition to current input modalities with a combination of features that no other modality can offer. Unconstrained by what is physically possible, it might also be a very natural interaction modality, allowing gamers to express themselves in their own unique way.

Some of such valuable features have already been uncovered. In human computer interaction the amount of information the user can provide is limited. In addition to control commands, BCI can provide new kinds of information, specifically on the user's mental state. There have been reports by users that the system seems to recognize a decision before they were consciously aware of it themselves. As with LRP, it may also be possible to detect actions before they are actually executed.

The medical research that lies at the foundation of current BCI research has been and still is very important. However, to move BCI forward as a viable interaction modality for everybody, the human element has to be given a more prominent place in the research. Whether the system is a 'pure BCI' is of secondary importance to healthy users. Usability and user experience, which lie at the core of human-computer interaction, should be considered when designing systems and applications, in order to increase the user satisfaction and acceptance of this new technology.

We believe that BCI could be seamlessly integrated with traditional modalities, taking over those actions which it can detect with sufficiently reliable accuracy. For game adaptation, affective BCI could be a fast and sensitive method on its own, or combined with other user state indicators it could help to create more robust and reliable systems. Timing and fine-grained control are important topics to look into, as these features are important for many applications. Artifacts and noise that are inherent to using BCI in a real-world environment should be dealt with or even better, used as additional information about the user.

We need to move beyond feasibility tests, to prove that BCI is also applicable in realistic, real-world settings. Only the study of BCI under ecologically valid conditions—that is within realistic HCI settings and with behaving users naturally—will reveal the actual potential, and also the real challenges, of this promising new technology. Another way of thinking is required to make BCI part of HCI. 'The subject' should become 'the user'. The first steps have already been taken.

Acknowledgements This work has been supported by funding from the Dutch National Smart-Mix project BrainGain on BCI (Ministry of Economic Affairs) and the GATE project, funded by the Netherlands Organization for Scientific Research (NWO) and the Netherlands ICT Research and Innovation Authority (ICT Regie).

References

Aftanas LI, Reva NV, Varlamov AA, Pavlov SV, Makhnev VP (2004) Analysis of evoked EEG synchronization and desynchronization in conditions of emotional activation in humans: Temporal and topographic characteristics. Neurosci Behav Physiol 34(8):859–867

Allanson J, Mariani J (1999) Mind over virtual matter: Using virtual environments for neurofeedback training. In: IEEE Virtual Reality Conference 1999 (VR'99), pp 270–273

Bayliss JD (2003) Use of the evoked potential P3 component for control in a virtual apartment. IEEE Trans Neural Syst Rehabil Eng 11(1):113–116

Bayliss JD, Ballard DH (2000) A virtual reality testbed for brain-computer interface research. IEEE Trans Rehabil Eng 8(2):188–190

Bayliss JD, Inverso SA, Tentler A (2004) Changing the P300 brain computer interface. CyberPsychol Behav 7(6):694–704

Benovoy M, Cooperstock JR, Deitcher J (2008) Biosignals analysis and its application in a performance setting. In: Proceedings of the International Conference on Bio-Inspired Systems and Signal Processing, pp 253–258

Bianchi-Berthouze N, Kim W, Patel D (2007) Does body movement engage you more in digital game play? And why? In: Affective Computing and Intelligent Interactions. Lecture Notes in Computer Science, vol 4738. Springer, Berlin, pp 102–113

Blankertz B, Kawanabe M, Tomioka R, Hohlefeld FU, Nikullin V, Müller KR (2007) Invariant common spatial patterns: Alleviating nonstationarities in brain-computer interfacing. Neural Inf Process Syst (NIPS) 20:113–120

Blankertz B, Tomioka R, Lemm S, Kawanabe M, Müller KR (2008) Optimizing spatial filters for robust EEG single-trial analysis. IEEE Signal Process Mag 25(1):41–56

Blizzard Entertainment®, Inc (2008) World of Warcraft® subscriber base reaches 11.5 million worldwide. http://www.blizzard.com/us/press/081121.html

Bussink D (2008) Towards the first HMI BCI game. Master's thesis, University of Twente

Cantero J, Atienza M, Gómez C, Salas R (1999) Spectral structure and brain mapping of human alpha activities in different arousal states. Neuropsychobiology 39(2):110–116

Chanel G, Kronegg J, Grandjean D, Pun T (2006) Emotion assessment: Arousal evaluation using EEG's and peripheral physiological signals. In: Multimedia Content Representation, Classification and Security. Lecture Notes in Computer Science, vol 4105. Springer, Berlin, pp 530–537

Chanel G, Rebetez C, Bétrancourt M, Pun T (2008) Boredom, engagement and anxiety as indicators for adaptation to difficulty in games. In: MindTrek '08: Proceedings of the 12th International Conference on Entertainment and Media in the Ubiquitous Era. ACM, New York, NY, USA, pp 13–17

Chanel G, Kierkels JJ, Soleymani M, Pun T (2009) Short-term emotion assessment in a recall paradigm. Int J Hum Comput Stud 67(8):607–627

Cho BH, Lee JM, Ku JH, Jang DP, Kim JS, Kim IY, Lee JH, Kim SI (2002) Attention enhancement system using virtual reality and EEG biofeedback. In: IEEE Virtual Reality Conference 2002 (VR 2002), p 156

Cover TM, Thomas JA (2006) Elements of Information Theory, 2nd edn. Wiley, New York

Csikszentmihalyi M (1990) Flow: The Psychology of Optimal Experience. Harper and Row, New York

Davidson RJ (1992) Anterior cerebral asymmetry and the nature of emotion. Brain Cogn 20(1):125–151

Doppelmayr M, Klimesch W, Stadler W, Pöllhuber D, Heine C (2002) EEG alpha power and intelligence. Intelligence 30(3):289–302

Fairclough SH (2009) Fundamentals of physiological computing. Interact Comput 21(1–2):133–145

Ferrez P, Millán JdR (2008) Error-related EEG potentials generated during simulated brain-computer interaction. IEEE Trans Biomed Eng 55(3):923–929

Finke A, Lenhardt A, Ritter H (2009) The MindGame: A P300-based brain-computer interface game. Neural Netw 9(22):1329–1333

Galán F, Ferrez P, Oliva F, Guardia J, Millán JdR (2007) Feature extraction for multi-class BCI using canonical variates analysis. In: IEEE International Symposium on Intelligent Signal Processing, pp 1–6

Garcia Molina G, Tsoneva T, Nijholt A (2009) Emotional brain-computer interfaces. In: Proceedings of the 3rd International Conference on Affective Computing and Intelligent Interaction (ACII 2009). IEEE Computer Society Press, Los Alamitos, pp 138–146

Goodwin NC (1987) Functionality and usability. Commun ACM 30(3):229–233. DOI http://doi.acm.org/10.1145/214748.214758

Guger C, Edlinger G, Harkam W, Niedermayer I, Pfurtscheller G (2003) How many people are able to operate an EEG-based brain-computer interface (BCI)? IEEE Trans Neural Syst Rehabil Eng 11(2):145–147

Hettinger LJ, Branco P, Encarnacao LM, Bonato P (2003) Neuroadaptive technologies: Applying neuroergonomics to the design of advanced interfaces. Theoretical Issues in Ergonomics Science, pp 220–237

Hiltz SR, Johnson K (1990) User satisfaction with computer-mediated communication systems. Manag Sci 36(6):739–764. http://www.jstor.org/stable/2631904

Hjelm SI (2003) Research + design: The making of brainball. Interactions 10(1):26–34

Hjelm SI, Eriksson E, Browall C (2000) Brainball—using brain activity for cool competition. In: Proceedings of the First Nordic Conference on Human-Computer Interaction, p 59

Hwang HJ, Kwon K, Im CH (2009) Neurofeedback-based motor imagery training for brain–computer interface (BCI). J Neurosci Methods 179(1):150–156

IJsselsteijn W, de Kort Y, Poels K (2008) The game experience questionnaire: Development of a self-report measure to assess the psychological impact of digital games. Manuscript submitted for publication

International Organization for Standardization (1991) ISO 9126—Information technology—Software product evaluation—Quality characteristics and guidelines for their use

Ives B, Olson MH, Baroudi JJ (1983) The measurement of user information satisfaction. Commun ACM 26(10):785–793. DOI http://doi.acm.org/10.1145/358413.358430

Jackson MM, Mappus R, Barba E, Hussein S, Venkatesh G, Shastry C, Israeli A (2009) Continous control paradigms for direct brain interfaces. In: Human-Computer Interaction. Novel Interaction Methods and Techniques. Springer, Berlin, pp 588–595

Kaul P (2006) Neurological gaming environments. In: SIGGRAPH '06: ACM SIGGRAPH 2006 Educators Program. ACM, New York, NY, USA, p 25

Kayagil TA, Bai O, Lin P, Furlani S, Vorbach S, Hallett M (2007) Binary EEG control for two-dimensional cursor movement: An online approach. IEEE/ICME International Conference on Complex Medical Engineering, pp 1542–1545

Keil A, Müller MM, Gruber T, Wienbruch C, Stolarova M, Elbert T (2001) Effects of emotional arousal in the cerebral hemispheres: A study of oscillatory brain activity and event-related potentials. Clin Neurophysiol 112(11):2057–2068

Kim J, André E (2008) Emotion recognition based on physiological changes in music listening. IEEE Trans Pattern Anal Mach Intell 30(12):2067–2083

Krepki R, Blankertz B, Curio G, Müller KR (2007) The Berlin brain-computer interface (BBCI)—towards a new communication channel for online control in gaming applications. Multimed Tools Appl 33(1):73–90

Lalor EC, Kelly SP, Finucane C, Burke R, Reilly RB, McDarby G (2004) Brain computer interface based on the steady-state VEP for immersive gaming control. Biomed Tech 49(1):63–64

Lalor EC, Kelly SP, Finucane C, Burke R, Smith R, Reilly RB, McDarby G (2005) Steady-state VEP-based brain-computer interface control in an immersive 3D gaming environment. EURASIP J Appl Signal Process 19:3156–3164

Lécuyer A, Lotte F, Reilly RB, Leeb R, Hirose M, Slater M (2008) Brain-computer interfaces, virtual reality, and videogames. IEEE Comput 41(10):66–72

Lee U, Han SH, Kim HS, Kim YB, Jung HG, Lee HJ, Lang Y, Kim D, Jin M, Song J, Song S, Song CG, Shin HC (2006) Development of a neuron based internet game driven by a brain-computer interface system. In: Proceedings of the International Conference on Hybrid Information Technology, pp 600–604

Leeb R, Pfurtscheller G (2004) Walking through a virtual city by thought. In: Proceedings of the 26th Annual International Conference of the IEEE Engineering in Medicine and Biology Society, 2004. IEMBS '04, vol 2, pp 4503–4506

Leeb R, Scherer R, Lee F, Bischof H, Pfurtscheller G (2004) Navigation in virtual environments through motor imagery. In: Proceedings of the 9th Computer Vision Winter Workshop, CVWW, vol 4, pp 99–108

Leeb R, Keinrath C, Friedman D, Guger C, Neuper C, Garau M, Antley A, Steed A, Slater M, Pfurtscheller G (2005) Walking from thoughts: Not the muscles are crucial but the brain waves! In: Proceedings of the 8th Annual International Workshop on Presence, pp 25–32

Lehtonen J, Jylanki P, Kauhanen L, Sams M (2008) Online classification of single EEG trials during finger movements. IEEE Trans Biomed Eng 55(2 Part 1):713–720

Lin TA, John LR (2006) Quantifying mental relaxation with EEG for use in computer games. In: Proceedings of the International Conference on Internet Computing, pp 409–415

Lin YP, Wang CH, Wu TL, Jeng SK, Chen JH (2009) EEG-based emotion recognition in music listening: A comparison of schemes for multiclass support vector machine. In: Proceedings of the IEEE International Conference on Acoustics, Speech and Signal Processing 2009, pp 489–492

Liu C, Agrawal P, Sarkar N, Chen S (2009) Dynamic difficulty adjustment in computer games through real-time anxiety-based affective feedback. Int J Hum Comput Interact 25(6):506–529

Lotte F, Renard Y, Lécuyer A (2008) Self-paced brain-computer interaction with virtual worlds: A quantitative and qualitative study "out of the lab". In: Proceedings of the 4th International Brain-Computer Interface Workshop and Training Course, pp 373–378

Lucas HC (1975) Why Information Systems Fail. Columbia University Press, New York

Mandryk RL, Inkpen KM, Calvert TW (2006) Using psychophysiological techniques to measure user experience with entertainment technologies. Behav Inf Technol 25(2):141–158

Marosi E, Bazán O, Yañez G, Bernal J, Fernández T, Rodríguez M, Silva J, Reyes A (2002) Narrow-band spectral measurements of EEG during emotional tasks. Int J Neurosci 112(7):871–891

Martinez P, Bakardjian H, Cichocki A (2007) Fully online multicommand brain-computer interface with visual neurofeedback using SSVEP paradigm. Comput Intell Neurosci 2007(1):13

Mason SG, Bohringer R, Borisoff JF, Birch GE (2004) Real-time control of a video game with a direct brain-computer interface. J Clin Neurophysiol 21(6):404

McFarland D, Miner L, Vaughan T, Wolpaw J (2000) Mu and beta rhythm topographies during motor imagery and actual movements. Brain Topogr 12(3):177–186

Microsoft® (2009) Project natal. Internet http://www.xbox.com/en-US/live/projectnatal/

Middendorf M, McMillan G, Calhoun G, Jones KS (2000) Brain-computer interfaces based on the steady-state visual-evoked response. IEEE Trans Rehabil Eng 8(2):211–214

Mingyu L, Jue W, Nan Y, Qin Y (2005) Development of EEG biofeedback system based on virtual reality environment. In: Proceedings of the 27th Annual International Conference of the Engineering in Medicine and Biology Society. IEEE-EMBS 2005, pp 5362–5364

Morris JD (1995) SAM: The Self-Assessment Manikin. An efficient cross-cultural measurement of emotional response (observations). J Advert Res 35(6):63–68

Mühl C, Heylen D (2009) Cross-modal elicitation of affective experience. In: Proceedings of the Workshop on Affective Brain-Computer Interfaces, pp 42–53

Mühl C, Gürkök H, Plass-Oude Bos D, Scherffig L, Thurlings ME, Duvinage M, Elbakyan AA, Kang SW, Poel M, Heylen D (2010) Bacteria Hunt: A multimodal, multiparadigm BCI game. In: Proceedings of the 5th International Summer Workshop on Multimodal Interfaces eNTER-FACE'09, to appear

Müller MM, Keil A, Gruber T, Elbert T (1999) Processing of affective pictures modulates right-hemispheric gamma band EEG activity. J Clin Neurophysiol 110(11):1913–1920

Müller-Tomfelde C (2007) Dwell-based pointing in applications of human computer interaction. In: Proceedings of the 11th IFIP TC13 International Conference on Human-Computer Interaction (INTERACT 2007), vol 4662. Springer, Berlin, pp 560–573

Nacke L, Lindley CA (2008) Flow and immersion in first-person shooters: Measuring the player's gameplay experience. In: Proceedings of the 2008 Conference on Future Play. Future Play '08. ACM, New York, NY, USA, pp 81–88

Nelson WT, Hettinger LJ, Cunningham JA, Roe MM, Haas MW, Dennis LB (1997) Navigating through virtual flight environments using brain-body-actuated control. In: Proceedings of the IEEE 1997 Virtual Reality Annual International Symposium, pp 30–37

Nielsen J (1993) Usability Engineering. Morgan Kaufmann Publishers, San Mateo

Nielsen J (1996) Usability metrics: Tracking interface improvements. IEEE Softw 13(6):12–13

Nijholt A, Tan D (2007) Playing with your brain: Brain-computer interfaces and games. In: Proceedings of the International Conference on Advances in Computer Entertainment Technology. ACM, New York, NY, USA, pp 305–306

Nijholt A, van Erp JBF, Heylen DKJ (2008a) Braingain: BCI for HCI and games. In: Proceedings of the AISB Symposium Brain Computer Interfaces and Human Computer Interaction: A Convergence of Ideas, The Society for the Study of Artificial Intelligence and Simulation of Behaviour, pp 32–35

Nijholt A, Tan D, Pfurtscheller G, Brunner C, Millán JdR, Allison B, Graimann B, Popescu F, Blankertz B, Müller KR (2008b) Brain-computer interfacing for intelligent systems. IEEE Intell Syst, pp 76–83

Nijholt A, Oude Bos D, Reuderink B (2009) Turning shortcomings into challenges: Brain-computer interfaces for games. Entertain Comput 1(2):85–94

Obaid M, Han C, Billinghurst M (2008) "Feed the fish": An affect-aware game. In: IE '08: Proceedings of the 5th Australasian Conference on Interactive Entertainment. ACM, New York, NY, USA, pp 1–6

Oude Bos D, Reuderink B (2008) BrainBasher: A BCI game. In: Extended Abstracts of the International Conference on Fun and Games 2008, Eindhoven, Netherlands. Eindhoven University of Technology, Eindhoven, The Netherlands, pp 36–39

Palke A (2004) Brainathlon: Enhancing brainwave control through brain-controlled game play. Master's thesis, Mills College

Picard RW (1997) Affective Computing. The MIT Press, Cambridge, MA, USA

Picard RW, Vyzas E, Healey J (2001) Toward machine emotional intelligence: Analysis of affective physiological state. IEEE Trans Pattern Anal Mach Intell 23(10):1175–1191

Pineda JA, Silverman DS, Vankov A, Hestenes J (2003) Learning to control brain rhythms: Making a brain-computer interface possible. IEEE Trans Neural Syst Rehabil Eng 11(2):181–184

Pope AT, Palsson OS (2001) Helping video games "rewire our minds". Tech. rep., NASA Langley Research Center

Reuderink B, Nijholt A, Poel M (2009) Affective Pacman: A frustrating game for brain-computer interface experiments. In: 3rd International Conference on Intelligent Technologies for Interactive Entertainment. Lecture Notes of the Institute for Computer Sciences, Social-Informatics and Telecommunications Engineering, vol 9. Springer, Berlin, pp 221–227

Rushinek A, Rushinek SF (1986) What makes users happy? Commun ACM 29(7):594–598

Saari T, Turpeinen M, Kuikkaniemi K, Kosunen I, Ravaja N (2009) Emotionally adapted games—An example of a first person shooter. In: Human-Computer Interaction. Interacting in Various Application Domains. Lecture Notes in Computer Science, vol 5613. Springer, Berlin, pp 406–415

Sander D, Grandjean D, Scherer KR (2005) A systems approach to appraisal mechanisms in emotion. Neural Netw 18(4):317–352

Scherer R, Schlögl A, Lee F, Bischof H, Janša J, Pfurtscheller G (2007) The self-paced Graz brain-computer interface: Methods and applications. Comput Intell Neurosci 2007:9

Shibasaki H, Hallett M (2006) What is the bereitschaftspotential? Clin Neurophysiol 117(11):2341–2356

Shim BS, Lee SW, Shin JH (2007) Implementation of a 3-dimensional game for developing balanced brainwave. In: Proceedings of the 5th ACIS International Conference on Software Engineering Research, Management & Applications. IEEE Computer Society, Los Alamitos, CA, USA, pp 751–758

Sobell N, Trivich M (1989) Brainwave drawing game. In: A Delicate Balance: Technics, Culture and Consequences. IEEE Los Angeles Council, Torrance, CA, USA, pp 360–362

Solovey ET, Girouard A, Chauncey K, Hirshfield LM, Sassaroli A, Zheng F, Fantini S, Jacob RJ (2009) Using fNIRS brain sensing in realistic HCI settings: Experiments and guidelines. In: Proceedings of the 22nd Annual ACM Symposium on User Interface Software and Technology. ACM, New York, NY, USA, pp 157–166

Tangermann MW, Krauledat M, Grzeska K, Sagebaum M, Blankertz B, Vidaurre C, Müller KR (2009) Playing pinball with non-invasive BCI. In: Advances in Neural Information Processing Systems 21. MIT Press, Cambridge, MA, USA, pp 1641–1648

Tijs T, Brokken D, Ijsselsteijn W (2009) Creating an emotionally adaptive game. In: Proceedings of the 7th International Conference on Entertainment Computing. Lecture Notes in Computer Science, vol 5309. Springer, Berlin, pp 122–133

Tonet O, Marinelli M, Citi L, Rossini PM, Rossini L, Megali G, Dario P (2008) Defining brain-machine interface applications by matching interface performance with device requirements. J Neurosci Methods 167(1):91–104

Tschuor L (2002) Computer game control through relaxation-induced EEG changes. Student project report

Tyson P (1987) Task-related stress and EEG alpha biofeedback. Appl Psychophysiol Biofeedback 12(2):105–119

van den Broek E, Janssen JH, Westerink J, Healey JA (2009) Prerequisites for affective signal processing (ASP). In: Proceedings of the International Conference on Bio-inspired Systems and Signal Processing, pp 426–433

van de Laar B, Bos DO, Reuderink B, Heylen D (2009) Actual and imagined movement in BCI gaming. In: Proceedings of the International Conference on Artificial Intelligence and Simulation of Behaviour, pp 9–16

van Reekum CM, Johnstone T, Banse R, Etter A, Wehrle T, Scherer KR (2004) Psychophysiological responses to appraisal dimensions in a computer game. Cogn Emot 18(5):663–688

Vidal JJ (1977) Real-time detection of brain events in EEG. Proc IEEE 65(5):633–641

Vidaurre C, Schlögl A, Cabeza R, Scherer R, Pfurtscheller G (2006) A fully on-line adaptive BCI. IEEE Trans Biomed Eng 53(6):1214–1219

Wang C, Zhang H, Phua KS, Dat TH, Guan C (2007) Introduction to NeuroComm: A platform for developing real-time EEG-based brain-computer interface applications. In: Proceedings of the 29th Annual International Conference of the IEEE Engineering in Medicine and Biology Society, pp 4703–4706

Witmer B, Singer M (1998) Measuring presence in virtual environments: A presence questionnaire. Presence 7(3):225–240

Wolpaw JR, Birbaumer N, McFarland DJ, Pfurtscheller G, Vaughan TM (2002) Brain-computer interfaces for communication and control. Clin Neurophysiol 113(6):767–791

Zander TO, Kothe C, Welke S, Roetting M (2009) Utilizing secondary input from passive brain-computer interfaces for enhancing human-machine interaction. In: Foundations of Augmented

Cognition. Neuroergonomics and Operational Neuroscience. Lecture Notes in Computer Science, vol 5638. Springer, Berlin, pp 759–771

Zeng Z, Pantic M, Roisman GI, Huang TS (2007) A survey of affect recognition methods: Audio, visual and spontaneous expressions. In: Proceedings of the 9th International Conference on Multimodal Interfaces. ACM, New York, NY, USA, pp 126–133

Zhao Q, Zhang L, Cichocki A (2009) EEG-based asynchronous BCI control of a car in 3D virtual reality environments. Chin Sci Bull 54(1):78–87

Part III
Brain Sensing in Adaptive User Interfaces

Chapter 11
Enhancing Human-Computer Interaction with Input from Active and Passive Brain-Computer Interfaces

Thorsten O. Zander, Christian Kothe, Sabine Jatzev, and Matti Gaertner

Abstract This chapter introduces a formal categorization of BCIs, according to their key characteristics within HCI scenarios. This comprises classical approaches, which we group into active and reactive BCIs, and the new group of passive BCIs. Passive BCIs provide easily applicable and yet efficient interaction channels carrying information on covert aspects of user state, while adding little further usage cost. All of these systems can also be set up as hybrid BCIs, by incorporating information from outside the brain to make predictions, allowing for enhanced robustness over conventional approaches. With these properties, passive and hybrid BCIs are particularly useful in HCI. When any BCI is transferred from the laboratory to real-world situations, one faces new types of problems resulting from uncontrolled environmental factors—mostly leading to artifacts contaminating data and results. The handling of these situations is treated in a brief review of training and calibration strategies. The presented theory is then underpinned by two concrete examples. First, a combination of Event Related Desynchronization (ERD)-based active BCI with gaze control, defining a hybrid BCI as solution for the midas touch problem. And second, a passive BCI based on human error processing, leading to new forms of automated adaptation in HCI. This is in line with the results from other recent studies of passive BCI technology and shows the broad potential of this approach.

T.O. Zander (✉) · C. Kothe · S. Jatzev · M. Gaertner
Team PhyPA, TU Berlin, Berlin, Germany
e-mail: thorsten.zander@mms.tu-berlin.de

T.O. Zander · C. Kothe · S. Jatzev · M. Gaertner
Department of Psychology and Ergonomics, Chair for Human-Machine Systems, Berlin Institute of Technology, Berlin, Germany

D.S. Tan, A. Nijholt (eds.), *Brain-Computer Interfaces,*
Human-Computer Interaction Series,
DOI 10.1007/978-1-84996-272-8_11, © Springer-Verlag London Limited 2010

11.1 Accessing and Utilizing User State for Human-Computer Interaction

Today's interaction between machines and human beings in general is dominated by discrete and overt events, demanding a high degree of awareness from the user. Commands are messaged by explicit manual actions, like button presses, or speech control, and information is fed back from the machine through visual, auditory and/or tactile displays. Further, in the last decades—especially in Human-Computer Interaction (HCI)—a strong development towards increasing diversity in information flow could be observed, approaching a complexity of interaction which can saturate the user's capabilities. User-friendly design of HCI has therefore become an important part of current research. New approaches evolved such as adaptive or interpretative HCI heading for optimal support of the user (Chen and Vertegaal 2004; Rötting et al. 2009). With that, *context-sensitivity* is added to already existing human-machine systems. The key information for the design of such systems is knowledge about the *current* user state within the interaction.

11.1.1 Utilizing User State for Human-Computer Interaction

Relevant information in human-computer interaction comprises state of the technical system and of the system environment, as well as state of the user, In particular, cognitive processes like the user's internal interpretation of the situation are of high interest. This can be made clear by taking a look at another type of interaction—that between humans. One fraction of social interaction is explicit—by intentionally sending a message to another actor. In addition, there is an *implicit* information flow. By observing aspects of user state accompanying the explicit interaction, such as gestures, mimics, or body posture, actors gain access to information about inner states of each other. Reading interpretations and intentions of others is an important ability that involves representing and embedding the mental states of others in one's own mind, as, for example, postulated by the "theory of mind" (Premack and Woodruff 1978). Such information might also be relevant for a more intuitive HCI (Asteriadis et al. 2009; Moldt and von Scheve 2002). Consequently, integrating information on *aspects of user state* into HCI could lead to a more natural way of interaction between human and machine. Here cognitive aspects are of special interest, as they might reflect highly complex information of the current user state—which is mainly encoded in the human brain.

One can divide these aspects of user state into two roughly distinct groups, both of which can carry relevant (and implicit) information. First, there are latent cognitive processes, such as arousal, fatigue and more complex examples like the perceived loss of control (Jatzev et al. 2008). And second, there are time-bounded cognitive processes, known as cognitive events from neuro-science. First investigated examples from this area are perception and processing of errors (Blankertz et al.

2002; Zander et al. 2008; Ferrez and del Millán 2008), moments of bluffing in a game context (Reissland and Zander 2009) or surprise (Farwell and Donchin 1988).

In a system which captures user state for implicit communication, this information flow can be seen as input from the user to the machine which is not sent intentionally—hence as *implicit* commands. Due to the fact that such implicit commands are generated automatically in the course of interaction, there is an increase of information flow, while the effort of the user is *not increasing*. Hence, the use of information on cognitive user state is a highly efficient way for enhancing HCI. But—unfortunately—especially these aspects are hard to observe with technical systems, as will be explored next.

11.1.2 Accessing User State with Psycho-Physiological Measures

User state has covert parts, which are hard to access from the outside. Examples for these parts are physiological processes within the human body or the aforementioned processes of cognition. There are approaches to utilize overt measures, like the users behavior, and of extracting information correlated to aspects of user state (Becker et al. 2007). Further, physiological measures like haptic data (Park et al. 2005) or eye gaze (Asteriadis et al. 2009; Rötting et al. 2009) have been shown to provide useful information on user state. Yet, the scope of these methods is limited, as they can only generate information which is weakly correlated to the actual user state (Müller et al. 2008). This gives the basis to define these parts as *covert aspects of user state* (CAUS), analogously to covert attention (Posner and Cohen 1984).

11.1.3 Covert Aspects of User State

A covert aspect of user state is a process occurring within the user which can only be detected with weak reliability by using overt measures. As the user's cognition is inherently hard to access by overt measures, a big portion of cognitive processes are CAUS. Hence, we need an elaborate and continuous measure of accessing and providing those as input to HCI like proposed in the previous section. Since the electroencephalogram (EEG) gives insight into the processes of the human brain, the source of all cognition, in high temporal resolution, it is a potentially suitable measure. In the field of Brain-Computer Interfacing EEG has been used for online detection and interpretation of distinct cognitive processes. Applied in a broader context, such BCIs provide a powerful tool for enriching HCI in general with information on CAUS like cognitive events and conditions. In the next section, a view on classical BCI technology from an HCI perspective will be given, followed by an overview of broader definitions of the term *Brain-Computer Interfaces*, including passive and *hybrid BCIs*, and extending them from medical applications to HCI in general.

11.2 Classical BCIs from an HCI Viewpoint

BCIs are primarily considered to be means of communication and control for their users (Wolpaw et al. 2002). These "classical" BCIs can be divided into two sub-groups, which we now summarize from the perspective of HCI.

- *Directly controlled BCIs* Some BCIs allow for direct communication with a technical system, by mapping consciously controlled mental activity onto a new artificial output channel. Thereby, they can bypass the natural outputs of the brain, which is integral for their clinical applications. Examples are BCIs based on sensorimotor imagery (Blankertz et al. 2007), where the type of mental imagery is mapped to a multi-valued control signal. Despite its power and novelty, applying this type of control to general Human-Computer Interfaces is a challenge. Complementing conventional (e.g. manual) means of human-computer interaction with it faces the problem that the user's resources for parallel conscious communication are limited, creating a conflict between BCI and conventional control. Second, brain activity which can be both consciously controlled and at the same time measured with present non-invasive equipment largely overlaps with the brain's primary output modality—muscular control—creating another resource conflict. This limitation may eventually vanish with further advances in detecting more subtle cognitive processes and commands. Finally, if taken as a replacement to manual control instead of a complement, BCIs are currently slower, more prone to errors, and more difficult to use.
- *Indirectly controlled BCIs* BCIs in the second group rely on conscious modulation of brain activity, as it arises in response to external stimulation. In these, the modulated activity is mapped to an artificial control signal. Examples are P300 spellers (Farwell and Donchin 1988): systems which detect a characteristic brain response, the P300, which is elicited whenever an on-screen letter focused by the user lights up. Thus, brain activity is indirectly controlled by shifting attention. In this interaction technique, another resource of the user—the attention focus in visual, auditory, or tactile perception—is modulated for the purpose of communication, and thereby occupied. For this reason, this subgroup of BCIs, as well, is not easily applied meaningfully in Human-Computer Interfaces.

11.3 Generalized Notions of BCIs

We can re-express the previously identified groups in a framework which captures additional types of BCIs, by shifting the perspective from the user side to the application side. This shift allows for the following definition of BCIs, which covers a broader spectrum of human-computer interaction.

A BCI is a system to provide computer applications with access to real-time information about cognitive state, on the basis of measured brain activity.

Further, in this context, it is beneficial to not restrict the information available to BCIs to brain activity alone. Instead, context parameters may be used by BCIs to help improve the accuracy of their predictions, leading to hybrid BCIs (Pfurtscheller et al. 2006). Specifically, when moving from controlled laboratory conditions to highly varying real-world situations, context parameters help factoring out variations in brain activity which could otherwise bury features of interest under noise. These parameters may include state of the application, such as program events, state of the environment, or state of the user as acquired by other physiological measures, such as body posture, voice tone, or gaze direction. Section 11.5 gives a complete example of how careful hybridization can allow to successfully integrate otherwise impractical BCI control into HCIs.

The classical BCI occupies, in the framework of the above definition, the role of providing information which is actively messaged or modulated by the user in order to control the application. What is not covered by classical notions, however, is information which is not consciously sent by the user, spanning a large fraction of implicit user state. BCIs which sidestep voluntary control are clearly restricted, but they have several benefits which are critical for their effective use in Human-Computer Interfaces. These will be outlined in the following.

11.3.1 BCI Categories

We have proposed a categorization of BCIs into three types (Zander et al. 2008).

- *Active BCI* An active BCI is a BCI which derives its outputs from brain activity which is directly consciously controlled by the user, independently from external events, for controlling an application.
- *Reactive BCI* A reactive BCI is a BCI which derives its outputs from brain activity arising in reaction to external stimulation, which is indirectly modulated by the user for controlling an application.
- *Passive BCI* A passive BCI is a BCI which derives its outputs from arbitrary brain activity without the purpose of voluntary control, for enriching a human-computer interaction with implicit information.

Active and reactive BCIs match the subgroups of classical BCIs for direct and indirect control, respectively, and passive BCIs account for all other BCIs. These categories form a partition of the space of BCIs, since first, conscious control does either depend on external influences, rendering it reactive, or works independently from it, making it active, and second, passive BCIs are defined as complementary, in purpose, to this conscious control. The inter-category boundaries are smooth.

11.3.2 Passive BCIs

Restricted forms of passive BCIs predating these notions have been proposed in the past, for example for detecting forms of mental workload (Kohlmorgen et al.

2007) and perception of self-induced errors (Blankertz et al. 2002). Such applications have been referred to as "BCI as a measure" by some, since they give rise to physiological measures of the user's cognitive state (specifically of CAUS). They have, however, not been analyzed and evaluated with respect to an ongoing Human-Computer Interaction, and focus on user-state detection alone. More recent cases include measuring working memory load (Grimes et al. 2008), and detecting and correcting machine-induced errors (Zander et al. 2008). A complete example, one of the first cases of using passive BCIs to enhance human-computer interaction, is found in Section 11.6. Passive BCIs can be seen as secondary communication channels in Human-Machine Systems: a Human-Machine System linked by some primary communication channel (e.g. manual input) can be complemented by an optional secondary channel formed by a passive BCI, influencing and enriching the ongoing primary interaction with implicit user information (Zander and Jatzev 2009). The performance of passive BCIs is therefore best measured by the cost or benefit of their use in a particular scenario, rather than in terms of their bitrate.

11.3.2.1 Key Properties

Passive BCIs have the following three distinguishing aspects which account for their practical prospects in Human-Computer Interfaces:

- *Complementarity* The concept of passive BCI is complementary to other means of Human-Machine Interaction, in the sense that it does not interfere with it, in contrast to most forms of active or reactive BCIs, for reasons mentioned earlier. A passive BCI can be reliant on either the presence or the absence of an ongoing conventional Human-Computer Interaction, or be invariant under it.
- *Composability* An application can make use of arbitrarily many passive BCI detectors in parallel with no conflicts, which is more difficult for active and reactive BCIs due to the user's limited ability of consciously interacting with them.
- *Controlled Cost* Since no conscious effort is needed for the use of passive BCIs (besides preparation), their operational cost is determined by the cost of their mis-predictions. Passive BCIs producing probabilistic estimates, together with the *a priori* probability of predicting correctly, are sufficient for arbitrary cost-optimal decision making at the application level, with zero benefit in the worst case.

Since passive BCIs are so easily applicable in real-world systems, the only remaining cost factors of preparation and calibration come much more into focus. Therefore, calibration and related issues are given a treatment in Section 11.4.

11.3.2.2 Accessible State and Potential Applications

A broad spectrum of cognitive state can be accessed with passive BCIs. This includes latent cognitive state such as arousal (Chanel et al. 2006), fatigue (Cajochen et al. 1996), vigilance (Schmidt et al. 2009), working memory load (Grimes et al. 2008), visual/auditory/tactile/cross-modality attention focus (Kelly et al. 2005), and possibly some emotional state, etc. on one hand, and temporary cognitive events such as surprise, perception of user/machine errors (Blankertz et al. 2002; Zander et al. 2008; Ferrez and del Millán 2008), or decision-making load (Heekeren et al. 2008), etc. on the other hand. Significantly more subtle state could be accessed with better, but not easily deployable, measurement equipment (Shinkareva et al. 2008). For EEG or Near Infrared Spectroscopy, a simple rule of thumb is: what is represented in a large and compact area of the cortex and is close to the scalp should also be detectable. Thus, brain atlases (Toga and Mazziotta 2000) give a useful overview of what could potentially be accessed by passive BCIs.

Various potential applications arise from this data, such as for augmenting or improving existing systems, e.g. by improving safety and usability via operator monitoring. In this role, they allow to better respect the human factor in a Human-Machine System. Another application is for creating highly interactive and sensitive Human-Machine Interfaces: having information about the ongoing activity profile of the user, the system can adapt to avoid cognitive overload, and further, information about the interpretation of events by users can serve as a better basis for making decisions. As a third example, passive BCIs can help better connect multiple users by accounting for more aspects of user state, both in professional multi-operator scenarios as well as in recreation environments.

11.4 Refining the BCI Training Sequence

Applying BCI technology as proposed in the previous sections poses new challenges—especially regarding the acceptance by healthy users. The time-consuming *preparation phase* of EEG systems and the *calibration* of BCI detectors limit the scope of possible applications. The calibration phase can be optimized in several ways, though.

First, in spite of the strong variability between EEG sessions, there are approaches for porting information between sessions (Krauledat 2008). In line with this thought, there might even be the possibility of defining universal detectors applicable to users or groups of users with short or no re-calibration. However, a prerequisite for that would be the existence of an aspect of cognitive state which is consistent and represented invariantly across subjects. Beyond these problems, there are still other hurdles to take. Shifting BCI applications into the context of general HCI leads to a more complex, and hence noisier, environment, and diversified user state induced by rich forms of interaction. Also, applications will not only be controlled by BCI input but will still rely on standard input forms, like mouse or keyboard, and other input methods may be combined with BCI input into a hybrid BCI. Another problem is defined by the increasing number of artifacts recorded in the EEG data in a more complex context. These can be divided into parts resulting from the environment or uncorrelated user state and those resulting from correlated user state, such as correlated eye blinks and other types of behavior. As the first category of artifacts always decreases the signal to noise ratio, these should be filtered out for BCI applications. In contrast, artifacts from the second category may be used as features, but it is unclear whether these signals are as robust as cognitive events and states, with respect to context variation.

As there is a high variability in the signals recorded between sessions or between subjects, and even within sessions (mostly due to changes in context), an initial system calibration used for detecting patterns in brain activity is necessary. In classical BCI applications, this calibration and the user's learning of the task in the application are the only methods of learning about the state of the interacting system. This defines the first stage of *adaptation*. With that, we address the adaptation of the machine to the user as well as the adaptation of the user to the machine. But it is very likely that the user still will be learning while interacting within the application. Hence, the user state will change in time which might lead to later performance drops. Then, a readaptation of the classifier can be of use (Shenoy et al. 2006; Jatzev et al. 2008), defining the second stage of adaptation. In general, one faces the problem of two adaptive systems which may diverge in time. Both machine and user have to be trained to let their adaptations converge. To cope with the previously defined problems, the definition of procedures defining BCI applications has to be more elaborate. Therefore, we propose the following sequence consisting of five stages, for structuring a BCI session:

- *User Training*
  In this stage the user gets familiar with the task of the Machine Training stage. This task could be generating BCI detectable signals, mostly in active or reactive BCIs, or a predefined Human-Computer Interaction usually independent from BCI input, for generating passive signals.
- *Machine Training*
  In a standardized paradigm the user is guided to generate prototypes of brain activity which can be used as input for the proposed BCI application. In this stage all artifacts should be controlled. The outcome of this stage is a system, usually a combination of feature extraction and classifier, able to distinguish the intended commands or to infer an aspect of cognitive state. We call this system a detector.
- *Confluence Stage*
  Here, a simple BCI application is defined which can be controlled by the outcome of the previously defined detector. Depending on the performance of the detector in the initial application, parameters of the detector might be adjusted or, in active BCIs, the user can learn how to interact with the system.
- *Validation Stage*
  This stage is the first test of the intended BCI application. Its outcome is a performance estimate of the defined detector. Depending on this, it can be decided to repeat some of the previous three stages to obtain better results.
- *Application Stage*
  The defined and validated detector is applied for generating input to the technical system resulting from brain activity of the user. Methods capable of online adaptation might be used to (continuously) adjust parameters of the detector to relevant changes of user state.

11.5 An Active and Hybrid BCI: Combining Eye Gaze Input with BCI for Touchless Interaction

The integration of new input modalities into HCI has been pursued by various researchers. Already in 1982 Bolt and others investigated eye movements as an alternative input modality to improve efficiency in HCI (Bolt 1982). Moving the mouse cursor via eye movements has been shown to be intuitive and facilitate search (Engell-Nielsen et al. 2003; Nilsson et al. 2007; Jacob 1993; Murata 2006; Hutchinson 1993). However, defining adequate mechanisms for the selection command or click operation remained a challenge. The prevalent solution for Gaze-controlled User Interfaces are dwell times, where items are selected when they are fixated by the user for a pre-defined duration. This allows for a faster interaction than using a mouse (Sibert and Jacob 2000), but creates the problem of finding the appropriate dwell times for complex stimuli or icons. The user cannot rest the gaze anywhere without making a selection (Jacob et al. 1993), which is stressful when complex icons must be understood, leading to the "Midas Touch" problem (Pierce et al. 1999). In real-world scenarios this problem is amplified by unpredictable variations in stimulus complexity, making it almost impossible to define an appropriate dwell time.

11.5.1 A Hybrid BCI Solution

In this study, an active Brain-Computer Interface (BCI) is added as a second input modality, serving as an action selection device within an eye gaze controlled environment (Vilimek and Zander 2009). A two-dimensional cursor control is realized by tracking the user's gaze and a BCI-detectable mental gesture, an imagination of a two-handed movement, serves as the selection command. The integration of an active BCI application within HCI allows for direct conscious control and communication via BCI. This way, disadvantages of the two modalities can be counterbalanced: the Eye Gaze based system compensates for the BCI restriction to binary inputs, not suitable for cursor movements, while the BCI enables a natural and selection command under complete user control.

For an application, the hybrid BCI system must not be significantly slower than dwell times, but large speed gains can not be expected either, since the activation thought and BCI processing add their own latency. Secondly the BCI-based solution should result in lower error rates (false selections), especially in the presence of complex stimuli, since it is based on an explicit conscious action. It was investigated whether this hybrid BCI provides a successful solution to the "Midas Touch" problem, not dependent on stimulus complexity.

11.5.1.1 Experimental Task

The proposed BCI-based target selection was compared against two dwell time solutions on two stimulus complexities. Ten participants (five female, five male) took

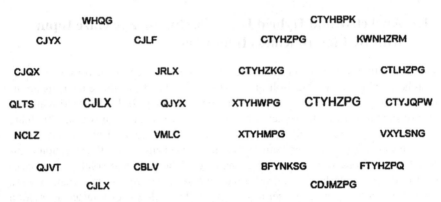

Fig. 11.1 Examples for easy (*left*) and difficult (*right*) search tasks

part in the study, performing a search-and-select task. Within a circular arrangement of 11 similar distractor strings, subjects had to find the string identical to the target string, which was presented in the middle of the circle (see Fig. 11.1). The task included two levels of difficulty: an "easy" condition presenting strings of four characters and a "difficult" one (seven characters), at the upper boundary of working memory capacity (Miller 1994), where the user is forced to rest gaze for encoding. The appropriate dwell times were found in pre-experiments: a long, well controllable dwell time of 1.300 ms and a short dwell time of 1.000 ms, not perceived as slowing down performance.

11.5.1.2 Experimental Design

The structure of the experimental blocks was chosen in accordance with the training sequence described in Section 11.4. During the user training phase, participants were assisted to imagine the hand movement, followed by a 15 minute machine training phase. Subsequently, the BCI command was practiced during the confluence stage, enabling readjustments of the threshold probability for selection. The mental gesture chosen for the BCI activation thought was: "imagine wringing a towel with both hands into opposite directions". Then, during the application stage, the main task was performed by the participants, using the three activation modes for each of the two levels of task difficulty. To ensure robustness of the detector, the user training task was a variant of the application stage, with the difference that a grey box containing the word "search" was occluding strings from the circle at random. Participants were to follow the box until the word "select" appeared. In this case, they had to perform the imagined hand movement. This training elicits prototypes for two mental conditions or BCI classes. One class was characterized by search (following the "search box"), the other one was characterized by the selection command (motor imagery).

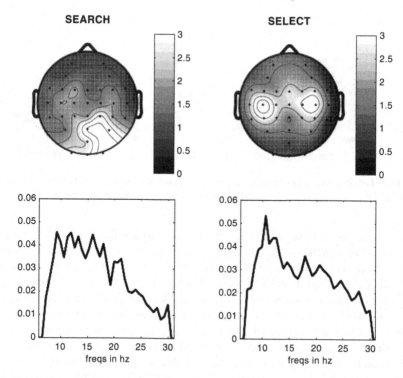

Fig. 11.2 Grand averages of electrode and frequency weighting calculated by the Spec-CSP algorithm. Units of all weights are arbitrary. Features show evidence for ERD during selection

11.5.1.3 BCI Control

For BCI analysis, 32 EEG channels were used, with a focus on sensorimotor areas around the C3/C4 locations. BCI feature extraction focused on sensorimotor synchronization/desynchronization (Pfurtscheller et al. 1997). The Spec-CSP (Tomioka et al. 2006) feature extractor was used to find optimal linear combinations of weights for each electrode and frequency.

11.5.1.4 Results

Advantages of the hybrid BCI were investigated by measuring effectiveness, efficiency, cognitive demand (mental workload) and user acceptance. Effectiveness of task performance was measured by errors (false target selections), and accuracy of target selection, respectively, or the "easy" condition, the subject's accuracy using the BCI-based solution was slightly lower (88%) compared to the long dwell times (93%), with short dwell times resulting in the lowest accuracy (83.3%) (see Fig. 11.3). Remarkably, the BCI achieves the best results in accuracy for the "difficult" condition (78.7% correct), but only the difference to the short dwell

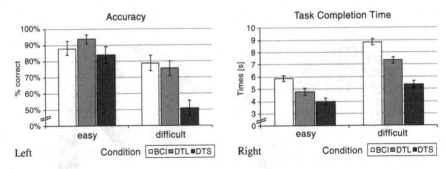

Fig. 11.3 *Left*: Percentage of correct selection: Brain-Computer Interface (BCI), long dwell times (DTL) and short dwell times (DTS). *Right*: Task completion times for the respective conditions

time (51.1% correct) was significant. With respect to efficiency, indicated by time needed for task completion, the BCI solution was significantly the slowest activation method over both conditions (5.90 s; 8.84 s) (see Fig. 11.3). Overall mental work-load effects, measured via NASA task Load Index, showed no differences, except for one subscale: 'amount of frustration'. Here, the BCI method was rated significantly lower ($p < 0.05$) than dwell time solutions. In addition, nine out of ten participants preferred using the combined BCI/Eye Gaze Interface. Many participants stated to use a strategy to avoid mis-selection by dwell times, moving their eyes shortly to an item and then quickly to a 'safe area'. With respect to BCI classification, the mean cross-validation accuracy was 89% (standerd deviation of 10.1%). Spec-CSP showed highest electrode weights over motor cortex (see Fig. 11.2) and highest weights for frequency range was in the alpha band, characteristic for sensorimotor rhythm (SMR).

11.5.1.5 Discussion

The more accurate interaction regarding the 'difficult' stimuli, a strong user prefer-ence and low frustration ratings support the idea of applying a BCI as an additional input modality in Eye Gaze based systems. This study demonstrates that an active BCI can be successfully integrated into HCI by hybridization, ensuring an accu-rate selection command for Gaze-controlled User Interfaces, which is, in contrast to dwell time based solutions, independent from stimulus complexity.

11.6 A Passive BCI: Automated Error Detection to Enhance Human-Computer Interaction via Secondary Input

The example for passive BCIs is taken from the domain of erroneous human-computer interaction. The recent rapid development of automation technology has increased the precision and efficiency of HCI, but has also been shown to be a source of errors in such systems. Sometimes, these systems are even referred to as "clumsy automation" (Wiener 1989), causing additional cognitive workload for the human instead of reducing it. We developed an *Error-BCI* (Zander et al. 2008) that enables single trial detection of brain responses to machine errors as caused by such automation processes, but is not restricted to them. Errors, as perceived by the user, are fed back to the system and thus enable a correction or adaptation. The direct access to the cognitive state results in a more suitable and context-sensitive adaptation compared to other automation technologies which have to rely on behavioural or other implicit data (Wiener 1989). Since BCI error detection is based on a non-intended and automatic reaction of the brain to the environmental context, this defines a passive BCI, with no additional cognitive effort for the user, and no conflict with the primary mode of interaction.

11.6.1 Experimental Design

The applicability of the Error-BCI to enhance HCI efficiency was investigated by utilizing a game as experimental task, in order to simulate a real-world-like situation and to ensure proper user motivation. The goal of the player is to rotate one of two letters, drawn randomly from the set {L, R} and presented in front of a circle, until a given target configuration is reached. Reaching the target completes a round of the game. The letter L can be rotated clockwise by a left key press and the letter R counter-clockwise by a right key press (see Fig. 11.4). The letters are automatically

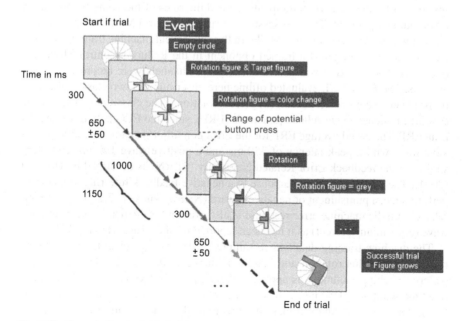

Fig. 11.4 Example for single trial of the RLR-Design

changing colors in 1000 ms intervals, where color indicates the angle of rotation upon key press. The following mapping rules hold: red indicates rotation by 90 degrees and green indicates rotation by 30 degrees upon key press. Only one press is possible per color phase, and there is an intermittent grey phase, where no rotation is possible. Players are free to choose the time point of the key press, and therefore can build up an efficient strategy in order to achieve the goal: be as fast as possible without making mistakes, such as over-rotating or pressing the wrong key.

The game is played in two modes: in the first mode, the subject has full control over the game (Full Control Mode). During the second mode (Reduced Control Mode) false rotation angles (machine errors) appear randomly. In these, rotation angles are smaller than expected: in 30% of all key presses, red letters would rotate by 30 degrees instead of 90 degrees and the green letter would not rotate by 30 degrees, but not at all. To build up motivation for the task, a second player competing in speed to the first one is participating in the RLR game. Performance is measured and fed back to both players, by presenting the score after each round. The artificially induced machine errors have a negative valence for the user, since they decrease the performance and also lead to frustration.

11.6.2 Offline Experiment

The first of two experiments took place under controlled laboratory conditions, involving 14 participants (6 F/8 M, age: 21–30 years). During two initial user training sessions (40 rounds each), participants learned the rules of the game by practicing it without an opponent. The first session was in Full Control Mode, and the second session was in Reduced Control Mode. In the subsequent machine training session, participants played against a trained opponent in the Reduced Control Mode. No online feedback by BCI was given, but 54 EEG channels were recorded for later analysis. The Error-BCI, evaluated offline here, discriminates two classes of conditions: (1) erroneous rotations and (2) correct rotations. The classification scheme is designed to detect event related potentials (ERP), since the EEG pattern of interest is an ERP. The grand average ERP for the Error condition is characterized by a negative wave with a peak latency of 350 ms and a positive wave 100 ms later, very similar to the feedback Error Related Negativity (f-ERN) as described by Holroyd (2004). The f-ERN occurs in response to a negative feedback referring to incorrect performance, a punishment or negative reward (Nieuwenhuis et al. 2004). The ERP related with the machine error response is also present for the respective difference wave (error minus correct) as it has been reported for the f-ERN (Holroyd 2004).

The machine training data was re-sampled at 100 Hz, epoched from 0–800 ms relative to stimulus rotation and bandpass-filtered at 0.1–15 Hz. Subsequently, a pattern matching method was applied (Blankertz et al. 2002), using six consecutive time windows of 50 ms each, yielding 6 × 54 features per trial. A regularized Linear Discriminant Analysis classifier was trained on these features. Performance evaluation was done offline by 10-fold outer and 8-fold nested cross validation.

The mean classification error for the automated error detection was 11.8% with a mean standard deviation of 5.0%. The false positive (FP) and false negative (FN) rates were moderately balanced with a mean FP rate of 9.54% and a mean FN rate of 16.42%.

11.6.3 Online Experiment

The second experiment was conducted at the Open House of the Berlin Institute of Technology (LNdW 2007). Four times two different players from the audience played the RLR game against each other. The setting at the LNdW served as an uncontrolled environment to test whether the classifier is robust enough to work properly in such situations. Each pair played three sessions, consisting of 40 trials per class, and lasting for about 15 minutes. First, the user training included one session without error states. The machine training followed introducing machine error trials with a probability of 30%. A classifier was trained based on the sample trials of the machine training phase.

For BCI classification, the same pattern matching method as in the offline experiment was utilized. Automatic error detection and adaptation via Error-BCI was applied in the last session, but only for one player. While points were equally distributed between session 1 and 2, the performance of all BCI-supported players increased significantly during the third passive BCI session. This is indicated by a substantially higher score of the BCI-supported player, compared to the opponent and to his own former sessions, plotted in Fig. 11.5 as difference in points between players. The classifier had an accuracy of 81.2% with error rates equally distributed over the two classes.

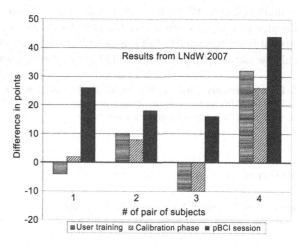

Fig. 11.5 Results of the LNdW 2007. The bars indicate difference in points of Player A (up if better) and Player B (down if better). Horizontally striped bars show the results from the user training (no machine errors). Results from the machine training (machine errors included) are represented by the *diagonally striped bars*. In the application stage, results shown in *black*, BCI support was given to Player A

11.6.4 Discussion

The studies presented in this part show that it is possible to enhance the efficiency of HCI via passive BCI, constituting an additional information channel. By providing the technical system with information about the perceived errors, the system was able to adapt the actions to the user's covert cognitive state of perceiving an error. Especially the second study shows that this significantly optimizes the Human-Machine Interaction in real-world environments.

11.7 Conclusion

In this chapter, BCIs have been identified as possible means to access a particularly interesting portion of a human-computer system's state—Covert Aspects of User State—which holds promise to enable a more intuitive and context-sensitive HCI. The canonical notion of BCI as control device was revisited from an HCI standpoint and its two main categories have been integrated into the definitions of active and reactive BCI. A third distinct type of BCI has been defined as passive BCI, whose applications are potentially far-reaching, only limited by present preparation and calibration procedures. As a way forward, a sequential structure for the entire process of BCI usage was proposed, followed by two complete examples of (B+H)CIs from the newly defined categories: a passive one, and an active hybrid one. The question whether BCI technology could be applied in a useful way for a broader sense of HCI can thus be answered positively. At least the here presented framework of passive and hybrid BCIs embedded in an elaborated training sequence leads to new and more efficient ways of interaction between human and machine. Adding BCI-Technology to a given gaze-based interaction system leads to a more natural and less erroneous way of interaction (see 11.5). Access to the users situational interpretation (see 11.5) allows for higher levels of automated adaptation and, hence, to highly efficient HCI. This approach finds an application also in navigation (see Chapter 4), computer games (see Chapter 10) and task balancing (see Chapter 13). Also, it is not restricted to EEG signals (see Chapter 9). As these studies show, it is only the starting point of the new and highly interdisciplinary field of (B+H)CI.

Acknowledgements   We gratefully thank Matthias Roetting for continuous financial support, and Roman Vilimek, Siemens AG, as well as Jessika Reissland, TU Berlin, for their professional co-working, their beneficial comments, and their support.

References

Asteriadis S, Tzouveli P, Karpouzis K, Kollias S (2009) Estimation of behavioral user state based on eye gaze and head pose—application in an e-learning environment. Multimed Tools Appl 41:469–493

Becker H, Meek C, Chickering DM (2007) Modeling contextual factors of click rates. In: Proceedings of the Twenty-Second AAAI Conference on Artificial Intelligence, Vancouver

Blankertz B, Schäfer C, Dornhege G, Curio G (2002) Single trial detection of EEG error potentials: A tool for increasing BCI transmission rates. In: Artificial Neural Networks—ICANN 2002, pp 1137–1143

Blankertz B, Dornhege G, Krauledat M, Müller K, Curio G (2007) The non-invasive Berlin Brain–Computer Interface: Fast acquisition of effective performance in untrained subjects. NeuroImage 37(2):539–550

Bolt RA (1982) Eyes at the Interface. In: Proceedings of the 1982 Conference on Human Factors in Computing Systems. ACM Press, New York, pp 360–362

Cajochen C, Kräuchi K, von Arx M, Möri D, Graw P, Wirz-Justice A (1996) Daytime melatonin administration enhances sleepiness and theta/alpha activity in the waking EEG. Neurosci Lett 207(3):209–213

Chanel G, et al (2006) Emotion assessment: Arousal evaluation using EEG's and peripheral physiological signals. Multimedia Content Representation, Classification and Security, pp 530–537

Chen D, Vertegaal R (2004) Using mental load for managing interruptions in physiologically attentive user interfaces. Extended Abstracts of SIGCHI 2004 Conference on Human Factors in Computing Systems, pp 1513–1516

Engell-Nielsen T, Glenstrup AJ, Hansen JP (2003) Eye gaze interaction: A new media—not just a fast mouse. In: Itoh K, Komatsubara A, Kuwano S (eds) Handbook of Human Factors/Ergonomics. AsakuraPublishing, Tokyo, Japan, pp 445–455

Fang F, Liu Y, Shen Z (2003) Lie detection with contingent negative variation. Int J Psychophysiol 50(3):247–255

Farwell LA, Donchin E (1988) Talking off the top of your head: Toward a mental prosthesis utilizing event-related brain potentials. Electroencephalogr Clin Neurophysiol 70(6):510–523

Ferrez PW, del Millán R (2008) Error-related EEG potentials generated during simulated brain-computer interaction. IEEE Trans Biomed Eng 55(3):923–929

Grimes D, Tan DS, Hudson SE, Shenoy P, Rao RP (2008) Feasibility and pragmatics of classifying working memory load with an electroencephalograph. In: Proceeding of the Twenty-Sixth Annual SIGCHI Conference on Human Factors in Computing Systems (Florence, Italy, 2008). ACM, New York, pp 835–844

Heekeren HR, Marrett S, Ungerleider LG (2008) The neural systems that mediate human perceptual decision making. Nat Rev Neurosci 9:467–479

Holroyd CB (2004) A note on the oddball N200 and the feedback ERN. In: Ullsperger M, Falkenstein M (eds) Errors, Conflicts, and the Brain. Current Opinions on Performance Monitoring. Max-Planck Institute for Human Cognitive and Brain Sciences, Leipzig, pp 211–218

Hutchinson TF (1993) Eye gaze computer interfaces: Computers that sense eye positions on the display. Computer 26:65–67

Jacob RJK (1993) What you look at is what you get. IEEE Comput 26:65–66

Jacob RJK, Legett JJ, Myers BA, Pausch R (1993) Interaction styles and input/output devices. Behav Inf Technol 12:69–79

Jatzev S, Zander TO, DeFilippis M, Kothe C, Welke S, Rötting M (2008) Examining causes for non-stationarities: The loss of controllability is a factor which induces non-stationarities. In: Proceedings of the 4th Int BCI Workshop & Training Course, Graz University of Technology. Publishing House, Graz, Austria

Kelly S, Lalor E, Reilly R, Foxe J (2005) Visual spatial attention tracking using high-density SSVEP data for independent brain–computer communication. IEEE Trans Rehabil Eng 13(2):172–178

Kohlmorgen J, Dornhege G, Braun M, Blankertz B, Müller K, Curio G, Hagemann K, Bruns A, Schrauf M, Kincses W (2007) Improving human performance in a real operating environment through real-time mental workload detection. In: Toward Brain-Computer Interfacing. MIT Press, incollection 24:409–422

Krauledat M (2008) Analysis of nonstationarities in EEG signals for improving brain-computer interface performance. PhD thesis, Technische Universität Berlin, Fakultät IV—Elektrotechnik und Informatik

Miller GA (1994) The magical number seven, plus or minus two: Some limits on our capacity for processing information. Psychol Rev 101(2):343–352

Moldt D, von Scheve C (2002) Attribution and adaptation: The case of social norms and emotion in human-agent interaction. In: Proceedings of "The Philosophy and Design of Socially Adept Technologies", Workshop Held in Conjunction with CHI'02, April 20th, Minneapolis/Minnesota, USA. National Research Council Canada, Ottawa

Müller K, Tangermann M, Dornhege G, Krauledat M, Curio G, Blankertz B (2008) Machine learning for real-time single-trial EEG-analysis: From brain-computer interfacing to mental state monitoring. J Neurosci Methods 167:82–90

Murata A (2006) Eye gaze input versus mouse: Cursor control as a function of age. Int J Hum Comput Interact 21:1–14

Nieuwenhuis S, Holroyd CB, Mol N, Coles MG (2004) Reinforcement-related brain potentials from medial frontal cortex: Origins and functional significance. Neurosci Biobehav Rev 28:441–448

Nilsson S, Gustafsson T, Carleberg P (2007) Hands free interaction with virtual information in a real environment. In: Proceedings of COGAIN 2007, Leicester, UK, pp 53–57

Park N, Zhu W, Jung Y, McLaughlin M, Jin S (2005) Utility of haptic data in recognition of user state. In: Proceedings of HCI International 11. Lawrence Erlbaum Associates, Mahwah

Pfurtscheller G, Neuper C, Flotzinger D, Pregenzer M (1997) EEG-based discrimination between imagination of right and left hand movement. Electroencephalogr Clin Neurophysiol 103(6):642–651

Pfurtscheller G, Leeb R, Keinrath C, Friedman D, Neuper C, Guger C, Slater M (2006) Walking from thought. Brain Res 1071(1):145–152

Pierce J, Stearns B, Pausch R (1999) Voodoo dolls: Seamless interaction at multiple scales in virtual environments. In: Tagungsband Symposium on Interactive 3D graphics, Atlanta, GA, USA. ACM Press, New York, pp 141–145

Posner MI, Cohen Y (1984) Components of visual orienting. In: Bouma H, Bouwhuis DG (eds) Attention and Performance, vol 10. Erlbaum, Hillsdale, NJ, pp 531–556

Popescu F, Fazli S, Badower Y, Blankertz B, Müller K-R (2007) Single trial classification of motor imagination using 6 dry EEG electrodes. PLoS ONE 2(7). DOI 10.1371/journal.pone.0000637

Premack D, Woodruff G (1978) Does the chimpanzee have a "theory of mind"? Behav Brain Sci 4:515–526

Reissland J, Zander TO (2009) Automated detection of bluffing in a game—Revealing a complex covert user state with a passive BCI. In: Proceedings of the Human Factors and Ergonomics Society Europe Chapter Annual Meeting, Linkoeping, Sweden

Rötting M, Zander T, Trösterer S, Dzaack J (2009) Implicit interaction in multimodal human-machine systems. In: Schlick C (ed) Methods and Tools of Industrial Engineering and Ergonomics. Springer, Berlin

Schmidt EA, Kincses WE, Schrauf M, Haufe S, Schubert R, Curio G, Ag D (2009) Assessing driver's vigilance state during monotonous driving, June 2009

Shenoy P, Krauledat M, Blankertz B, Rao RPN, Müller K-R (2006) Towards adaptive classification for BCI. J Neural Eng 3(1):R13–R23

Shinkareva SV, Mason RA, Malave VL, Wang W, Mitchell TM, Just MA (2008) Using fMRI brain activation to identify cognitive states associated with perception of tools and dwellings. PLoS ONE 3(1):e1394

Sibert LE, Jacob RJK (2000) Evaluation of eye gaze interaction. CHI'00. In: Proceedings of the SIGCHI Conference on Human Factors in Computing Systems. ACM Press, New York, pp 281–288

Toga AW, Mazziotta JC (2000) Brain Mapping. Gulf Professional Publishing, Amsterdam

Tomioka R, Dornhege G, Nolte G, Blankertz B, Aihara K, Müller K-R (2006) Spectrally weighted common spatial pattern algorithm for single trial EEG classification.Technical Report, 21. Dept. of Mathematical Engineering. Tokyo, Japan: University of Tokyo

Vilimek R, Zander TO (2009) BC(eye): Combining eye-gaze input with brain-computer interaction. In: Proceedings of the HCII 2009. Springer, Heidelberg

Wiener EL (1989) Human factors of advanced technology ("glass cockpit") transport aircraft. NASA Contractor Report 177528, NASA Ames Research Center

Wolpaw JR, Birbaumer N, McFarland DJ, Pfurtscheller G, Vaughan TM (2002) Brain-computer interfaces for communication and control. Clin Neurophysiol Off J Int Fed Clin Neurophysiol 113(6):767–791. PMID: 12048038

Wriessnegger S, Scherer R, Mörth K, Maier C, Pfurtscheller G (2006) CN. Heart rate-controlled EEG-Based BCI: The Graz hybrid BCI. In: Proc of the 3rd Int BCI Workshop & Training Course, Graz, Austria, 2006. Graz University of Technology Publishing House, Graz

Zander TO, Kothe C, Welke S, Roetting M (2008) Enhancing human-machine systems with secondary input from passive brain-computer interfaces. In: Proc of the 4th Int BCI Workshop & Training Course, Graz, Austria, 2008. Graz University of Technology Publishing House, Graz

Zander TO, Jatzev S (2009) Detecting affective covert user states with passive brain-computer interfaces. In: Proceedings of the ACII 2009. IEEE Computer Society Press, Los Alamitos, CA

Chapter 12
Brain-Based Indices for User System Symbiosis

**Jan B.F. van Erp, Hans (J.A.) Veltman,
and Marc Grootjen**

Abstract The future generation user system interfaces need to be user-centric which goes beyond user-friendly and includes understanding and anticipating user intentions. We introduce the concept of operator models, their role in implementing user-system symbiosis, and the usefulness of brain-based indices on for instance effort, vigilance, workload and engagement to continuously update the operator model. Currently, the best understood parameters in the operator model are vigilance and workload. An overview of the currently employed brain-based indices showed that indices for the lower workload levels (often based on power in the alpha and theta band of the EEG) are quite reliable, but good indices for the higher workload spectrum are still missing. We argue that this is due to the complex situation when performance stays optimal despite increasing task demands because the operator invests more effort. We introduce a model based on perceptual control theory that provides insight into what happens in this situations and how this affects physiological and brain-based indices. We argue that a symbiotic system only needs to intervene directly in situations of under and overload, but not in a high workload situation. Here, the system must leave the option to adapt on a short notice exclusively to the operator. The system should lower task demands only in the long run to reduce the risk of fatigue or long recovery times. We end by indicating future operator model parameters that can be reflected by brain-based indices.

J.B.F. van Erp (✉) · J.A. Veltman
TNO Human Factors, P.O. Box 23, 3769DE Soesterberg, The Netherlands
e-mail: jan.vanerp@tno.nl

J.A. Veltman
e-mail: hans.veltman@tno.nl

M. Grootjen
EagleScience, Lommerlustlaan 59, 2012BZ Haarlem, The Netherlands
e-mail: marc@eaglescience.nl

D.S. Tan, A. Nijholt (eds.), *Brain-Computer Interfaces*,
Human-Computer Interaction Series,
DOI 10.1007/978-1-84996-272-8_12, © Springer-Verlag London Limited 2010

12.1 Introduction

Since the era of the industrial revolution, the interaction between human and machine changed drastically. At first, machines were only capable of replacing human physical labor, which made the interaction between both purely physical. Later, introduction of computing systems and the personal computer suddenly opened up the possibility to allocate cognitive tasks to a system. These developments caused a paradigm shift in Human-Computer Interaction (HCI).

In 2006, Nature predicted that the achievements of computing power, networks and humans will grow beyond human creativity within the next 15 years (Vinge 2006). This prediction illustrates the skills that computing systems are developing, inevitably leading to a new paradigm shift from an HCI perspective. System and user will not remain separate entities but will confluent into a symbiotic cooperation; or as Boff (2006) foresees: how systems can collaborate symbiotically with humans to enhance human capabilities "... *well outside the range of normal biological variation thereby altering traditional boundary constraints on the adaptability of humans in complex system design...*" The symbiosis Boff refers to requires adequate knowledge about the user's capacities, emotions and intentions and is an extension of human-centered design which should still be central in the development of new technologies in order to make human machine symbioses a success (Hancock 2009). This chapter is about the importance of brain measures in the endeavour of reaching user-system symbiosis.

12.1.1 Evolution of Human Computer Interaction

Before the introduction of computing systems, the interaction between a human and a machine was purely physical. Optimizing performance of the total human-machine system meant improving the machine or automated component, for example by automation of any task that could be done faster, cheaper or more accurate by the machine. With the introduction of the computer this changed. Fitts (1951) was one of the first to acknowledge that both entities have different aptitudes and he crafted a list describing where each entity excels. Following this approach, allocation of tasks was based on the aptitudes of each entity, leading to a categorized list of whether the human, machine, or a combination of both should implement a function (Sheridan 1997). However, the Fitts list assumed the aptitudes to be static and was not intended to incorporate dynamic situations (Dongen and Maanen 2005). In reality, the environment or context can change rapidly creating a different demand for aptitudes. This leads to the conception that function allocation should also be dynamic. Adaptive automation takes the dynamic division of labour between man and machine as a starting point. The terms adaptive automation, dynamic task allocation, dynamic function allocation, or adaptive aiding (Rouse 1988; Scerbo 1996) all reflect the real-time dynamic reallocation of work in order to optimize performance. They are based on the conception of actively aiding the operator only when human information processing limitations emerge.

In the last decades, a number of different dynamic function allocation taxonomies have been proposed (Sheridan and Verplank 1978; Endsley 1987; Endsley and Kaber 1999). The latest and widely accepted taxonomy by Parasuraman et al. (2000) suggests to apply automation to four broad classes of functions: information acquisition, information analysis, decision support and action implementation. Within each of these types, automation can be applied across a continuum of levels (i.e. from fully manual to fully automatic) depending on the cognitive state of the human.

However, ongoing automation and the application of new sensor and information technologies give rise to new challenges for the human. The increase in system complexity, information volume, autonomy, and task integration from different domains cause extreme differences in human demands, for example between normal working conditions and emergency situations. These challenges ask for new paradigms in HCI to ensure that performance is continually optimized. The concept of augmented cognition extends the adaptive aiding paradigm by integration of user and system in a closed-loop system whereby the operator's cognitive state and the operational context have to be taken into account by the system (Kruse and Schmorrow 2005). One of the challenging factors in the development of a successful closed-loop system concerns the question of *when* optimization must be effectuated. Currently, workload[1] is generally considered as the key concept to invoke such a change of authority, but most researchers agree that "*workload is a multidimensional, multifaceted concept that is difficult to define. It is generally agreed that attempts to measure workload relying on a single representative measure are unlikely to be of use*" (Gopher and Donchin 1986). The next section looks more closely at the variables necessary for future symbioses.

12.1.2 Information Models for Future Symbiosis

To deal with the challenges of today, the future generation interfaces need to be user-centric and include understanding and anticipating user intentions. These interfaces will move away from the static keyboard and monitor, must be personalized, and may have a human like appearance and communication channels that resemble those used by people interacting with each other. To achieve this new human-computer symbiosis, *integration* of an operator model (i.e. the user's capacity and task demands) with other information models is required. Literature shows a large variety of models, for example Schneider-Hufschmidt et al. (1993) describe 13 elementary models which focus on the various functional aspects relevant to adaptive interaction. However, to keep the system controllable, we select the following models: (1) operator model (or user model), (2) task model, (3) system model, and (4) context model (or domain model). All of this information is combined in (5) an Adaptation Model (see Fig. 12.1).

---

[1] We consider workload here as the experienced load as function of task demands and user effort, see Section 12.3.1 for more details.

Fig. 12.1 Required
information models for
human-computer symbiosis

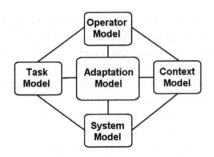

- Task model. The task model is a static representation of the possible tasks for an operator (e.g., a goal hierarchy for solving specific error messages), containing information on the task demands that affect human operator performance and effort. The task model is not a definition of the operator's cognitive state: The effects these tasks have on the operator depends on the interaction between the tasks and the operator model (Neerincx 2003). For some operators a certain level of task demands results in low workload, whereas for other (less experienced) operators this will result in high workload.
- System model. The system model contains technical information about the different system components (e.g. layout, software applications and dependencies). Special cases of system models are for example application models and dialogue (interaction) models (Brown et al. 1990).
- Context model. The context model (or domain model) contains high level information of the human in its environment, such as information about the importance of tasks, the hierarchy of events and organisational context (e.g. is a system part of another system). The context model is dynamic.
- Operator model. The operator model can contain a large variety of information of the individual operator, for instance general performance, preferences and capacities (and in the future possibly data on affective processes: emotions, engagement, frustration, surprise, intention, and boredom). The operator model also contains information about the current active task from the task model. Information about the task load, that comes from the task model and the static information about the capacity of the operator, result to an expected workload level. This should be supplemented by an indication about the actual workload level. The system will require every data source available for continuous updating of information, especially when in-the-loop adaptation is implemented. Examples of data sources are: gestures, facial expression, emotion from voice, and more than ever: physiological measures including brain-based indices to indicate the momentary workload level.

This chapter focuses mainly on the role of brain-based indices as an element of an operator model. However, it should be kept in mind that the integration of information is essential in our human-system symbiosis. Isolated information from only one of the models provides insufficient data for an accurate and useful interpretation.

12.1.3 This Chapter

From the five models mentioned above, we focus on the operator model. The development of adaptive automation in the last 15 years gave an impulse to measure physiological parameters to drive the dynamic allocation of tasks. It will not come as a surprise that neurophysiological signals are generally seen as very relevant for the implementation of adaptive automation and the realization of (future) human system symbiosis. In Section 12.2, we present an overview of the current state of brain-based indices useful for adaptive interaction, restricting ourselves to indices related to workload (being the key concept to adapt the user-system interaction). In Section 12.3, we introduce a state regulation model and discuss how these brain-based indices fit into an operator model. We conclude by identifying the potential and restrictions of using brain-based indices in the endeavour of developing user-system symbiosis and what needs to be done to achieve this symbiosis.

12.2 Brain-Based Indices for Adaptive Interfaces

As stated above, workload is considered a key parameter in adaptive automation and the majority of the physiological measures deal with workload. In this section, we will further look into the possibilities of using brain signals as real time indicators, possibly in combination with other (subjective, performance or physiological) indictors (Byrne and Parasuraman 1996; Parasuraman and Wilson 2008). We discuss workload indices separately from indices for vigilance. We categorize the EEG measures in reactive and passive measures according to the nomenclature introduced by Zander (see Chapter 11 of this Volume). Reactive measures are based on the brain response (e.g., Event Related Potentials—ERPs) to specific probe stimuli while passive measures are based on brain patterns that occur during task execution.

12.2.1 Brain-Based Workload Indices

12.2.1.1 Reactive Workload Indices

An ERP is a brain response that is the result of an internal or external stimulus. ERP components are either positive or negative deflections in the EEG (denoted with a P or N, respectively) that occur within a certain interval after stimulus presentation (often denoted in milliseconds, e.g. the P300 component is a positive deflection with a peak after 300 ms, or with a single number as a simple counter, e.g. the P3 is the third positive peak). Specific ERP components reflect different stages of processing. Generally speaking, the earlier components reflect perceptual processing while later components reflect central cognitive processing. During the 1970-s and 80-s, the idea arose that a user's ERPs to (task irrelevant) probe stimuli could serve as an indicator of workload and processing capacity. The general hypothesis is that ERP components are delayed and/or have a lower amplitude under high workload conditions as compared to lower workload conditions.

With respect to workload measurements, mainly the P300 (or P3) has been investigated under the assumption that the P300 relates to the capacity for processing (task relevant) stimuli (Isreal et al. 1980a; Prinzel et al. 2003). However, there has been some controversy as to how workload affects the P300. Both the amplitude of the peak and/or the latency may be affected. Watter et al. (2001) used the n-back task (n0 – n-3) to study the P300. In the n-back task, observers are presented with a continuous stream of items and have to indicate for each item whether it is the same as the item 1, 2, or n positions back. P300 latency was constant across n-back tasks, but P300 amplitude decreased with increasing memory load. However, lack of sensitivity of the P300 amplitude was shown by Fowler (1994) in a simulated visual flight rules final approach and landing scenario with different levels of workload. Fowler did find effects on the P300 latency reflecting the slowing of perceptual/cognitive processing caused by workload. Isreal et al. (1980b) had participants perform tracking tasks with different levels of difficulty and measured P300 amplitude to be counted tones and also found no effects on P300 amplitude as function of task difficulty. After performing an extensive review on the P300 as index for workload, Kok (2001) concludes that the utility of P300 amplitude as a sensitive and diagnostic measure of processing capacity remains limited. Kok suggests that in many tasks, an increase in difficulty transforms the structure or actual content of the flow of information in the processing systems, thereby interfering with the processes that underlie P3 generation.

Besides the P300, other ERP components have been investigated as well. For instance, Ullsperger et al. (2001) investigated the P3 and the N1 components of an auditory oddball task while participants performed a monitoring and mental arithmetic task separately and together. In an oddball task, one rare item differs from a continuous stream of similar items. The measures were found to be sensitive to perceptual processing (N1) and central processing (P3). Allison and Polich (2008) recently investigated ERP amplitude to tones while subjects played a first-person shooter game at different difficulty levels and reported decreasing amplitudes with increasing difficulty level. Much earlier work of Kramer et al. (1995) already indicated that the P300 component may not be the most sensitive. In their experiment, operators performed a low and high workload radar-monitoring task in the presence of a series of irrelevant auditory probes. P300 amplitude was sensitive only to the introduction of the radar-monitoring task, but could not distinguish between the low and high workload condition. Contrary to the amplitude of the N100, N200, and early and late mismatch negativity (MMN) components. These components decreased from the baseline to the low load condition and from the low load to the high load condition.

12.2.1.2 Passive Workload Indices

A second category of EEG indicators is based on analyzing the different frequency bands in EEG signals. Generally, EEG frequency is divided into the following bands of which each is linked to a different state or activity: delta (<4 Hz; linked to sleeping), theta (4–7 Hz; drowsy or aroused), alpha (8–12 Hz; relaxed), beta (12–30 Hz; alert, concentrated, active) and gamma (>30 Hz; specific cognitive and motor functions). As with the ERP studies, which combination of spectral bands has the highest sensitivity and the best diagnostic value is a matter of debate. Several authors found theta to be a good workload indicator with increasing load corresponding to increasing theta (e.g Fournier et al. 1999; Gevins et al. 1998). For instance, Hankins and Wilson (1998) found increased power in the theta band during flight segments which required mental calculations. Alpha was also identified as sensitive to workload, but with decreasing power corresponding to increasing workload (Gevins et al. 1998; Fournier et al. 1999). Finally, also gamma was found to be sensitive. Laine et al. (2002) used EEG power in the 31–40-Hz band combined with eye movement features to obtain a classification accuracy of 87% distinguishing low and high workload conditions.

12.2.1.3 Discussion on Brain-Based Workload Indices

We have sketched two approaches in identifying EEG indices for workload. The first is based on monitoring the brain's reaction to probe stimuli, the second is based on analysing the brain at work. In analogy to the nomenclature introduced by Zander et al. (see Chapter 11 of this Volume), these approaches result in reactive and passive indices, respectively. The presented results clearly show that there is not a single, simple workload indicator in the brain, and the most sensitive index may depend on tasks, environmental and individual characteristics (as already stated by Humphrey and Kramer 1994). As reactive indices, mainly the N100 and P300 delay and decreased amplitude seem of relevance. As passive indices, increased theta and decreased alpha are most suitable (Gevins et al. 1998). Interestingly, we are not aware of studies that directly compared these two types of indices. This is not to say that there is no good diagnostic value in EEG workload indices. For a two-level situation, discrimination rates above 90% correct are often reported (Fournier et al. 1999), reaching almost 100% correct when combined with physiological measures such as eye movements and heart rate. For instance Wilson and Russell (2003) report 98% correct classification in distinguishing between acceptable load and overload in a simulated air traffic control task. However, an important question is to what extend we can generalise the reported results. This question has mainly been researched across days and across group of individuals, but not so much over tasks and environments. Also relevant is the question to what extend decreased theta and increased alpha are due to other factors than workload. For instance, Smith et al. (2001) found the same effects as function of task difficulty, which is not necessarily the same as workload as we will show in Section 12.3.

12.2.2 Brain-Based Vigilance and Drowsiness Indices

Experts can easily distinguish between the EEG of an alert and a drowsy individual, and Vuckovic et al. (2002) showed that this expertise can also be formalised in an artificial neural network (with a 95% match on average). Although from an HCI perspective, a finer state classification is desirable it shows that EEG potentially contains useful features, and reliable drowsiness detection may be of great value in many (safety critical) environments e.g. (Lal and Craig 2001). Interestingly, this research area focuses on passive indices in either the EEG or the cerebral blood flow, but hardly on reactive indices.

12.2.2.1 Reactive Vigilance and Drowsiness Indices

We know of only a limited number of studies looking into reactive indices of drowsiness. Boksem et al. (2005) used a three-hour visual attention task and compared ERPs to relevant and irrelevant stimuli. Vigilance corresponded with a decreasing N1 amplitude and a decreasing difference between the N2B amplitude of relevant and irrelevant stimuli. The latter indicates that subjects encounter more difficulties in ignoring irrelevant stimuli during a vigilance task. The authors claim that mental fatigue results in a reduction in goal-directed attention, leaving subjects performing in a more stimulus-driven fashion. Trejo et al. (1995) used a visual display-monitoring task (including a signal detection task) to evaluate the relation between ERP components and performance but their experiment is not conclusive with respect to vigilance effects.

12.2.2.2 Passive Vigilance and Drowsiness Indices

Similar to the spectral bands used as indices for levels of workload, indices for vigilance are mainly based on the theta and alpha power in the EEG. Generally, increased theta power correlates with poor performance in sleep deprived subjects (Makeig et al. 2000), in vigilance tasks (Paus et al. 1997; Boksem et al. 2005), and in continued video data terminal work (frontal midline theta rhythm; Yamada 1998). Lal and Craig (2001) concluded based on an extended review that changes in theta and delta activity are strongly linked to transition to fatigue.

Stampi et al. (1995) showed the usefulness of alpha activity as index for sleepiness. More precisely, they validated the Alpha Attenuation Test (AAT) as index for sleepiness with sleep deprived subjects. The AAT is based on the observation that when operators get sleepier, alpha activity with eyes open increases and with eyes closed decreases. The relation between theta, alpha and sleepiness was also reported by Torsvall and Akerstedt (1987) who followed train drivers during night and day drives. They report high intra-individual correlations between rated sleepiness and alpha and theta power density.

12.2.2.3 Blood Flow Vigilance and Drowsiness Indices

Besides EEG, cerebral blood flow (CBF) may contain correlates to vigilance or sleepiness. Paus et al. (1997) investigated CBF as function of time on task in an auditory vigilance task. Increased CBF was found in both left and right visual cortical areas, but decreased CBF was found in the right hemisphere only in both subcortical and cortical areas. The latter may correspond to a shift from controlled to automatic attentional processing of the auditory stimuli, similar to the findings of Boksem et al. (2005) on the N2B amplitude.

Schnittger et al. (1997) measured blood flow velocities in the middle cerebral arteries during a 30-minute visual vigilance task. They found reduced velocities to both hemispheres that corresponded with time on task and reduced performance. However, Warm et al. (2009), Shaw et al. (2006) also measured CBF velocity for both visual and auditory vigilance tasks. They confirm the decrease in CBF but do find differences between left and right hemisphere.

12.2.2.4 Discussion on Brain-Based Vigilance and Drowsiness Indices

So far, vigilance indicators are mainly based on passive indices. Although there may be diagnostic value in ERP components that signify a shift from top-down to bottom-up processing, there are several passive EEG and CBF measures that correlate well with vigilance or sleepiness. The general picture is clearer than in the previous section on workload: power in both the theta and alpha band are the best indices, although tools have been developed that use all major bands (Lal et al. 2003). As with the section on workload, we have to ask ourselves the question to what extend the findings can be generalised. Interestingly, the indices seem to transfer well across tasks, environments and even participants. However, Lal and Craig (2001) mention several factors that may influence fatigue, including personality, temperament, anxiety and mood.

12.2.3 Discussion on Brain-Based Indices

One of the things researchers have been interested in is the correlation between EEG indices and performance. Often, high correlations are reported between for instance EEG and rapid and slow reaction times (Besserve et al. 2008) and/or subjective measures (Prinzel et al. 2003). Although this is generally considered desirable, a valid question is what the added value of EEG indices is in case performance measures are available. Performance measures may be easier to obtain and more stable across individuals than EEG data, which makes the latter useless in case there is a high correlation with the obtained performance measures. However, we argue that workload and performance will correlate in specific circumstances only, so performance indices alone cannot validate a workload index. We will further explain the relation between workload and performance in Section 12.3. A similar investigation should be made between brain-based measures and other physiological measures to see to what extend these are additional or complementary.

The presented overview also shows that indices are reasonably successful in the lower workload range (i.e., vigilance, drowsiness), but reliable indices in high load spectrum seem to be less reliable (see also Byrne and Parasuraman 1996). We will also interpret these results using a model of state regulation presented in Section 12.3.

Finally, are passive indices preferred over reactive indices? Apart from differences in diagnositcity, both have practical pros and cons. Most prominent is that reactive indices need probe stimuli possibly disturbing task performance. However, reactive indices may need less electrodes than passive indices, namely along the central line versus spatially distributed (although some passive systems are based on as few as two electrodes, e.g. Jung et al. 1997).

12.3 Input for an Operator Model

12.3.1 Relation Between Workload, Task Demand and Performance

A complete operator model is very complex and would require knowledge of the relation between the components of such model such as taskload, emotional state, capacities, experience to name just a few. However, a complete operator model is not required for all applications and also not to implement adaptive automation. In this section we describe relations between important components of such an operator model. We describe the relation between task demands, workload, effort and performance after which we present a model that provides insight into the dynamic relation between effort regulation and operator state.

An operator model should contain information that is critical for the system to be able to realize symbiosis. At this moment, workload is one of the crucial parameters of the operator model. An adaptive system may for instance apply the following rule: under normal workload full information can be given in text and images, while under high workload only critical information should be given using images. Furthermore, tasks can be reallocated to the system or the user, depending on the workload level. For example if the user's performance degrades because of low workload, a reallocation of tasks can bring workload levels back to normal and optimize performance.

Figure 12.2 describes the relation between workload, task demands and operator performance. We argue that this relation is not as straightforward as is often assumed. And therefore, information about the task demands is not sufficient.

Optimal performance can be reached under normal workload levels when the operator is interacting with the system on a regular basis, and under high workload

Fig. 12.2 Hypothetical relation between task demands, performance, effort and workload

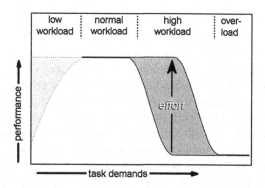

levels when the operator is able to maintain a high level of performance when additional effort is exerted. This can not be prolonged for a long time without costs. Operators become more fatigued, which might result in more errors. Furthermore, the recovery time after the work period will be longer. Suboptimal performance emerges when the workload is low (low task demands) and the task requires little attention. In this situation, human beings have difficulty to remain alert. Therefore, when new information is presented, operators are likely to miss it and the performance can decrease considerably. Suboptimal performance is also present in an overload situation. For example, when too much information must be processed, the operator cannot get an acceptable level of performance any more (despite exerting additional effort). It is likely that the operator will even stop to exert additional effort, because this will not help him anymore.

Figure 12.2 provides insight into the relation between workload and task performance. We argue that the following three conditions are undesirable and require a symbiotic system to intervene:

- Under low workload conditions it is important to know if the operator is still in an alert state. If not, the system should intervene, for example by adding additional tasks to the operator. This intervention should be immediately.
- Under high workload conditions, the system should monitor the ability of the operator to invest additional effort. Intervention does not need to be immediately, but in due time to prevent the operator from becoming fatigued or requiring a long recovery time.
- Under overload conditions, the system should intervene immediately to reduce the task demands to a level where the operator can reach good performance with additional effort and eventually reduce the task demands further to normal workload levels.

These conditions illustrate the importance of operator state information, or in other words: How are these three conditions reflected in brain-based (and other physiological) measures? In the previous section, we concluded that there are relatively reliable measures to identify vigilance and drowsiness. Several experiments show promising results for the use of brain measures for adapting the task load to the state of the operator e.g. (Scerbo et al. 2000) in this range of low task demands.

Scerbo and his colleagues showed that overall task performance improves when the state of the operator is used as a parameter to reallocate tasks between an operator and a computer. They calculated the relative high frequency of an EEG spectrum as an index of the operator state (which they called engagement index). Based on this index, a computer algorithm decided to give the operator more or less tasks. If the engagement index was low, providing additional tasks to the operator improved the overall task performance. Also, detecting overload is relatively simple and can be based on task demands and operator performance. However, the biggest challenge for a symbiotic system is to identify the high workload conditions where the operator reaches optimal performance by adding more effort. This is the complex situation where the operator him or herself is adapting to the task demands. To help identify possible indices, we present a state regulation model to explain the relation between operator state, workload and performance.

12.3.2 Operator State Regulation, Workload and Performance

The model in Fig. 12.3 is based on perceptual control theory (PCT; Powers 1973). This model provides insight into the dynamic relation between task load and the coping behaviour of operators. PCT is also used in similar models such as the model of Hockey (2003) and of Hendy et al. (2001). The model of Hockey uses PCT to

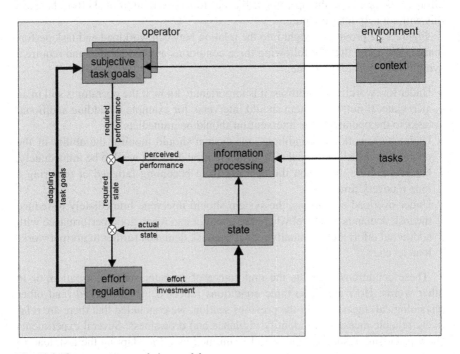

Fig. 12.3 Operator state regulation model

describe state regulation, whereas Hendy et al. use the PCT to describe information processing. The present model combines state regulation and information processing. The PCT assumes that the difference between the required situation (goal) and the actual situation (sensor information) is crucial for the adaptive behaviour of biological systems. Adaptive changes will occur when differences exist (error signals). According to PCT, goals can be defined at several levels and an error signal is often a new goal for a lower order system. The model in Fig. 12.3 includes two levels: 'subjective task goals' at the highest level and 'required state' at a lower level.

The model includes an information processing loop and a state regulation loop. The state is crucial for the information processing. There are many models of information processing. Most of them do not include state regulation. It is well known that it is difficult to perform a cognitively demanding task when we are in a suboptimal state, for example due to sleep loss or fatigue. The information-processing loop includes the stages of information processing of an operator dealing with a system (perception, decision making and action selection). These details are not relevant for the present purposes and therefore, the model in Fig. 12.3 contains only a single information processing box without further details.

Information to be processed can come from the environment (tasks) or from an internal model of the system that is built up by the operator. The perceived information, and in particular, the perceived actual performance is compared with the required performance. As long as the perceived performance matches the required performance, no state change is required. If there is a difference between the required and the actual state, there are two possible solutions to bring back equilibrium:

- Operators can invest more effort into the task. This will change the state in such a way that information processing becomes more appropriate.
- Operators can change the task goals in such a way that the level of the required performance is lowered (e.g. by accepting less accurate performance, take more time to perform the tasks or by skipping less relevant sub-tasks).

The first option will result in physiological changes and can be measured by the brain indices described in the previous section and other physiological indicators such as blood pressure, heart rate and heart rate variability (Veltman and Gaillard 1998).

12.3.2.1 State Regulation

A state should be regarded as the result of many physiological and psychological processes that regulate brain and body in an attempt to put an individual in an optimal condition to meet the demands of the work environment (Gaillard and Kramer 2000). Figure 12.3 assumes that there is a complex relation between task demands and task performance. By investing more effort, operators can keep the performance at a high level for some time. The model in Fig. 12.3 goes deeper into this relation. Effort investment changes the state of the operator to improve information processing. Consequently, the difference between the actual and the required performance will become smaller. As described above, an alternative reaction of the operator to increased task load can be a lowering of the subjective task goals. If this option is chosen, then an increase in task load will not result in an increase in effort invest-ment and as a consequence no physiological changes will be measured.

The likelihood of adapting the *task goals* is affected by the context. For exam-ple, in a flight simulator, reducing the task goals often does not have serious con-sequences. In a real aircraft this can have serious consequences and therefore, the effort investment is often much higher in a real aircraft (e.g. Wilson et al. 1987). However, when the context of the flight simulator is a selection to become a pi-lot, then the effort, measured with physiological measures, is the same as in a real aircraft (Veltman 2002).

Another example of the effect of context on subjective task goals is the existence of other goals. In many situations, the subjective task goals are just one set of goals among many other goals such as keeping rest, going to a toilet, have a social con-versation, going away for a cigarette etc. The context is important for keeping the task goal the primary one. During vigilance for example, performance will often deteriorate after some time because it is difficult to keep the task goal the primary goal among other competing goals as getting rest or counteracting boredom.

These effects are important for the choices of physiological measures. We dis-cussed many brain-based indicators in this chapter, most of them have been tested as a measure for mental workload. Some of the measures provide information about additional effort expenditure in high workload situations (such as high frequency EEG and P300) and others provide information about the alert state or engagement in low workload situations (e.g. low frequency EEG). There is still not enough in-formation about how these measures can be used adequately for human computer symbioses.

12.3.2.2 Operator Adaptation

One of the aspects that we want to make clear with the present model is that the operator is almost continuously adapting to changing task demands. This adaptation process can be measured with physiological measures that should not only provide information about the workload of an operator but also about the way the operator is adapting to changing task demands.

Based on the model in Fig. 12.3, we argue that it is not likely that simple adaptive automation principles will work in high-workload situations in which an operator is continuously adapting to changing task demands. If the task becomes more difficult, the operator may adapt by investing more effort. Human beings are very efficient in adapting to changing task demands. In fact, that is essential of all biological systems. We favour an approach in which the system allows periods of high workload but continuously monitors the ability of the operator to maintain an adaptive state and reduces task demands on a longer term to prevent fatigue.

12.4 Discussion

12.4.1 Sense and Non-sense of Brain-Based Adaptation

We argued that several models (operator, context, task and system model) are required for an efficient human computer symbioses system. The model we presented in this chapter can not be used directly as an operator model for this purpose. However, we think that the present model provides insight into the way brain measures can be used for human computer symbioses.

In the future, computers can take over complex tasks from human operators. In many situations it is not desirable that computers take over all tasks. The human operator can perform optimally when he is in the loop. It would be a huge step forward when computer systems can take over tasks from the human operator and still let the operator have control over the whole situation.

We argue that it is important to distinguish between high and low workload situations. In low workload situations, chances are that the operator will loose attention and is not in the loop any more. He is then likely to make errors due to missed information. In other words, the operator is not in an adaptive mode in such a situation. Measuring the operator state in these situations is relevant because a computer system can use this information to provide extra information to the operator to make the operator more alert. We have provided data that this state can be quite accurately identified with brain-based indices.

Information about the operator state in high workload situations can not be used in the same straight forward way. It seems obvious that a computer system can take away some tasks when the operator experiences high workload. However, when brain measures and other physiological measures indicate that the operator is investing additional effort, than the operator is actually in an adaptive state. If the computer takes away tasks from the operator directly, this may lead to undesirable situations. In fact, both the computer system and the operator are adapting at the same time. The operator tries to adapt to changing task demands, and the computer system tries to adapt to the state of the operator. Adaptive systems that try to adapt to each other will not work together.

There are several possibilities how to use the state information during high workload situations. One possibility is that the task model monitors the relevance of all possible tasks that have to be performed by the operator. When the operator is in a high workload situation, information about less relevant tasks might be postponed until the workload level reached normal values again. Another possibility is that the brain measures are used to monitor the effort expenditure and use this to estimate the fatigue level of an operator. This can be used to reduce task load after some time instead of reducing it momentarily.

12.4.2 Opportunities for Brain-Based Indices in User-System Symbiosis

As we sketched in the introduction, for future user-system symbiosis, an operator model needs to contain more parameters than workload, including for instance engagement, confusion, and emotional state. Recently, investigations started to identify EEG patterns that reflect some of these parameters. Several authors developed an engagement factor. For instance, Freeman et al. (1999) and Pope et al. (1995) developed engagement indices based on patterns in the theta, alpha and beta band to control automation. Fairclough and Venables (2006) measured several EEG and other physiological measures and used multiple regression to explore the relation with task engagement, distress and worry, of which the first two could be predicted quite well. However, one can argue that these (engagement) indices are on the same continuum as workload and vigilance. Only very recently, efforts are made to identify neural correlates from completely different categories such as spatial disorientation and situational awareness (Van Orden et al. 2007; Viirre et al. 2006) and emotions (Petrantonakis and Hadjileontiadis 2009). The latter is an interesting new field: emotions are both critical to "understand" the user and also interact with cognitive capabilities such as attention and reasoning (Dolan 2002).

Acknowledgements   The authors gratefully acknowledge the support of the BrainGain Smart Mix Programme of the Netherlands Ministry of Economic Affairs and the Netherlands Ministry of Education, Culture and Science.

References

Allison BZ, Polich J (2008) Workload assessment of computer gaming using a single-stimulus event-related potential paradigm. Biol Psychol 77(3):277–283

Boff KR (2006) Revolutions and shifting paradigms in human factors & ergonomics. Appl Ergon 37(4 SPEC. ISS.):391–399

Besserve M, Philippe M, Florence G, Laurent F, Garnero L, Martinerie J (2008) Prediction of performance level during a cognitive task from ongoing EEG oscillatory activities. Clin Neurophysiol 119(4):897–908

Boksem MAS, Meijman TF, Lorist MM (2005) Effects of mental fatigue on attention: An ERP study. Cogn Brain Res 25(1):107–116

Brown D, Totterdell P, Nonnan M (eds) (1990) Adaptive User Interfaces. Academic Press, London

Byrne EA, Parasuraman R (1996) Psychophysiology and adaptive automation. Biol Psychol 42(3):249–268

Dolan RJ (2002) Neuroscience and psychology: Emotion, cognition, and behavior. Science 298(5596):1191–1194

Dongen K, Maanen PP (2005) Design for dynamic task allocation. In: Proceedings of the 7th International Conference on Naturalistic Decision Making

Endsley M (1987) The application of human factors to the development of expert systems for advanced cockpits. In: Proceedings of the Human Factors Society 31st Annual Meeting, pp 1388–1392

Endsley MR, Kaber DB (1999) Level of automation effects on performance, situation awareness and workload in a dynamic control task. Ergonomics 462–492

Fairclough SH, Venables L (2006) Prediction of subjective states from psychophysiology: A multivariate approach. Biol Psychol 71(1):100–110

Fitts PM (1951) Human engineering for an effective air navigation and traffic control system. Ohio State University Foundation Report, Columbus, OH

Fournier LR, Wilson GF, Swain CR (1999) Electrophysiological, behavioral, and subjective indexes of workload when performing multiple tasks: Manipulations of task difficulty and training. Int J Psychophysiol 31(2):129–145

Fowler B (1994) P300 as a measure of workload during a simulated aircraft landing task. Hum Factors 36(4):670–683

Freeman FG, Mikulka PJ, Prinzel LJ, Scerbo MW (1999) Evaluation of an adaptive automation system using three EEG indices with a visual tracking task. Biol Psychol 50(1):61–76

Gaillard AWK, Kramer AF (2000) Theoretical and methodological issues in psychophysiological research. In: Backs RW, Boucsein W (eds) Engineering Psychophysiology: Issues and Applications. Lawrence Erlbaum Associates, Mahwah (NJ), pp 31–58

Gevins A, Smith ME, Leong H, McEvoy L, Whitfield S, Du R, Rush G (1998) Monitoring working memory load during computer-based tasks with EEG pattern recognition methods. Hum Factors 40(1):79–91

Gopher D, Donchin E (1986) Workload—An examination of the concept. In: Boff K, Kaufman L, Thomas J (eds) Handbook of Perception and Human Performance, vol 41(1). Wiley, New York, pp 41–49

Hancock PA (2009) Mind, Machine and Morality; Toward a philosophy of Human-Technology Symbioses. Ashgate Publishing Limited, Farnham (UK)

Hankins TC, Wilson GF (1998) A comparison of heart rate, eye activity, EEC and subjective measures of pilot mental workload during flight. Aviat Space Environ Med 69(4):360–367

Hendy KC, East KP, Farrell PSE (2001) An informationprocessing model of operator stress and performance. In: Hancock PA, Desmond PA (eds) Stress, Workload and Fatigue. Lawrence Erlbaum Associates, Mahwah (NJ), pp 34–82

Hockey GRJ (2003) Operator functional state as a framework for the assessment of performance degradation. In: Hockey GRJ, Gaillard AWK, Burov A (eds) Operator Functional State: The Assessment and Prediction of Human Performance Degradation in Complex Tasks. NATO Science Series. IOS Press, Amsterdam, pp 8–23

Humphrey DG, Kramer AF (1994) Toward a psychophysiological assessment of dynamic changes in mental workload. Hum Factors 36(1):3–26

Isreal JB, Chesney GL, Wickens CD, Donchin E (1980a) P300 and tracking difficulty: Evidence for multiple resources in dual-task performance. Psychophysiology 17(3):259–273

Isreal JB, Wickens CD, Chesney GL, Donchin E (1980b) Event-related brain potential as an index of display-monitoring workload. Hum Factors 22(2):211–224

Jung T-P, Makeig S, Stensmo M, Sejnowski TJ (1997) Estimating alertness from the EEG power spectrum. IEEE Trans Biomed Eng 44(1):60–69

Kok A (2001) On the utility of P3 amplitude as a measure of processing capacity. Psychophysiology 38(3):557–577

Kramer AF, Trejo LJ, Humphrey D (1995) Assessment of mental workload with task-irrelevant auditory probes. Biol Psychol 40(1–2):83–100

Kruse AA, Schmorrow DD (2005) Session overview: Foundations of augmented cognition. In: Schmorrow DD (ed) Foundations of Augmented Cognition. Lawrence Erlbaum Associates, Mahwah, NJ, pp 441–445

Laine TI, Bauer KW Jr, Lanning JW, Russell CA, Wilson GF (2002) Selection of input features across subjects for classifying crewmember workload using artificial neural networks. IEEE Trans Syst Man Cybern Part A, Syst Hum 32(6):691–704

Lal SKL, Craig AA (2001) Critical review of the psychophysiology of driver fatigue. Biol Psychol 55(3):173–194

Lal SKL, Craig A, Boord P, Kirkup L, Nguyen H (2003) Development of an algorithm for an EEG-based driver fatigue countermeasure. J Saf Res 34(3):321–328

Makeig S, Jung T-P, Sejnowski TJ (2000) Awareness during drowsiness: Dynamics and electrophysiological correlates. Can J Exp Psychol 54(4):266–273

Neerincx MA (2003) Cognitive task load design: Model, methods and examples. In: Hollnagel E (ed) Handbook of Cognitive Task Design. Lawrence Erlbaum Associates, Mahwah, NJ, pp 283–305

Parasuraman R, Wilson GF (2008) Putting the brain to work: Neuroergonomics past, present, and future. Hum Factors 50(3):468–474

Parasuraman R, Sheridan T, Wickens C (2000) A model for types and levels of human interaction with automation. IEEE Trans Syst Man Cybern 286–297

Paus T, Zatorre RJ, Hofle N, Caramanos Z, Gotman J, Petrides M, Evans AC (1997) Time-related changes in neural systems underlying attention and arousal during the performance of an auditory vigilance task. J Cogn Neurosci 9(3):392–408

Petrantonakis PC, Hadjileontiadis LJ (2009) EEG-based emotion recognition using hybrid filtering and higher order crossings. In: International Conference on Affective Computing & Intelligent Interaction. IEEE, New York

Pope AT, Bogart EH, Bartolome DS (1995) Biocybernetic system evaluates indices of operator engagement in automated task. Biol Psychol 40(1–2):187–195

Powers WT (1973) Behavior: The Control of Perception. Aldine, Chicago

Prinzel LJ III, Freeman FG, Scerbo MW, Mikulka PJ, Pope AT (2003) Effects of a psychophysiological system for adaptive automation on performance, workload, and the event-related potential P300 component. Hum Factors 45(4):601–613

Rouse WB (1988) Adaptive aiding for human/computer control. Hum Factors 30(4):431–443

Scerbo M (1996) Theoretical perspectives on adaptive automation. In: Parasuraman R, Mouloua M (eds) Automation and Human Performance: Theory and Applications. Lawrence Erlbaum Associates, Mahwah, pp 37–63

Scerbo MW, Freeman FG, Mikulka PJ (2000) A biocybernetic system for adaptive automation. In: Backs RW, Boucsein W (eds) Engineering Psychophysiology: Issues and Applications. Lawrence Erlbaum Associates, Mahwah (NJ), pp 241–254

Schneider-Hufschmidt M, Kühme T, Malinowski U (1993) Adaptive User Interfaces—Principles and Practice. Elsevier, Amsterdam

Schnittger C, Johannes S, Arnavaz A, Munte TF (1997) Relation of cerebral blood flow velocity and level of vigilance in humans. NeuroReport 8(7):1637–1639

Shaw TH, Warm JS, Matthews G, Riley M, Weiler EM, Dember WN, Tripp L, Finomore V, Hollander TD (2006) Effects of sensory modality on vigilance performance and cerebral hemovelocity. In: Proceedings of the Human Factors and Ergonomics Society, pp 1619–1623

Sheridan TB (1997) Function allocation: algorithm, alchemy or apostasy. In: ALLFN'97, pp 307–316

Sheridan TB, Verplank WL (1978) Human and computer control of undersea teleoperators. MIT Man-Machine Systems Laboratory, Cambridge, MA, Tech. Rep

Smith ME, Gevins A, Brown H, Karnik A, Du R (2001) Monitoring task loading with multivariate EEG measures during complex forms of human-computer interaction. Hum Factors 43(3):366–380

Stampi C, Stone P, Michimori A (1995) A new quantitative method for assessing sleepiness: The alpha attenuation test. Work Stress 9(2–3):368–376

Torsvall L, Akerstedt T (1987) Sleepiness on the job: Continuously measured EEG changes in train drivers. Electroencephalogr Clin Neurophysiol 66(6):502–511

Trejo LJ, Kramer AF, Arnold JA (1995) Event-related potentials as indices of display-monitoring performance. Biol Psychol 40(1–2):33–71

Ullsperger P, Freude G, Erdmann U (2001) Auditory probe sensitivity to mental workload changes—An event-related potential study. Int J Psychophysiol 40(3):201–209

Van Orden KF, Viirre E, Kobus DA (2007) Augmenting task-centered design with operator state assessment technologies. In: Lecture Notes in Computer Science (including subseries Lecture Notes in Artificial Intelligence and Lecture Notes in Bioinformatics), LNAI 4565, pp 212–219

Veltman JA (2002) A comparative study of psychophysiological reactions during simulator and real flight. Int J Aviat Psychol, pp 33–48

Veltman JA, Gaillard AWK (1998) Physiological workload reactions to increasing levels of task difficulty. Ergonomics 5:656–669

Viirre E, Wing S, Huang R, Strychacz C, Koo C, Stripling R, Cohn J, Chase B, Jung T (2006) EEG markers of spatial disorientation. In: Proc 2nd Int Conf Aug Cog, 1

Vinge V (2006) 2020 computing: The creativity machine. Nature 440(7083):411

Vuckovic A, Radivojevic Chen V, ACN Popovic D (2002) Automatic recognition of alertness and drowsiness from EEG by an artificial neural network. Med Eng Phys 24(5):349–360

Warm JS, Matthews G, Parasuraman R (2009) Cerebral hemodynamics and vigilance performance. Mil Psychol 21(SUPPL 1):1

Watter S, Geffen GM, Geffen LB (2001) The n-back as a dual-task: P300 morphology under divided attention. Psychophysiology 38(6):998–1003

Wilson GF, Russell CA (2003) Operator functional state classification using multiple psychophysiological features in an air traffic control task. Hum Factors 45(3):381–389

Wilson GF, Purvis B, Skelly J, Fullenkamp P, Davis I (1987) Physiological data used to measure pilot workload in actual flight and simulator conditions. In: Proceedings of the Human Factors Society, 31th Annual Meeting, pp 779–783

Yamada F (1998) Frontal midline theta rhythm and eyeblinking activity during a VDT task and a video game: Useful tools for psychophysiology in ergonomics. Ergonomics 41(5):678–688

Chapter 13
From Brain Signals to Adaptive Interfaces: Using fNIRS in HCI

Audrey Girouard, Erin Treacy Solovey, Leanne M. Hirshfield, Evan M. Peck, Krysta Chauncey, Angelo Sassaroli, Sergio Fantini, and Robert J.K. Jacob

Abstract Functional near-infrared spectroscopy (fNIRS) is an emerging non-invasive, lightweight imaging tool which can measure blood oxygenation levels in the brain. In this chapter, we describe the fNIRS device and its potential within the realm of human-computer interaction (HCI). We discuss research that explores the kinds of states that can be measured with fNIRS, and we describe initial research and prototypes that can use this objective, real time information about users' states as input to adaptive user interfaces.

A. Girouard (✉) · E.T. Solovey · L.M. Hirshfield · E.M. Peck · K. Chauncey · R.J.K. Jacob
Computer Science Department, Tufts University, Medford, MA 02155, USA
e-mail: audrey.girouard@tufts.edu

E.T. Solovey
e-mail: erin.solovey@tufts.edu

L.M. Hirshfield
e-mail: leanne.hirshfield@tufts.edu

E.M. Peck
e-mail: evan.peck@tufts.edu

K. Chauncey
e-mail: krysta.chauncey@tufts.edu

R.J.K. Jacob
e-mail: robert.jacob@tufts.edu

A. Sassaroli · S. Fantini
Biomedical Engineering Department, Tufts University, Medford, MA 02155, USA

A. Sassaroli
e-mail: angelo.sassaroli@tufts.edu

S. Fantini
e-mail: sergio.fantini@tufts.edu

D.S. Tan, A. Nijholt (eds.), *Brain-Computer Interfaces,*
Human-Computer Interaction Series,
DOI 10.1007/978-1-84996-272-8_13, © Springer-Verlag London Limited 2010

13.1 Introduction

The field of brain-computer interfaces (BCI) is beginning to expand beyond its original clinical focus. While traditional BCIs were designed to function using the brain as the sole means of communication for disabled patients (Millán et al. 2004), current research investigates the brain as an additional input to the interface, designed for a broader range of users (Grimes et al. 2008). Neural signals can act as a complementary source of information when combined with conventional computer inputs such as the mouse or the keyboard. We present work in this chapter that illustrates this direction in BCI and shows how to move from controlled experiments exploring task-specific brain activity to a more general framework using mental activity to guide interface response. Our work, grounded in the field of human-computer interaction (HCI), suggests the practicality and feasibility of using normal untrained brain activity to inform interfaces.

While most BCIs use the electroencephalogram (EEG) to measure brain activity, we adopt the relatively less-explored technique of functional near-infrared spectroscopy (fNIRS), a non-invasive measurement of changes in blood oxygenation, which can be used to extrapolate levels of brain activation (Fig. 13.1, see also Chapter 8 of this Volume). Ideally, for HCI research, the fNIRS signals would be robust enough to remain unaffected by other non-mental activities, such as typing, occurring during the participant's task performance. In fact, one of the main benefits of fNIRS is that the equipment imposes few physical or behavioral restrictions on the participant (Hoshi 2009).

We identify two research questions that shape this chapter: (1) what kind of states can we measure using fNIRS? (2) how should we use this information as input to an adaptive user interface?

To address our first question, we will start by discussing practicality and applicability of the technology in realistic, desktop environments (Solovey et al. 2009). We will then describe studies investigating the use of fNIRS to obtain meaningful data related to mental workload, both with workload as an overall cognitive function (Girouard et al. 2009; Hirshfield et al. 2007), and with specific components of it

(a)   (b)

Fig. 13.1 Functional near-infrared spectroscopy: (**a**) typical setup with a sensor secured on forehead with a headband, (**b**) the sensor containing near-infrared light sources and a light detector

(Hirshfield et al. 2009b). Our studies progress from very controlled experiments that help us identify centers of brain activity, to experiments using simple user interfaces, showing how this technique may be applied to more realistic interfaces. Throughout all studies in this chapter, we show the use of novel machine learning techniques applied to fNIRS, in order to classify and use the brain activity information in real time.

Our second goal focuses on creating new interactive, real-time user interfaces, which can adapt behavior based on brain measurements. The design challenge is to use this information in a subtle and judicious way, as an additional, lightweight input that could make a mouse or keyboard-driven interface more intuitive or efficient. Specifically, we are exploring situations and interfaces that can be adapted slowly, in a manner that is subtle and unobtrusive to the user, which could increase productivity and decrease frustration. At the end of this chapter, we describe two early prototypes of user interfaces that can adapt to the user's workload profile or other brain activity in real time.

13.2 fNIRS Background

fNIRS provides a measure of blood oxygen concentration, indicative of brain activity when measured on the head (Villringer and Chance 1997). Near-infrared light is pulsed into the forehead where it is refracted from the tissues of the cortex up to depths of 1–3 cm. Oxygenated and deoxygenated hemoglobin are the main absorbers of light at these wavelengths, and thus the diffusely reflected light picked up by the detector correlates with the concentration of oxygen in the blood, as well as the overall amount of blood in the tissue. The basic technology is common to all systems, but the measured signal differs depending on the location of the probe and the amount of light received.

There are many possible placements of fNIRS probes, allowing the study of multiple brain regions. The most common placements are on the motor cortex (Sitaram et al. 2007) and the prefrontal cortex (PFC) (Ehlis et al. 2008; Mappus et al. 2009), although other regions have also been explored (Herrmann et al. 2008). We chose to study the anterior PFC (aPFC), an active region that deals with high-level processing such as working memory, planning, problem solving, memory retrieval and attention (Ramnani and Owen 2004). Thus, our considerations below are intended for researchers investigating the aPFC; methods that reflect activity in other parts of the brain will vary considerably. However, we expect our results to be valid for other experimental setups and contexts that use the PFC.

13.3 fNIRS Considerations for HCI Research

Because most brain imaging and sensing devices were developed for clinical settings, they often have characteristics that make them less suitable for use in realistic

HCI settings. For example, although functional magnetic resonance imaging (fMRI) is effective at localizing brain activity, it is susceptible to motion artifacts, and even slight movement (more than 3 mm) will corrupt the image. The most common technology used for brain measurement in HCI is EEG, since it is non-invasive, portable, and relatively inexpensive compared with other brain imaging devices (Lee and Tan 2006). EEG is not ideal for HCI, either: it is susceptible to artifacts from eye and facial movement, as well as nearby electronic devices, requires gel in the participant's hair, and takes time to set up properly.

Recently, fNIRS has been used in HCI because it has many characteristics that make it suitable for use outside of clinical settings (Girouard et al. 2009; Hirshfield et al. 2009b; Mappus et al. 2009). Benefits include ease of use, short setup time, and portability, making it a promising tool for HCI researchers. In addition, there are no technical restrictions for using EEG and fNIRS together (Hirshfield et al. 2009a), and the two technologies could complement one another. While EEG measures electricity—a direct result of neuronal activity—and is thus very fast, it is also spatially indeterminate; as previously mentioned, fNIRS measures blood oxygenation, an indirect measure of neuronal activity which is much slower to change than the EEG signal.

Our goal is to observe brain signals that can be used in a relatively ordinary computer task environment; so we do not expect the participant to be physically constrained while using the computer. In most studies using brain sensors, researchers expend great effort to reduce the noise picked up by the sensors. Typically, participants are asked to remain still, avoid head and facial movement, and use restricted movement when interacting with the computer. In addition, many factors cannot be controlled, so researchers sometimes throw out data that may have been contaminated by environmental or behavioral noise, or they develop complex algorithms for removing the noise from the data. By doing this, the researchers hope to achieve higher quality brain sensor data, and therefore better estimates of cognitive state information. However, it is not clear that all of these factors contribute to problems in fNIRS data or that these restrictions improve the signal quality, so a series of experiments were conducted in order to observe directly the effect of such artifacts on the data. Below, we identify several fNIRS considerations and explain best practices for working with fNIRS in HCI research.

13.3.1 Head Movement

Several fNIRS researchers have brought attention to motion artifacts in fNIRS sensor data, particularly those from head movement (Devaraj et al. 2004; Matthews et al. 2008). They note that these issues are significant if the head is not restricted, and even more so in an entirely mobile situation. However, other researchers indicate that fNIRS systems can "monitor brain activity of freely moving subjects outside of laboratories" (Hoshi 2009). While fNIRS data may be affected by head movements, they only become a problem when present at a fairly gross level; this should be contrasted with fMRI where movement over 3 mm will blur the image. Because of the lack of consensus in the community, we investigated the artifacts associated with head movements during typical computer usage to determine their effect on fNIRS sensor data in a typical HCI setting (Solovey et al. 2009). From our experiments, we suggest that participants minimize major head movements, although we believe these artifacts may be corrected using filtering techniques.

13.3.2 Facial Movement

fNIRS sensors are often placed on the forehead, and as a result, it is possible that facial movements could interfere with accurate measurements. Coyle et al. (2004) point out that "slight movements of the optodes on the scalp can cause large changes in the optical signal, due to variations in optical path". These forehead movements could be caused by talking, smiling, frowning, or by emotional states such as surprise or anger, and many researchers have participants refrain from moving their face, including talking (Chenier and Sawan 2007). However, as there is little empirical evidence of this phenomenon, we examined it further (Solovey et al. 2009).

We found that frowning data could always be distinguished from non-frowning. We also learned that if all the data includes frowns, then we cannot differentiate the cognitive task from the rest condition. However, we found that if we combine the data that contains frowning and that without frowning, we can then discriminate the cognitive task, which shows interesting potential to identify which examples to reject because of frowns. Those results clearly indicate that frowning is a problematic artifact, and should be avoided as much as possible.

Because fNIRS sensors are placed on the forehead, frowning was expected to have a large impact on this data. It is possible that other facial movements would not have as strong of an effect. Eye movements and blinking are known to produce large artifacts in EEG data, which leads to the rejection of trials; experimenters often ask their participants to refrain from blinking entirely, or to blink during a specific, non-critical period in each trial (Izzetoglu et al. 2004). In contrast to EEG, fNIRS is less sensitive to muscle tension and researchers have reported that no artifact is produced in nearby areas of the brain (Izzetoglu et al. 2004). It would also be unrealistic to prevent eye blinks and movement in HCI settings. Overall, we conclude eye artifacts and blinks should not be problematic for fNIRS, and we do not constrain participants in our studies.

13.3.3 Ambient Light

Because fNIRS is an optical technique, light in the environment could contribute to noise in the data. Coyle et al. (2004) advise that stray light should be prevented from reaching the detector. Chenier and Sawan (2007) note that they use a black hat to cover the sensors, permitting the detector to only receive light from the fNIRS light sources. While this is a concern for researchers currently using raw fNIRS sensors that are still under development, we feel that future fNIRS sensors will be embedded in a helmet or hat that properly isolates them from this source of noise. Therefore, we have not examined how the introduction of light can affect fNIRS data. Instead we caution that excess light should be kept to a minimum when using fNIRS, or the sensors should be properly covered to filter out the excess light.

13.3.4 Ambient Noise

During experiments and regular computer usage, one is subjected to different sounds in the environment. Many studies using brain sensors are conducted in sound-proof rooms to prevent these sounds from affecting the sensor data (Morioka et al. 2008). However, this is not a realistic setting for most HCI research. Therefore, we conduct all of our studies in a setting similar to a normal office. It is mostly quiet (although the room is not soundproof), and there may be occasional noise in the hallway, or from climate control systems. We have successfully run many studies using the fNIRS system in these conditions.

13.3.5 Respiration and Heartbeat

The fNIRS signals picks up respiration and heartbeat, by definition, as it measures blood flow and oxygenation (Coyle et al. 2004; Matthews et al. 2008). These systemic noise sources can be removed using validated filtering techniques. For a discussion of techniques, see Matthews et al. (2008) and Coyle et al. (2004).

13.3.6 Muscle Movement

In clinical settings, it is reasonable to have participants perform purely cognitive tasks while collecting brain sensor data. This allows researchers to learn about brain function without interference from other factors such as muscle movement. However, to move brain imaging methods into HCI settings, this constraint would have to be relaxed, or methods for correcting the artifacts must be developed.

One of the main benefits of fNIRS is that the setup does not physically constrain participants, allowing them to use external devices such as a keyboard or mouse. In addition, motion artifacts are expected to have less of an effect on the resulting brain sensor data (Girouard et al. 2009). We examined physical motions that are common in HCI settings, typing and mouse clicking, to determine whether they are problematic when using fNIRS (Solovey et al. 2009).

Overall, while typing artifacts could be detected when there was a cognitive task being performed, we could still distinguish the cognitive task itself from a rest state.

This confirms our hypothesis and validates that typing is an acceptable interaction when using fNIRS. From this, we can also assume that simple key presses (e.g. using arrow keys) would also be acceptable with fNIRS since it is a more limited movement than typing with both hands.

We found that mouse clicking might affect the fNIRS signal we are collecting. When the participant was at rest, we found a significant difference in the signal between the presence and absence of clicking. The difference in activation is not surprising as we did not have a "random clicking" task, but one where subject had to reach targets, which may have activated the area being probed (the anterior prefrontal cortex). However, because we still were able to distinguish the cognitive task from rest, the cognitive task may produce a different signal from clicking. Hence, results indicate that when we want to observe a cognitive task that contains clicking, we need to have the rest task contain clicking as well. Overall, we believe that mouse clicking is acceptable if the experiment is controlled.

13.3.7 Slow Hemodynamic Response

The slow hemodynamic changes measured by fNIRS occur in a time span of 6–8 seconds (Bunce et al. 2006). This is important when designing interfaces based on fNIRS sensor data, as the interface would have to respond in this time scale. While the possibility of using event-related fNIRS has been explored (Herrmann et al. 2008), most studies take advantage of the slow response to measure short term cognitive state, instead of instantaneous ones.

13.3.8 Summary of Guidelines and Considerations

According to our research, mouse clicking and typing are not problematic, but large-scale head and facial movements should be minimized; minor movements as well as heartbeat and respiration can be corrected using filtering techniques. Many limitations that are inherent to other brain sensing and imaging devices such as long setup time, highly restricted position, and intolerance to movement are not factors when using fNIRS. By using the guidelines described above, researchers can detect aspects of the user's cognitive state in realistic HCI laboratory conditions. In our work, we have focused on mental workload, and have conducted several experiments described below exploring the feasibility of recognizing mental workload states with fNIRS.

13.4 Measuring Mental Workload

Acquiring measurements about the mental state of a computer user is valuable in HCI, both for evaluation of interfaces and for real time input to computer systems.

Although we can accurately measure task completion time and accuracy, measuring factors such as mental workload, frustration and distraction are typically limited to qualitatively observing users or administering subjective surveys. These surveys are often taken after the completion of a task, potentially missing valuable insight into the user's changing experiences throughout the task. They also fail to capture internal details of the operator's mental state.

As HCI continues to move out of the workplace and into the real world, users' goals and uses for computers are changing and the analysis involved in the evaluation and design of new interfaces is shifting from "*usability* analysis to *user experience* analysis" (Mandryk et al. 2006). New evaluation techniques that monitor user experiences while working with computers are increasingly necessary. To address these evaluation issues, current research focuses on developing objective techniques to measure in real time user states such as workload, emotion, and fatigue (Gevins and Smith 2003; John et al. 2004; Marshall et al. 2003). Although this ongoing research has advanced user experience measurements in the HCI field, finding accurate, non-invasive tools to measure computer users' states in real working conditions remains a challenge. Measuring user workload with objective measures such as galvanic skin response (John et al. 2004), EEG (Gevins and Smith 2003), ERP (Kok 1997), pupil dilation (Iqbal et al. 2004), and facial EMG (Fuller et al. 1995) has been a topic of much research. It is well understood that a reliable measure of user workload could have a positive impact in many real life interactions (Guhe et al. 2005; Iqbal et al. 2004; John et al. 2004).

We conducted a study to demonstrate the feasibility and potential for using fNIRS in HCI settings (Hirshfield et al. 2007). We distinguished several discrete levels of workload that users experienced while completing different tasks. In this experiment, four subjects completed thirty tasks where they viewed all sides of a rotating three-dimensional (3D) shape comprised of eight small cubes. The cubes could be colored with two, three, or four colors, which we hypothesized would lead to different workload levels. During each task, subjects counted the number of squares of each color displayed on the rotating shape in front of them. A blank screen represented the baseline state (no colors).

The main goal of this experiment was to establish whether fNIRS data is sufficient for determining the workload level of users as they perform tasks. To accomplish this, a graphical interface displayed the rotating shapes.

At the completion of each task, the subject was prompted for his or her count for each color. Then, the subject rested for thirty seconds, allowing the brain to return to a baseline state. After completing the tasks, the subject was presented with an additional example of each workload level and asked to fill out a NASA-Task Load Index (Hart and Staveland 1988), administered to compare our results with an established measure of workload. The results of the NASA-TLX assessment validate our manipulation of workload levels: increased number of colors led to higher workload level.

We classified the data with a multilayer perceptron classifier using the sliding windows approach (Dietterich 2002). We tested distinguishing all four workload levels from each other, as well as comparisons of two, three, and four workload conditions of the graphical workload level. When we consider the results comparing workload levels 0, 2, and 4, classification accuracies range from 41.15% to 69.7% depending on the subject. Considering that a random classifier would have 33.3% accuracy, the results were promising. We could predict, with relatively high confidence, whether the subject was experiencing no workload (level zero), low workload (level two), or high workload (level four).

Our goal was to test the ability of the fNIRS device to detect levels of workload in HCI, to develop classification techniques to interpret its data, and to demonstrate the use of fNIRS in HCI. Our experiment showed several workload comparisons with promising levels of classification accuracy.

13.5 Separating Semantic and Syntactic Workload in the Brain

In our initial work described above, we verified that fNIRS sensors provide researchers with a measure of the mental workload experienced by users working on a task with a given user interface (UI). However, detecting a high workload while a user works with a system is not necessarily a bad thing; it could indicate that the user is immersed in the task. How can UI evaluators and designers of adaptive systems know if a high workload measurement is due to the UI or to the underlying task?

To solve the question, we were influenced by Shneiderman's theory of semantic and syntactic components of a user interface (Shneiderman and Plaisant 2005). In this theory, the semantic component involves the effort expended by a user to complete a given task. The syntactic component involves the effort required to understand and work with the interface, which includes interpreting the interface's feedback, and formulating and inputting commands to the interface. We propose to conceptually separate mental workload into multiple components, where the total workload required to perform a task using a computer is composed of a portion attributable to the difficulty of the task itself plus a portion attributable to the complexity of operating the user interface.

We designed a protocol to aid usability experts to measure workload as a dependent variable while a user works with an interface and/or task. The general protocol is as follows: Given an interface to evaluate and an underlying task, researchers conduct a task analysis on both the interface and task. For each subtask, they determine the cognitive subsystems that one would use while conducting the subtasks (i.e., spatial working memory, visual search, etc.). Next they gather benchmark exercises from cognitive psychology designed to elicit high and low levels of workload on the target cognitive resources associated with the interface. Researchers then run an experiment where users complete the benchmark cognition exercises, providing a measure of their brain activity while they experience high and low workload levels in their various cognitive subsystems. Users also work with the user interface that the researchers are attempting to evaluate. Lastly, researchers use fNIRS data analysis tools to find similarities and differences in the users' brain activity while working with the interface under evaluation and with the cognitive psychology exercises.

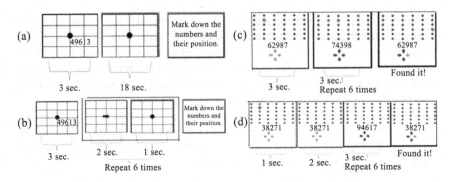

Fig. 13.2 Experimental Tasks. There were two benchmark tasks from cognitive psychology:
(**a**) low spatial working memory: recall digits and location, and (**b**) high spatial working memory: use arrows to update location of digits. There were two interface exercises where participants had to traverse a group of linked web-pages to find matching zip code, and remember current location at all times: (**c**) informed UI, and (**d**) uninformed UI

We used this protocol while conducting an experiment to shed light on the syntactic (interface) components of workload of two specially constructed interfaces that involve users traversing through a group of web pages that are linked together while conducting an information retrieval task (Hirshfield et al. 2009b). We kept the retrieval task constant between the two conditions, while we varied the design of the interface in each condition (Figs. 13.2c and 13.2d). In the first user interface, subjects were continually informed about their location within the space, whereas in the other condition, subjects were unaware of their current location. We refer to these interface variations as the *informed location UI* and the *uninformed location UI*, and we hypothesize that the uninformed location UI caused subjects to experience higher loads on their spatial working memory than the informed location UI.

We chose two benchmark tasks from cognitive psychology experiments that are known to involve both spatial and verbal working memory (Figs. 13.2a and 13.2b). Both of these exercises had low verbal working memory demands (mirroring the information retrieval task). However, one of these exercises had *high spatial working memory (HSWM)* demands, and the other involved *low spatial working memory (LSWM)* demands. We also had a controlled *rest* condition where subjects simply rested, with no workload for a set period of time. We used these tasks to provide us with benchmark brain activity for each subject where the spatial WM needed to complete the *rest* task was less than that needed to complete the *LSWM* task, which was less than that needed to complete the *HSWM* task.

A randomized block design with nine trials was used during the experiment. Ten subjects (6 female) completed the experiment. Results indicated that we could distinguish between the benchmark cognition tasks, the controlled rest, and the two user interface variations conditions using analysis of variance (ANOVA) with 95% confidence on one or both sides of subjects' heads (Hirshfield et al. 2009b).

We expected the *uninformed UI* to cause higher spatial WM load than the *informed UI*. We used hierarchical clustering with a Euclidian distance measure to cluster our data, which helped to validate this expectation. Clustering results showed that for 90% of subjects, the *uninformed UI* was grouped closer to benchmark tasks of *HSWM* load than the *informed UI* (Hirshfield et al. 2009b). Therefore, we established that the *informed UI* caused a lower load on users' spatial working memory than the *uninformed UI*. This is not surprising, as web site designers are well aware of the benefits of keeping users oriented.

We expect this novel protocol to work in a similar manner with more realistic UIs, where the established cognitive psychology tasks may not parallel the user interfaces as closely as they did in this experiment. However, the fNIRS analysis algorithms will still show useful similarities and differences between brain activity induced by the interfaces and by the cognition exercises. While separating semantic and syntactic workload may not be possible in more complex UIs, evaluators can make informed changes to UI designs based on the level of workload measured in users' various cognitive resources while they work with a user interface.

These workload levels also may be useful input to an adaptive system if classified in real time. With this goal in mind we used a k-nearest-neighbor classifier and a distance metric computed via dynamic time warping to make comparisons between brain activity induced by the experiment conditions on a single trial basis. It was possible to distinguish between the benchmark *LSWM* tasks and the *HSWM* tasks with nearly 70% average accuracy, between each condition and the *rest* condition with nearly 80% average accuracy, and between the two UI conditions with 68% average accuracy. This shows promise for detecting workload changes in various cognitive resources in real-time adaptive interfaces.

In this study, we did not separate semantic and syntactic workload in the brain directly, but rather we constructed our UI and task so that the syntactic portion maps directly onto spatial working memory, and the semantic portion maps onto verbal working memory. We also developed an experimental protocol that merges low-level cognition experiments with high-level usability evaluation. Our experiment protocol and data analysis algorithms can help usability experts, or designers of adaptive systems, to acquire information about the cognitive load placed on users' various cognitive resources while working with a user interface.

13.6 fNIRS Sensing During Interactive Game Play

Moving away from traditional psychology experiments, where one can isolate, manipulate, and measure mental workload with great precision, we chose to apply our brain measurements techniques to a real user interface, that of an arcade game. The goal of the study was to distinguish between different levels of game difficulty using fNIRS data collected while subjects played a computer game (Girouard et al. 2009). This study was a step forward, as previous work only evaluated the activeness of the user during video games using fNIRS (Matsuda and Hiraki 2006; Nagamitsu et al. 2006). The study was designed to lead to adaptive games and other interactive interfaces that respond to the user's brain activity in real time, and we believe this work to be a stepping stone to using fNIRS in an adaptive user interface, in this case a passive brain-computer interface. *Passive BCIs* are interfaces that detect brain activity that occurs naturally during task performance for use as an additional input, in conjunction with standard devices such as keyboards and mice (Cutrell and Tan 2007). This is in contrast with *active BCIs*, which use brain activity as the primary input device, often requiring the user to be trained to generate specific brain states, which are interpreted as explicit input.

We asked participants to play the game of Pacman (Namco, Japan) for periods of thirty seconds, and then rest for thirty seconds. They completed ten sets of two levels of difficulty, an easy level and a hard level, during which their brain activity was measured using fNIRS. We also collected performance data, and analysis of this data showed a clear and significant distinction between the two levels. An objective measure of workload was collected using NASA-TLX (Hart and Staveland 1988), which confirmed two levels of mental workload.

We performed two analyses of the data to confirm the presence of differences in hemoglobin concentrations for each condition: a classic statistical analysis to establish the differences between conditions, and a more novel task classification to show the possibility of using this data in real-time adaptive systems.

The statistical analysis revealed that we can distinguish between subjects being active and passive in their mental state (playing versus resting), as well as between different levels of game complexity (difficulty level). The classification was consistent with those results, but indicated more difficulty at distinguishing the game levels (94% to classify playing versus resting, while 61% for the easy versus hard levels). This could indicate that the mental process for this activity manifests itself at another, unmeasured location in the brain, or that the difference was simply not strong enough to cause changes in activation.

While some might argue that performance data is sufficient to classify the difficulty level of a game and can be obtained without interference, the goal of this study was to investigate the use of the brain measurements with fNIRS as a new input device. In a more complex problem, performance and fNIRS brain data might not be as related, e.g. if the user is working hard yet performing poorly at some point. In addition, distractions may also produce workload increases that would not obvious from monitoring game settings and performance, and thus may necessitate brain measurements. That is, a participant playing a simple game while answering difficult questions might also show brain activity relating to increased workload that would be incomprehensible based only on performance data (e.g. Nijholt et al. 2008). In non-gaming situations, we might not have performance data like in the present case, as we don't always know what to measure. The use of the brain signal as an auxiliary input could provide better results in these situations.

13.7 Moving Towards an Adaptive fNIRS Interface

Now that we have established a foundation for fNIRS measurements, the focus shifts to our second question: How do we use these measurements in the context of adaptive interfaces? How do we responsibly apply a measurement of workload in a useful way? To answer these questions we first need to find a class of problems where fNIRS may be helpful.

Given the temporal limitations of hemodynamic response in the brain, we are drawn towards problems where millisecond snapshots are not necessary, eliminating activities that are instant states or extremely time-sensitive. For example, users who are monitoring constant streams of data fit nicely into this framework.

From one perspective, the temporal limitation of fNIRS can be viewed as a healthy one—a slow hemodynamic response pushes us towards creating interfaces that are gentle and unobtrusive. This is important. If we aren't careful, brain-computer interfaces can suffer the same Midas Touch problems identified in eye tracking research (Jacob 1993). It is a safe assumption that users do not expect an interface to change with every whim and daydream during the course of their work-day. We must be judicious with our design decisions.

As a general rule for implicit interfaces, any visual modifications to the interface should be done carefully enough that the user hardly notices the change until he or she needs to (Fairclough 2009). The eye is very sensitive to movement, and any adaptation that robs the attention of the user will be counterproductive to the primary task. A pop-up dialog box is a distracting response to a user in the middle of a task, even if we occasionally guess exactly what the user wants. Fading, overlaying information, or changing an application's screen real estate are options that, if done slowly enough, may impact the user's focus in a positive way. Visually altering the interface is just one response we can make to real-time fNIRS measurements. We can also choose to change the underlying information of the interface while keeping the general visualization stable.

While work in this direction is still in its infancy, we propose two prototypes to demonstrate how real-time, lightweight adaptive interfaces may be used with fNIRS measurements.

13.7.1 The Stockbroker Scenario

A stockbroker is writing a sensitive email to a client. At the same time, he is trying to track critical, minute-by-minute stock information on the same screen. While his email is of the upmost importance, he doesn't want to completely abandon the stock information. What if he were to miss a significant spike?

Unfortunately, the detailed visualization of stock data is mentally taxing to look at and prevents the broker from focusing on his email. As a solution, our stockbroker prototype gently changes the visualization of the data depending on the workload we associate with the emailing task.

If the stockbroker is not exerting a high mental workload on his email, we show his stock visualization as highly detailed, giving the stockbroker as much informa-tion as possible (Fig. 13.3, left). If the stockbroker is working exceptionally hard at his email and cannot afford to be distracted by complex stock information, we simply lower the level of detail. The broker will still recognize major changes in the data without getting bogged down in the details (Fig. 13.3, right).

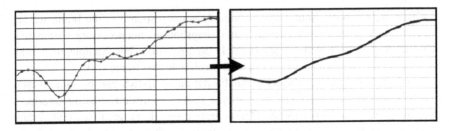

Fig. 13.3 An example of high detailed graph (*left*), and one of low detail (*right*)

13.7.2 Many Windows Scenario

Users are often juggling four or five windows at once—writing a paragraph in one window, displaying a page of notes in another, glancing at an academic paper in a third, and tracking email in a fourth. While, like the stockbroker, the user may prefer not to get rid of any of the windows, their presence detracts from the primary task. The user may wish that the windows were only there when needed.

While fNIRS may not be able to take on the role of both mind-reader and task-driver, fNIRS can help us guess which windows are most important. We can monitor the amount of workload required in each task, and fade the other windows accordingly. If glancing at email is relatively low-workload, then it may not be distracting. If keeping track of email is mentally expensive, then we can gradually fade the window. When the surrounding windows do not demand many mental resources, we may keep them transparent. In this way, we can think of them as being cheap to keep around.

13.7.3 Looking Ahead

These two scenarios offer a brief glimpse into brain-computer interfaces with fNIRS. They are gentle and unobtrusive. They are more concerned with long-term workload and trends than an immediate snapshot. Looking ahead, we can imagine numerous situations where fNIRS is a valuable input to adaptive interfaces. What if we could adjust teaching methods to best suit a child's learning style? What if we could dynamically filter streams of information (Twitter, RSS, email) to accommodate the current workload of the user?

13.8 Conclusion

We began this chapter by dealing with two major questions: (1) what kind of things can we measure using fNIRS? (2) how should we use this information as input to an adaptive user interface? Our response to the first question was three pronged:

First, we explored the practical considerations for using fNIRS in HCI. We looked at the impact of head, facial, and muscle movement on fNIRS readings. We also took into account environmental factors such as ambient light and ambient noise. Next, we investigated the feasibility of using fNIRS as a measure of workload in general before measuring differences in syntactic and semantic workload in the brain, a measurement that helps us separate the interface and the underlying task. Finally, we measured a real interface, identifying a workload measurement that increased or decreased according to the complexity of the task (in this case, a game of Pacman). To address our second goal, we first outlined general characteristics for the design space of user interfaces that adapt based on fNIRS measurements. We then described two scenarios that could take advantage of such an interface design. From our experience, we believe that fNIRS brain sensing has great potential for both user interface evaluation and adaptive user interfaces, and will open new doors for human-computer interaction.

Acknowledgements   The authors would like to thank the HCI research group at Tufts University; Michel Beaudoin-Lafon, Wendy Mackay, and the In |Situ| research group; and Desney Tan and Dan Morris at Microsoft Research. We thank the NSF (Grant Nos. IIS-0713506 and IIS-0414389), the Canadian National Science and Engineering Research Council, the US Air Force Research Laboratory, and the US Army NSRDEC for support of this research. Any opinions, findings, and conclusions or recommendations expressed in this chapter are those of the authors and do not necessarily reflect the views of these organizations.

References

Bunce SC, Izzetoglu M, Izzetoglu K, Onaral B, Pourrezaei K (2006) Functional near infrared spectroscopy: An emerging neuroimaging modality. IEEE Eng Med Biol Mag 25(4):54–62. Special issue on Clinical Neuroengineering

Chenier F, Sawan M (2007) A new brain imaging device based on fNIRS. Paper presented at the BIOCAS 2007, pp 1–4

Coyle S, Ward T, Markham C (2004) Physiological noise in near-infrared spectroscopy: Implications for optical brain computer interfacing. Paper presented at the Proc EMBS, pp 4540–4543

Cutrell E, Tan DS (2007) BCI for passive input in HCI. Paper presented at the ACM CHI'08 Conference on Human Factors in Computing Systems Workshop on Brain-Computer Interfaces for HCI and Games

Devaraj A, Izzetoglu M, Izzetoglu K, Onaral B (2004) Motion artifact removal for fNIR spectroscopy for real world application areas. Proc SPIE 5588:224–229

Dietterich TG (2002) Machine learning for sequential data: A review. Struct Syntactic Stat Pattern Recognit 2396:15–30

Ehlis A-C, Bähne CG, Jacob CP, Herrmann MJ, Fallgatter AJ (2008) Reduced lateral prefrontal activation in adult patients with attention-deficit/hyperactivity disorder (ADHD) during a working memory task: A functional near-infrared spectroscopy (fNIRS) study. J Psychiatr Res 42(13):1060–1067

Fairclough SH (2009) Fundamentals of physiological computing. Interact Comput 21(1–2):133–145

Fuller D, Sullivan J, Essif E, Personius K, Fregosi R (1995) Measurement of the EMG-force relationship in a human upper airway muscle. J Appl Physiol 79(1):270–278

Gevins A, Smith M (2003) Neurophysiological measures of cognitive workload during human-computer interaction. Theor Issues Ergon Sci 4:113–131

Girouard A, Solovey E, Hirshfield L, Chauncey K, Sassaroli A, Fantini S, et al (2009) Distinguishing difficulty levels with non-invasive brain activity measurements. In: Human-Computer Interaction—INTERACT 2009, pp 440–452

Grimes D, Tan DS, Hudson SE, Shenoy P, Rao RPN (2008) Feasibility and pragmatics of classifying working memory load with an electroencephalograph. Paper presented at the Proc CHI'08, pp 835–844

Guhe M, Liao W, Zhu Z, Ji Q, Gray WD, Schoelles MJ (2005) Non-intrusive measurement of workload in real-time. Paper presented at the 49th Annual Conference of the Human Factors and Ergonomics Society, pp 1157–1161

Hart SG, Staveland LE (1988) Development of NASA-TLX (Task Load Index): Results of empirical and theorical research. In: Hancock P, Meshkati N (eds) Human Mental Workload, Amsterdam, pp 139–183

Herrmann MJ, Huter T, Plichta MM, Ehlis A-C, Alpers GW, Mühlberger A, et al (2008) Enhancement of activity of the primary visual cortex during processing of emotional stimuli as measured with event-related functional near-infrared spectroscopy and event-related potentials. Hum Brain Mapp 29(1):28–35

Hirshfield LM, Girouard A, Solovey ET, Jacob RJK, Sassaroli A, Tong Y, et al (2007) Human-computer interaction and brain measurement using functional near-infrared spectroscopy. Paper presented at the Proceedings of the ACM UIST'07 Symposium on User Interface Software and Technology

Hirshfield LM, Chauncey K, Gulotta R, Girouard A, Solovey ET, Jacob RJ, et al (2009a) Combining electroencephalograph and functional near infrared spectroscopy to explore users' mental workload. Paper presented at the Proceedings of the 5th International Conference on Foundations of Augmented Cognition. Neuroergonomics and Operational Neuroscience: Held as Part of HCI International 2009, San Diego, CA, pp 239–247

Hirshfield LM, Solovey ET, Girouard A, Kebinger J, Jacob RJK, Sassaroli A, et al (2009b) Brain measurement for usability testing and adaptive interfaces: An example of uncovering syntactic workload with functional near infrared spectroscopy. Paper presented at the Proceedings of the 27th International Conference on Human Factors in Computing Systems, Boston, MA, USA, pp 2185–2194

Hoshi Y (2009) Near-infrared spectroscopy for studying higher cognition neural correlates of thinking, pp 83–93

Iqbal ST, Zheng XS, Bailey BP (2004) Task-evoked pupillary response to mental workload in human-computer interaction. Paper presented at the CHI'04 extended abstracts on Human Factors in Computing Systems, Vienna, Austria, pp 1477–1480

Izzetoglu K, Bunce S, Onaral B, Pourrezaei K, Chance B (2004) Functional optical brain imaging using near-infrared during cognitive tasks. IJHCI 17(2):211–231

Jacob RJK (1993) Eye movement-based human-computer interaction techniques: Toward non-command interfaces. In: Hix HRHaD (ed) Advances in Human-Computer Interaction, vol. 4. Ablex Publishing Co, Norwood, NJ, pp 151–190

John MS, Kobus D, Morrison J, Schmorrow D (2004) Overview of the DARPA augmented cognition technical integration experiment. Int J Hum Comput Interact 17(2):131–149

Kok A (1997) Event-related-potential (ERP) reflections of mental resources: A review and synthesis. Biol Psychol 45:19–56

Lee JC, Tan DS (2006) Using a low-cost electroencephalograph for task classification in HCI research. Paper presented at the Proc ACM Symposium on User Interface Software and Technology 2006, pp 81–90

Mandryk R, Atkins M, Inkpen K (2006) A continuous and objective evaluation of emotional experience with interactive play environments. Paper presented at the Proceedings of the SIGCHI conference on Human factors in computing systems, Montreal, Quebec, Canada, pp 1027–1036

Mappus RL, Venkatesh GR, Shastry C, Israeli A Jackson MM (2009) An fNIR Based BMI for Letter Construction Using Continuous Control. Paper presented at the Proc CHI 2009 Extended Abstracts, pp 3571–3576

Marshall S, Pleydell-Pearce C, Dickson B (2003) Integrating psychophysiological measures of cognitive workload and eye movements to detect strategy shifts. Paper presented at the IEEE Proceedings of the 36th Annual Hawaii International Conference on System Sciences, 130b

Matsuda G, Hiraki K (2006) Sustained decrease in oxygenated hemoglobin during video games in the dorsal prefrontal cortex: A NIRS study of children. NeuroImage 29(3):706–711

Matthews F, Pearlmutter BA, Ward TE, Soraghan C, Markham C (2008) Hemodynamics for brain-computer interfaces. Signal Process Mag IEEE 25(1):87–94

Millán JdR, Renkens F, Mouriño J, Gerstner W (2004) Brain-actuated interaction. Artif Intell 159(1-2):241–259

Morioka S, Yamada M, Komori T (2008) Frontal lobe activity during the performance of spatial tasks: fNIRS study. J Phys Ther Sci 20:135–139

Nagamitsu S, Nagano M, Tamashita Y, Takashima S, Matsuishi T (2006) Prefrontal cerebral blood volume patterns while playing video games—A near-infrared spectroscopy study. Brain Develop 28:315–321

Nijholt A, Tan D, Allison B, Millán JdR, Graimann B (2008) Brain-computer interfaces for HCI and games. Paper presented at the CHI'08 extended abstracts on Human Factors in Computing Systems, Florence, Italy, pp 3925–3928

Ramnani N, Owen AM (2004) Anterior prefrontal cortex: insights into function from anatomy and neuroimaging. Nat Rev Neurosci 5(3):184–194

Shneiderman B, Plaisant C (2005) Designing the User Interface: Strategies for Effective Human-Computer Interaction, 4th edn. Addison-Wesley, Reading, Mass

Sitaram R, Zhang H, Guan C, Thulasidas M, Hoshi Y, Ishikawa A, et al (2007) Temporal classification of multichannel near-infrared spectroscopy signals of motor imagery for developing a brain-computer interface. NeuroImage 34(4):1416–1427

Solovey ET, Girouard A, Chauncey K, Hirshfield LM, Sassaroli A, Zheng F, et al (2009) Using fNIRS brain sensing in realistic HCI settings: Experiments and guidelines. Paper presented at the ACM UIST'09 Symposium on User Interface Software and Technology, pp 157–166

Villringer A, Chance B (1997) Non-invasive optical spectroscopy and imaging of human brain function. Trends Neurosci 20:435–442

Part IV
Tools

Chapter 14
MATLAB-Based Tools for BCI Research

Arnaud Delorme, Christian Kothe, Andrey Vankov, Nima Bigdely-Shamlo, Robert Oostenveld, Thorsten O. Zander, and Scott Makeig

Abstract We first discuss two MATLAB-centered solutions for real-time data streaming, the environments FieldTrip (Donders Institute, Nijmegen) and DataSuite (Data- River, Producer, MatRiver) (Swartz Center, La Jolla). We illustrate the relative simplicity of coding BCI feature extraction and classification under MATLAB (The Mathworks, Inc.) using a minimalist BCI example, and then describe BCILAB

A. Delorme (✉) · A. Vankov · N. Bigdely-Shamlo · S. Makeig
Swartz Center for Computational Neuroscience, Institute for Neural Computation, University of California San Diego, La Jolla, CA, USA
e-mail: arno@ucsd.edu

A. Vankov
e-mail: avankow@ucsd.edu

S. Makeig
e-mail: smakeig@ucsd.edu

A. Delorme
Université de Toulouse, UPS, Centre de Recherche Cerveau et Cognition, Toulouse, France

A. Delorme
CNRS, CerCo, Toulouse, France

C. Kothe · T.O. Zander
Team PhyPA, TU Berlin, Berlin, Germany

C. Kothe
e-mail: christiankothe@googlemail.com

C. Kothe · T.O. Zander
Department of Psychology and Ergonomics, Chair Human-Machine Systems, Berlin Institute of Technology, Berlin, Germany

R. Oostenveld
Donders Institute for Brain, Cognition and Behaviour, Radboud University Nijmegen, Nijmegen, The Netherlands
e-mail: r.oostenveld@donders.ru.nl

D.S. Tan, A. Nijholt (eds.), *Brain-Computer Interfaces,*
Human-Computer Interaction Series,
DOI 10.1007/978-1-84996-272-8_14, © Springer-Verlag London Limited 2010

(Team PhyPa, Berlin), a new BCI package that uses the data structures and extends the capabilities of the widely used EEGLAB signal processing environment. We finally review the range of standalone and MATLAB-based software currently freely available to BCI researchers.

14.1 Introduction

Brain-computer Interface (BCI) systems and algorithms allow the use of brain signals as volitional communication devices or more generally create some sort of useful interconnection between the operation of a machine system and the brain activity of a human or animal subject using, engaged with, or monitored by the system. Because of its portability, most BCI systems use electroencephalographic (EEG) signals recorded from one or more scalp channels. Although most of the approaches we review here are also applicable to single-channel recordings, we will focus on software for processing multi-channel EEG data in the MATLAB computing environment (The Mathworks, Inc., Natick MA), a widely available commercial platform-independent numerical computing and visualization software environment. Although, MATLAB applications are rarely used outside of research environments, they offer a valuable tool for developing, prototyping, and testing BCI approaches.

While freely available MATLAB-compatible software alternatives exist (e.g., Octave, see www.gnu.org/software/octave) and alternative open-source software is slowly emerging (www.sagemath.org), MATLAB is presently used in most research centers and is widely considered the tool of choice for developing and, often, applying computational methods in cognitive neuroscience and beyond. While early versions of MATLAB 5.3 were much slower than compiled versions of the same code, the most recent version of MATLAB has more than doubled in speed, a fact that increasingly makes MATLAB a suitable environment for real-time processing. As of its 2009 release, MATLAB processes may also make use of multiple cores. MATLAB also sells a dedicated package, the Realtime target, designed to facilitate real-time operations.

Several requirements for a research BCI software development environment arise from the demands of the BCI research field:

- *Flexibility*. BCI is an active and rapidly advancing field. Thus, any BCI environment not supporting development and testing of more advanced uses than those initially anticipated will necessarily be of limited value. BCI software environments should therefore allow, invite, and facilitate flexibility in methods extension and re-definition.
- *Ease of Use*. BCI software users include psychologists, human factors experts, human interface designers, signal processing engineers, computer scientists, and mathematicians. All these users cannot be expected to have comprehensive knowledge of the mathematical and neurophysiological bases of BCI operation. While lack of relevant scientific background among a BCI project team might impact their productivity, BCI software environments may minimize or at least

mitigate serious errors and misunderstandings by establishing and documenting best practices, providing reasonable default values, flagging and detailing mistakes in usage, and by making common tasks simple to perform.

- *Efficiency.* The choice of algorithms that can be applied under given conditions is often determined by the computation time required and available. Therefore, the computational efficiency of the BCI environment is a critical element. Moreover, prototyping and testing of new methods and applications itself should be efficient, because successful designs will typically require many iterations to perfect. Thus, the BCI environment should allow users to quickly update and test new designs.
- *Performance.* Since current BCI system performance levels are often at best close to the lower boundary of what is considered practical, inference performance, or the accuracy of the predictions, is a most critical aspect of BCI system design. Higher levels of performance are reached by newer state-of-the-art methods whose inventors may not have the resources to perform extensive testing. Ideally, therefore, BCI software environments should include measures and methods for fairly evaluating BCI system performance.
- *Robustness.* BCI research often involves making empirical estimates about the performance of a given BCI design from limited amounts of training and test data, making the problem of overfitting acute and ever present. Because of this, current designs may not adequately model and compensate for the massive diversity and non-stationarity of brain EEG signals. Lack of adequate training and testing data means that BCI systems should have a tendency to work best in the precise subject situations and contexts in which they were developed, and may fail to prove robust as the recording situation or context changes. Thus, performance estimates based on limited testing data are almost always optimistic. Yet dependability of BCI solutions must be an important goal if BCI systems are to find uses outside the laboratory. Ideal BCI software environments should therefore facilitate routine collection of relatively large amounts of training and test data.

The three main components of a BCI system are data streaming and online data processing, plus delivery of user feedback. Data streaming includes channel selection, data filtering and buffering, and extracting epochs in real time based on event presentation. Online data processing involves data preprocessing followed by feature extraction and classification. User feedback involves selection and promotion of desired user interactions based on classification results. Feedback methods of choice depend on the specific application and will not be dealt with here. Below, we discuss first data streaming and then online data processing.

14.2 Data Streaming

Processing of EEG data in (near) real time in BCI software applications requires, first and foremost, access to the data. Data acquired by an acquisition system must therefore first be streamed into the BCI processing pipeline. Currently, there is no fundamental problem in reading data acquired by a digital recording system in near real time using any general purpose programming language including MATLAB. Many EEG acquisition systems provide some way to interface custom software to their output EEG data stream. For example, Biosemi and TMSI both offer a dynamically-linked library (dll) for interfacing with the hardware, while BrainProducts provides the specification of a TCP protocol under which data can be streamed over a network. Under MATLAB, it is possible to directly interface this EEG data stream by direct calls to DLL routines, by interfacing acquisition cards using the RealTime Workshop (The Mathworks), or by using TCP/IP and the Instrument Control Toolbox (The Mathworks). MATLAB may collect either one sample or one block of data at a time, and then populate data blocks into a larger data matrix of dimensions channels-by-samples. This data matrix may then be processed under MATLAB using feature extraction and translation algorithms.

However, since MATLAB is a single-threaded application, collecting the continuously streaming data *and* processing it in near-real time may be challenging. Imagine acquiring samples of the EEG data stream and then performing a CPU-intensive computation on those samples, e.g. overlapping fast Fourier transforms (FFTs). During the time that MATLAB requires to compute each FFT, new data arriving in the EEG stream from the acquisition system may be ignored. To allow for full control of the timing of a processing pipeline in MATLAB, incoming data must be buffered to avoid gaps whenever repeated computation is taking place. While the low-level TCP/IP network stack of the operating system will buffer the data for some time, the duration that the data remains in the network stack buffer cannot be guaranteed.

Therefore, instead of having MATLAB itself read one sample at a time from the data stream, another standalone application or thread should read the incoming samples and copy them into a fixed-length or data-adaptive circular buffer. MATLAB can then read new data from this buffer at any time appropriate, e.g., after completion of each computation. Successively separating the buffering of the data stream from computation on segments of that data stream depends on a having fast interface between MATLAB and the buffering software, so that little time is lost in copying data from the buffer into MATLAB memory. In the next sections we present two MATLAB-centered solutions that use this approach: FieldTrip and DataSuite. FieldTrip aims only to provide a usable interface to a single online data stream, while DataSuite in addition allows synchronization of dissimilar data streams, including streams output by online computational clients running on the same or different machines on the network, plus integrated, flexible, and if desired distributed stimulus control.

14.2.1 FieldTrip

The FieldTrip toolbox (R. Oostenveld, www.ru.nl/neuroimaging/fieldtrip) for EEG/MEG-analysis under MATLAB provides an open-source implementation of a realtime data buffering scheme. The FieldTrip buffer is implemented as a network transparent TCP server, which allows the acquisition client to stream EEG data to it sample by sample or in small blocks, while at the same time any data that is present in the buffer can be retrieved and processed by another application. The buffer is implemented as a multi-threaded application in C/C++, allowing multiple clients to connect simultaneously to read/write data and event codes.

The FieldTrip buffer may be used more generally to communicate between separate applications. One application program is responsible for data acquisition, writing the data (and optionally also event codes) to the buffer. Another application can connect to the server to read some of the data and event codes (typically, the most recent), and may optionally also write new event codes (e.g., as the output of a classification algorithm) into the same buffer. Source code for the buffering can be integrated into any EEG/MEG acquisition or analysis system, first writing the header information and describing the number of channels and sampling frequency, then delivering the stream of data and/or event codes. The TCP protocol controls reading and writing to the buffer and can issue a flush/empty command when data collection is restarted

The buffer code is compiled into a MATLAB 'mex' file. This allows processing of small segments of streaming EEG data under MATLAB while incoming new data is buffered in a separate thread. Since the buffer allows multiple concurrent read connections, multiple MATLAB clients can connect to it, each analyzing a specific aspect of the data concurrently. The MATLAB mex file can also be used to access a remote buffer linked to the acquisition software running as a separate program, possibly even on a separate computer, to instantiate a local buffer linked to the MATLAB process as a separate thread.

14.2.2 DataSuite: DataRiver and MatRiver

DataSuite (www.sccn.ucsd.edu/wiki/DataSuit) is a distributed data acquisition, synchronization, online processing, and stimulus delivery system based around DataRiver (A. Vankov), a unique data management and synchronization real-time engine. DataRiver is based on a real-time data management core, previously developed for the ADAPT data acquisition and analysis system and language (Adapt © and Varieté 1987–2003). Producer (A. Vankov) is a DataRiver client for flexibly controlling stimulus presentation using an original scripting language. MatRiver (N. Bigdely-Shamlo), described below, is a MATLAB client toolbox for DataRiver. Data acquired by independent devices are by definition asynchronous, even when they are acquired at the same nominal sampling rate, because of the independent clocks typically used to pace data acquisition. Moreover, sampling rates for different data sources can differ significantly: while EEG is typically sampled between 250 Hz and 2000 Hz, concurrent body motion capture or button press data, for example, may be sampled at much lower rates. Another major source of time delays is data acquisition hardware buffering to ensure regularity of the data samples. For data acquired through an IP socket connection, network delays can also be significant. Finally, Windows (or any other multi-user) operating system itself introduces variable delays in processing of asynchronous streams through its pre-emptive multitasking—in a multitasking scheme, typically data are processed only when the corresponding thread is activated, not when data become available.

14.2.3 DataRiver

DataRiver was developed to solve these synchronization issues. DataRiver is a flexible and universal system for high precision synchronization of data streams, providing a dynamic, near real-time mechanism for synchronizing concurrent data streams with designed and tested precision better than 2 ms on current workstations.

The flexibility of DataRiver derives from its modular design—data output by a variety of hardware devices are handled by specialized device drivers that convert each of them into a device-independent data stream. Those data streams are then continuously merged together in real time into a data "river." DataRiver device drivers, currently available for several types of data input devices and systems, allow ready development of a wide range of interactive experimental paradigms in a wide variety of application environments. Data in incoming data streams can be used in real time by "stream recipient" modules for recording, online data processing, and/or stimulus control. DataRiver has built-in support for a real-time data exchange with one or more remote computers in a local area network (LAN), allowing a distributed, cooperative experimental environment (Fig. 14.1). New DataRiver routines can easily be added at any time, ensuring expandability to meet evolving research goals.

14.2.4 MatRiver

MatRiver is a MATLAB toolbox that includes a MATLAB DataRiver client optimized for real-time data processing, buffering and visualization with emphasis on EEG analysis. It calls DLL functions under Windows OS to communicate with DataRiver and provides a pipeline for EEG pre-processing and classification. In addition to performing common EEG processing steps such as channel selection, re-referencing, frequency filtering and linear spatial filtering (ICA (Makeig et al. 1996) or other linear models), MatRiver includes simple-to-use routines for dynamic noisy 'bad' channel detection and compensation (taking into account the ICA source model if any). The preprocessed activities of channels or independent components (ICs) are accumulated in MATLAB and may be used for event-based classification or continuous visualization of derived EEG features such as alpha band power.

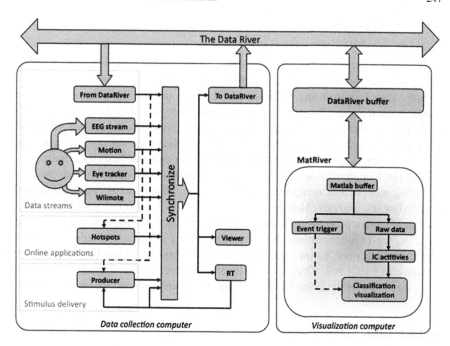

Fig. 14.1 DataSuite data flow. Two computers each running an instance of DataRiver are presented. One acquires data (*left*); the other (*right*) uses MatRiver to perform data classification and feedback visualization. *Dashed lines* indicate control signals

Event-based EEG classification is facilitated in MatRiver using MATLAB callback functions that are executed at predefined latencies after selected events (triggers). This architecture allows for use of any classifier function accessible in MATLAB, for example from other toolboxes such as BCILAB (described below). Since MatRiver uses MATLAB timers running in the background for real-time processing, it operates in a non-blocking manner—the MATLAB command line stays available throughout the session, allowing for interactive exploration of incoming data. Online sessions can also be simulated in MatRiver using previously recorded data.

MatRiver is optimized for speed of computation and display; EEG preprocessing and most event-related data classifications can be performed in less than 10 ms on contemporary (2010) hardware. Also, continuous visualizations of derived EEG features (for example, alpha band power) may be rendered at more than 19 frames per second using the Open-GL based Simulink 3-D (The MathWorks, Inc.). The computer gaming industry generally considers screen response latencies of less than 80 ms to be imperceptible for human subjects. MatRiver can thus achieve comparable or better response latency in a wide range of applications. Visualization in MatRiver also complements the C++-based DataSuite stimulus delivery environment ('Producer') optimized for real-time use with DataRiver. Producer clients may also be used to visualize results of MatRiver computations that are merged via MatRiver routines to the ongoing data river.

14.2.5 EEGLAB

EEGLAB is a general offline analysis environment for EEG and other electrophysiological data (Delorme and Makeig 2004) (http://www.sccn.ucsd.edu/eeglab) that complements Datariver and Matriver. EEGLAB is an interactive menu-based and scripting environment for processing electrophysiological data based under MATLAB. EEGLAB provides command line and interactive graphic user interface (GUI) allowing users to flexibly and interactively process their high-density electrophysiological data (up to several hundred channels) or other dynamic brain data time series. Its functions implement several methods of electroencephalographic data analysis including independent component analysis (ICA) (Makeig et al. 1996, 2002) and time/frequency analysis (Makeig and Inlow 1993). EEGLAB has become a widely used platform for processing biophysical time series and sharing new techniques. At least 28 plug-in functions have been implemented by a variety of user groups. Both MatRiver (described below) and BCILAB (described later) use the EEG dataset structure of EEGLAB. Thus BCI applications written in either environment may make direct use of the many EEGLAB data processing and visualization functions.

14.2.5.1 Other Solutions

Other packages also allow performing data acquisition and processing under MATLAB. rtsBCI in BIOSIG uses MATLAB Simulink and the RealTime Workshop to interface ADC cards. Similarly, the g.tec company uses MATLAB Simulink for high-speed online processing via specially-developed hardware interrupt-controlled drivers. These approaches are not further discussed here.

14.3 Online Data Processing

Online BCI processing often consists of first a BCI-specific portion involving custom signal processing and/or feature extraction for which there is already quite a large palette of published algorithms, followed by a generic machine learning/inference portion, for which many toolboxes and simple yet powerful algorithms like Linear Discriminant Analysis (LDA) (Fisher 1936) are available. In view of the wide range of available tools, flexibly prototyping custom data processing and classification methods is a main reason to use MATLAB for BCI research applications.

```
n = 300; % Number of samples
d = 10; % Number of features
labels = sign(randn(1,n)); % Labels -1 and 1
% Data (1 distributions' distance)
data = [randn(d,n) + 0.5*randn(d,1)*labels];

for i = 1:10 % 10-fold cross-validation
% Test indices
```

```
tst = [round(n/10)*(i-1)+1:round(n/10)*i];

% Train indices
trn = logical(ones(1,n)); trn(tst) = 0;

% Train LDA
w = inv(cov(data'))*data(:,trn)*labels(trn)';

% Test LDA
c = w'*data(:,tst);

% Compute percentage correct
p(i) = sum(sign(c)==labels(tst))/length(tst);
end

% Result (~95% accuracy)
fprintf('Perf.: %2.1f%%(+-%1.1f)\n',100*mean(p),100*std(p));
```

MATLAB code, see figure 14.2

14.3.1 A Minimalistic BCI Script Using Native MATLAB Code

MATLAB itself allows easy prototyping of complex algorithms. For instance, the implementation of LDA projection requires 286 lines of C++ code in the OpenViBE toolbox, whereas in MATLAB it can essentially be implemented as the single line $\gg result = sign(w' * x - b)$, wx being the data, w the weights and b the bias factor. This is one reason why many new computational methods are tested under MATLAB before implementing them in a more structured application-oriented language. For example, MATLAB functions can be used directly to perform learning with and rigorous testing of Linear Discriminant Analysis (LDA), using only simple matrix manipulation (Fisher 1936). The sample code in Fig. 14.2 above creates two classes of Gaussian-distributed data and then performs training and testing. The script performs 10 fold cross-validation (10 training repetitions on 90% of the data; testing on the remainder) using LDA, and returns mean and std. dev. detection classification accuracy.

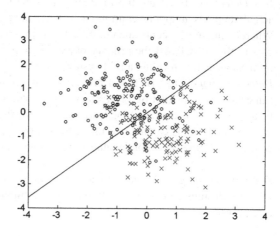

Fig. 14.2 Listing above: Minimal MATLAB code for training and testing a simple LDA classifier and performing ten-fold cross-validations. Figure right: The test data versus LDA solution hyperplane in the first two dimensions

MATLAB scripts may also perform more advanced classification. For instance, the Common Spatial Pattern (CSP) algorithm for oscillatory data processing (Ramoser et al. 1998) is used in many BCI systems. Implementations of CSP often involve manually tuning its frequency filter and time window. Methods to automatically adapt these parameters exist (e.g., Spec-CSP; Tomioka et al., 2006) but are significantly more difficult to implement. Fig. 14.3 shows a minimalistic BCI script performing CSP classification that would require thousands of lines of C or C++ code. Despite its simplicity, it can perform online BCI control whose performance may rival that of much more complex BCI software.

Here, the data involved imagined left and right hand movements plus rest periods. The learned test function can also be applied in real time to a new incoming data stream using a MATLAB timer. The only usage guideline for *test_bci* is that whenever the user wants a prediction of the current mental state, he must feed it all raw EEG samples that have been collected since the previous call to the function.

The spatiotemporal filters associated with the example from Fig. 14.3 are shown in Fig. 14.4 above. Figure 14.4C shows the output of the model and the data labels.

14.3.2 BCILAB

BCILAB is a system for easily constructing new BCI systems with a strong focus on advancing the state of the art. BCI systems constructed using BCILAB can be applied online and/or evaluated offline. Many BCI designs are permitted, from the simplest signal processing chain to advanced machine learning systems. BCILAB is designed to become (likely in 2010) a freely available toolbox for the creation, evaluation, and application of BCI systems. BCILAB also provides tools to explore and visualize datasets offline for basic research purposes. As there is no clear boundary between data analysis for BCI and for neuroscience, here BCILAB blends into EEGLAB on which it is built. BCILAB system design is based on three concepts:

- *BCI Detectors*. These are the fundamental component of any BCI system, the actual methods mapping continuous EEG data measures to a control signal. Whereas in environments such as EEGLAB, the primary object of study is the data itself, in BCILAB the primary object of study are BCI Detectors, with one or more Detectors forming a BCI system.
- *Detector components*. BCILAB provides a large collection of components that can be used to construct BCI Detectors. Three categories exist: Signal processing, feature extracting, and machine learning. Custom signal processors and machine learning algorithms can also be implemented by the user, subject to framework contracts guiding the implementation which are sufficiently general to encompasses most approaches.
- *Detection paradigms*. Detection paradigms are prototypes of commonly re-used Detector designs consisting of multiple BCI components, usually from all three categories.

```
% [S,T,w,b] = train_bci(Raw-Signal, Sample-Rate, Markers,
%       Epoch-Wnd, Spectral-Flt, Flt-Number, Flt-Length)

%%%%%%%%% TRAINING BCI FUNCTION  %%%%%%%
function [S,T,w,b] = train_bci(EEG,Fs,mrk,wnd,f,nof,n)

% frequency filtering and temporal filter estimation
[t,c] = size(EEG); idx = reshape(1:t*c-mod(t*c,n),n,[]);
FLT = real(ifft(fft(EEG).*repmat(f(Fs*(0:t-1)/t)',1,c)));
T = FLT(idx)/EEG(idx);

% data epoching, class-grouping and CSP
wnd = round(Fs*wnd(1)):round(Fs*wnd(2));
for k = 1:2
    EPO{k} = FLT(repmat(find(mrk==k),length(wnd),1) +
                 repmat(wnd',1,nnz(mrk==k)),:);
end
[V,D] = eig(cov(EPO{1}),cov(EPO{1})+cov(EPO{2}));
S = V(:,[1:nof end-nof+1:end]);

% log-variance feature extraction and LDA
for k = 1:2
    X{k} = squeeze(log(var(reshape(EPO{k}*S, length(wnd),[],2*nof))));
end
w = ((mean(X{2})-mean(X{1}))/(cov(X{1})+cov(X{2})))';
b = (mean(X{1})+mean(X{2}))*w/2;

%%%%%%%%%%%%% TEST BCI %%%%%%%%%%%%%%%%%
% Prediction = test_bci(Raw-Block, Spatial-Flt, Temporal-Flt, Weights, Bias)
function y = test_bci(X,S,T,w,b)

global B; % B is the buffer
if any(size(B) ~= [length(T),length(S)])
    B = zeros(length(T),length(S));
end
B = [B;X]; B = B(end-length(T)+1:end,:);
y = log(var(T*(B*S)))*w - b;

%%%%%%%%%%%%% OFFLINE TEST %%%%%%%%%%%%%
load data_set_IVb_al_train
flt = @(f)(f>7&f<30).*(1-cos((f-(7+30)/2)/(7-30)*pi*4));
[S,T,w,b] = train_bci(single(cnt), nfo.fs, ...
    sparse(1,mrk.pos,(mrk.y+3)/2),[0.5 3.5],flt,3,200);

load data_set_IVb_al_test
for x=1:length(cnt)
    y(x) = test_bci(single(cnt(x,:)),S,T,w,b);
end

load true_labels
plot((1:length(cnt))/nfo.fs,[y/sqrt(mean(y.*y)); true_y']);
xlabel('time (seconds)'); ylabel('class');

%%%%%%%%%%%%%% R-T %%%%%%%%%%%%%%%%%%%%%
y = [];
start(timer('R = get_rawdata; y(end+1) = test_bci(R,S,T,w,b);
plot(y(max(1,length(y)-20):end);', 'InstantPeriod', 0.1));
```

Fig. 14.3 A minimalistic BCI script (C. Kothe). The top function (train_bci) performs temporal filtering and training of a CSP filter. The second function (test_bci) applies the model to incoming blocks of raw data, and can be used for online processing. The scripts load data (here from the BCI Competition III), perform training and testing, and display results as in Fig. 14.2. Assuming a function "get_rawdata" allows asynchronous data collection (for example to DataRiver or Field-trip), the fourth script performs real-time (R-T) classification and displays an evolving time course of classification over the past 2 seconds with a refresh rate of 100 ms. Figure 14.4 shows the spatial and temporal filters learned and used. For more details see www.sccn.ucsd.edu/minimalistBCI

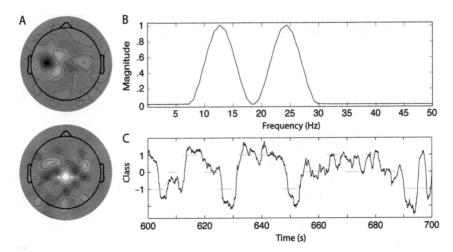

Fig. 14.4 Spatial and temporal filters associated with the code in Fig. 14.3. *Left*. CSP 118-channel spatial filter weights for the best two of six CSP filters used. *Topright*: The temporal filter tailored to the BCI data. This filter was learned by the Test BCI script in Fig. 14.3. *BottomRight*: BCI performance over a 100 second window. The *black curve* indicates the output of the test_bci function. *Gray plateaus* indicate the detected class (1 is imagined left hand movement; 0 is rest; −1 is imagined right hand movement)

BCILAB data processing capabilities are reviewed in Table 14.1.

BCILAB natively implements some default BCI paradigms. These allow the researcher to simply provide data and designate a paradigm name: CSP for imagined movements with LDA (Fisher 1936), Spec-CSP for imagined movements with LDA (Tomioka et al. 2006) logarithmic band-power estimates with Hjorth surface Laplacian filter (Vidaurre and Schlögl 2008), multi-segment averages with LDA (for using the Lateralized Readiness Potential) (Blankertz et al. 2002a), adaptive autoregressive models on band-pass filtered channels with LDA (Schlögl 2000), common spatial patterns for slow cortical potentials (Dornhege et al. 2003a), multi-band CSP, ICA-decomposed logarithmic band-power estimates and, as meta-algorithms, feature combinations (Dornhege et al. 2003b) as well as multi-class classification by panels of experts. These default detection paradigms are massively adaptable. For example, the CSP paradigm for imagined movements can easily be parameterized to measure aspects of mental workload or relaxation. Much BCILAB design work amounts to re-parameterization of existing paradigms for new goals (epoch length, filtering, etc.). In principle, the entire preprocessing chain of the paradigm can be replaced element by element as desired. The ease of adding new components to the toolbox has allowed ready implementation of a variety of methods from EEG and BCI research.

Automated Parameter Search is a particularly convenient feature of the design interface. Instead of a parameter, the special expression *search*(...) can be given, to specify a parameter range. This can be used, for example, to auto-determine the best model parameters, or to regularize a classifier. The BCILAB Detector Design

Table 14.1 Signal processing, feature extraction, and machine learning algorithms in the BCILAB/EEGLAB framework

Signal processing	Feature extraction	Machine Learning Algorithms
• Channel selection • Resampling • Deblinking • Envelope extraction • Epoch extraction • Baseline filtering • Re-referencing • Surface Laplacian filtering[n] • ICA methods (Infomax, FastICA, AMIGA)[p,q] • Spectral filters (FIR, IIR) • Spherical spline interpolation[s]	• Multi-window averaging for detection based on slow cortical potentials[a,b] • Common Spatial Patterns (CSP)[d] • Spectrally-weighted Common Spatial Patterns[f] • Adaptive Autoregressive Modeling, from BioSig[h]	• Linear Discriminant Analysis (LDA)[c] • Quadratic Discriminant Analysis (QDA)[e] • Regularized LDA and QDA[g] • Linear SVM[i] (implemented using LIBLINEAR) • Kernel SVM[i] (implemented using SVMPerf, with LibSVM fallback) • Gaussian Mixture Models (GMM three methods[j,k,l] implemented using GMMBAYES) • Variational Bayesian Logistic Regression[m] (contributed by T. Klister) • Deep Restricted Boltzmann Machines[o] (contributed by F. Bachl) • Relevance Vector Machines (RVM)[r] (implemented using SparseBayes)

[a,b]Blankertz et al. (2002a, 2002b), [c]Fisher (1936), [d]Ramoser et al. (1998), [e]Friedman (2002), [f]Tomioka et al. (2006), [g]Friedman (2002), [h]Schlögl (2000), [i]Schölkopf and Smola (2002), [j,k,l]Bilmes (1998), Vlassis et al. (2002), Figueiredo and Jain (2002), [m]Jaakkola and Jordan (1997), [n]Babiloni et al. (1995), [o]Hinton et al. (2006), [p,q]Makeig et al. (1996), Palmer et al. (2007), [r]Tipping (2001), [s]Perrin et al. (1987)

Interface (DDI) is the primary interface for configuring, training, and evaluating Detectors offline. There are three interface functions covering this area of BCI research. *bci_preproc*, *bci_train* and *bci_predict* are command line interfaces, though a GUI wrapper for each of them is planned. The data are first preprocessed by *bci_preproc* with the help of EEGLAB functions. *bci_train* then finds the optimal Detector given the paradigm; this Detector function can then be used for online data processing. The *bci_preproc* function can apply customization to the whole flow, from raw data to a final online-ready Detector, on the fly. Real-time use of the toolbox is similar to the minimalist BCI.

When attempting new BCI applications, often not much is known about the nature of the data at hand, and therefore not much about how Detector parameters should be chosen. This is where strong visualization functions can help. It is relatively easy to get a BCI running under MATLAB (cf. *train_bci* in Fig. 14.3), but it involves much more work to visualize the data in time and frequency and to plot scalp maps, tasks which are practical when tuning the parameters of these functions and checking the neurophysiological plausibility of the learned models. BCILAB contains a function (*vis_hyperspectrum*) to display accuracy-coded time/frequency

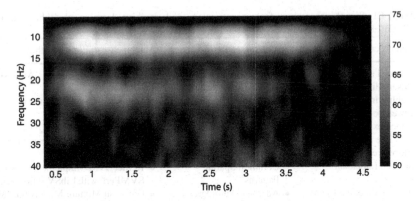

Fig. 14.5 Illustration of estimated accuracy of a CSP-based time/frequency Detector in a two-class imagined movement task (Kothe 2009) using Logistic Regression to classify every time/frequency voxel during the 5 seconds after stimulus presentation. Here the spectral time windows were Hann windows with 90% overlap. Time/frequency estimates were obtained by computing 150-sample FFTs. The cross-validated performance of a CSP+LDA classifier was then estimated and mapped to an oversamples and interpolated color (or here grey-scale) image

images that encode, for every time/frequency voxel, the cross-validated performance estimates of a CSP Detector, as shown in Fig. 14.5. A variant of it allows inspection of the similarity of optimal filters over time and frequency: similar colors imply similarly successful filters.

Another function displays class-colored distributions of slow cortical potentials over time, thus showing at which times the slow potentials for the contrasted conditions become discriminative. These functions allow quick identification of good parameters for Detectors, using spectral power and/or (near DC) SCP classifiers. For instance, Fig. 14.5 was used to select an optimal frequency filter for the model implemented in the minimalistic BCI code (Fig. 14.3). A collection of additional visualization functions display internal properties of trained Detectors, for example showing linear classifier weights as scalp map plots using EEGLAB plotting functions.

To summarize, the BCILAB toolbox can fit the online processing slot in most research BCI environments. For example, it can be linked as processing node into DataSuite, FieldTrip, BCI2000, or OpenViBE systems, or be connected to a proprietary acquisition and stimulus presentation system. As it is fully scriptable, when MATLAB is available it can in principle also be embedded into research prototype systems for use outside the laboratory. In addition to functioning as processing block, BCILAB has a user interface for developing, customizing, training, evaluating, and tuning Detectors using a array of methods likely to grow wider before release. Finally, BCILAB can also serve as a tool to explore discriminative questions about data, and can be viewed as a plug-in extension to EEGLAB for this purpose.

Table 14.2 Free and commercial classifiers running under MATLAB. The double horizontal line separates the EEG-tailored tools from more general all-purpose classification tools. GPL refers to software freely available under the Gnu Public Licence

Package	License	Content
BCILAB	GPL	See Table 14.1
g.BSanalyse	Commercial	LDA, Minimum Distance Classifier (MDC), QDA, MultiLayer Perceptron (MLP), Radial Basis Function (RBF), Kmean
BIOSIG	GPL	Various LDA, QDA/MDA, Regularized Discriminant Analysis (RDA), MDC, Partial Least Square (PLS), RBF, various SVM and Bayesian classifiers
NMLT	GPL	This toolbox is associated with FieldTrip. Currently in development
MATLAB	Commercial	LDA; Minimum Distance Classifier, QDA, HMM (Statistic Toolbox); MLP (Neural Network Toolbox), SVM, Kmean (Bioinformatics Toolbox)
CVX	GPL	Logistic regression, SVM, Gaussian process regression
GPML toolbox	GPL	Gaussian process classification
LibSVM	GPL	SVM, supports multi-class
MLOSS	Mostly GPL	Various Machine Learning Open Source Software

14.3.3 Other MATLAB BCI Classification Tools

Various classification methods may be implemented using functions in the commercial MATLAB add-on toolboxes. The *classify* function of the MATLAB Statistics toolbox performs LDA, its variants Quadratic Discriminant Analysis (QDA) (Friedman 2002), and classification using Mahalonobis distance (MDA). The *hmmtrain* function allows training of Hidden Markov Models (HMM). The Neural Network toolbox adds Multilayer Perceptrons. The Bioinformatics toolbox adds support vector machine (SVM) and K-means classification, and also contains a user-friendly and versatile function *crossvalind* to produce cross-validation indices, plus a function *classperf* to store and accumulate classifier performances and statistics. It is beyond the scope of this chapter to review all the MATLAB commercial and free tools available to perform classification and data processing, especially since these tools are in constant evolution. Instead, in Table 14.2 we list some commonly used tools (as of early 2010) for classifying data.

Other BCI software also offers comprehensive solutions on different platforms and operating systems. We review them briefly below.

14.3.4 Other Existing MATLAB and Non-MATLAB BCI Tools

- *BioSig* (Schlögl and Brunner 2000) (www.biosig.sourceforge.net) emerged from the original Graz BCI system as a MATLAB/Octave toolbox. This software (as of version 2.31), supports a wide range of functionality in statistics and time-series analysis, with a focus on online biosignal processing. It includes the most complete adaptive auto-regression implementation (Schlögl 2000) as well as blind source separation (Bell and Sejnowski 1995), Common Spatial Patterns classification (Ramoser et al. 1998) and code to perform classification according to a variety of methods including kernel Support Vector Machines (Schölkopf and Smola 2002) as well as basic cross-validation methods for estimating classiffier performance (see Table 14.1 for the list of classification algorithms suported). Most implemented features are linked to full paper references. Online and real-time operation is implemented in "rtsBCI", a module based on Simulink and the RealTime Workshop from The Mathworks. Using the BioSig software tends to require strong programming abilities and in-depth knowledge of code internals.

- *OpenViBE* (www.irisa.fr/bunraku/OpenViBE) is a relatively new project developed in France quite different from BioSig. The current implementation (version 0.4.0) is a clean-slate approach to BCI written in C++ with a focus on online processing and virtual reality integration. Most of OpenViBE is a visual programming toolkit for low-level signal processing and higher-level classification, implemented via building blocks that can be graphically combined, making it an ambitious programming project. OpenViBE has been used together with a relatively versatile machine learning library (BLiFF++). OpenViBE also contains a module to run MATLAB code in real-time, although currently this only deals with real-time data processing (or offline streaming of data). When eventually completed, OpenViBE could become one of the easier-to-use tools for BCI signal analysis.

- *BCI2000* (Schalk et al. 2004) (www.bci2000.org) is also a native C++ implementation headed by Gerwin Schalk at the Wadsworth Center (Albany NY) that focuses on online data collection, processing, and feedback. BCI2000 is a complete research BCI toolkit including a data recording module with integrated processing, a simple stimulus presentation module, an operator control module, and a feedback module. It is a robust and sufficient tool for testing simple and established BCI approaches such as 'P300'-based spellers (Sellers et al. 2006) and mu rhythm demodulation (Miner et al. 1998). In theory, it can also handle more complex workloads such as adaptive spatiotemporal filtering, non-linear classification, and BCI performance evaluation. The BCI2000 software is reliable and has a large user base and several extensions are available, including an implementation of the Common Spatial Patterns algorithm. BCI2000 has support for executing functions in MATLAB in real time, and includes some basic functions for offline processing of data from disk in MATLAB.

- *The BBCI Toolbox* (www.bbci.de) is an in-house, closed-source, BCI toolkit developed by Berlin Institute of Technology, the Fraunhofer FIRST institute and the Charité University Medicine (Berlin, Germany). Though not much is known about its internal structure, there is reason to believe that it is flexibly designed. Its functionality, judging by the authors' publications (i.e. Blankertz et al., 2002a, 2002b), may make it the most complete BCI toolbox written to date. Its feedback system is currently being rewritten in Python and has been released as open source software (Venthur and Blankertz 2008).

- *g.BSanalyze* (www.gtec.at) is a commercial biosignal analysis toolbox developed
  by the Austrian company g.tec and written in MATLAB. A feedback application
  based on MATLAB's Simulink can be obtained separately. Its documentation implies that its level of BCI functionality can be compared to that of BioSig plus a
  large subset of EEGLAB (Delorme and Makeig 2004). Clearly a massive amount
  of work went into optimizing its GUI design and usability. However, the most
  advanced classifiers and feature extractors are currently not yet implemented.
- *Other projects.* The EU funded Tobi project (www.tobi-project.org) is a multi-
  million euro project that includes both the Graz BCI team and the BBCI teams. It
  is currently developing a common software platform for BCI operation and calibration. The Dutch government funded Braingain project (www.braingain.nl) is
  supporting the development of real-time FieldTrip (described above) and Brain-
  Stream (www.brainstream.nu), a simplified MATLAB-based BCI environment
  for non-programmers.

14.4 Conclusion

BCI research now underway has at least three objectives. First, much BCI research
attempts to identify efficient and low-latency means of obtaining volitional control
over changes in EEG features, thus forming 'mental signals' usable for BCI communication (see Chapter 12 of this Volume). A second class of BCI systems attempt
to use modulation of brain activity in response to external stimulation, often by
volitional control of user attention. The modulated brain activity, for instance the
P300 target stimulus complex (Farwell and Donchin 1988), is mapped to an artificial control signal such as a speller that detects a characteristic brain dynamic response elicited when an on-screen letter attended by the user is highlighted. A third
objective performs passive cognitive monitoring of user state including actions or
intention, so as to enhance overall human-system productivity, safety, enjoyment, or
equilibrium. Applications in this area are as diverse as alertness monitoring (Jung et
al. 1997), systems to detect user confusion (Zander and Jatzev 2009), neurofeedback
(Birbaumer et al. 2009), and systems proposed to automatically detect and quench
epileptic seizures.

Current BCI technology is quite young, much in flux, and is likely moving toward
eventual convergence on robust and flexible mental state inference methods. Real-
world BCI applications for healthy or disabled users can be efficiently designed
and prototyped using currently available MATLAB tools and toolboxes, but break-
through into widely-applicable methods will probably not occur until dry, wireless EEG systems are readily available (Lin et al. 2008), and more advanced signal
processing methods are developed based on more complete understanding of distributed brain processes. The introduction of machine learning techniques from BCI
research into cognitive neuroscience may facilitate development of more comprehensive models of brain function. Despite their efficiency and simplicity, many current BCI algorithms such as Common Spatial Patterns (CSP) are not directly based
on or interpretable in terms of EEG source neurophysiology. Incorporating advances

in understanding EEG and brain function will likely help BCI systems mature and improve in performance.

Finally, although early work in BCI-based communication systems designed for use with 'locked-in' patients took appropriate care to exclude use of potentials arising from muscle activity in normal control subjects, there is no reason that BCI systems need rely on EEG signals alone. Rather, the prospect of using mobile brain/body imaging (MoBI) (Makeig et al. 2009) to model concurrent motor behavior and psychophysiology (including body movements and muscle activities) as well as EEG *and* electromyographic (EMG) data should open up a much wider range of BCI (or perhaps brain/body computer interface) concepts (Makeig et al. 2009). Components of such systems are already being developed commercially for computer gaming, and will likely be soon applied to much broader classes of human-system interaction research.

References

Adapt © 1987–2003 and Variété, © 2000, 2001 are property of EEG Solutions LLC, and are used under free license for scientific non-profit research

Bell AJ, Sejnowski TJ (1995) An information-maximization approach to blind separation and blind deconvolution. Neural Comput 7(6):1129–1159

Babiloni F, et al (1995) Performances of surface Laplacian estimators: A study of simulated and real scalp potential distributions. Brain Topogr 8(1):35–45

Bilmes J (1998) Gentle Tutorial of the EM Algorithm and its Application to Parameter Estimation for Gaussian Mixture and Hidden Markov Models. International Computer Science Institute

Birbaumer N, et al (2009) Neurofeedback and brain-computer interface clinical applications. Int Rev Neurobiol 86:107–187

Blankertz B, Curio G, Müller K (2002a) Classifying single trial EEG: Towards brain computer interfacing. In: Diettrich T, Becker S, Ghahramani Z (eds) Advances in Neural Inf Proc Systems (NIPS 01), pp 157–164

Blankertz B, et al (2002b) Single trial detection of EEG error potentials: A tool for increasing BCI transmission rates. In: Artificial Neural Networks—ICANN 2002

Delorme A, Makeig S (2004) EEGLAB: An open source toolbox for analysis of single-trial EEG dynamics including independent component analysis. J Neurosci Methods 134(1):9–21

Dornhege G, Blankertz B, Curio G (2003a) Speeding up classification of multi-channel brain-computer interfaces: Common spatial patterns for slow cortical potentials. In: First International IEEE EMBS Conference on Neural Engineering

Dornhege G, et al (2003b) Combining features for BCI, In: Becker S, Thrun S, Obermayer K (eds), Proc Systems (NIPS 02), pp 1115–1122

Farwell L, Donchin E (1988) Talking off the top of your head: Toward a mental prosthesis utilizing event-related brain potentials. Electroencephalogr Clin Neurophysiol 70(6):510–523

Figueiredo M, Jain A (2002) Unsupervised learning on finite mixture models. IEEE Trans Pattern Anal Mach Intell 24(3)

Fisher R (1936) The use of multiple measurements in taxonomic problems. Ann Eugen 7:179–188

Friedman J (2002) Regularized discriminant analysis. J Am Stat Assoc 84(405):165–175

Hinton G, Osindero S, Teh Y (2006) A fast learning algorithm for deep belief nets. Neural Comput 18:1527–1554

Jaakkola T, Jordan M (1997) A variational approach to Bayesian logistic regression models and their extensions. In: Sixth International Workshop on Artificial Intelligence and Statistics

Jung T-P, et al (1997) Estimating alertness from the EEG power spectrum. IEEE Trans Biomed Eng 44(1):60–69

Kothe C (2009) Design and Implementation of a Research Brain-Computer Interface. Berlin Institute of Technology, Berlin. Section 8.2.1

Lin C-T, et al (2008) A noninvasive prosthetic platform using mobile & wireless EEG. Proc IEEE 96(7):1167–1183

Makeig S, et al (2009) Linking brain, mind and behavior. Int J Psychophysiol 73(2):95–100

Makeig S, et al (2002) Dynamic brain sources of visual evoked responses. Science 295(5555):690–694

Makeig S, Inlow M (1993) Lapses in alertness: Coherence of fluctuations in performance and EEG spectrum. Electroencephalogr Clin Neurophysiol 86(1):23–35

Makeig S, et al (1996) Independent component analysis of electroencephalographic data. In: Touretzky D, Mozer M, Hasselmo M (eds), Advances in Neural Information Processing Systems, pp 145–151

Miner LA, McFarland DJ, Wolpaw JR (1998) Answering questions with an electroencephalogram-based brain-computer interface. Arch Phys Med Rehabil 79(9):1029–1033

Palmer JA, et al (2007) Modeling and estimation of dependent subspaces with non-radially symmetric and skewed densities. In: 7th International Conference on Independent Component Analysis and Signal Separation, London, UK

Perrin F et al (1987) Mapping of scalp potentials by surface spline interpolation. Electroencephalogr Clin Neurophysiol 66(1):75–81

Ramoser H, Müller-Gerking J, Pfurtscheller G (1998) Optimal spatial filtering of single trial EEG during imagined hand movement. IEEE Trans Rehabil Eng 1998(8):441–446

Schalk G, et al (2004) BCI2000: A general-purpose brain-computer interface (BCI) system. IEEE Trans Biomed Eng 51(6):1034–1043

Schlögl A (2000) The electroencephalogram and the Adaptive Autoregressive Model: Theory and Applications. Shaker Verlag, Aachen. ISBN3-8265-7640-3

Schlögl A, Brunner C (2000) Biosig: A free and open source software library for BCI research. Computer 41(10):44–50

Schölkopf B, Smola A (2002) Learning with Kernels. MIT Press, Cambridge, MA

Sellers E, et al (2006) A p300 event-related potential brain-computer interface (BCI): The effects of matrix size and inter stimulus interval on performance. Biol Psychol 73(3):242–252

Tipping M (2001) Sparse Bayesian learning and the relevance vector machine. J Mach Learn Res 1:211–244

Tomioka R et al (2006) An iterative algorithm for spatio-temporal filter optimization. In: 3rd International BCI Workshop and Training Course. Verlag der Technischen Universität Graz, Graz

Venthur B, Blankertz B (2008) A platform-independent open-source feedback framework for BCI systems. In: 4th International Brain-Computer Interface Workshop and Training Course

Vidaurre C, Schlögl (2008) A comparison of adaptive features with linear discriminant classifier for brain computer interfaces. In: Engineering in Medicine and Biology Society. EMBS 2008. 30th Annual International Conference of the IEEE

Vlassis N, Likas A, Greedy EM (2002) Algorithm for Gaussian Mixture Learning. Neural Processing Letters, vol 15. Kluwer Academic Publishers, Dordrecht

Zander T, Jatzev S (2009) Detecting affective covert user states with passive brain-computer interfaces. In: ACII 2009. IEEE Computer Society Press, Los Alamitos, CA

Chapter 15
Using BCI2000 for HCI-Centered BCI Research

Adam Wilson and Gerwin Schalk

Abstract BCI2000 is a general-purpose software suite designed for brain-computer interface (BCI) and related research. BCI2000 has been in development since 2000 and is currently used in close to 500 laboratories around the world. BCI2000 can provide stimulus presentation while simultaneously recording brain signals and subject responses from a number of data acquisition and input devices, respectively. Furthermore, BCI2000 provides a number of services (such as a generic data format that can accommodate any hardware or experimental setup) that can greatly facilitate research. In summary, BCI2000 is ideally suited to support investigations in the area of human-computer interfaces (HCI), in particular those that include recording and processing of brain signals. This chapter provides an overview of the BCI2000 system, and gives examples of its utility for HCI research.

15.1 Introduction

BCI2000 is a general-purpose software suite designed for brain-computer interface (BCI) research. It can also be used for data acquisition, stimulus presentation, and general brain monitoring applications. The core goal of the BCI2000 project is to facilitate research and development of new applications in these areas. It is designed to be a tool to simplify the considerable challenge of setting up, configuring, and maintaining a BCI system. It provides a consistent framework that encourages collaboration between labs. BCI2000 has been in development since 2000 in a collaboration between the Wadsworth Center of the New York State Department of

A. Wilson (✉)
Department of Neurosurgery, University of Cincinnati, Cincinnati, USA
e-mail: wilso3jn@uc.edu

G. Schalk
Wadsworth Center, New York State Dept. of Health, Albany, USA
e-mail: schalk@wadsworth.org

D.S. Tan, A. Nijholt (eds.), *Brain-Computer Interfaces*,
Human-Computer Interaction Series,
DOI 10.1007/978-1-84996-272-8_15, © Springer-Verlag London Limited 2010

Health in Albany, New York, and the Institute of Medical Psychology and Behavioral Neurobiology at the University of Tübingen, Germany. Since its initial release in 2001, BCI2000 has had a substantial impact on BCI research. As of late 2009, BCI2000 has been acquired by close to 500 laboratories around the world. Because BCI2000 is available for free to academic and educational institutions, many other individuals at different institutions around the world have contributed to this project.

BCI2000 was designed primarily as a framework for implementing a general-purpose BCI. However, as this chapter will show, it is also ideally suited for studying human-computer interfaces (HCI). BCI2000 is capable of presenting stimuli (e.g., visual and audio) with high temporal resolution, while simultaneously recording brain signals and subject responses, such as joystick movement, button presses, and even eye tracker data, all synchronized and stored in a generic data format. The capability of logging data from any input device synchronized with stimulus presentation, and requiring little or no programming should be of immediate utility to many HCI-centered labs. Furthermore, since BCI2000 is designed to be a closed-loop system, i.e., it reacts and adapts to the user's actions, more complex HCI experiments could be designed in which the stimulus presentations changes based on how the user is performing. At the same time, as the basic technological, algorithmic, and neurological concepts of BCIs have become better understood, and BCIs have begun moving out of the realm of lab-based "proof-of-concept" projects, there has been increased interest in the *interface* aspect of brain-computer interfaces, and finding ways to improve the BCI for the end user (Allison 2009). Since the BCI2000 framework is so configurable, and the core applications are simple to modify, BCI2000 is a natural platform to assist improving the interface and usability of BCIs, without needing to worry about the system details, or whether a care-taker is capable of running the BCI. In fact, with minimal training, it is literally possible for the operator to run BCI2000 and press start, without *any* intermediate configuration.

BCI2000 facilitates the implementation of different BCI systems and other psychophysical experiments by substantially reducing the time that would otherwise be spent developing the BCI software framework. It does this by providing a number of BCI and stimulus presentation paradigms that can be configured by the investigator or adapted by a software engineer. Furthermore, a number of standard configurations are included with the software, so that if BCI2000-compatible hardware is used, BCI experiments can be started within minutes of downloading the system. Because BCI2000 is based on a system model that can describe any BCI system, because its underlying framework is highly generic, and because execution of BCI2000 does not require third-party components, its use is most beneficial in large collaborative research programs with many concurrent and different experiments in different locations.

In this chapter, we will introduce the reader to the BCI2000 system, outline common scenarios for its use, and provide a brief technical overview of the system.

15.2 Advantages of Using BCI2000

In this section, the advantages of using BCI2000 are discussed, generally as it relates to BCI applications. However, since a brain-computer interface is a specific type of human-computer interface (i.e., the interface is with brain signals, as opposed to a different type of input device), nearly all of the concepts discussed are just as relevant for HCI research as BCI research. In fact, the BCI2000 framework already provides methods for acquiring data from many different input devices, and therefore can immediately be used for HCI experiments with few if any modifications.

Many scientific articles or book chapters have described the basics of BCI systems using different brain signals (e.g., sensorimotor rhythms or evoked responses). A student with moderate knowledge of a programming language such as Matlab and some understanding of the necessary signal processing routines could write a BCI demonstration in a matter of days. Why, then, is BCI2000 even necessary? Writing "in-lab" BCI software has many disadvantages. First, it requires considerable expertise, time, and thus cost to build a BCI system that is robust. That is, while it may be possible and seem attractive to write a BCI system within a few days, perhaps using a rapid prototyping system such as Matlab, it is likely that such a prototype will contain bugs that may invalidate collected data when they are carefully analyzed after data collection is completed. Even more problematically, it is very complex and difficult to verify correct system function. It is not unreasonable to assume that it can take a technically highly competent graduate student at least a semester to have a working system before experimental data can be collected confidently. Even in such an optimistic scenario, the next student will need to understand how to run the program and modify the code (which was likely undocumented), or, more typically, simply start from scratch.

Thus, the main benefit of using BCI2000 is that it implements a standard, modular BCI framework that can describe any BCI system, and that handles many of the system details that are secondary to the algorithms and application output but nonetheless are critical for a successful experiment. For example, data collected with BCI2000 are stored using a standard data format that contains all experimental parameters (so that all details of experimental configuration can be reconstructed offline), all experimental event markers (such as when and where stimuli are presented), and all brain signal data. This data format is the same regardless of the specific BCI implementation, i.e., for any amplifier system, signal processing algorithm, and application output, the data format is identical. Hence, offline analysis routines can be designed to work with the same type of data irrespective of the details of the experiment. This fact alone provides a tremendous advantage for multi-site collaborative studies, for which different institutions may not have the same hardware configurations, or even for in-house studies that involve more than one person. Beyond the data format, the graphical interface that allows the investigator to set up and control an experiment is the same for any hardware configuration regardless of the specific algorithms or applications that are used. This interface is dynamically generated based on the details of the hardware, processing, and experimental paradigm. Thus, this interface does not need to be rewritten for every possible combination of these different experimental aspects. Furthermore, all of the necessary experimental configuration data can be saved in a textual parameter file and distributed to other collaborators, even if different amplifiers or other hardware are used, and the experiment will run identically at all locations.

Another advantage to using BCI2000 is that it uses a modular format that separates the core BCI system components into completely separate programs running simultaneously. There is a Source module that handles data acquisition from the amplifier (and other input devices) and data storage, a Signal Processing module that extracts brain signal features and translates them into device control signals, a User Application module that controls the feedback to the user (e.g., a computer display), and finally an Operator module that controls the other modules and provides configuration and a configuration interface for the investigator. These four modules run independently of each other, meaning that the Source module can be switched for a different amplifier system needing to modify the Signal Processing or User Application modules; and the graphical interface in the Operator will be updated appropriately to reflect the required parameters for the new Source module.

Finally, this framework allows BCI2000 to easily be extended beyond its core capabilities. If a new user input device is desired, it is straightforward to insert the acquisition code into a new logger, which is used with a Source module, and the framework will handle all of the other details. For example, all of the necessary configuration parameters required for the new input device will appear in the BCI2000 configuration window, and will be saved in the data file. Furthermore, the input device will automatically work with the existing applications, due to the standard data transfer protocol between the modules. Similarly, if a new experimental feedback paradigm is desired, a new Application module can be written to display the new paradigm, and all parameters and events introduced by the new module will be recorded in the data file. Additionally, since the modules communicate using the TCP/IP network protocol, new programs could be written in any programming language such as Python or Java, and communicate with the other BCI modules using the BCI2000 data format.

In summary, BCI2000 provides a core set of common BCI implementations within a standard BCI framework. BCI2000 is provided with fully documented components that have proven to work robustly in many different BCI and other experiments. By its modular design, BCI2000 tries to avoid redundancies in code, and re-uses modules and code in multiple contexts rather than re-duplicating it. One of the advantages of this approach is that it maximizes the effect of errors that may exist in any single component, greatly increasing the likelihood to detect such errors early. Furthermore, because of its flexible and modular design, BCI2000 allows combination of existing software components with relatively little effort. This ranges from simple re-combination of modules (e.g., using the same signal processing algorithm with different feedback paradigms), to modification of the kind and order of signal processing components, and to modification of existing components or creation of new components. For these reasons, BCI2000 provides a distinct advantage over BCIs written in-house.

In the following section, we will first present different scenarios with relevance to the HCI community in which BCI2000 can be beneficial, and then give a technical overview of the BCI2000 system.

15.3 Usage Scenarios

15.3.1 Performing an HCI/Psychophysical Experiment

BCI2000 can be valuable for laboratories specialized in the fields of electrophysiology and psychophysiology, including those investigating aspects of human-computer interaction. Typical psychophysiological experiments involve visual, auditory, or other types of stimulation, and simultaneous recording of brain signal responses. They often also require recording from multiple input devices, including mice, keyboards, joysticks, eye trackers, and motion trackers. For such experiments, BCI2000 may be used as software system that is capable of capturing human input from multiple devices that is synchronized with stimulus presentation and neurological recordings.

An example of such experiments are those that investigate Fitts's law model of information transfer rates in human movement (Fitts 1954). These experiments measure the tradeoff between speed and accuracy with a particular input modality by requiring the subject to move back and forth between two targets as quickly and accurately as possible using a particular body part or input device, such as a stylus (Fig. 15.1).

Both the width (W) of the targets and the distance between them (D) are systematically altered, and assigned an index of difficulty (ID) that describes the relative difficulty of the task (see (15.1)). The movement times for the desired IDs are measured during the experiment, and a model of the movement time as a function of the ID is derived (see (15.2)). The equations for this model are given as:

$$ID = \log_2\left(\frac{2A}{W}\right), \tag{15.1}$$

$$MT = a + b * ID. \tag{15.2}$$

The regression equation (15.2) includes the expected reaction time (a) and the information transfer rate ($1/b$, in bits/sec) for a given modality. In the original re-

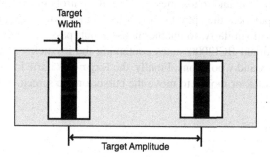

Fig. 15.1 In the original Fitts's law study, the subjects quickly moved a stylus back and forth between two targets of a particular width and distance apart. By altering the target widths and distances (which determine the index of difficulty), and measuring the movement times, it is possible to calculate the information transfer rate of the human motor system for a particular input modality

Fig. 15.2 Fitts's law applied to the BCI2000 cursor movement task. The subject moves the cursor from the center of the screen to the highlighted target of width *W* over a distance *A*. At the end of the trial, the cursor is returned to the center, and the next target is presented

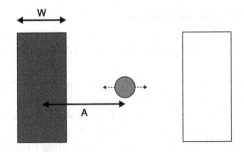

ciprocal tapping task, which involved moving a stylus back and forth between two targets, the information transfer for all tasks was 10–12 bits/sec, which thus gave the performance capacity of the human motor system for such tasks (Fitts 1954).

Using BCI2000, it is possible to design a reciprocal tapping experiment to measure the information transfer rate using multiple input modalities (e.g., mouse, joystick, and brain control), as was done in Felton et al. (2009). Implementation of the Fitts's task paradigm in BCI2000 requires three steps. First, the Cursor Task feedback paradigm that comes with BCI2000 must be extended to support a dwell period during target acquisition, so that the cursor must remain within the target region for a short time before it is selected. Thus, the BCI2000 source code needs to be downloaded, and a compatible compiler installed in order to build the new customized Cursor Task.

The second step is to configure BCI2000 to display all of the target locations; a wide range of IDs should be tested for each dimension of control; in Felton et al. (2009), 14 targets with an ID range of 0.58 to 3.70 were used. In BCI2000, the targets are defined in a table called *Targets* that lists their positions and geometries in the *x*, *y*, and *z* planes. Additionally, to ensure that all targets are presented in a run, the *NumberOfTrials* parameter should be set to equal the number of targets in the *Targets* table, or some may not be presented. The BCI2000 application that is displayed to the user is shown in Fig. 15.2.

The final step is to configure BCI2000 to record from different input devices during the experiment, and to use these devices to control cursor movement. To use a joystick for input, pass the option -LogJoystick=1 (to the Source module) on the command line; similarly, to enable mouse input, pass -LogMouse=1. These will create additional BCI2000 states containing the joystick's x and y positions, and the mouse's x and y positions. Finally, the ExpressionFilter can be used to allow the joystick or mouse to move the cursor on the screen. To allow joystick control, enter

```
JoystickXPos
JoystickYPos
```

in the ExpressionFilter table; replace these with MousePosX and Mouse-PosY for mouse input. For brain control, BCI2000 should be configured for the Mu/Beta rhythm task. Detailed instructions for all of the BCI2000 configuration steps are available in the BCI2000 documentation and tutorials.

When the tests have been completed, an analysis environment such as Matlab can be used to import the data and calculate the movement times as a function of the ID for all three conditions.

15.3.2 Patient Communication System

As a real-world application of BCI technology, a patient communication system uses a BCI as an input device similar to a computer keyboard or mouse. Once a particular BCI system has been designed and tested in laboratory experiments, BCI researchers may want to deploy the system to the target population—typically, severely paralyzed people that depend on caregivers. A BCI may improve their quality of life by allowing communication with caregivers, loved ones, or others through email or other electronic means, and by providing a degree of independence by allowing control of the environment, such as turning lights on and off, controlling a television or radio, etc.

One of the primary challenges in developing a robust patient communication system is making it simple enough for non-expert users, such as the caregiver, to setup and use daily. Additionally, many people with severe motor disabilities already have some form of augmentative communication technology (e.g., a predictive speller), which may need to be integrated with the BCI system. In these instances, the BCI essentially functions as an input device, and therefore will not require many advanced interface options.

BCI2000 facilitates implementation of such a patient communication system mainly in two ways. First, by integration and optimization of its graphical interface, i.e., its Operator module; and second, by connecting its output to external devices or software. Integration of BCI2000's graphical interface is possible through a number of means. First, the parameter configuration dialog may be restricted to only show those parameters that are changed by operators. Second, system behavior can be controlled via command-line parameters. Using command-line parameters, it is possible to automatically load parameter files, start system operation, and quit BCI2000 at the end of a run. In addition, beginning with BCI2000 version 3, the system will be further modularized so that the graphical interface to the operator can be completely replaced with an application-specific (rather than a generic) interface. BCI2000 may also be integrated with external devices or applications. One way to accomplish this is to use BCI2000's external application interface, which provides a bi-directional link to exchange information with external processes running on the same or a different machine. Via the external application interface, read/write access to BCI2000 state information and to the control signals is possible. For example, in a μ rhythm-based BCI, an external application may read the classification result, control the user's task, or get access to the control signal that is calculated by the Signal Processing module so as to control an external output device (such as a robotic arm or a web browser).

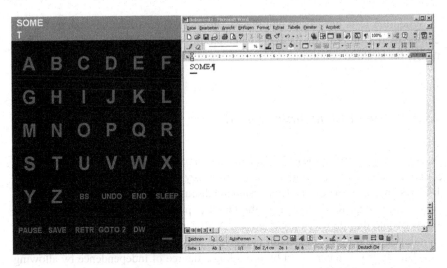

Fig. 15.3 A P300 Speller-based patient communication system to enter text into a word processor

As an example of BCI2000's inter-operability capabilities, we will discuss the scenario of a patient control system that allows paralyzed patients to use brain activity to control a standard word processor. Such a scenario has several requirements. First, in an initial training phase, the BCI needs to be configured and adapted to the patient. This usually requires expert supervision. In further sessions, the system should be operated by nursing staff, with a minimum of interactions. Next, the system should be based on the P300 speller paradigm, and choosing individual matrix entries should correspond to entering letters into a standard word processor (Fig. 15.3). Finally, the system should include standard word processing commands, including a backspace, save and load file commands, and other essential features.

In this scenario, the standard P300 speller configuration will serve as a starting point. To implement the required connectivity to external devices, one would begin by extending the existing speller system to recognize additional selection commands, and act upon them by sending appropriate device commands. In the present example, no software modification is necessary, since the standard P300 speller module is capable of sending information about letter selection to the same or another computer via UDP, where it may be picked up by any external program. Thus, to connect speller selections to a standard word processor, it is only necessary to create a small interfacing program that reads letter selections from the speller's UDP port, and uses the operating system to send appropriate key-press events to the word processing application.

Once basic functionality is established, the entire system including BCI2000, the interfacing program, and the word processor should be packaged into a larger system, which will use a simplified user interface to be operated by nursing staff. The simplified user interface may request a user name at startup, and a very limited number of additional parameters. Once acquired, these parameters will then be concatenated with a user-specific parameter file that contains the actual BCI configuration. Then, the system will start up the word processor, the interfacing program, and BCI2000. Using operator module command line parameters, it will automatically load the temporarily created parameter file, and begin BCI operation. Once the user selects a "quit" command, BCI2000 will quit automatically. By using this configuration methodology, i.e., configuring BCI2000 using a combination of simple dialogs and command-line interfaces, it is possible to avoid all references to the BCI2000 user interface on the operator's screen, and to only retain the application module's user screen (i.e., the speller matrix).

15.3.3 Other Directions

The two experiments shown here are two simple examples of how HCI concepts could be explored using BCI2000. However, there are many possibilities for utilizing BCI2000 for improving human-computer interaction by studying exactly how people use various input devices, while tracking eye position using the eye tracker, attention from the brain signals, and other physiological signals (heart rate, skin conductance) to measure stress and frustration, for example. Thus, existing input devices could be improved by measuring not only how the primary input device is used, but also the mental and physiological states of the user while the device is used.

15.4 Core Concepts

15.4.1 System Model

The BCI2000 system model (Fig. 15.4) was designed to describe any kind of BCI, which generally consists of three components: (1) a *data acquisition* component that records neural signals; (2) a *signal processing algorithm* that extracts signal features that represent the user's intent and translates them into commands for an output device; and (3) a *user application* component that sends these commands to the output device, thus providing feedback to the user. These components are present in any BCI system, and are described in Wolpaw et al. (2002).

In BCI2000, these three components correspond to three core BCI2000 modules, which are implemented as independent executables that exchange data and communicate using a network-capable protocol. These modules are called the *Source Module*, the *Signal Processing Module*, and the *User Application Module*. There is a Source module for each type of data acquisition hardware amplifier, a Signal Processing module for each type of signal processing algorithm, and a User Application module for each type of feedback or output device. These modules are usually independent of each other, e.g., the Source module does not require any knowledge of the Signal Processing or User Application modules, and vice versa. Therefore, these

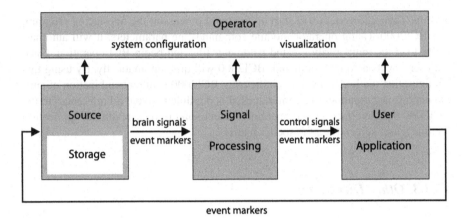

Fig. 15.4 The BCI2000 system model. Acquired data are processed sequentially be three modules (i.e., Source, Signal Processing, and User Application). The modules are controlled by an additional Operator module (from Schalk et al. 2004)

modules my be recombined by choosing a different set of executables when starting BCI2000.

As an example, conducting sensorimotor rhythm (SMR) feedback using the g.tec g.USBamp acquisition system will involve the g.USBamp Source module (for data acquisition and storage), the ARSignalProcessing module (for spatial filtering, autoregressive spectral estimation, linear classification, and signal normalization), and the CursorTask module (which provides visual feedback to the user in the form of cursor movement). If a different amplifier system is used at another location, the appropriate Source module is simply substituted.

15.4.2 Configuration

Once BCI2000 has been started, further configuration and control is performed through a dedicated *Operator Module*. That module provides the experimenters user interface. While it may show different parameters that are specific to a particular experiment, the Operator module is the same program for all possible configurations of BCI2000. In other words, the BCI2000 graphical interface to the investigator does not have to be rewritten for different configurations. The Operator module provides a user interface to start, pause, and resume system operation. In addition, it is able to display logging information, signal visualization, and a reduced copy of the user's screen during system operation (Fig. 15.5).

The functional details of individual modules are configured by parameters that are requested by the individual components that make up each module. For example, the data acquisition component of the BCI2000 Source module typically requests a parameter that sets the device's sampling rate. The parameters of all modules are displayed, modified, and organized in the Operator module's configuration dialog

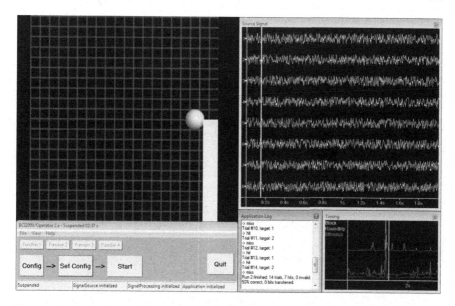

Fig. 15.5 BCI2000 Operator module, displaying source signal (*top right*), timing information (*bottom right*), a downsampled copy of the application window (*top left*), and an application log (*middle bottom*)

(Fig. 15.6). As mentioned before, a different configuration of BCI2000 (i.e., using different Source, Signal Processing, or User Application modules) will result in different parameters displayed in this dialog and written in the data file. All of these automatic adaptations in the BCI2000 system to different configurations are handled by the BCI2000 and are transparent to the user and even the BCI2000 programmer.

15.4.3 Software Components

Inside core modules, software components act on blocks of brain signal data in sequence, forming a chain of "filters" (Fig. 15.7). Module operation may be adapted by writing new filters, modifying existing ones, or simply by rearranging them. These filters are written in C++, so their adaptation requires the requisite programming skills. However, BCI2000 provides a programming framework that is designed to achieve slim and transparent coding inside filter components, and thus simplifies filter modification. Also, we provide a filter that employs user-provided Matlab™ code for online data processing.

Filters usually do not have their own user interface. Rather, they typically request configuration *parameters* from the programming framework, which will then be displayed and organized in the Operator module's configuration window (e.g., in Fig. 15.6), with no specific programming effort required. Parameters may be characters or numbers, and may be single values, lists, or matrices, and do not change during an experimental session.

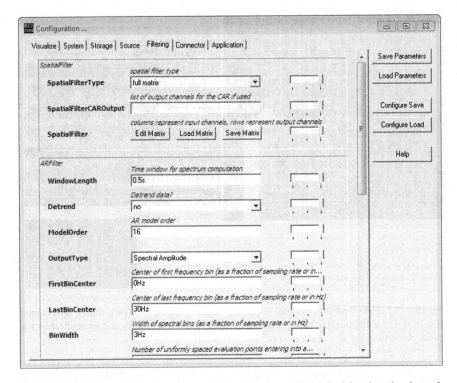

Fig. 15.6 The BCI2000 parameter configuration dialog. The "Filtering" tab is selected and reveals the configuration details relating to signal processing. Using the sliders on the right side, individual parameters can be assigned user levels so that only a subset of them will be visible at lower user levels; this is useful for clinical applications of BCI systems. "Save" and "Load" buttons provide storage and retrieval of parameters, the "Configure Save" and "Configure Load" buttons allow users to determine a subset of parameters to store or retrieve, respectively. The "Help" button provides instant access to parameter documentation

In addition to the concept of parameters, which are static during a defined period of experimentation, BCI2000 also supports the concept of event markers called *states*. BCI2000 states encode those aspects of the system state during an experiment that are necessary to reconstruct the timing of events. During the experiment, state values are changed based on the current state of the BCI system, providing a means of recording event markers, and encoding information about stimulation or user task for later data analysis. The values for all states are saved along with the brain signals at every sample regardless of whether the state value changed. For example, during the P300 Speller task, the row and column that are currently being flashed are stored in state values, which allows to reconstruct the entire experiment. Similarly to parameters, states are requested by filters, and then propagated and recorded transparently by the framework.

During operation, a filter may access parameters and states using a simple programming interface that allows setting and obtaining parameter and state values in a manner similar to assigning values to or from variables. The advantage of using this

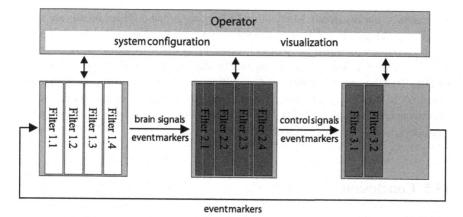

Fig. 15.7 BCI2000 Filter Chain. Inside core modules, individual filter components are indicated. This figure demonstrates that the initial brain signals undergo several subsequent processing steps in the three core modules prior to application output

software infrastructure is that requested parameters automatically appear in particular tabs in the configuration dialog, parameters are automatically stored in the header of the data file (so that all aspects of system configuration can be retrieved offline), and that state variables are automatically associated with data samples and stored in the data file. In other words, BCI2000 system operation, data storage, and real-time data interchange can be adapted substantially to the needs of particular situations by only making local changes to individual BCI2000 filters within modules.

15.4.4 Getting Started with BCI2000

Getting started with BCI2000 requires appropriate hardware, which consists of a computer system and recording equipment. The computer system may be standard desktop or a laptop computer running Windows.[1] The computer should come with a dedicated 3D-capable video card. For most experiments, it is advantageous to use separate video screens for the experimenter and the subject, respectively. When using a desktop computer, this implies a two-monitor configuration; when using a laptop computer, a separate monitor for the subject, i.e., the BCI user.

The recording equipment consists of an amplifier, a digitizer, and appropriate sensors. Today, many amplifiers come with an integrated digitizer. For example, this includes the g.tec™ amplifiers supported in the core distribution of BCI2000: the 16-channel g.USBamp that connects via USB, and the 8-channel g.MOBIlab+

---

[1]We have comprehensively tested BCI2000 on Windows NT, Windows 2000, and Windows XP. While BCI2000 operates under Windows Vista, Vista's timing performance, in particular with regards to audio and video output, is substantially reduced compared to Windows XP.

that connects via Bluetooth. Many other EEG systems and digitizer boards are supported through additional Source modules that have been provided by BCI2000 users. Examples comprise EEG/ECoG recording systems by Biosemi, Brainproducts (BrainAmp, V-Amp), Neuroscan, and Tucker-Davis, as well as digitizer boards by Data Translations, Measurement Computing, and National Instruments. In most situations in humans, BCI systems will record from sensors placed on the scalp (electroencephalography (EEG)). EEG caps are usually offered in conjunction with amplifiers, or may be purchased separately.

15.5 Conclusion

BCI2000 provides a number of important capabilities useful to researchers performing BCI, psychophysical, and human-computer interaction studies. Because the BCI2000 framework handles much of the internal functions necessary for executing and maintaining successful experiments, and can be expanded for and adapted to a wide range of possible applications, BCI2000 allows scientists to focus on only those aspects that are unique to their experiments. Thus, BCI2000 greatly reduces the complexity, time, and thus cost, of creating and maintaining experiments in the area of real-time biosignal processing and feedback.

References

Allison B (2009) The I of BCIs: Next generation interfaces for brain-computer interface systems that adapt to individual users. In: Human-Computer Interaction. Novel Interaction Methods and Techniques. Lecture Notes in Computer Science, vol 5611. Springer, Heidelberg, pp 558–568

Felton E, Radwin R, Wilson J, Williams J (2009) Evaluation of a modified Fitts law brain–computer interface target acquisition task in able and motor disabled individuals. J Neural Eng 6(5):056002

Fitts P (1954) The information capacity of the human motor system in controlling the amplitude of movement. J Exp Psychol 47(391):1088

Schalk G, McFarland D, Hinterberger T, Birbaumer N, Wolpaw J (2004) BCI2000: A general-purpose brain-computer interface (BCI) system. IEEE Trans Biomed Eng 51:1034–1043

Wolpaw JR, Birbaumer N, McFarland DJ, Pfurtscheller G, Vaughan TM (2002) Brain-computer interfaces for communication and control. Electroencephalogr Clin Neurophysiol 113(6):767–791

Index

D.S. Tan, A. Nijholt (eds.), *Brain-Computer Interfaces,*
Human-Computer Interaction Series,
DOI 10.1007/978-1-84996-272-8, © Springer-Verlag London Limited 2010